Business Decision Making
and
Government Policy

Business Decision Making and Government Policy

Cases in Business and Government

DAN H. FENN, JR.

Commissioner
United States Tariff Commission

DONALD GRUNEWALD

Associate Professor
Graduate School of Business Administration
Rutgers—The State University

ROBERT N. KATZ

Attorney at Law and
Visiting Lecturer
Georgetown University

PRENTICE-HALL, INC., *Englewood Cliffs, N.J.*

PRENTICE-HALL INTERNATIONAL, INC., *London*
PRENTICE-HALL OF AUSTRALIA, PTY. LTD., *Sydney*
PRENTICE-HALL OF CANADA, LTD., *Toronto*
PRENTICE-HALL OF INDIA (PRIVATE) LTD., *New Delhi*
PRENTICE-HALL OF JAPAN, INC., *Tokyo*

Dedication

We wish to dedicate this first published casebook in the new and growing field of business-government relations to George P. Baker, Dean of the Harvard Graduate School of Business Administration, and to Paul W. Cherington, James J. Hill Professor of Transportation at Harvard. It was Dean Baker and Professor Cherington who first saw that the business manager needed something more than the traditional economic approach to government regulation if he was to deal effectively with the range of relationships with local, state, and national officials, which would develop during his management career. Their pioneering concept inspired the manager to see himself as a participant and shaper of public policy where it affected his company rather than as a defensive querulous victim of mysterious forces operating in an alien and frightening world of their own. It is our hope that this book will serve to broaden, deepen, and sharpen that concept and thus further its impact on the thinking of students of business management.

Acknowledgments

Numerous persons have had a hand in the successful completion of this casebook. First of all, we wish to acknowledge our great debt to the many business firms and businessmen who gave us valuable time and information. Unfortunately, lack of space and the need to preserve anonymity for some firms precludes individual acknowledgments of all this help and encouragement. These firms and businessmen deserve much credit for their contributions to business education.

The copyright on the following cases in this book is held by the President and Fellows of Harvard College, and they are published herein by express permission:

Worcester National Bank
The Federal Government and the Sale of Cranberries
Mohawk Republican Town Committee
Sindall Lumber Company

In case material of the Harvard Graduate School of Business Administration names, quantities, and other identifying details may be disguised, although basic relationships are maintained. Cases are prepared as the basis for class discussion rather than to illustrate either effective or ineffective handling of administrative situations. We appreciate the kindness of Dean George P. Baker and Professor Paul W. Cherington in granting us the permission to include these cases. We also acknowledge the contribution of Mr. George C. Lodge, Lecturer at the Harvard Graduate School of Business Administration, to the collection of material for the Somali American Fishing Co. case.

We gratefully acknowledge permission by Northwestern University

School of Business to include the Photographic Equipment Industry and Tariffs and the Follansbee Steel Company cases. We also appreciate the kind permission of Dean T. R. Martin of the Robert A. Johnson College of Business Administration of Marquette University to include the Allis-Chalmers and the T.V.A. case, written by Professor T. Healy.

We acknowledge the permission of the *Harvard Business School Bulletin* to reproduce part of "They Said It Couldn't Be Done," by Charles C. Bowen, from Vol. 36, No. 5, of the October, 1960 issue of the *Bulletin*.

The courtesy of *The New York Times* and *The Wall Street Journal* in permitting the reproduction of published material in the Antitrust and the 29 Electrical Manufacturers case; and of the *Newark Star-Ledger* in permitting the reproduction of published material in The Port of New York Authority case is gratefully acknowledged.

We wish to express our appreciation to Holt, Rinehart and Winston, Inc. for their permission for us to include the Lynn Cocktail Lounge case. This case was first published in *Cases in Business Policy* by Donald Grunewald, copyright 1964 by Holt, Rinehart and Winston, Inc.

We wish especially to acknowledge the contributions by the individual casewriters at Harvard, Marquette, and Northwestern for their contributions. We also thank the graduate students at Rutgers who gathered much of the material and wrote first drafts of several of the cases. The contribution to scholarship and to business education of writing a case has, unfortunately, not often been given sufficient credit at many institutions. Successful casewriting is a difficult task, probably more difficult than the writing of an article for an academic journal.

We wish also to express our appreciation to our past students in our various graduate and senior courses in government and business for serving as guinea pigs and for their helpful ideas, suggestions, and constructive criticisms of the cases. Thanks are also due to our colleagues at various institutions for their helpful contributions and advice, and to Dr. Paul J. Garfield, Foster Associates, Inc., and Professor Vernon A. Mund, Department of Economics, University of Washington, for their valuable comments and suggestions.

We wish especially to thank Miss Lilian A. Shaw for her careful typing of the manuscript in several drafts, her meticulous work in assisting in the preparation of materials for the manuscript, and her help in proofreading.

All cases in this book have been prepared for the purposes of class discussion rather than to illustrate either effective or ineffective handling of administrative situations.

D.H.F.
D.G.
R.N.K.

Contents

ACCESS TO A LEGISLATURE

ACCESS TO THE EXECUTIVE BRANCH

ANTITRUST PROBLEMS

POLITICAL ACCESS

SPECIAL SITUATIONS

Business Decision Making and Government Policy

Introduction

According to the traditional view of business-government relations, our economy is divided into neat, measurable, solid blocks called interest groups which collide and conflict. According to the practicing business manager, our economy operates through a whole series of contacts between people which produce a continuing, complex ebb and flow of collision and cooperation. It is to this latter view of business-government interactions that this book is dedicated.

In fact, the government official is sometimes an antagonist, sometimes a servant, sometimes responsive, sometimes rigid, sometimes a useful tool against competitors, sometimes a nuisance, sometimes an advisor, sometimes a friend, and sometimes a competitor for the business manager. In this regard, he is not unlike the other businessmen with whom an executive deals. The problem the manager faces, then, is simply this: how can I deal most effectively with this government man in this situation and secure what I feel is in the best interests of my company?

This is not to say that the government agency holds the same objectives, fills the same role, has the same problems, and represents the same constituency as the business organization. It does not. Consequently, in many circumstances, there are bound to be significant differences in viewpoint. But the overarching fact is that the areas of satisfactory accommodation and even common interest far exceed the more dramatic areas of conflict.

The authors of this book have proceeded on two premises: (1) the government, as a business participant; and (2) in an increasingly complicated and interrelated world, with ever-mounting conflicts of interest be-

1

tween individuals and between organizations, the participation of government in the affairs of men is likely to grow rather than to decrease.

Many characteristics of our society indicate that the role of the
government in the everyday life of most business managers will be even
larger in the future. The rising population, the increasing trend to urban-
ization, and the focus on poverty promise a growth in government services
and controls to deal with the problems that arise when more and more
people live closer and closer together and are ever more dependent on
one another. The rapid growth of technology and automation, coupled
with the civil rights movement, make it likely that there will be more
conflict in labor relations, with consequent pressures for further government intervention. The continued growth of large firms by merger and
market expansion may lead to increased antitrust and regulatory activity
by various government agencies. The accelerating trend toward an international orientation by United States business, with the development of
blocs like the European Common Market, the Central American community, and the developing countries generally will likely bring increased
government activity in the area of foreign trade policy. Finally, the demands placed on our society by a world in turmoil will inevitably require
more government intervention in the economy.

Therefore, the authors of this text are adopting an approach which
opens up the entire range of a businessman's relationship with government. The cases in this book deal not only with the relationships between
the corporate giant and the federal agency but also include the individual
small businessman and the local planning board. The material covers not
only areas of conflict, but areas of cooperation.

We have chosen to include a number of state and local cases because, for most businessmen, by far the bulk of their contacts will be on
these levels. In the early history of mankind, the cave man presumably
disposed of trash and garbage by throwing it outside his cave. When the
disadvantages of this practice became painfully obvious, he moved on.
Today men cannot do this. We have established local ordinances controlling the disposal of garbage and sewage as well as zoning regulations
which dictate what an individual may or may not do on his property.
This kind of government regulation touches directly upon every businessman in an urban area.

In this text, we neither justify nor condemn government regulation
of business. Presumably some is useful, some is capricious. We hope the
students will think through that matter as they deal with the individual
cases. But we hope also that they will recognize that, because of the
complexity of our society today, government involvement is a fact of life
and will continue to be one as long as there are men with economic and
social purposes which may at times be inconsistent with the economic and
social purposes of other men. In this context, the general concept of government participation in business decisions can be treated as a fact of

life with which the businessman must live, whether he approves or disapproves. We trust that he will, however, speak up and act to rectify specific situations, judged on their own merits. To do this effectively, he needs to understand the government and government personnel, to learn when and how to protect himself against what he determines are harmful actions, and when and how he can use government as a tool in the operation of his enterprise. Cases have been chosen to illustrate typical ways in which the businessman can deal with government in these terms.

We do not present the law as such, for we believe that any student at the level at which this text will be used can read the law, and the businessman, of course, will have his attorney to advise him. Rather, these cases are chosen to illustrate how the law might be used, applied, and influenced. The cases are designed to expose the student to the broad management decisions which the manager must make rather than to acquaint him with the details of ever-changing legislation.

The text begins with cases involving the government's granting licenses and providing services. It finishes with the problems of access to the various divisions and levels of government. The latter material touches upon the businessman's responsibilities to society and the businessman's role in helping to develop governmental policies. It is, of course, impossible to separate the businessman's responsibilities as a citizen from any discussion of business-government relations, and we hope that the reader will consider this aspect in pursuing this course, even though it is not the specific topic of any one case.

The authors hope that this casebook will help students (including practicing businessmen, since government regulation is constantly changing) to utilize government as a management tool skillfully, to work more effectively with those in whose hands the regulation of business is placed, and to assert their influence in bringing about greater understanding in the relationships between government and business in the interests of a dynamic and expanding economy.

Because Wisdom Can't Be Told[1]

So he had grown rich at last, and thought to transmit to his only son all the cut-and-dried experience which he himself had purchased at the price of his lost illusions; a noble last illusion of age. . . .—BALZAC

It can be said flatly that the mere act of listening to wise statements and sound advice does little for anyone. In the process of learning, the learner's dynamic cooperation is required. Such cooperation from students does not arise automatically, however. It has to be provided for and continually encouraged.

Thus, the key to an understanding of the Business School case plan of teaching is to be found in the fact that this plan dignifies and dramatizes student life by opening the way for students to make positive contributions to thought and, by so doing, to prepare themselves for action. Indeed, independent, constructive thinking on the part of students is essential to the sound operation of the plan. This result is achieved in two ways.

In the first place, students are provided with materials which make it possible for them to think purposefully. For the benefit of those unfamiliar with Business School cases, it is merely necessary to explain that, as now used, a case typically is a record of a business issue which *actually* has been faced by business executives, together with surrounding facts, opinions, and prejudices upon which executive decisions had to depend. These real and particularized cases are presented to students for con-

[1] Charles I. Gragg. Reprinted by permission from the *Harvard Alumni Bulletin*, October 19, 1940.

4

BECAUSE WISDOM CAN'T BE TOLD   5

sidered analysis, open discussion, and final decision as to the type of action which should be taken. Day by day, the number of individual business situations thus brought before the students grows and forms a backlog for observing coherent patterns and drawing out general principles. In other words, students are not given general theories or hypotheses to criticize. Rather, they are given specific facts, the raw materials, out of which decisions have to be reached in life and from which they can realistically and usefully draw conclusions. This opportunity for students to make significant contributions is enhanced by the very nature of business management. Business management is not a technical but a human matter. It turns upon an understanding of how people—producers, bankers, investors, sellers, consumers—will respond to specific business actions, and the behavior of such groups always is changing, rapidly or slowly. Students, consequently, being people, and also being in the very stream of sociological trends, are in a particularly good position to anticipate and interpret popular reactions.

In the second place, the desired result of student participation is achieved by the opening of free channels of communication between students and students, and between students and teachers. The confidence the student can be given under the case system that he can, and is expected to, make contributions to the understanding of the group is a powerful encouragement to effort. The corollary fact that all members of the group are in the same situation provides the student with exercise in receiving as well as in giving out ideas. In short, true intercommunication is established.

In these facts lies the answer to the unique values of the case system, and from these facts also arise certain difficulties encountered in its use. It is not easy for students to accept the challenge of responsible activity in the face of realistic situations. Nor is it always easy for teachers to preserve the needed open-mindedness toward their students' contribution. Nevertheless, the very existence of the assumption, implicit in the case system, that students are in a position to and will exert themselves to think with a lively independence toward a useful end in itself provides a real stimulus. By the same token, the stage is so set as to simplify the teacher's task of encouraging students to participate actively in the process of learning. The students are given the raw materials and are expected to use them. The teacher, for his part, has every opportunity and reason to demonstrate an encouraging receptivity as well as to inform and guide.

Thinking out original answers to new problems or giving new interpretations to old problems is assumed in much undergraduate instruction to be an adult function and, as such, one properly denied to students. The task of the student commonly is taken to be one chiefly of familiarizing himself with accepted thoughts and accepted techniques, these to be actively used at some later time. The instruction period, in other words, often is regarded both by students and by teachers as a time for absorption.

Thus many students entering graduate schools have become habituated to the role of the receiver. The time inevitably arrives, however, when young people must engage in practical action on their own responsibility. Students at professional school have a little time, at the [Harvard] Graduate School of Business [Administration] two years, to achieve the transition from what may be described as a childlike dependence on parents and teachers to a state of what may be called dependable self-reliance.

If the hearts of the young men entering a graduate school of business administration could be clearly read, it is likely there would be found in many a cherished hope that upon graduation they would find positions of authority and power awaiting them. This is a carefully guarded hope, because for some reason there is a general feeling that it is an unseemly one for young men to harbor. Yet, although the students who possess this hope may be said to be unrealistic under conditions as they exist, they cannot be said to be other than logical. For if a young man more or less permanently is to occupy a humble position in the business hierarchy, he can make better use of two years of his time than spending it at a school of business administration. The apprentice system is open to the young man who wishes to enter business in a fuller way than it is to the young man who seeks to work in the field of law or of medicine, for example. Except in a few instances, such as the plumbing and electrical trades, there are no restrictions similar to those imposed by bar or medical examinations as to who can start in business. And, if a young man who is to spend his life as a salesman, floorwalker, clerk, or minor official has several years to devote to acquiring background, he is likely to find that study of sonnets, or operas, or fishing, or philosophy will be more sustaining to his soul than a broad knowledge of business operations.

The work of a graduate school of business consequently must be aimed at fitting students for administrative positions of importance. The qualities needed by businessmen in such positions are ability to see vividly the potential meanings and relationships of facts, both those facts having to do with persons and those having to do with things, capacity to make sound judgments on the basis of these perceptions, and skill in communicating their judgments to others so as to produce the desired results in the field of action. Business education, then, must be directed to developing in students these qualities of understanding, judgment, and communication leading to action.

Furthermore, since young men who contemplate entering a graduate business school customarily have an alternative opportunity to enter business immediately, the business school must be able to do more for its students than could be accomplished in a corresponding period of actual business experience. Formal professional education necessarily postpones the time of responsible action. Yet a principal object of professional education is to accelerate the student's ability to act in mature fashion under conditions of responsibility. A young man who completes a professional course is expected to demonstrate a more mature judgment, or to demonstrate mature judgment at an earlier period, than the young man who enters upon a career of action without benefit of formal training. The presumption in this situation obviously must be that it is possible to arrange programs of training in such a way as to do more than offset the effect of prolonging the student's period of ostensible immaturity.

It would be easy to accept the unanalyzed assumption that by passing on, by lectures and readings, to young men of intelligence the accumulated experience and wisdom of those who have made business their study, the desired results could be achieved. Surely, if more or less carefully selected young men were to begin their business careers with the advantage of having been provided with information and general principles which it has taken others a lifetime to acquire and develop, they might be expected to have a decided head start over their less informed contemporaries.

This assumption, however, rests on another, decidedly questionable one: namely, the assumption that it is possible by a simple process of telling to pass on knowledge in a useful form. This is the great delusion of the ages. If the learning process is to be effective, something dynamic must take place in the learner. The truth of this statement becomes more and more apparent as the learner approaches the inevitable time when he must go into action.

We are all familiar with the popular belief that it is possible to learn how to act wisely only by experience—in the school of hard knocks. But everyone knows that, from a practical point of view, strict adherence to the literal meaning of this belief would have a decidedly limiting effect upon the extent of our learning. Time is all against it. So we all try to tell others what we know or what we think we know. A great part of our educational system, perhaps necessarily, rests on this basis. It is the simple, obvious way of passing the torch of culture from hand to hand.

Entirely aside from the seemingly sound logic of this course, there exists a natural and strong tendency for people to tell others what is what—how to think, or feel, or act. Often this tendency seems, to the one having it, like an urge to duty. A friend of ours, for example, may remark that he is worried because he doesn't seem to be getting anywhere with the president of the company. "He doesn't seem to know I'm around," our friend explains. Ah ha! We know the answer to that one and will tell our friend how to solve his problem. "Look here, old boy, the trouble with you is you are too shy. Just speak up, loudly and firmly. Tell him what's what. The old buzzard won't ignore you then!"

It is possible that our desire to pass on our knowledge springs in part from the fact that such activity places us, for the time being, in the superior position. From our earliest beginnings there have been people around to tell *us* what to do, to pass on to us their experience and wisdom. There is no little gratification in turning the tables. For a while we will be the parents and someone else can be the child. It is only necessary to listen to a six-year-old lecturing a three-year-old to see vividly the strength of this urge.

Teachers, since it is their avowed objective to extend the knowledge boundaries of others, are particularly beset by the temptation to tell what they know—to point out right paths of thought and action. The areas in which their help is called for are ones they have penetrated many times. They have reflected, presumably, upon their subjects from all angles. They feel that they know the answers and, with unselfish abandon, they are willing to tell all. Their students thus will be saved all the time and effort it would have taken them to work things out for themselves, even granted they ever could work out such excellent answers.

Yet no amount of information, whether of theory or fact, in itself improves insight and judgment or increases ability to act wisely under conditions of responsibility. The same statistical tables covering all aspects of a business may be available to every officer of the organization. Nevertheless, it does not follow that it makes no difference to the business which officer makes the decisions. Likewise, the whole body of generally accepted business theory may be equally familiar to all executives, yet the decisions reached by the various individuals are unlikely to be the same or to have equal merit.

We cannot effectively use the insight and knowledge of others; it must be our own knowledge and insight that we use. If our friend, acting solely on our advice, undertakes to tell the president what is what, the chances are he will make himself conspicuous but not impressive. For him to use our words effectively, granted our diagnosis of the situation is sound, they must become his own through a process of active thought and feeling on his part. Then, if he agrees with us, he will be able to act as we suggest, not on our advice, but from his own heart. The outstanding virtue of the case system is that it is suited to inspiring activity, under realistic conditions, on the part of the students; it takes them out of the role of passive absorbers and makes them partners in the joint processes of learning and of furthering learning.

The case plan of instruction may be described as democratic in distinction to the telling method, which is in effect dictatorial or patriarchal. With the case method, all members of the academic group, teacher *and* students, are in possession of the same basic materials in the light of which analyses are to be made and decisions arrived at. Each, therefore, has an identical opportunity to make a contribution to the body of principles governing business practice and policy. Business is not, at least not yet, an exact science. There is no single, demonstrably right answer to a business problem. For the student or businessman it cannot be a matter of peeking in the back of a book to see if he has arrived at the right solution. In every business situation, there is always a reasonable possibility that the best answer has not yet been found—even by teachers.

Exercise of mature judgment obviously is inconsistent with a program of blindly carrying out someone else's instructions. Moreover, no matter how worthy those instructions may be, they cannot cover every exigency. Tommy's mother says: "On your way home from school never cross the street until the policeman tells you to and, when he does tell you to, run." Perhaps one day no policeman is there. Is Tommy to wait forever? Or, perhaps a driver fails to observe the policeman's signals. Is Tommy to dash under the speeding wheels?

So far as responsible activity in the business world is concerned, it is clear that a fund of ready-made answers can be of little avail. Each situation is a new situation, requiring imaginative understanding as a prelude to sound judgment and action. The following sad limerick, aimed at describing what might happen to business students without benefit of cases, has been contributed by a friend who prefers to remain anonymous.

> A student of business with tact
> Absorbed many answers he lacked.
>   But acquiring a job,
>   He said with a sob,
> "How *does* one fit answer to fact?"

A significant aspect of democracy in the classroom is that it provides a new axis for personal relationships. No longer is the situation that of the teacher on the one hand and a body of students on the other. The students find their attention transferred from the teacher to each other. It is not a question of dealing more or less *en masse* with an elder; it is a question of dealing with a rather large number of equals and contemporaries whose criticism must be faced and whose contributions need to be comprehended and used. Everyone is on a par and everyone is in competition. The basis is provided for strong give and take both inside and outside the classroom. The valuable art of exchanging ideas is cultivated, with the object of building up some mutually satisfactory and superior notion. Such an exchange stimulates thought, provides a lesson in how to learn from others, and also gives experience in effective transmission of one's own ideas.

Under the case system, the instructor's role is to assign the cases for discussion, to act as a responsible member of the group delegated to provoke argumentative thinking, to guide discussion by his own contributions and questions toward points of major importance, and, if he chooses, to take a final position on the viewpoints which have been threshed out before him. The more powerful are the student arguments, the heavier is the burden on the instructor; he must understand and evaluate each contribution, many of which are new to him, regardless of how thoroughly he has studied the cases or how many times he has used them with previous classes. To the instructor, every class meeting is a new problem and a new opportunity both to learn and to help others to learn. The important question under these circumstances is not whether the student pleases the instructor, but whether he can either support his views against the counterattacks and disagreement of others in the group or, failing to do so, can accept cooperatively the merits of his antagonists' reasoning.

For both teachers and students, the disciplines of the case method of learning are severe. Sometimes the shock is devastating to young men who previously have been dominated by patriarchal instructors and thus have been faced merely with the relatively simple task of more or less passive reception and verbatim repetition of facts and ideas. Not all students can bear the strain of thinking actively, of making independent judgments which may be challenged vigorously by their contemporaries. Many people will always prefer to have answers handed to them. Teachers, for their part, particularly those unused to the system, sometimes find it straining to leave the safe haven of dogmatism and meet their students on a democratic plane. The inherently dramatic and challenging character of the case system, however, although it may produce anxiety and confusion for the newcomer, also arouses his deep interest and leads him to make the effort required for adjustment.

In making the adjustment to the democratic disciplines of the case system, students typically pass through at least three objectively discernible phases. The first phase is that of discovering the inability of the individual to think of everything that his fellow students can think of. In many instances, to be sure, the challenge to original thought is pleasing from the first. Yet perhaps more often confusion and a feeling of helplessness set in: "But it's so discouraging to prepare a case as well as I can and then listen for an hour in class to other students bringing out all sorts of interpretations and arguments that I had never thought of."

The second phase is that of accepting easily and naturally the need for cooperative help. During the last half of the first year and the first half of the second year, students learn to draw more and more fully upon each other's ideas in the working out of problems. Competition for high academic standing grows more keen, to be sure, but the mutual giving and taking of assistance ceases to be a matter of secret anguish. The young men are making common cause and thereby learning the pleasure of group pooling of intellectual efforts.

The third and final phase in the march toward maturity usually comes well on in the second year with the recognition that the instructors do not always or necessarily know the "best" answers and, even when they do seem to know them, that each student is free to present and hold to his own views. When this phase is reached, the student is ready to make independent progress and to break new ground on his own account. He is operating as a responsible member of the community, taking help, to be sure, from both contemporaries and elders, but making his own decisions without fear of disapproval or search for an authoritative crutch to lean upon. An outstanding effect of the case system, in other words, is to put upon students the burden of independent thinking.

No method is foolproof. A badly handled case system cannot but be an academic horror. Improperly handled, a case is merely an elaborate means for confusing and boring students. If, moreover, the teacher insists on being a patriarch—if he is sure he has the right and only answers and visualizes his task as one of forcing the students, the case facts, and *his* answers into an affectionate rapport—it will be found that the out-and-out lecture system is infinitely less costly and less straining to everyone concerned. Such authoritarian use of cases perverts the unique characteristics of the system. The opportunity which this system provides the students of reaching responsible judgments on the basis of an original analysis of the facts is sacrificed.

In addition to the possibility that the case system will be misused, and so become merely a wasteful way of telling the students what the teacher thinks, it must be recognized that the case does not provide a perfect replica of a business situation. In the properly conducted class using business cases, the students are put in the position of the executives who must arrive at definite conclusions to be followed by specific actions whose merits will be tested by resulting developments. Yet there is no escaping the fact that the students' decisions are not tested in this way. As Winston Churchill is reported to have remarked on one occasion, there is a great deal of difference between being responsible for an order which may lose several valuable ships and expressing an opinion without such responsibility. It is too much to expect that anything except experience can be exactly like experience.

Nevertheless, a training period which allows students this relative responsibility has great advantage. The serious student gets the essential background for responsible decisions without the risks to himself and to his firm which are inseparable from amateurish action. He is led to active consideration of a tremendous number of diverse and related real situations, which it would take him at least a lifetime of experience to encounter, and he is thus given a basis for comparison and analysis when he enters upon his career of business action.

The case system, properly used, initiates students into the ways of independent thought and responsible judgment. It confronts them with situations which are not hypothetical but real. It places them in the active role, open to criticism from all sides. It puts the burden of understanding and judgment upon them. It provides them the occasion to deal constructively with their contemporaries and their elders. And, at least in the area of business, it gives them the stimulating opportunity to make contributions to learning. In short, the student, if he wishes, can act as an adult member of a democratic community.

As for the teacher, the case method of instruction provides him richly with the basic means of research. Not only does the existence of a stream of recorded business experience enable him to keep in touch with businss life and to make continuous necessary modifications in his inductions and general conclusions. In addition, the relations which the case system sets up between himself and his students give the teacher the continual benefit of fresh, imaginative points of view which always hold the possibility of true advance.

Worcester County Trust Company[1]

The Worcester County Trust Company, oldest and largest commercial bank in Worcester County, Massachusetts, traces its history back to 1804 when its predecessor, the Worcester Bank, was organized by a group of citizens of the area. In 1864, as a result of a merger, it became one of the first institutions to join the National Banking System. In 1934, it surrendered its federal charter and reverted to its former status as a state bank.

By the end of 1958, with assets of nearly $137 million, 470 employees, and thirteen offices in nine Worcester County cities and towns, it was the fifth largest bank in Massachusetts and the second largest state bank. It had 130,000 shares outstanding, and 882 stockholders. Some 55,000 shares were held by 49 Massachusetts savings banks; about 65 per cent of this block was in the hands of saving institutions in Worcester County.

The bank is a member of several trade associations, including the American Bankers Association and the Massachusetts Bankers Association. The latter is an organization made up of all the commercial and many of the savings banks in the state. The MBA operated with a budget of about $100,000 in 1958, and employed a full-time staff including legislative counsel. Policy formation is in the hands of an Executive Council which meets monthly. The president of the Worcester County Trust Company, Edward L. Clifford, served as a member of the Council for one three-year term.

[1] Copyright © 1960 by the President and Fellows of Harvard College.

Mr. Clifford came to the Worcester County Trust as president in 1950 after nearly twenty years of experience in both state and national banks. At the time of his appointment as chief executive officer of the Worcester institution, he was a vice president of the Rhode Island Hospital Trust Company in Providence. His father, a lawyer, was once Assistant Secretary of the Treasury and subsequently practiced law in Washington for some fourteen years.

Mr. Clifford had been active in community affairs throughout his business career and was especially interested in politics. He first became involved in 1934, when he worked as a clerk at the polls and helped get out the vote. From 1938 to 1950, he was a member of the Second Ward Republican Committee in Providence; from 1946 to 1948, he served as treasurer of the Rhode Island Republican State Central Committee. In addition, he worked for twelve years as a member of the State Republican Finance Committee.

When he moved to Massachusetts, he maintained his political interests and associations. In 1956, for example, he was chairman of the United Republican Victory Committee in Worcester. He made it a rule to keep in touch with state legislators of both parties, and held an annual dinner for the group at the bank.

Mr. Clifford explained his continuing and vigorous political activity in an interview with a reporter from *The American Banker* in the summer of 1956 with these words:

> Political campaigns and platforms are increasingly based on economic matters and their effect on every kind of family unit and business, large and small. Many politicians distort the economic facts of our free enterprise system and such misinformation has had a bad effect from an immediate and long-term standpoint on banks. In every political campaign, it seems to me, it is essential that bankers, whether Democrats or Republicans, play an active part in the interpretation of the facts.
>
> Bankers should participate as actively in politics as in other less controversial community activities because creating good government is vital to our civic life. Bank officials are often too cautious in committing themselves on political issues for fear of losing business, but we have found that a forthright stand has worked to our advantage. In 24 years of banking, I cannot think of a customer our bank has lost because of political activity. I can think of a good many customers, Democrats as well as Republicans, whom I came to know first through politics and later as customers.

As president of the Worcester County Trust Company, Mr. Clifford urged the employees to participate in politics by raising the topic in conversations, at meetings, and through *The Mirror,* the bank's monthly staff newsletter. In one such article, for instance, he said:

> There appears to be an increasing interest on the part of businessmen in participating actively in government and politics at the local and state

levels. In order that there be no misunderstanding on the part of any employee of this Bank, I wish to make it perfectly clear that management is wholeheartedly behind this movement.

This Bank cannot and will not take a stand pro or con on partisan issues, nor condone participation of any of its employees in so-called 'Gutter Politics.' Aside from this, however, we encourage your participation, particularly in local politics, in the interest of good government. By participation, I mean working for the party or candidate *of your choice,* running for local elective office or serving in an appointive capacity. Within the practical limits of doing justice to your own position here, we will make every effort to see that those who aspire to office, as well as those who are successful, are given the time to do a good job.

To back up his words, he made it plain that community service generally would be taken into account in promotion decisions, and that special credit would be given for work in activities that were controversial.

Because of his knowledge of the advantages and disadvantages of both state and federal charters, Mr. Clifford often considered the possibility of converting the Worcester County Trust to a national bank. He knew that such a conversion would be unusual—the national trend is in the other direction—and that only one Massachusetts bank in a position like his had made such a request for many years. But he and his associates believed that the treasurers of national companies respond more rapidly to the idea of doing business with national banks than state ones, and he saw real growth possibilities for his institution in such concerns. Secondly, he was continuously watching his operating costs and felt that he could achieve a significant reduction in the number and variety of required reports if the bank converted. Reports demanded by the Comptroller of the Currency are similar to those submitted to the Federal Reserve Board, while the statements sent to the State Banking Department in Massachusetts are quite different and make necessary a separate bookkeeping arrangement. In the third place, he believed that the move would be a logical one in view of the bank's growth in resources and number and type of depositors.

Finally, he was not altogether pleased with the state regulatory agency and the Massachusetts political climate. The Worcester County Trust had had some disagreements with the state banking department over out-of-state mortgages which, Mr. Clifford felt, might have impeded the institution's growth to some degree. A Stock Option Bill which he had submitted to the legislature with the backing of the MBA had been pocket-vetoed by the Governor in the early fall of 1958. This bill would have permitted the institution of a restricted stock option plan for executives similar to those used in industry. His request for a deposit of state funds from the Massachusetts Turnpike Authority had been turned down in favor of a small national bank in a nearby town. This decision was consistent with state policy; national banks rather than state banks were the state's chief depositories. His bank, therefore, had almost no state money on deposit. When the 1958 elections produced a Democratic sweep of considerable proportions, placing both branches of the legislature, the Governor's Council and all the constitutional offices including the governorship in the hands of the Democrats, he became further concerned about the business climate in Massachusetts and felt that this turn of events made improvement in the prevailing conditions unlikely.

The sweep extended throughout the state, and changed the nature of the Worcester delegation to the State House considerably. The two Senators—William D. Fleming, Democrat, a veteran legislator of considerable stature, and Harold R. Lundgren, Republican, a long-time leader in his party and chairman of the Committee on Banks and Banking in the outgoing legislature—both retained their seats, but two Republican Representatives were defeated. This left the House group with two Republicans and eight Democrats. One of the Republicans and four of the Democrats were freshmen; two of the Democrats, Domenic V. DePari and Leo J. Reynolds, were veterans with a fair amount of influence. By and large, the other Democrats were expected to follow the party line.

By late November of 1958, Mr. Clifford decided to pursue the matter of conversion seriously. After meeting with the Comptroller of the Currency in Washington, he began to hold conferences with his legal advisers and asked the treasurer of the bank to start drawing up the necessary papers. In so doing, he was well aware that he faced two potentially serious obstacles.

1. The Bank Commissioner, Edward A. Counihan III, could be expected to oppose the conversion because of the size and importance of the Worcester bank. His office would lose $15,000 of examining fees, and would suffer a loss of prestige if its second largest institution left the system. Mr. Counihan, a well-known Democrat, was the eldest son of a Supreme Court judge and came from a family that had long been closely identified with Democratic party politics and political figures. Governor Furcolo, re-elected in November of 1958, had appointed him in 1957.

2. A bill which would, if passed, essentially prevent state banks from converting without the approval of the Bank Commissioner was pending before the new legislature, which was due to convene on January 7, 1959. The measure was designed to prevent possible conversions, though, in fact, there had been only one request to change status from state to federal in the Commonwealth for at least thirty years. Proponents claimed it should be passed to balance similar federal restrictions on conversions from national to state pending the report of a recently-appointed legislative commission in Massachusetts which was studying the whole issue.

Proposed by the Bank Commissioner, the current bill (House Bill #10) was similar to one that had been defeated in an earlier session, but most observers believed that it could be passed fairly quickly by the incoming House and Senate. Similar last-minute legislative action, in combination with delaying tactics by the Bank Commissioner, had thwarted a proposed merger of two Massachusetts banks several years before, and it seemed more than possible to Mr. Clifford that the General Court might take the same sort of step in his case.

Faced with these problems, Mr. Clifford set to work with all speed, taking care to keep the project confidential. He established contact with a Washington attorney, a former Deputy Comptroller of the Currency, who agreed to represent the bank at that end. The necessary work on the papers was completed between December 10 and December 21, the Executive Committee met on December 17 and voted to recommend conversion to the directors; and a board meeting was held December 23. At this meeting the conversion was approved and a special stockholders' meeting was called for January 2, 1959.

Notices to shareholders went in the mail that afternoon. As soon as the board had voted, a representative of the bank who had gone to Washington the day before was called and instructed to present the papers to the comptroller's office for tentative approval. By 3:30 P.M. on December 23 the federal authorities had processed the documents and given their assent, pending the stockholders' meeting.

On Wednesday, December 24, timed for the afternoon papers, the bank's public relations office issued the first news release about the pending conversion.

Five days later—on Monday, December 29—a representative of the Bank Commissioner's office telephoned to inquire about the "rumors." The board vote of December 23 was reported to him by an official of the bank. The next day the Commissioner himself called asking for a list of stockholders, which was made available to him after clearing with the bank's counsel.

At 11:00 A.M. on December 31, the Washington Savings Bank of Lowell, holders of 260 shares of Worcester County Trust stock, filed a suit in Suffolk County Superior Court. Though the bank's attorneys were heard on the matter, Judge Jesse W. Morton issued a temporary injunction restraining the stockholders from meeting on January 2 to approve the conversion. A hearing on the petition to prevent the conversion was set for January 12, five days after the new legislature was to go into session. Since Mr. Clifford had received the proxy of the Washington

Savings Bank on the morning of the day their suit was filed, he suspected that they were acting at the behest of the Bank Commissioner.

The same day, Mr. Counihan sent the following telegram to the 49 savings banks who were stockholders on the Worcester County Trust:

> Urge you vote against proposal to convert Worcester County Trust Company to national bank, January 2. Your deposits invested in Worcester County Bank stock will no longer be tax exempt under state law and your depositors will thus suffer from conversion.—Edward A. Counihan III, Commissioner of Banks.

At about the same time, the Comptroller of the Currency received a message from Massachusetts Congressman John W. McCormack, long-time power in the House of Representatives in Washington and currently Democratic Majority Leader, requesting him not to approve any conversion without talking to Massachusetts Bank Commissioner Counihan.

On the late afternoon of December 31, Mr. Clifford sat down to review his position. He realized that Mr. Counihan would almost surely persuade Governor Furcolo to send a special message to the legislature immediately following the Governor's inauguration on Wednesday, January 7, asking that House Bill #10 be passed at once as an emergency measure. This process could take as little time as one day. The House was under the leadership of a strong Furcolo man as Speaker, Representative John F. Thompson of Ludlow; the Senate was tightly controlled by Senate President John E. Powers, Democrat, of South Boston. Senator Powers, a powerful and respected political veteran, was to be a candidate for mayor of Boston in the 1959 fall elections. He had run against Mayor John B. Hynes several years before, but had lost, partly because he had been unable to win over the "respectable" elements in town. With Mayor Hynes' decision not to seek another term, Senator Powers had decided to make a second try. He was very concerned with assembling all the strength he could. Though they were both Democrats, Senator Powers and Governor Furcolo had been at odds for some time both personally and ideologically.

From information that came to him, Mr. Clifford had good reason to think that Mr. Counihan was anxious to reach some kind of compromise. Three possibilities were suggested by sources close to the Commissioner: a deposit of $3 million of state funds in the Worcester County Trust; a guarantee that the Stock Option Bill would pass and, this time, be signed by Governor Furcolo; and a suggestion that the bank drop two of its major branches, allowing them to stay in the state system when it converted.

Mr. Clifford thought it very likely that the Commissioner would follow up his telegrams to the savings banks. Since the tax loss mentioned in the telegram could only amount to $2,800 even for the largest stockholder institution, the substance of this argument seemed thin but Mr.

Clifford was not sure of its impact. Further, he knew that there were bills pending in the legislature which could have a very damaging effect on savings banks if passed, and he was not sure of the weight of this fact in the minds of these institutions which held 55,000 shares of Worcester County Trust stock. Perhaps they might not want to get involved in any disputes at this particular time.

PART TWO

THE GOVERNMENT AS A LICENSER

"They Said It Couldn't Be Done"[1]

Can a business in a declining industry be restored to financial and economic good health if, during its period of rehabilitation, it must overcome such handicaps as:

Granting a series of wage hikes and fringe benefits nearly doubling the pay of hundreds of workers—while gross business volume was shrinking to less than one quarter of its starting total;

Paying off several millions of dollars in debts;

Operating under multiple regulation of municipal and state authorities, which at times met head on with conflicting ideas, orders and demands;

Waging (and winning) a proxy battle;

Having to engage repeatedly in costly litigation to gain self-evident justice;

Overcoming public ill will and winning good will—replacing irrational conflict with realistic cooperation.

These obstacles were faced by Portland Transit Company, a private corporation whose subsidiaries provide public transportation and freight operations in the area around Portland, Oregon.

Our organization—Charles C. Bowen & Co. of San Francisco—does not seek business and financial troubles in the enterprises in which we

[1] Charles C. Bowen '23, Partner, Charles C. Bowen & Co. Reprinted from *The Harvard Business School Bulletin*, Vol. 36, No. 5, Oct., 1960, by permission.

engage. We do not insist upon handicaps as a condition precedent to taking a financial and managerial interest in a given situation. Still, it must be admitted that obstacles add zest to an undertaking—especially in retrospect—and we certainly had our share!

This mass transportation system proposition is quite a story, which really starts back in the thirties when I became increasingly interested in the link between accounting and management consulting. I had been graduated from the College of Commerce, University of California at Berkeley, in 1921, and received my M.B.A. from the Harvard Business School in 1923. I then went on to acquire my CPA in 1925. An extended period of practical experience in commercial, investment and trust banking followed, capped by "postgraduate" work in a national management consulting firm.

My interest has always been in the end use of accounting, rather than in the practice of the profession for its own sake, so the establishment of our firm was a logical step. Charles C. Bowen & Co., Certified Public Accountants and Management Consultants, began business in San Francisco in 1939. It was, I believe, the first West Coast CPA firm to establish a department of management services. Today there are many local and national firms with Pacific Coast offices operating in this field.

This firm turned out to be the key to our venture in the public transportation business. The idea of an accounting firm in the consulting field attracted substantial investors seeking advice in the use of their funds. We became appraisers of businesses for prospective buyers and sellers and were asked to represent banks and investment houses on the boards of various companies. Through these channels we became interested, in 1945, in the situation which later developed into Portland Transit Company.

Portland Electric Power Company was in reorganization under the District Court of the United States, under Chapter X of the Federal Bankruptcy Act. The trustees representing the Court were seeking a purchaser for Portland Traction Company, a subsidiary of the power company, which operated its mass transportation and terminal freight systems.

I was extremely intrigued by the venture. The company's record in the prospectus was highly profitable, and professional appraisals showed a promising future. Furthermore, there was a substantial sum of cash accumulated in a reserve fund and set aside for modernization. The only problems that we could see were an unspecified tax liability—which I shall mention later—and the fact that the trustees were insisting that the purchaser take over an interurban railroad along with the city transportation system. Everyone seemed to agree that the railroad was a real dog. But all in all, the package seemed to be a good one.

This was a $5.8-million deal—a bit hefty for us to swing alone. So I sought out my old roommate at the Business School, Duke O. Hannaford '24, who was head of the San Francisco securities firm of Hannaford

& Talbot. Assured of Duke's interest, we next turned to First California Company, one of the largest distributors of securities on the Pacific Coast, and, finally, to Bank of America.

Portland Transit Company was formed as the parent organization, and a financing program set up to provide the $5.8 million. It consisted of a $2.5-million bank loan to the Transit Company, and two issues of stock: $1.5-million preferred and $1.8-million common.

One of the conditions of purchase was the stipulation that the buyer had to assume a tax liability of a substantial but undetermined amount. A competing bidder lost out through his inability to arrive at a reasonable estimate of the commitment; our organization, being more tax conscious, was able to assume this liability without reservation, and as a result we were the successful bidder.

We needed a down payment of $500,000, subject to possible forfeiture, and raised the money by creating Pacific Associates, Inc., an investing firm. Duke Hannaford and I were substantially interested in this new company and served as officers and directors of it. Since its organization for the Portland Transit deal, Pacific Associates has expanded and diversified its activities by purchasing controlling interest in Kaar Engineering Corporation of Palo Alto, California, one of the oldest electronic firms specializing in communications equipment, and Klamath Machine & Locomotive Works of Ukiah, California, manufacturer of sawmill machinery.

So we acquired Portland Traction, but what did we have? Portland Traction Company consisted of two main divisions: the Portland city lines and the interurban serving Oregon City and other communities. The interurban handled a substantial volume of freight, which turned out to be a very fortunate circumstance since it gave us a hedge against the passenger patronage shrinkage which developed later.

The company had had a long and checkered career (which seems to be the history of just about every transit operation in the country)— many managements, many company names, and many problems over the years. Portland Traction had, however, emerged from World War II in excellent shape. Business had been unusually good because Portland had been a shipbuilding center, employing thousands of workers to be transported from place to place. Rationing of gasoline and tires had forced many automobile owners to use public transportation. So business was good—at least at the start.

The first job was to find a top man to run the company. Fortunately, we convinced Fred G. Stevenot, an extremely able man with sound banking and management experience, to take over as president—more recently he has become chairman of Portland Transit. He had served on the California Railroad Commission, predecessor to California Public Utilities Commission, and, as a Bank of America officer, had accomplished many successful reorganizations. At the time, he was president of the

Puget Sound Pulp and Timber Company, which he had built up into a top company, but he and I had met twenty years before when we were serving in the state government of California. It was agreed that this outstanding executive was just the man for us.

From the beginning the parent company, Portland Transit, determined to keep the local managemnt of Portland Traction intact, since its operating heads and the Portland Board of Directors were composed of prominent local citizens. David B. Simpson, an outstanding property management man and a former "First Citizen of Portland," is still closely associated with us, as is my friend and HBS classmate, Dick Montgomery '23, who was elected to the Board in 1948 and was to play an important role in the fortunes of the Company, as we will see later.

Public offering of Portland Transit Company's preferred and common stocks was made in November, 1946, by a group of 22 national and Pacific Coast underwriters headed by First California Company. The offering was made through a prospectus of 99 pages—a most complex but frank statement making full disclosure of the facts. And when I say "frank," I really mean it. The document was a pretty negative one, actually, stressing the complexity of the company's affairs, the state of the railroad, the tax liability, the extent of borrowing involved in the deal, and the fact that none of the new group had any previous transit experience.

"Full disclosure" does not, for obvious reasons, include prediction, prophecy, or fortune telling. Perhaps it is better that way, for in the Portland instance the road ahead was to be a rough one; in fact, it began to get bumpy right away. We offered the stock at $7.50 a share. Just then the market broke, and this unhappy event, when combined with some further legal problems with the SEC, meant that the underwriters had a very tough time getting rid of the stock.

Then came the second complication. It was not long after we set up shop that a downtrend in volume of riders appeared which was destined to continue for many years. With the end of gas rationing and resumption of automobile manufacturing, passenger traffic declined sharply, not only in Portland but all over the United States. Thus began a long struggle to keep overhead in line with diminishing revenues so as to maintain a profit with which to meet debt obligations and in other ways protect the interests of stockholders. In 1959 city passenger traffic was down to one-fourth of its 1946 total. During this same period wages were raised 73 per cent, and on top of that came layer upon layer of fringe benefits.

Our third difficulty turned on the matter of equipment. We were operating old-fashioned trolley cars. However, we inherited a fleet of trolley coaches, which represented little, if any, improvement, since trolley coaches cost more to operate than do diesel buses. In addition, a large, expensive, and unnecessary headquarters-shop building, which was dubbed the Taj Mahal, had been put up. This, too, proved to be a drain on our dwindling resources and was soon abandoned due to our reduced traffic. It was later sold at a large sacrifice.

In the face of all this, we decided we had to take some forceful action. As volume and revenue fell, we raised fares and redrew the bus lines and schedules. But we did this with some degree of anxiety because, under our charter, we had to go to the City Council for approval each time, and they sometimes objected to such changes. Furthermore, we were all too conscious of the fact that the company's 20-year franchise was to come up again in 1956. We were concerned that it might not be renewed.

As we approached the franchise renewal date, we had more and more reason to be worried. Private automobiles competed for our business and clogged the streets, interfering with bus running time. Bus service suffered. Bus riders suffered. Tempers became frayed all around. Then we decided that we had to get rid of the trolley buses and operate less expensive equipment. That set off another explosion—people liked them because they were quiet and comfortable.

By this time, due to circumstances and despite my sincere efforts to do a job, I had become the villain of a drama. Somebody had to be the "goat," and perhaps I was the most logical candidate, as an absentee landlord. However, I never lost faith that some day all of this would change.

In such an atmosphere, it seemed impossible to negotiate a satisfactory operating city-lines franchise, then coming up for renewal. The City Council finally decided to let us continue operating the city lines through a series of short-term permits. Then, as if all this weren't enough, some of our opponents put a resolution on the ballot for the next city election which called for municipal ownership of the company.

CHART ONE

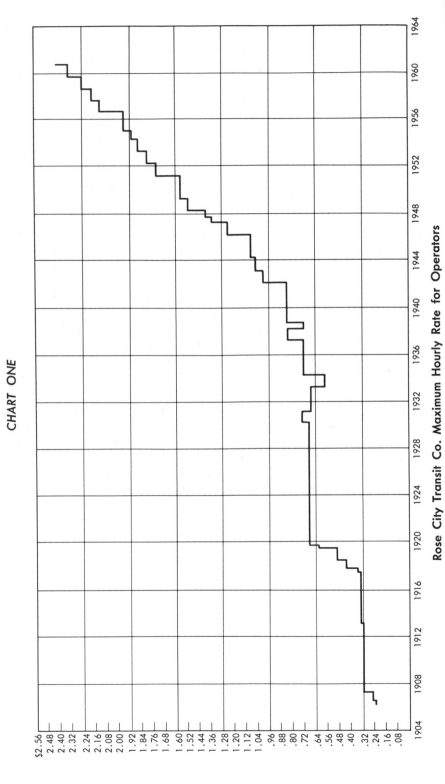

Rose City Transit Co. Maximum Hourly Rate for Operators

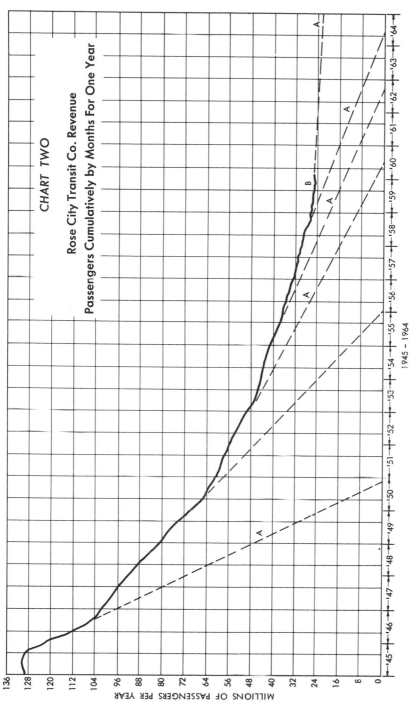

CHART TWO

Rose City Transit Co. Revenue

Passengers Cumulatively by Months For One Year

1945 – 1964

MILLIONS OF PASSENGERS PER YEAR

Each point on the chart represents the millions of revenue passengers carried in the twelve month period ending with that month. For example, for the year ending November, 1959, 24,658,761 revenue passengers were carried. This is indicated by point B on the chart.

Light lines (marked A) are trend lines indicating the number of passengers that might have been expected if the then existing trend had continued.

CHART THREE

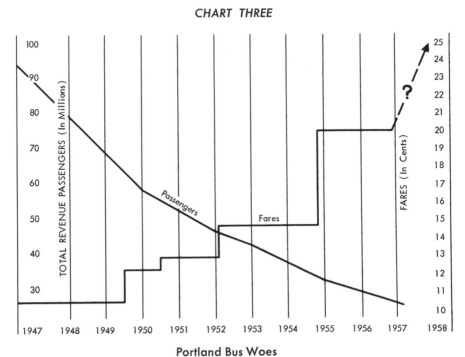

Portland Bus Woes
Fares Up—Passengers Down

The 1789

Georgetown University is located in the exclusive Georgetown section of Washington, D.C. Across the street from one of the classroom buildings of the University is a strip of commercial enterprise. Among these are a haberdasher, laundromat, a small restaurant, and a barber shop. While this area was commercial, these shops possessed a certain charm and lent an atmosphere to the area not ordinarily found in residential areas today. Also on that block for many years was a medium-sized restaurant known as the Hilltop. The Hilltop served wines and beer, in addition to food, and possessed what was known as a "Class D" license from the Alcoholic Beverage Control Board of the District of Columbia, which permitted the Hilltop to serve beer and light wines.

In 1960, Georgetown University became the owner of the property on which the Hilltop stood. At the same time, the business of the Hilltop was purchased by a corporation identified as R. J. M., Inc. R. J. M., Inc. then became the lessee from the university, and, by virtue of having purchased the business of the Hilltop, became the transferee of the Class D license. The occupancy of the premises and R. J. M'.s plans for that location eventually became the subject of extensive litigation. The pleadings and testimony developed at various administrative hearings and court proceedings indicated that some people in positions of authority at Georgetown University were desirous of there being an establishment similar to Mory's at Yale, where students could gather, and it was hoped that R. J. M. would develop such an establishment. R. J. M., Inc., began operating under the name The 1789, which was the year of the adoption of the United States Constitution, the date of the incorporation of the village of Georgetown, and the date of founding of Georgetown University. When R. J. M. had applied for transfer of the Class D license from the Hilltop to R. J. M., citizens in the area objected, but filed their objection too late, and the transfer was made without incident. In the past, citizens of Georgetown had never questioned possession of the Class D license by the Hilltop.

In 1961, Richard J. McCooey, president of R. J. M., Inc., an alumnus of Georgetown University and former advertising executive, applied to the Alcoholic Beverage Control Board for a Class C license. A Class C license permitted the sale of liquor, as well as beer and light wines permitted under a Class D license. When some residents of the neighborhood had objected to the transfer of the Class D license from the Hilltop to R. J. M., Inc., Mr. McCooey thought that perhaps the citizens and residents did not understand what he was trying to accomplish, or realize the nature of the establishment which he envisioned. Accordingly, he attempted to speak with some of the residents who had objected. Some of the residents had indicated at that time that they had no desire to speak to Mr. McCooney and declined to communicate with him. Others wrote what some people would describe as "crank letters."

As might have been expected, when R. J. M., Inc., applied for a Class C license from the Alcoholic Beverage Control Board, a hue and cry was raised in opposition to the application of R. J. M., Inc., before the Alcoholic Beverage Control Board. Two local Citizens' Associations, the Georgetown Citizens Association and the Progressive Citizens Association, opposed a granting of a Class C license at the hearings conducted before the Alcoholic Beverage Control Board. The newspapers gave extensive coverage to the fight that ensued. At the hearings, nine citizens testified in opposition to the granting of the license, and the Board received fifteen letters from citizens in opposition. The opponents of issue of the license submitted extensive surveyors' plats, drawings, photographs, and movies. Much of this appealed to the emotions; words which some observers considered inflammatory, such as "saloon," "tavern," etc., were used extensively. The movies showed children in the neighborhood going to school not far from the location of The 1789. The citizens' groups were well organized, even to the extent of having block captains to solicit petitions in opposition. Apparently, it is fairly easy for one neighbor to obtain another's signature on a petition of this type; it later developed, according to the court files, that some signers of the petitions had allegedly been misled at the time of signing the petitions. Those who allegedly were misled stated that they were not aware of the apparent approval of Georgetown University of the establishment of, and plans for, The 1789.

At the hearings before the Alcoholic Beverage Control Board, Mr. McCooey testified about his plans for the restaurant and what he envisioned. Mr. McCooey had long felt that there was a real need for an establishment such as The 1789 near the University, and he had left the field of advertising because of his belief in this need. In addition to Mr. McCooey, three area residents and landowners testified that they had no opposition to the granting of a Class C license to The 1789. It should be noted that private homes were located both immediately behind and across the street from the premises occupied by The 1789. A police captain from the precinct also testified that precinct records and his experience indicated no complaints about activities in or around the location of The 1789 resulting from operation of The 1789 or the Hilltop for the past twenty years. R. J. M., Inc., also urged residents to write their opinions to the Alcoholic Beverage Control Board. R. J. M., Inc., felt that letters had more effect upon the board than did petitions.

After the hearing in late 1961, the Alcoholic Beverage Control Board issued to R. J. M., Inc., the Class C license for which it had applied. Such approval of the license was contingent, however, upon R. J. M., Inc., meeting certain conditions. Such conditions had included obtaining an occupancy permit and completing remodeling of the premises. Mr. McCooey had developed plans for remodeling the premises to a style which was reminiscent of British and other European restaurants, inns, and taverns, and for inclusion of a rathskeller. The plans, though once turned down, had been approved by the Fine Arts Commission of the District of Columbia in August, 1960. The Fine Arts Commission is a body whose purpose it is to ensure that public buildings in the District of Columbia were in conformity with other surrounding buildings, and in good taste, and that buildings of historical and aesthetic interest are not disturbed and are kept in conformity with the surrounding district and traditions. Accordingly, since The 1789 was a commercial establishment and in a historical area, it was necessary that the Fine Arts Commission approve the remodeling of the premises. (Although not relevant to this case, it is interesting to note that private property owners whose property is adjacent to public parks or parkways must obtain approval of the Fine Arts Commission before they can even do so much as place a fence on their property.) R. J. M. had begun alterations to the premises on November 1, 1961.

On January 19, 1962, 23 plaintiffs who were residents of the neighborhood brought an action in the U. S. District Court for the District of Columbia, challenging the decision of the Alcoholic Beverage Control Board, and asking that the license issued by the board be revoked. The neighborhood residents who vigorously opposed the plans of R. J. M., Inc. were far from "crackpots," meddlers, or similar types. One of the plaintiffs who lived quite close to The 1789 was H. Struve Hensel, who was at one time General Counsel of the Department of Defense. Leaders of the opposition to The 1789 were H. Alexander Smith and John Colie. Others among the plaintiffs were of similar reputation and prestige and were considered extremely responsible citizens.

During the pendency of this action, the time within which R. J. M.,

Inc., was to have complied with conditions imposed by the Alcoholic Beverage Control Board in order to get its Class C license had expired. This, then, raised the question of whether or not the matter before the court involved a moot issue, since the license had not become perfected. However, R. J. M., Inc., filed a new application for a Class C license. The application was opposed, of course, by the residents of the area. Some legal maneuvering and "fancy footwork" on the part of both plaintiffs and defendents ensued. The net result was that the court retained jurisdiction of the matter and determined the issue of the validity of issuance of a Class C license to R. J. M., Inc., by the Alcoholic Beverage Control Board.

An alcoholic beverage license is issued for a period of one (1) year, and most are renewed without objection on an annual basis. The citizens' associations sought to enjoin the Alcoholic Beverage Control Board from holding hearings on the second application until after the court had ruled on the first application of R. J. M., Inc. This injunction did not materialize. These activities took place in February and March of 1962. After the injunction was denied, hearings were held. The residents obtained a postponement of the first hearings set by the Alcoholic Beverage Control Board due to allegations that adequate notice had not been posted. Some of the residents testified that they had not seen notices and that notices which were posted were removed before the expiration of the period during which notices were to be posted. One plaintiff testified that, as he was passing The 1789 one day, he observed what appeared to be an official notice posted on a wall at The 1789. In order to get a closer look at the notice, however, he, according to his affidavit, had to climb between the rails of a barricade and stand on a pile of sand and lumber. According to another affidavit in the record, a citizen plaintiff observed the notice and thought it might be important, so she went home and got her opera glasses so she could read the notice. The purpose of these affidavits was to develop the allegations that sufficient notice had not been given by the Alcoholic Beverage Control Board of the pending hearing. During this time renovations which were estimated at a cost in excess of $300,000 were being made at The 1789. The Alcoholic Beverage Control Board's action in approving issuance of a Class C license to R. J. M., Inc., was upheld by the District Court. The plaintiffs appealed the decision in March of 1962. The appeal was denied in July of 1963. Meanwhile, the license was issued to R. J. M., Inc. in July of 1962. R. J. M., Inc., opened The 1789 for business in August of 1962.

Although this litigation was originally brought against the Alcoholic Beverage Control Board in order to set aside its decision, R. J. M., Inc., had sought to be included and was granted permission to be included as a co-defendant in order to protect its interests in this matter. The Alcoholic Beverage Control Board was represented by the District of Columbia Corporation Counsel (in other areas this would be the city or county attorney). R. J. M., Inc., was represented by its own counsel, who were Eugene Stewart, who later became president of the Georgetown Alumni Association, and J. E. Bindeman, also a Georgetown alumnus.

The plaintiffs had alleged that the granting of the license would create irreparable injury to the plaintiffs and would deprive them of property without due process of law. The defendants introduced expert testimony concerning evaluation of property to establish that the existence of The 1789 would not lower property value. The main thrust of the plaintiffs rested on the regulation which prohibits granting of a Class C license to an establishment which would be within 400 feet of a public, private or parochial school, church, or university. The same prohibition applied to a Class D license. The court upheld the board. On appeal, the decision of the lower court was upheld, since the Hilltop had begun operation in 1928, and the license, which had originally been issued in 1936, had been in effect prior to the 400-foot restriction set forth in the regulations. Such restriction did not apply to businesses which were already in operation. This is what is known as a grandfather clause and is not uncommon. Other aspects of the board's decision were primarily administrative in nature and, as such, were a discretionary matter with which the court would not interfere, since the court would not overrule discretionary administrative decisions unless such were clearly arbitrary, capricious or contrary to law. It is also interesting to note that most of the nearby property owners and the owners of the largest parcels of property in the area were not opposed to the plans of The 1789.

Seeing difficulty in prevailing in the action against the Alcoholic Beverage Control Board, the opposing residents also presented an action in connection with zoning regulations in order to thwart the plans of R. J. M., Inc. They approached the Zoning Administrator for the District of Columbia and asked that he find that The 1789 would be in violation of the zoning regulations. They based their protest on grounds that the plans of The 1789, in calling for use of the basement as a rathskeller, increased the maximum amount of occupiable area which could be located on a certain parcel of property and that insufficient parking spaces were provided for by The 1789. The Zoning Administrator's decision was taken to the Board of Zoning Adjustment, which denied the relief sought by the area residents. Here again, considerable testimony was introduced and hearings were held. At this point, Mr. Stewart brought in lawyers who were experts in the field of zoning matters. The decision of the Board of Zoning Adjustment did not issue for considerable time, and the board called some witnesses back to testify. Some observers feel that the board took considerable time to reach a decision because the board was aware of the fact that no matter which way it decided, litigation would result. The Board of Zoning Adjustment found in favor of R. J. M., Inc. The area residents then filed an action against the Board of Zoning Adjustment in the U.S. District Court for the District of

Columbia. Again, R. J. M., Inc., appeared as co-defendant. R. J. M., Inc., closed off part of its premises in order that it not exceed the questionable area-usage limitation and made arrangements for additional parking. This, of course, did not satisfy the protesting residents, as they had sought to shut down The 1789 completely. The court found in favor of the plaintiffs and set aside the decision of the Board of Zoning Adjustment. This would have meant that R. J. M., Inc., would have to have reduced its operation. R. J. M., Inc. filed an appeal. Prior to a decision on the appeal, the case was dismissed by mutual agreement. About this time, Mr. Smith died, and the other protesting citizens seemed to have lost their zeal for pursuing this matter, since it no longer appeared that The 1789 would be closed completely. Also, at about this same time, two of the plaintiffs requested that their names be stricken from the list of plaintiffs, alleging that they knew nothing about the action and were not knowingly plaintiffs. Although there was evidence in the file which may have rebutted these plaintiffs' allegations that they were not knowingly aware of or parties to the action, the court permitted their withdrawal.

After the dismissal of the appeal, R. J. M., Inc. continued its operation of The 1789. Had the tactics of the protesting residents been successful, The 1789 might perhaps have been able to operate as a private club, since the regulations involved would not have applied in those circumstances. The promoters of The 1789 did not want to move from that location because they could not then accomplish what they wanted: establishment of a superior, respectable gathering place for students. Some observers felt that Mr. McCooey must have had considerable motivation to establish The 1789 and considerable financial resources or backing. Otherwise, he would have been forced at some point to yield to the pressure of the residents, which was not only emotionally taxing, but also financially burdensome.

During the course of the testimony, there was some inference that the objection to the plans of The 1789 was based on objection to the university's impact and future growth in the Georgetown area. While it appears that The 1789's immense problems have been resolved, it is continually faced with the problem of community and neighbor relationships. The relationship of Georgetown University to the Georgetown citizens may be a factor in the citizens' acceptance or lack of acceptance of The 1789. It is noteworthy that, three years after the litigation involving The 1789 began, a group of prominent citizens was formed to purchase land surrounding the university in order to prevent further encroachments by the university upon the historical residential area. Implicit in this was the question of whether or not such strenuous objections would have been raised to The 1789 if the university had not owned the property. Conversely, had the university not had any interest in the property, would R. J. M., Inc., have prevailed in the dispute?

Channel Eight, West Coast City

Mr. Kevin Traynor has been asked to join with 35 other businessmen in the metropolitan area of West Coast City in submitting an application to the Federal Communications Commission to operate a new television station on Channel Eight, in West Coast City. Traynor has further been asked to head the group which would incorporate as West Coast Television, Inc., as president of the new corporation.

West Coast City, located in the state of West Coast, is a large metropolitan area similar in size to San Francisco or metropolitan Scattle-Tacoma. Clearly, West Coast City is a major market for television.

There are only two commercial VHF (Very High Frequency) television channels in operation in West Coast City. VHF channels (Channels Two through Thirteen) were in scarce supply generally throughout the nation, since widespread separation of channels was necessary to prevent interference with the signals, and there were many other competing uses for VHF facilities (such as for military uses) that prevented more VHF channels from being assigned to television for commercial broadcast purposes. The higher band UHF (Ultra High Frequency) channels did not satisfy adequately the demand for more commercial television channels in cities such as West Coast City, since few television sets were equipped to receive UHF signals, and UHF home television antennas were somewhat more complex and expensive than VHF antennas. In addition, the UHF channels were assigned to television some years after the VHF channels and the public was still somewhat skeptical of them. All FCC and industry efforts to promote UHF television had been so far generally unsuccessful, particularly in communities like West Coast City which had existing VHF television stations in operation.

WXXP-TV, Channel Three, had gone on the air in 1948 in West Coast City. Together with four other VHF stations in leading cities, it was owned by a well-known manufacturer of electrical products (including television sets) with corporate headquarters in a large east coast city. WXXP-TV was a primary affiliate of the NBC television network. WCYY-TV, Channel Ten, had also gone on the air in 1948 in West Coast City. WCYY-TV was owned by the broadcasting subsidiary of a major rubber company with headquarters in Ohio. The latter station had a primary affiliation with the CBS television network and also carried some programs of the ABC television network. WCYY-TV could not physically carry all the programs of both networks.

In addition to the two commercial VHF stations, a non-commercial VHF education license had been granted to the West Coast State University to operate an educational station on Channel Five, West Coast City. The educational station first went on the air in 1956. Also, permits had been granted for three UHF stations to operate in the metropolitan West Coast City area. Only one of these stations, WBBB-TV, so far has been placed in operation. WBBB-TV went on the air in 1957 on Channel 59. It had an affiliation with the ABC network but operated with little commercial success and was forced to suspend operations in 1958.

The demand by advertisers for time on commercial VHF television in West Coast City was probably greater than the two existing stations could fill. Mr. Traynor, on the basis of his own observations, believed that practically all the day and nighttime segments were sold on the two existing stations. From the point of view of the networks and the public, which wanted a full choice of network programs, the situation was also unsatisfactory. CBS and especially ABC were both unhappy with having to share WCYY-TV.

Because of this demand for three network stations in West Coast City and in other large cities with only two commercial VHF stations, and the failure (to date) of UHF to solve the problem, the FCC began in the early 1960's a policy of "dropping in" a third VHF channel wherever interference problems were not too great. The FCC had announced, early this year, that it was assigning Channel Eight to West Coast City and that applications would be accepted for a thirty-day period beginning July first.

Four groups had applied for permission to construct a station and operate on Channel Eight by July 15. If West Coast Television Inc. applied, it would make five groups all desiring the same channel. Mr. Traynor believed that there would be no additional applicants for the channel.

The first group to apply for Channel Eight was Publishers Broadcasting Co. Publishers Broadcasting was a wholly owned subsidiary of

West Coast Newspaper Corporation, publisher of the West Coast City daily and Sunday News and evening Star newspapers. Publishers Broadcasting owned and operated the leading full-power AM radio station in West Coast City and also operated an FM radio station in West Coast City. All of the officers and directors of Publishers Broadcasting resided in the metropolitan West Coast City area. Jonas M. Esterberry, president and director of the West Coast Newspaper Corporation since 1933, together with his family, held about 28 per cent of the stock of the corporation, which was the principal holding. Most of the rest of the stock was publicly held. However, much of the management of the News and the Star and their radio stations was delegated to Mr. Ephraim Tuttle, Jr., vice president and director of West Coast Newspaper Corporation and president of Publishers Broadcasting Co.

A second applicant for Channel Eight was Acme Pacific Telecasters, Inc. This corporation was formed especially to apply for Channel Eight. This group started out originally as a partnership but later became a corporation with 84 stockholders, mostly West Coast City area residents. Sol Cohen, president and director, held a 21.74 per cent stock interest in the new corporation. No other stockholder of Acme Pacific Telecasters held more than five per cent of the stock.

A third applicant was the Joseph DeWald Electronics Corporation, headed by Joseph DeWald, a pioneer in the development of commercial television. DeWald was a New Jersey corporation with headquarters in New York City. Thirty per cent of the voting stock of DeWald was controlled by a large motion picture company which named three of the eight DeWald directors. Mr. DeWald was the only other stockholder who owned more than three per cent of the stock. DeWald Electronics owned and operated three other commercial television stations in leading Eastern and Midwest cities.

Journal Publishing Corporation also applied for Channel Eight. This company published the daily and Sunday West Coast City Journal and owned and operated an AM radio station in West Coast City. Mr. Charles Atwood, who resided in Arizona but spent considerable time in West Coast City, was 100 per cent owner of the stock of the Journal Publishing Corporation.

West Coast Television Inc. would probably be the final applicant for Channel Eight. The company would be especially formed to apply for Channel Eight. Thirty-six predominantly local citizens would each buy 60 shares of $10 par value common stock. Thirty-five of these stockholders would sign agreements to purchase 2,440 additional shares each and the thirty-sixth (the proposed manager of the station) would be given 2,440 shares for services. Four other key employees would also be given contracts providing an opportunity to purchase equal amounts of stock. Thirty-eight of these 40 were long-time residents of the West Coast City area.

Before deciding whether to join West Coast Television, Inc., as a stockholder and as president, Mr. Traynor decided to contact Mr. James E. Killie, who had long experience in the television industry as a station manager in a smaller city in West Coast State. If the decision was made to go ahead with the application, Killie would be the proposed station manager. Killie suggested that Mr. Traynor join him and Mr. Peter Paolozzi for lunch to discuss the matter. Mr. Paolozzi was a member of a Washington, D.C. law firm that specialized in broadcast matters before the Federal Communications Commission.

At lunch, Messrs. Poalozzi and Killie explained the general outline of the FCC licensing process to Mr. Traynor. Once a channel has been allocated to a city, either in the general table of assignments (made in 1952 by the FCC) or by special action, such as the "drop-in" of Channel Eight, potential licensees of the channel file application for authority to construct a television broadcast station. Part I of the FCC's Rules, "Practice and Procedure," states the procedure to be followed. Each applicant must file three copies (in some cases more) of FCC Form 301, March 1960, which is a 23-page application form. This form consists of five sections. The first section requires such information as channel requested, type of station desired, location, and hours of operation. The second section calls for information about the nature of the applicants. Such information as citizenship, antitrust violations, past and present occupations of the principals, their officers and directors, and connections with existing radio and television stations is required. Section three concerns financial ability to build and operate the station. Sources of equipment, facilities, etc. and their cost must be listed, and financial resources to meet them must be shown. In section four, the applicant states his proposed programming policy and percentages for the different types of programming to be broadcast in a typical week in terms of program category (such as entertainment, news, educational, etc.) and percentages of network, local, and recorded programs. Details of the staffing of the proposed station must also be listed in this section. The final section concerns technical matters such as location of transmitter, studio and antenna site, contour diagrams for service, height of antenna, etc.

The applicant files Form 301 with the Commission Secretary. The Office of the Secretary dates the application and forwards it to the Broadcast Bureau. The Broadcast Bureau processes the application to see that it is complete. Assuming there are no omissions, the bureau submits a memorandum to the commission as to the legal, technical, and financial qualifications of each applicant. If there are omissions in the application, the bureau may accept the application for filing and request more information from the applicant, or if the omissions are substantial, it may return the application to the applicant with a statement explaining the defects.

If there is only one applicant for a channel, the commission examines the Broadcast Bureau memorandum and, assuming the bureau finds the applicant legally, technically, and financially qualified, would normally grant a construction permit. However, if the commission is unable to make a finding that a grant is in the public interest, the applicant is informed of any objections. The applicant must then prove that the grant will serve the public interest, if he is to be awarded a construction permit.

If there is more than one applicant for any one channel (as in the situation with regard to Channel Eight, West Coast City) the commission issues an order designating the applications for hearing in a consolidated proceeding, since all the applications are mutually exclusive. The order states what issues will be considered in the hearing and the basis on which the winner will be chosen. A copy of the order is mailed to each applicant and the notice of hearing is published in the *Federal Register*.

The seven commissioners, sitting *en banc*, or a panel of commissioners may hear the case itself. Usually, however, the commission designates a hearing examiner to hear the case in accordance with the Administrative Procedures Act. In fact, the Chief Hearing Examiner assigns the examiners to serve on cases through a mechanical rotation system based entirely on workload.

The examiner may add issues to the hearing as he sees fit. However, he may not eliminate any issues designated by the commission. The Administrative Procedures Act and Section 1.144 of the Commission Rules empower the examiner to administer oaths, issue subpoenas, examine witnesses, rule on questions of evidence, take depositions, hold prehearing and other conferences, and maintain decorum at the hearings.

After the taking of testimony is completed, the examiner officially closes the record and files it with the Secretary of the Commission. The applicants then file findings of fact and conclusions of law which become a part of the record in the case.

The examiner then weighs all the evidence and issues an initial decision which contains findings of facts and conclusions, and a decision recommending the grant of a construction permit to one applicant and denying all other applications. He may recommend that all applications be denied. In theory, the examiner reaches his decision by applying criteria evolved by the commission in previous cases to the facts in the case to determine which applicant (if any) best meets "the public interest, convenience, and necessity." Probably, however, the examiner's own judgment and "gut feelings" are important or even the determining factor in reaching his decision. He then may rationalize his judgments in terms of the FCC criteria in much the same way that Chief Justice Marshall reached his Supreme Court decisions and afterwards told Justice Story to find the precedents.

Mr. Traynor was unfamiliar with this use of examiners to preside over hearings and prepare initial decisions. Mr. Paolozzi stated that use of examiners (all of whom are trained lawyers) is not unique with the FCC. Other independent regulatory agencies, such as the Civil Aeronautics Board and the Federal Power Commission, also employ examiners for similar hearings. Although all agencies are bound by the Administrative Procedures Act, there are some differences among independent regulatory agency hearings, since each agency is bound as well by its own particular act (such as Civil Aeronautics Act) and since each agency promulgates its own particular rules (such as FCC Rules).

Any of the parties, including any of the applicants, the Broadcast Bureau, the Commission General Counsel, the Department of Justice or other interested parties, may file exceptions to the examiner's findings and initial decision within thirty days after the release of the decision. If no exceptions are filed, and the commission takes no action on its own initiative, the initial decision becomes final in fifty days, and the winning applicant may construct his station.

Assuming exceptions are filed or the commission decides to reopen the record on its own initiative, the commission designates a time when it will hear oral argument on the exceptions or issues raised by the commission. Any exception to the initial decision must point out in detail any alleged errors. Similarly, any party may file a statement in support of the initial decision. Any of the parties may also submit a brief which is limited to fifty typewritten pages. The commission also allows the submission of reply briefs, within a specified length of time.

The Office of Opinion and Review (O & R) prepares a memorandum for the commission summarizing the pleadings of each party. According to members of the FCC staff, O & R tries to make a completely impartial presentation to the commission. Each commissioner is also helped by his legal assistant, who will do any further research desired by the commissioner.

Those parties wishing to participate in the oral argument must file written notice of intention to appear and participate. Generally each party is given twenty or thirty minutes to state its case. Commissioners frequently ask questions of the counsel for the various parties during the oral argument.

Sometime after oral argument, the commissioners meet and discuss the issues among themselves. After their discussions they take a trial vote and issue instructions to O & R to write a decision supporting the trial vote designation of one applicant for the license. In recent years, the commission has made the results of the trial vote public.

Once the O & R decision has been prepared and submitted to commissioners, the commissioners meet, make charges, argue, discuss, and vote. The commission decision usually consists of a statement of facts regarding each applicant, the majority of the commissioners' view of how each applicant is rated on each of the FCC criteria, and the majority's reasons as to why one particular application should be granted and the rest denied. Dissenting commissioners often add short statements explaining their reasons for dissent. With its decision, the commission issues an order granting a construction permit to the applicant who received a majority vote of those commissioners present and voting. Once the station has gone on the air, a license is issued for the normal licensing period by the commission.

Petitions for reconsideration and rehearing of the commission decision may be filed within thirty days after the text of the decision is released. Any individual or group "aggrieved" or whose interests are adversely affected by the decision may file such petitions. In lieu of or in addition to a request for a rehearing, any applicant for a construction permit whose application has been denied by the commission may appeal the decision to the U.S. Court of Appeals for the District of Columbia. Section 10 (e) of the Administrative Procedures Act provides that the court may set aside the commission's decision provided the commission's findings and conclusions are "arbitrary, capricious, or involve an abuse of discretion, or otherwise are contrary to law, or if not supported by substantial evidence."

Section 402 (j) of the Communications Act states that the court's judgment shall be final, subject, however, to review by the Supreme Court of the United States. The appellant, the commission, any interested party intervening in the appeal, or the Court of Appeals itself, may petition the Supreme Court for a writ of *certiorari*.

Unless a stay is issued by the courts, the applicant designated by the commission may proceed with construction and operation of the station, pending results of the court appeal. If there is no petition to the courts, the commission's decision and order is final.

Mr. Traynor was somewhat overwhelmed by the complexity of the television licensing process. He asked Mr. Paolozzi what parts of the process are most significant. In Paolozzi's opinion, the central parts of the process are the hearing examiner's statement of facts and the decision of the commission as to who gets the channel and why.

In general, findings of fact are decided once and for all by the hearing examiner. The examiner, like a trial judge, has the benefit of both written and oral testimony. Hence, he is in a good position to evaluate testimony of witnesses, to consider evidence, and to decide questions of fact. The seven commissioners cannot carry out this task very well for themselves, because they ordinarily do not hear oral testimony by witnesses, and they seldom have time to read the entire hearing record for each case, since the docket for a case may be twelve feet thick. The commission often gives less weight to the examiner's decision, in part because it is a one-man decision.

Congress has given a very broad guideline to the commission and its examiners to be used in reaching decisions. The only Congressional requirement is that licenses be given to those who would operate in the "public interest, convenience, and necessity." In order to meet this guideline and to regularize its process, the commission over a period of years, beginning with radio licensing and continuing with television licensing, evolved a list of criteria which it tries to apply to licensing cases.

In a letter to a U. S. Senate Committee in 1956, the then chairman of the FCC, George C. McConnaughey, listed the criteria as follows:

> A list of the comparative criteria, which have been evolved, and employed by the Commission in the comparative television cases, would include the following: Proposed programming and policies, local ownership, integration of ownership and management, participation in civic activities, record of past broadcast performance, broadcast experience, relative likelihood of effectuation of proposals as shown by the contacts made with local groups and similar effort, carefulness of operational planning for television, staffing, diversification of the background of the persons controlling, diversification of the control of the mediums of mass communications.

Besides its formally enunciated criteria, there is at least a suspicion that the commission has sometimes used political considerations in reaching its decisions. Even disregarding political factors, Mr. Paolozzi thought it would be difficult to predict which criteria the commission would emphasize in the Channel Eight case, as precedent is not binding on the commission and the commission has often been inconsistent in applying the criteria in what would seem to be similar cases. Indeed, some individual commissioners have sometimes reversed themselves on similar cases.

In view of the uncertainties of the licensing process, Mr. Traynor decided to review thoroughly the pros and cons of West Coast Television's applying for a license for Channel Eight.

First of all, Traynor decided to look at the financial considerations. Despite the limited number of television channels available, only about three quarters of all television stations in the United States have operated at a profit in recent years. Of those stations which are profitable, the median net income in recent years has been about $166,000 per station. Profit figures, however, are probably somewhat understated in view of generally liberal depreciation schedules.

Also, total figures for the United States include several markets which are not typical of the average major market. Television broadcasting in small towns tends to be less profitable than in major markets which are not typical because they have more than three VHF channels (such as Los Angeles with seven commercial VHF stations). It is the general industry opinion, according to Mr. Killie, that non-network stations, when faced with competition by stations affiliated with networks, have lower profits than the network affiliates. Mr. Killie believes non-network stations are generally losing money.

Profitability in some markets has been much higher than the average for the industry as a whole. For example, in 1960 Boston's three VHF commercial television stations shared net broadcast income after all expenses but before Federal Income Taxes of $8,942,617, and Detroit's three shared $8,226,101. In 1960, in the largest 25 markets ranked according to volume of revenues, 82 stations were profitable and had a median profit of $1,254,000. The other seventeen stations had a median loss of $237,000 per station.

On an aggregate basis, broadcasting as a whole, including the less profitable (relative to television) standard (AM) and FM radio broadcasting, is more profitable than the average manufacturing corporation. Broadcast returns on stockholders' equity averaged 13.5 per cent after tax, 1953-1958, compared to an average rate of 12.8 per cent for some 1,800 leading manufacturing corporations during the same period, and 10.6 per cent for some 3,400 major corporations in all sections of the economy.

Mr. Traynor was somewhat uncertain as to how these figures could be applied to Channel Eight, West Coast City. Since practically all of the day and nighttime segments were sold on the two existing stations, it was clear that some advertising could be sold on the new station. However, the two existing stations were well established in West Coast City, and it was clear that the new station would gain affiliation with the weakest of the three national television networks. Nevertheless, this network had in recent years been gaining a larger share of the audience and more sponsors than in earlier years. It appeared to be closing the gap that separated it from the two more successful networks.

Mr. Traynor was also somewaht concerned about future competition from UHF television stations in West Coast City. Although none were currently in operation, three UHF channels were allocated to West Coast City. As a result of a recent act by Congress, as implemented by the FCC, manufacturers were required to manufacture all television sets capable of receiving UHF channels as well as VHF channels beginning in 1964. As yet, the all-channel sets had not produced a great increase in the number of UHF television stations in operation. Clearly, however, the stage was set for UHF broadcasting to become economically feasible in cities such as West Coast City.

Mr. Killie pointed out to Mr. Traynor that the profitability of television broadcasting is reflected in capital gains as well as in net income. This capital gains feature has been a major factor leading to high demand for television stations. Since the tax laws allow capital gains to be taxed at lower rates than ordinary income, owners are encouraged to take their profits by selling their stations and transferring their licenses (with FCC approval required). In fact, transfer prices are often far in excess of the value of the physical assets of the station, with the result that the original licensees gather large capital gains.

One example of the capital gains possibilities was Storer Broadcasting Company's purchase of WBRC-AM-TV Birmingham from the original licensee for $2.4 million in May, 1953. Only four years later, Storer sold WBRC-AM-TV to the Taft Stations for $6,350,000—a capital gain of $4 million or almost $1 million per year of ownership. Another good example of multiple transfer is WDAF-AM-FM-TV in Kansas City. The original licensee, the Kansas City Star, was forced to sell the stations as part of a consent judgment. National Theaters paid the Star $7.6 million for these stations in 1958. In July, 1960, National resold WDAF-AM-FM-TV to Transcontinent Corp. for $9,750,000—a capital gain of more than $2 million to National in only two years. The record price for a radio-FM-television station combination was received by the Philadelphia Bulletin when it sold WCAU-AM-FM-TV to CBS for $15.6 million in July, 1958. Even stations that are probably not operating profitably can sometimes be sold for much more than the cost of the facilities. A New York educational group paid $6.2 million for seldom-profitable independent station WNTA-TV, Channel 13.

Mr. Traynor decided to look also at the costs of applying. Regardless of whether or not West Coast Television Inc. was awarded Channel Eight by the FCC, it would cost from $100,000 to $500,000 to go through the licensing process with a most likely cost of $225,000 based on other similar cases. Legal fees for Mr. Paolozzi's Washington law firm which would represent the applicant before the hearing examiner, the FCC itself, and the courts, if necessary, would be included in this estimated expenditure. Also, Mr. Killie's time and expenses in preparing detailed programming, staffing and other plans for the new station and his testimony before the hearing examiner as an expert witness would be included in this estimated expenditure. Other clerical and legal costs would be included—a single copy of the transcript of the hearings before the hearing examiner might cost as much as $25,000 by itself. All legal briefs must be printed in a standard manner for the use of the FCC staff and opposing counsel. Thus, if Channel Eight was awarded to another appplicant, the promoters of West Coast Television could lose up to $500,000.

If West Coast Television Inc. was awarded Channel Eight, it would have to construct studios, transmitting antennas, buy broadcasting equipment, etc. This might represent an investment of from $800,000 to $2 million. The promoters would not necessarily have to put up all this investment in cash, since much technical equipment could be bought on the installment plan and considerable bank support would doubtlessly be available to the successful applicant.

Another area Mr. Traynor was concerned about was how West Coast Television, Inc., might compare with the other applicants on the FCC criteria. Traynor, Killie, and Paolozzi decided to go down the list of the criteria as enumerated by Mr. McConnaughey and make a tentative comparison among the applicants.

The first criterion in Mr. McConnaughey's letter is "proposed programming and policies." Since the application period has not yet closed, the information on proposed programming of the applicants is not yet available to West Coast Television Inc. Mr. Killie believed, however, that West Coast Television Inc. would submit the most dynamic and original programming proposals, if it went ahead with its application—in part because of the diverse background and experience of the members of the group, each of whom would be asked for ideas for new formats and programs. Killie believed that much of the programming proposals of the other applicants would be prepared solely by their professional television consultants, with only a gesture or two made to local talent. However, Mr. Paolozzi was somewhat doubtful as to how much the FCC would emphasize this criterion, especially since most programming would, in fact, be furnished by the national network affiliation.

The second criterion, "local ownership," is often emphasized by the FCC, according to Mr. Paolozzi. The Joseph DeWald Electronics Corp. would be at a major disadvantage in this criterion because of its nonlocal control. Journal Publishing Company might also receive some disadvantage here because the sole owner is a legal resident of Arizona. All other applicants (Publishers Broadcasting, Acme Pacific Telecasters, and West Coast TV Inc.) would be equal under this criterion. The Commission might emphasize local ownership in this case as the other commercial television stations in West Coast City were nonlocally owned.

"Integration of ownership and management" would also be hard to predict in this case. Mr. Killie believed that the three locally owned applicants and possibly Journal Publishing Co. would have an advantage here over DeWald. Mr. Killie had suggested that West Coast TV establish a "town meeting" arrangement whereby all stockholders would have some responsibility for management. Mr. Paolozzi was not sure whether this "town meeting" device would give West Coast TV any comparative advantage on this criterion.

"Participation in civic activities" would probably be no advantage to any one applicant in this case, because all of the applicants involved were active in the civic affairs in their communities. The local applicants might be given a slight preference, since their civic activities were performed in the community where the station would be built. In forming the group, the promoters of West Coast TV were careful to invite into their group representatives of all aspects of the community. Various nationalities, races, and all the major religions were represented. So were different occupations; the group included educators, a labor union official, and businessmen of a wide variety. Acme Pacific Telecasters, Inc., would no doubt have a similar diversity in their group. Both of the publishers' groups were controlled and managed by old-time WASP families.

"Record of past broadcast performance" was ordinarily a minor factor unless some applicant could prove poor past broadcast performance in the record of a prior broadcaster. Mr. Killie believed there was some evidence that both publishers' radio broadcasting stations had gone in for overcommercialization and believed that the DeWald stations had somewhat ignored local broadcast needs. However, Mr. Paolozzi believed it would be very difficult to prove this to the satisfaction of the examiner or the commission.

"Broadcast experience" would clearly give preference to DeWald because of Mr. DeWald's long experience in the field and his high personal reputation in the industry as one of the "grand old men" of television. Both publishers would also gain some preference here because of their successful operation of radio stations. Publishers Broadcasting had also been experimenting by "dry running" television broadcasts over a closed-circuit system to train their people to operate a television station. Neither West Coast TV nor Acme Pacific Telecasters had any prior broadcast experience as a group. However, both of these groups had engaged station managers (e.g., Mr. Killie) with considerable experience in television broadcasting.

All groups would probably come out even, on balance, on the criteria of "relative likelihood of effectuation of proposals as shown by the contacts made with local groups and similar efforts," "carefulness of operational planning for television," and "staffing."

"Diversification of the background of the persons controlling" would probably give preference to West Coast TV and to Acme Pacific Telecasters because of their relatively large groups of owners. Mr. Killie thought his "town meeting" plan might give West Coast TV a slight edge on this criterion, since, in fact, Mr. Cohen probably owned controlling interest in Acme Pacific Telecasters. Journal Publishing Co. might be at the bottom of the list here because it was solely owned by one man.

"Diversification of the control of the mediums of mass communications" would clearly favor both West Coast TV and Acme Pacific Telecasters since none of the principals of either group had any ownership interest in other television stations, radio stations, newspapers, or magazines. DeWald Electronics would suffer a double disadvantage on this criterion, since it was at least partially controlled by a motion picture company and it owned other television stations. However, this would not necessarily be fatal, as it might be overbalanced by advantages in other criteria. Both publishers were at the maximum disadvantage on this criterion, compared with other applicants, since they owned both radio stations and newspapers in the same community. Some commissioners were opposed *per se* to giving a television license to a newspaper applicant when other qualified applicants were available in order to prevent a monopoly of communications in any one city. Other commissioners had sometimes argued, on the other hand, that the combination of a newspaper with a television station would benefit the public because of the complementary nature of their services. For example news gathered by the newspaper reporters could be presented over television as well.

Mr. Paolozzi believed there might be several other factors in this case, besides the standard criteria that might be relevant. Mr. Jonas M.

Esterberry, president of West Coast Newspaper Corporation, which in turn owned Publishers Broadcasting, was also chairman of the board of West Coast Petroleum Corporation. More than ten years earlier, West Coast Petroleum Corporation was convicted of violating the antitrust laws for conspiring to fix petroleum prices in West Coast City. The corporation was fined and ordered not to fix prices in the future. Mr. Esterberry, personally, had not been charged with violating the antitrust laws, but he was a major stockholder and chairman of the West Coast Petroleum Corporation at the time of the trial.

The motion picture company which partially controlled DeWald Electronics had also been found guilty of violating the antitrust laws some years earlier in its film distribution policies. It was, at that time, forced to sell its wholly owned film distributor and agree not to enter the film distribution business again.

Mr. Paolozzi believed that the FCC might take note of the antitrust violations of these two applicants' stockholders. Hopefully, the Justice Department might be persuaded to intervene in the case as *amicus curiae* and oppose granting the license to either DeWald or Publishers Broadcasting.

Mr. Traynor also had heard rumors that Journal Publishing Co. was in financial difficulties. The circulation of the *Daily Journal* had been declining in recent years, and rumors circulated that it would soon cease publication or would merge with the stronger *West Coast City Daily Standard,* which was the city's third newspaper published. The owner of the *Standard* had, however, publicly stated he was not interested in such a merger.

Mr. Traynor was also concerned about rumors of political activity by some of the applicants, even though it is illegal for anyone to make an off-the-record contact with any commissioner about a case while it is undergoing the licensing process. West Coast Newspaper Corp. was a staunch backer of the party that currently held the White House and a majority on the Federal Communications Commission. The state's senior U. S. Senator and a staff assistant to the President of the United States both owed at least some of their political success to support from the *West Coast City News and Star,* owned by West Coast Newspaper Corp.

One of the stockholders of Acme Pacific Telecasters Inc., a leading banker in West Coast City, was a good friend of the U. S. Secretary of Commerce and of the administrative assistant to the state's senior U. S. Senator. Mr. Atwood, owner of the Journal Publishing Co., had fought with leaders of both major parties but did have some friends in Congress. One of the FCC Commissioners had received his post largely at the urgings of one of Mr. Atwood's friends in Congress. The *Journal* supported the appointment in its editorial page. Mr. DeWald apparently had few political interests and contacts in Washington, aside from the Defense Department, which purchased considerable electronics equipment from

DeWald Electronics. Mr. Traynor was uncertain as to the political influence of the motion picture company affiliated with DeWald.

Mr. Traynor and many of his friends in West Coast TV were members of the minority party. Traynor himself was a close backer of the junior U. S. Senator from West Coast. Traynor was reluctant to take any action that might embarrass the Senator, as the Senator was a vice presidential possibility in the next election. However, Traynor was concerned with the rumors of political activity, especially since newspapers often have powerful influence in Washington. The *West Coast City Daily Standard* also traditionally backed the minority party. The publisher of the *Standard* did not want to apply for a television station for financial reasons. He encouraged both the West Coast TV and the Acme Pacific Telecasters groups to apply as he did not want one of his newspaper competitors to gain a television license in West Coast City.

Mr. Traynor also had to consider his personal interests. The group had asked him to assume the presidency of West Coast Television, Inc. As a rather wealthy forty-year-old investment banker with a small family, Mr. Traynor felt he could afford the investment in West Coast TV. He also felt he could spare the time to act as president of the new corporation. The challenge of television broadcasting also interested him. He did not believe that the present stations were doing all they could in the way of service to his community. On the other hand, failure of the venture could damage his investment banking business. Even if West Coast TV was awarded the station, Mr. Traynor was not sure that it would be worth getting involved in a power fight with such influential groups as two newspaper publishers and a leading local businessman like Mr. Cohen.

Fictiondale

The Fictiondale County Board of Commissioners had established a County Development Commission partly financed from funds contributed from local real estate developers and partly from funds contributed by the county. The purpose of the Development Commission was to lure new businesses and new industry into the county in order to promote land development and to build a tax base for the county. While located near the large city of Metropolia, the county was still considered substantially a farm and suburban locality. In area, it is one of the largest counties in the United States and is faced with a potential population explosion of residents working in Metropolia. Therefore, the County Commissioners believed that development of an industrial tax base was essential if the county was to continue providing services to its residents.

Late in 1957, George Hammer, the director of the Development Commission, had interested High-Rise bakeries in moving from Metropolia to the county. High-Rise had purchased an option on some land that was zoned for industrial use. The land was adjacent to Adamsville, a new residential development of homes which had recently been sold at prices ranging from $16,000 to $20,000. Access to the property was via an unimproved road which entered a paved street at a distance of approximately one mile from the entrance to Adamsville. High-Rise anticipated that its trucks and those of its suppliers and customers would use the route to reach its facilities. The area was also served by a railroad. The executives of High-Rise also anticipated, however, that two streets leading directly to its site from Adamsville would be used by its employees in coming to and from work. One of these streets ran along the side of and provided access to the Adamsville Recreation Center, which included a playground, swimming pool and tennis courts.

The residents of Adamsville had heard rumors that High-Rise was going to operate a retail store at its new plant site. Many of the residents of Adamsville were fearful that, if the streets leading directly to High-Rise were paved, an extremely heavy traffic flow through the residential areas would develop. Some residents foresaw streams of trucks lumbering down their quiet streets and, by July of 1958, feeling in the community began running high. The president of Adamsville Recreation Center wrote to the president of High-Rise, advising that the excavation work being done by High-Rise at the new site was endangering the center by taking away its lateral support. At about this time, a group of residents of Adamsville, through the Citizens Association, petitioned the Fictiondale Board of Commissioners to abandon the two streets which are involved as a public road. If the commissioners approved the petitions, such action would deny access to the streets to High-Rise. One commissioner publicly stated that so long as one of the streets was used for public access to the recreation center, it could not be abandoned by the county but must remain open.

The local newspapers gave full coverage to the dispute between High-Rise and the community. The company had proposed to the community that it would prohibit its trucks from using the residential streets, would discourage customers and suppliers from using the residential street and would seek to have signs prohibiting trucks placed on the residential streets. The community felt that this was not sufficient assurance that their streets would be protected from a large traffic buildup. When a letter to the newspaper appeared favoring closing the residential access route to the plant, Mr. Height, president of High-Rise, began consideration of abandonment of its plans to move to the county. High-Rise began to seek a new location elsewhere.

When Mr. Hammer, director of the Development Commission, learned of Mr. Height's consideration of other locations he attempted to speak to Mr. Height but could not reach him. Mr. Hammer investigated the matter further and learned that some overtures had been made to High-Rise by another nearby county, but that High-Rise was "pretty well committed" to pursuing its present plans to completion. However, Mr. Hammer felt compelled to forestall any further consideration by High-Rise of another location not only because he feared loss of High-Rise but also because other industry might fear a move into the county.

Members of the Realtors Association and Chamber of Commerce gave Mr. Hammer their support. Mr. Hammer wrote a letter to Mr. Height expressing the pleasure of the county over High-Rise as a new industrial member of the county and offered his assistance in acting as a go-between in the community relations problem. The County Commissioners also wrote High-Rise, welcoming them to the county. After receipt of the letter, High-Rise decided to stay in the county.

Hearing on the petitions to abandon the streets was scheduled for September. If the County Commission voted to "abandon," the intent to "abandon" would be advertised and parties would have thirty days in which to file a protest.

At the hearings the community was well represented. Car pools were organized to bring residents to the hearing. The commissioner from the district in which Adamsville was located voted to abandon the streets, as did one other commissioner. Three commissioners, however, voted to keep the streets open. While this officially closed the matter, High-Rise was concerned about the future relationship with its residential neighbors.

PART THREE

THE GOVERNMENT AS A PROVIDER OF SERVICES

Somali American Fishing Company[1]

In July, 1964, Herbert Farnsworth, chairman of the board of the Quincy Market Cold Storage and Warehouse Company, became highly interested in a report by the consulting firm of Checci and Company discussing the possibilities of a tuna fishing and freezing venture in the East African nation of the Somali Republic. The report had been brought to his attention by a group of his business associates in the Indo-American Seafood Corporation, an international trading company jointly owned by Gorton's Fish Company of Gloucester, Massachusetts, and a group of Boston businessmen. Quincy Market and Gorton's, one of the oldest and largest U. S. seafood companies, had collaborated on a number of projects, including a seafood center in Gloucester, and consequently kept in constant touch with each other.

Quincy Market had been in the fish cold storage business since 1881. In 1964, it operated three cold storage plants and an underground piped refrigeration service in Boston, three freezing and storage facilities in Gloucester, a small warehouse in Troy, New York, and a cold storage plant in Portland, Maine. Characterized in a U.S. government document as "conservatively financed and profitable," the company's gross sales for the year ending in March 1964 were $5 million, net income $532,716 and net worth stood at nearly $8 million on the company's books, though this figure was probably understated because old real estate was being carried at less than market value.

[1] The authors acknowledge with thanks the contribution made by Mr. George C. Lodge, lecturer at the Harvard Graduate School of Business Administration, to the collection of material for this case.

The firm had never invested in or established an overseas operation, but the Somali project nevertheless looked appealing to Farnsworth and to Paul Burrill, Quincy's president. Numerous surveys, including U. S. government studies going back at least as far as 1956, indicated that there were large concentrations of yellowfin and skipjack tuna in the Gulf of Aden. Using the long-line method of fishing (a technique developed by the Japanese, involving the use of baited hooks on separate strands hung at intervals along a heavy line) which was introduced into Somali by the fishing advisor on the staff of the U. S. foreign aid mission there, hooking rates have ranged up to 30 per cent with some individual sets as high as 90 per cent. (Hooking rates are the number of tuna caught per line per day.) Since the Japanese figure that a 5 per cent hooking rate represents the break-even point, Farnsworth was well impressed by the potential.

In addition, he knew that the world market for canned tuna was growing rapidly. Total world production had climbed from 256,000 metric tons in 1955 to 332,000 by 1963. A large part of the international trade in tuna is in the frozen product. The fish is cleaned and frozen where it is caught, and then shipped to a number of countries for processing and canning for their own internal markets. Thus, the tuna business fitted in well with Quincy's experience and knowhow.

Finally, he felt that his company might be able to make a genuine contribution to the national interest by working out some arrangement in this underdeveloped area.

According to Farnsworth's friends at Indo-American, the United States foreign aid agency, the Agency for International Development (AID) was extremely interested in this project and was anxious to find an American company which would participate in it. The Checci survey had been prepared for AID and for the development bank which it had established in Somalia, Credito Somalo. As a matter of fact, Indo-American had been seriously considering an arrangement with the International Basic Economic Corporation Packing Company, a leading fish processor with a large cannery in Puerto Rico, and had signed a letter of intent with a group of Somali businessmen, but the deal ultimately fell through. Therefore, they had good reason to believe that AID would be cooperative.

Indo-American's interpretation of the situation was entirely correct. The development of the Somali fishing industry had been a major objective of U. S. aid to the Somali Republic for some time. Technical assistance had been provided since 1957 and had contributed to a several-fold increase in catch, and a boatyard had been established in the capital city, Mogadiscio, which had turned out nearly forty small motorized fishing boats to supplement the canoes used by the local fishermen. In addition, the boatyard had served as a center of training for shipwrights, ship fitters, netmakers, and other specialists used in the fishing industry. In

1963, AID sponsored a tour for a group of Somali business leaders of U. S. fish companies. In these and other projects AID had spent over $450,000.

From an over-all standpoint, the AID program in this small, developing, infertile, one-time Italian colony had not been notably successful. Various projects, centered around the increase of the water supply, had not worked out, partly because of poor planning, but largely because of ineptitude and lack of interest on the part of the local government. AID's other projects tended to be infrastructure efforts—that is, long-range programs designed to lay the groundwork for economic progress like experimental farms, agricultural extension, a teacher training institute and a police academy—and AID was most anxious to create a project which would be immediately and demonstrably beneficial. The U. S. Ambassador in Mogadiscio, a career diplomat from New England named Horace G. Torbert, Jr., was also acutely conscious of some potential political problems: the Chinese Communists, taking advantage of a dispute between Somalia, Kenya and Ethiopia over the Somalia's attempt to "reunite" the "Somali people" by preempting pieces of their neighbors' territories, were increasingly active in the country. They were accusing the United States of supporting Kenya and Ethiopia at the expense of Somalia. Ambassador Torbert felt that the successful conclusion of the fishing project would strengthen the United States position in Somalia. Finally, as a stated policy, the United States Government was anxious to further the development of private enterprise in developing countries like Somalia.

The fish-processing project was particularly promising. Despite its long seacoast, Somalia had traditionally turned its back on the sea. As a U. S. government document put it, "By establishing a reliable market for fish, conducting commercial operations along the northern coast based on the resources of the sea, and marketing its product by sea, the proposed project will contribute to a diversified economy, more interested in the potentials of its coast line." The operation was to be based near the town of Alula, along the north coast of the Horn on the Gulf of Aden, an extremely underdeveloped area. (Somalia's 2,000,000 population has an annual per capita income of $51; the northern area is even worse off.) According to AID estimates, the fishing enterprise would employ thirty full-time Somalis on shore, part-time work for an additional fifty, construction employment for others, and stabilization of income for the fishermen who used some 2,000 canoes for their existing enterprise. Estimates of the total yearly payroll came to some $62,000 a not inconsiderable sum for the area; the project was expected to produce some $500,000 in free foreign exchange annually for the nation's economy after deductions for all requirements (including the profit on the American investment), and a reservoir of trained personnel would be created. Finally, AID expected that the byproduct of the operation, fishmeal, could be used either to expand the chicken and livestock industry in the Somali Republic or as an export to an expanding world market.

Thus, the project appeared particularly promising on both political and economic grounds to U. S. government officials in Washington and in the field.

Upon reading the Checci report, Farnsworth determined to pursue the matter further. He sent for AID's basic information pamphlet, "Memorandum to Businessmen," which described their various programs to assist and encourage companies interested in direct investment in developing countries, and called the firm's clerk and chief counsel, Allen Eaton, at his Boston law firm to have him investigate the relevant statutes and background material. The more he learned about both the economics and the politics of the venture, the more enthusiastic he became. He was confirmed in his original feeling that the proposition represented an opportunity for Quincy to assist in the United States program to help new nations advance themselves, and to make a profit at the same time.

From the start, Eaton and Farnsworth proceeded in an unusually sophisticated and careful fashion, so Farnsworth was well prepared when he held his first meeting at AID in Washington during late August. He knew that AID could provide specific risk guaranties against political upheavals and expropriation. He knew that the agency had also just been authorized by the Congress to offer extended risk guaranties to cover investments which would contribute to the development of a country and would not otherwise be made because of the commercial risk involved. He was familiar, also, with the availability of AID loans for private business ventures in underdeveloped areas, although from his conversations with Indo-American he assumed he would not need such help, because Credito Somalo had been established as a development bank in Somali for just this purpose.

As Farnsworth viewed the project, it would cost about $1.5 million. He decided that the best approach would be a joint venture with a Somali firm, already in existence, known as the Somali Fishing Company. As he viewed it, Credito Somalo would put $1.1 million into the project, and Quincy and the Somali company would each participate to the amount of about $225,000. Quincy would then ask for risk guaranties up to the full limit—one half of its investment. This total package, as Farnsworth saw it, would cover the costs of the construction of a sea wall and wharf for small boats, the construction and equipment of a fish freezing plant and ancillary facilities at Ras Filuch, the purchase and operation of fishing boats to augment the present local catch, housing, personnel training, vehicles and the various other necessary expenses.

It was with this program in mind that Farnsworth set up an appointment in Washington with Hon. Seymour Peyser, Assistant Administrator of AID for Development Finance and Private Enterprise during late August. Accompanied by Allen Eaton, his general counsel, and Eaton's assistant Edward Benjamin, he described his proposition to Peyser and found him most enthusiastic. Peyser indicated that the agency would follow a very flexible policy and, because of AID's intense interest in the project, would do everything it could to make the investment financially attractive.

AID, officially within the general Department of State complex along with the U. S. Mission to the United Nations and the Peace Corps, is, in fact, a semiautonomous agency. Only the Latin American Bureau of State and the equivalent part of AID (the Alliance for Progress) are merged. The Administrator of AID, Honorable David E. Bell, ranks as an Undersecretary of State, but the lines of authority—which are precise enough on paper—are somewhat vague in reality. AID itself is divided, basically, into four regional offices: Near East and South Asia, Africa, Far East and, with the distinction indicated above, Latin America. Each of these bureaus is headed by an assistant administrator appointed by the President and confirmed by the Senate. (There are only about 300 Presidential appointees in Washington who hold the top policy and administrative positions. Some 98 per cent of the 2,500,000 civilian employees of the federal government are covered by one or another of the career systems, which means that their jobs are subject to competitive examination and they do not move with changing administrations.)

Peyser's office, along with four other Presidential appointees, provides specialized staff services to the regional bureau administrators, who are the line officers of the agency. But over the years that the reorganized agency has been operating (it was established in 1961), these lines, too, have become somewhat eroded and unclear, and the assistant administrators of the nonregional bureaus are equipped with certain authorities on their own. Peyser, for example, served two major functions: to locate and promote opportunities for private participation in development ventures around the world, and to authorize the granting of specific and extended risk guaranties. Loans, however, are approved either by the regional assistant administrators (up to $2.5 million) or, in the case of larger amounts, by the administrator and a committee known as the Development Loan Committee.

After the highly encouraging conversation with Peyser, Farnsworth started on the project in earnest. He was in a hurry; because of Somali's violent summer winds off the desert which carry a blanketing dust with them, he determined that the facility had to be constructed completely by midsummer, 1965, if it was to be operational by October, 1965, when the fishing season was at its best. This meant that the equipment had to be ordered by November 1 at the latest, and it was already August, with verbal encouragement by AID but nothing signed and no in-depth studies completed by anyone. So Eaton, Theodore Love, his vice president and chief engineer, and a man from Indo-American headed for Mogadiscio in September and spent three weeks on the ground. Eaton, who had done an extremely effective piece of work in the earlier research and discussions with Washington, carried the main burden of the negotiations with the Somali government and the local businessmen in the Somali Fishing Company, of which Love did the work necessary for what proved to be an unusually complete and sophisticated engineering study. Within a few weeks, the task was complete and the joint company organized.

In the meantime, Benjamin started his negotiations with AID. He soon learned that, while Peyser's office was responsible for the risk guaranties, the loan end of the arrangement was housed in the African bureau under the authority of Honorable Edmond C. Hutchinson, a former RCA executive who joined AID in the winter of 1961. The project fell specifically in the Office of Capital Development and Finance of the bureau headed by Miles G. Wedeman.

Much to Benjamin's disappointment (and Farnsworth's, as well) AID did not look with favor on the idea of Credito Somalo advancing the entire $1.1 million. They had only $2 million to start with, and earlier loans left them with only $1.2 million; AID officials felt they should not devote virtually all their remaining capital to this one project, especially since there were other possibilities available. Since AID has to approve all Credito Somalo loans above $100,000, this decision effectively blocked the possibility.

Farnsworth was extremely concerned over this turn of events. However, AID did say that they would consider authorizing $500,000 from Credito Somalo, and loaning the new company $600,000 from their own funds. Farnsworth was not too pleased with this proposal. The arrangements with Credito Somalo had gone very smoothly and, in view of the time pressures, he was unenthusiastic about having to enter into what he was afraid might be extended discussions with AID over the terms and arrangements for their participation. Periodically, he considered abandoning the whole deal, and, as a matter of fact, so informed AID in cables from Mogadiscio. However, he ultimately decided that, despite his discouragement, the prospects were promising enough to make it worth pursuing, and he authorized Benjamin to proceed.

Loan applications of this kind are referred by Miles Wedeman to one of his fifteen loan officers. It is the loan officer's responsibility to work out all aspects of the venture in detail. He has technical experts in engineering, agriculture, law and so on available to him; he works with the desk officer (the AID official directly responsible in Washington for a country's program) and the mission in the field; and he must evaluate the feasibility of the loan against a long list of criteria established by Congress. (See Exhibit One for Statutory Checklist.)

Furthermore, AID loans are subject to Sec. 611 of the Foreign Assistance Act of 1961, as amended, which reads as follows:

SEC. 611. COMPLETION OF PLANS AND COST ESTIMATES—

(a) No agreement or grant which constitutes an obligation of the United States Government in excess of $100,000 under section 1311 of the Supplemental Appropriation Act, 1955, as amended (31 U.S.C. 200), shall be made for any assistance authorized under titles I, II, and VI of chapter 2 and chapter 4 of part I—

(1) if such agreement or grant requires substantive technical or financial planning, until engineering, financial, and other plans necessary to carry out such assistance, and a reasonably firm estimate of the cost to the United States Government of providing such assistance, have been completed; and

(2) if such agreement or grant requires legislative action within the recipient country, unless such legislative action may reasonably be anticipated to be completed in time to permit the orderly accomplishment of the purposes of such agreement or grant.

(b) Plans required under subsection (a) of this section for any water or related land resource construction project or program shall include a computation of benefits and costs made insofar as practicable in accordance with the procedures set forth in the Memorandum of the President dated May 15, 1962, with respect to such computations.

(c) To the maximum extent practicable, all contracts for construction outside the United States made in connection with any agreement or grant subject to subsection (a) of the section shall be made on a competitive basis.

(d) Subsection (a) of this section shall not apply to any assistance furnished for the sole purpose of preparation of engineering, financial, and other plans.

Thus the Congress, presumably acting in response to what it feels the American people want or would want if they knew the facts, has surrounded AID with a number of restrictions and provisions designed to insure that the taxpayers' money is well and wisely and prudently spent. AID officials are highly sensitive to Congressional wishes and mandates in this regard; each year they appear before four separate Committees of the House and Senate in order to secure the necessary funds for the forthcoming year, plus additional ones as special investigations arise, which probe every detail of every action of the agency and demand justification for it. In addition they are subject to an intensive review by the Bureau of the Budget acting as the President's agent.

Thus the loan officer is meticulous in examining all the details of a project. From his desk it goes to a so-called Development Finance Review Committee chaired by the Director of the Office of Capital Development, Miles Wedeman, where all interested parties can scrutinize the undertaking. This group, customarily in one sitting, authorizes a so-called "intensive review," which means that the project is virtually approved, assuming that no unforeseen developments occur. From there, Wedeman makes his recommendation to the Assistant Administrator for Africa, who signs off on the proposal. Wedeman's recommendation is sent forward in a forty-page mimeographed booklet which sets out a summary of the program, an analysis of its technical, economic, and political background, a financial analysis, a discussion of the impact on the U. S. economy, and a plan for implementation.

By the middle of September, AID's loan officer, Michael St. John, was working on an analysis of the project. At the same time, officers in Peyser's division were staffing out the application for extended risk guaranties, the first they had processed under the new law. The specific risk guaranty was approved quickly, but the other, because it was the initial action under the law, seemed to Benjamin to drag on interminably.

Similarly, first Benjamin and then Farnsworth became increasingly impatient through the early weeks of October with what they saw as the slow pace of the analysis of the loan application. The felt that the number of people participating in the over-all project was astonishingly large, and became frustrated and disillusioned by what seemed to them to be a maze of legal and technical requirements. A number of problems arose during the course of the discussions, including the following:

(1) Farnsworth learned that, under Somali law, any direct loan from a foreign power like this one required the formal approval of the Somali Parliament which, his local contacts told him, might or might not be forthcoming.

(2) A long technical discussion between AID and Love then developed over the question of the availability of water, a problem that concerned St. John and the AID engineers. The possibility of a solar distillation system was considered in some detail; wells seemed to be another possibility.

(3) Since the AID loan was prepayable in U. S. dollars, AID demanded evidence that the Somali government would allow conversion of Somali shillings and/or non-U. S. foreign exchange into U. S. dollars for payment of interest and repayment of principal. SAFCO—The Somali American Fishing Company—thought this would be no great problem, and was inclined to minimize the issue. Quincy did, however, investigate the Somali "Foreign Investments Law" (No. 10, dated 2/18/60), and discovered that "The investor can transfer each year up to 15% of the profit in /to/ the currency originally invested." (The law goes on to say that profits exceeding 15 per cent may be re-invested upon Government of Somali Republic approval over the first five years of operation until an amount equal to the initial investment has been plowed back, when the excess may be transferred. After the first five years, if double the initial capital has been invested, special application to the Government of Somali Republic must be made for transfers exceeding 15 per cent.) Dr. Giama of Credito Somalo, after informal discussions with the GSR Ministry of Industry and Commerce, told AID and Farnsworth (who was in Somali at the time) that he believed the servicing of the AID loan would

have to come out of the 15 per cent. Mr. Benjamin called AID to state that this would be unacceptable to Quincy and would end its interest in the project. Ultimately, the problem was negotiated to everyone's satisfaction—but at the cost of additional time and money.

(4) In conformity with statutory requirements, AID was concerned that U. S. tuna interests might be hurt by competition from the new venture. Although Quincy sincerely expected to market the entire product in Italy, Farnsworth was logically not inclined to burn bridges, and therefore objected strenuously to an AID-proposed clause guaranteeing that SAFCO would not export more than 20 per cent of its product to the U. S. Quincy reasoned that, since the U. S. was a net importer of frozen tuna, the SAFCO increment (a small percentage of U. S. imports) could not affect the market and therefore could not be considered competitive. (Quincy was aware, of course, that the second logical market for frozen tuna was Puerto Rico, which had a number of large canning plants for the U. S. market.) AID, however, was adamant on the point. Quincy had to swallow the clause.

(5) Fairly late in the process, AID decided to make the loan on a two-step basis, an arrangement which applies to loans for industrial and other income-producing projects when terms are "hard." The plan would allow the Government of Somali Republic to receive payment from SAFCO instead of AID if it wished and to take on the obligation to repay AID itself—on soft terms. The "spread" between the hard and soft terms (fifteen years vs. forty years; $5\frac{1}{2}$ per cent vs. $2\frac{1}{2}$ per cent) would then be available to the Government of Somali Republic for general budgetary and balance-of-payments purposes. This system is based on the theory that AID loans should consider a project's effect on the host *country,* and on the country's need for soft terms rather than the company's. This decision did not sit well with Quincy, who foresaw only added difficulties for them from the two-step procedure.

By the middle of October, Farnsworth was becoming deeply disturbed and discouraged again. He counted up the mounting out-of-pocket costs to Quincy, which were running much higher than planned, and the time he and his associates had spent on the venture. With an eye on the calendar, he asked AID for a promise that it would ultimately approve the loan even though it had not completed its analysis, and AID could not give him any such promise. Ambassador Torbert, who was intensely interested, kept in touch with AID Administrator Bell. Benjamin was in and out of Washington constantly, but the final agreement still was not forthcoming. Finally, Farnsworth told AID that he would abandon the whole idea if they could not complete their work and approve the arrangement by November 1, and asked if they would guarantee that date. This AID officials were unable to do, and Farnsworth again wondered whether he should withdraw from the venture altogether.

EXHIBIT ONE

Statutory Checklist *

1. *FA § 102.* Precautions that have been or are being taken to assure loan proceeds are not diverted to short-term emergency purposes (such as budgetary, balance of payments, or military purposes) or any other purpose not essential to the country's long-range economic development. Satisfied. (Section V. C). Also to be covered in Loan Agreement.

2. *FA § 201 (b).* Manner in which loan will promote country's economic development, emphasizing help for long-range plans and programs designed to develop economic resources and increase productive capacities. Satisfied. (Section V. B)

3. *FA § 201 (b)(1).* Information and conclusion on availability of financing from other free-world sources, including private sources within the United States. Satisfied. (Section V. B)

4. *FA § 201 (b)(2).* Information and conclusion on activity's economic and technical soundness, including the capacity of the recipient country to repay the loan at a reasonable rate of interest. Satisfied. (Sections III. C, III. D, IV., and V. F)

5. *FA § 201 (b)(3).* Information and conclusion on existence of reasonable promise activity will contribute to development of economic resources or increase of productive capacities. Satisfied. (Section IV. E)

6. *FA § 201 (b)(4).* Information and conclusion on activity's relationship to other development activities, and its contribution to realizable long-range objectives. Satisfied. (Sections IV. B and IV. E)

7. *FA § 201 (b)(5).* Country's self-help measures, including institution of Foreign Assistance Act investment guaranty programs. Satisfied. (Section V. B); Agreement signed 1/8/64.

8. *FA § 201 (b)(6).* Information and conclusion on possible effects on U.S. economy, with special reference to areas of substantial labor surplus. Satisfied. (Sections V. C and VI.)

9. *FA § 201 (b).* Information and conclusion on reasonable prospects of repayment. Satisfied. (Section V. F)

10. *FA § 201 (d).* Information and conclusion on legality (under laws of the country and the U.S.) and reasonableness of lending and relending terms. Satisfied. (Sections V. B, V. C, and V. F) Also to be covered in Loan Agreement.

11. *FA § 201 (e).* Information and conclusion on availability of an application together with sufficient information and assurances to indicate reasonably that funds will be used in an economically and technically sound manner. Satisfied. (Sections I. and III.)

12. *FA § 201 (f).* If a project, information and conclusion whether it will promote the economic development of the requesting country, taking

* The following abbreviations are used:

FA Foreign Assistance Act of 1961, as amended by the Foreign Assistance Act of 1964.

App. Foreign Assistance and Related Agencies Appropriation Act, 1965.

into account the country's human and material resource requirements and the relationship between the ultimate objectives of the project and the country's over-all economic development. Satisfied. (Section IV. E)

13. *FA § 201 (f)*. If a project, information and conclusion whether it specifically provides for appropriate participation by private enterprise. Satisfied. (Sections I., II., V. B)

14. *FA § 202 (a)*. Total amount of money under loan which is going directly to private enterprise, is going to intermediate credit institutions or other borrowers for use by private enterprise, is being used to finance imports from private sources, or is otherwise being used to finance procurements from private sources. Total loan to private borrower (Section II) to finance U.S. equipment. (Section V. C)

15. *FA § 601*. Information and conclusions whether loan will encourage efforts of the country to: (a) increase the flow of international trade; (b) foster private initiative and competition; (c) encourage development and use of cooperatives, credit unions, and savings and loan associations; (d) discourage monopolistic practices; (e) improve technical efficiency of industry, agriculture, and commerce; (f) strengthen free labor unions. (a), (b), (c), (d), and (e) satisfied. (Sections I., II., III., IV. A, IV. B, IV. E, V., and VI.) (f) not applicable.

16. *FA § 601 (d)*. Conclusions and supporting information on compliance with the Congressional policy that engineering and professional services of U.S. firms and their affiliates are to be used in connection with capital projects to the maximum extent consistent with the national interest. Not applicable.

17. *FA §§ 601, 602*. Information and conclusions whether loan will (a) encourage U.S. private trade and investment abroad; (b) encourage private U.S. participation in foreign assistance programs (including use of private trade channels and the services of U.S. private enterprise), and (c) permit American small business to participate equitably in the furnishing of goods and services financed by it. Satisfied. (Sections I, II, and III. E) (c) to be covered in Loan Agreement.

18. *FA § 604 (a)*. Compliance with restriction of commodity procurement to U.S. except as otherwise determined by the President and subject to statutory reporting requirements. Satisfied. (Section V. C) To be covered in Loan Agreement.

19. *FA § 604 (b)*. Compliance with bulk commodity procurement restriction to prices no higher than the market price prevailing in the U.S. at time of purchase. Not applicable.

20. *FA § 604 (d)*. Compliance with requirement that marine insurance be purchased on commodities if the participating country discriminates, and that such insurance be placed in the U.S. To be covered in Loan Agreement.

21. *FA § 611 (a)(1)*. Information and conclusion on availability of engineering, financial, and other plans necessary to carry out the assistance and of a reasonably firm estimate of the cost of the assistance to the United States. Satisfied. (Sections III., V. B, and VII)

22. *FA § 611 (a) (2)*. Necessary legislative action required within recipient country and basis for reasonable anticipation such action will be completed in time to permit orderly accomplishment of purposes of loan. To be covered in Loan Agreement.

23. *FA § 611 (b); App. § 101.* If water or water related land resource construction project or program, information and conclusion on benefit-cost computation. Not applicable.

24. *FA § 611 (c).* Compliance with requirement that contracts for construction be made on competitive basis to maximum extent practicable. Not applicable.

25. *FA § 619.* Compliance with requirement that assistance to newly independent countries be furnished through multilateral organizations or plans to maximum extent appropriate. Not applicable.

26. *FA § 620 (a); App. § 107.* Compliance with prohibitions against assistance to Cuba and any country (a) which furnishes assistance to Cuba or fails to take appropriate steps by February 14, 1964 to prevent ships or aircraft under its registry from carrying equipment, materials, or supplies from or to Cuba; or (b) which sells, furnishes or permits any ships under its registry from carrying items of primary strategic significance, or items of economic assistance. To be covered in Loan Agreement.

27. *FA § 620 (b).* If assistance to the government of a country, existence of determination it is not controlled by the international Communist movement. Not applicable.

28. *FA § 620 (c).* If assistance to the government of a country, existence of indebtedness to a U.S. citizen for goods or services furnished or ordered where such citizen has exhausted available legal remedies or where debt is not denied or contested by such government or the indebtedness arises under an unconditional guaranty of payment given by such government. Not applicable.

29. *FA § 620 (d).* If assistance for any productive enterprise which will compete with U.S. enterprise, existence of agreement by the recipient country to prevent export to the U.S. of more than 20 per cent of the enterprise's annual production during the life of the loan. Not applicable.

30. *FA § 620 (a).* If assistance to the government of a country, extent to which it (including government agencies or subdivisions) has, after January 1, 1962, taken steps to repudiate or nullify contracts or taken any action which has the effect of nationalizing, expropriating, or otherwise seizing ownership or control of property of U.S. citizens or entities beneficially owned by them without taking appropriate steps to discharge its obligations. Not applicable.

31. *FA § 620 (f); App. § 109.* Compliance with prohibitions against assistance to any Communist country. Satisfied. The Somali Republic is not considered to be a Communist country.

32. *FA § 620 (g).* Compliance with prohibition against use of assistance to compensate owners for expropriated or nationalized property. Satisfied. (Section V. C)

33. *FA § 620 (h).* Compliance with regulations and procedures adopted to insure against use of assistance in a manner which, contrary to the best interests of the U.S., promotes or assists the foreign aid projects or activities of the Communist-bloc countries. To be covered by Loan Agreement.

34. *FA § 620 (i).* Existence of determination that the country is engaging in or preparing for aggressive military efforts. No such determination has been made.

35. *FA § 620 (k).* If construction of productive enterprise where aggregate value of assistance to be furnished by U.S. will exceed $100 million, identification of statutory authority. Not applicable.

36. *FA § 620 (l).* Compliance with prohibition against assistance after 31 December 1965 for the government of a country which fails to institute investment guaranty program. Program instituted on 1/8/64.

37. *FA § § 636 (h); 612 (c).* Appropriate steps have been taken to assure that, to maximum extent possible, country is contributing local currencies to meet the cost of contractual and other services and foreign currencies owned by the U.S. are utilized to meet the cost of contractual and other services. Not applicable.

38. *App (§ Unnumbered).* Use of funds to carry out FA 205, which pertains to IDA. Not applicable.

39. *App. § 102.* Compliance with requirement that payments in excess of $25,000 for architectural and engineering services on any one project be reported to Congress. Not applicable.

40. *App. § 104.* Compliance with bar against funds to pay pensions, etc. for military personnel. Satisfied. (Section V. C)

41. *App. § 111.* Compliance with requirement for security clearance of personnel under contracts for services. Not applicable.

42. *App. § 112.* Compliance with requirement for approval of contractors and contract terms for capital projects. To be covered in Loan Agreement.

43. *App. § 114.* Compliance with bar against use of funds to pay assessments, etc. of U.N. member. Satisfied. (Section V. C)

44. *App. § 117.* Compliance with regulations on employment of U.S. and local personnel for funds obligated after 30 April 1964. Not applicable.

45. *App § 401.* Compliance with bar against use of funds for publicity or propaganda purposes within U.S. not heretofore authorized by Congress. Satisfied. (Section V. C)

The Small Busines
Administration

The material in this case is reprinted from literature distributed by the Small Business Administration.

**PART ONE
SBA—WHAT IT IS
—WHAT IT DOES**
The Small Business Administration is an independent, permanent agency established by Congress and the President to serve America's small businesses. The services it provides are authorized by the Small Business Act and the Small Business Investment Act. These direct SBA to help small firms obtain financing, overcome the effects of disasters, sell to or buy from the Federal Government, strengthen their management and production capabilities, and generally grow and prosper.

Financial Assistance

The small businessman with a financial problem has a ready source of advice and assistance in SBA. Agency financial specialists will review his problem with him and suggest possible solutions.

Where borrowing seems necessary, and the businessman's bank (or other commercial sources) cannot provide the needed funds on reasonable terms, SBA often can assist. The agency will consider participating with the bank in a loan to the businessman, or guaranteeing part of a loan made to him by the bank. The SBA may either provide or guarantee up to 90 per cent of a loan. If the bank cannot provide any of the funds, SBA will consider lending the entire amount as a "direct" government loan. However, about two-thirds of the agency's loans are made in participation with banks—concrete evidence of bank-SBA cooperation in meeting the term financing needs of small firms.

The SBA participates in loans, or makes direct loans, for these purposes:

- Business construction, expansion, or conversion.
- Purchase of machinery, equipment, facilities, supplies or materials.
- Working capital.

While most SBA business loans are small—some are for even less than $1,000—the agency may lend up to $350,000 as its share of a participation loan or as a direct loan.

SBA business loans may be for as long as ten years. The maximum interest rate is 5½ per cent. However, a bank may set a higher rate on its share of a participation loan and on SBA's share of a guaranteed loan until the agency actually provides its share. If a bank charges less than 5½ per cent on its share, SBA will match the bank's charge down to a minimum of 5 per cent.

Small Loan Plan

The SBA has a small loan plan tailored to the needs of small retail, service, and other firms. Under the plan, the agency will lend a business up to $15,000 for as long as six years. In judging an application, the primary consideration is the good character of an applicant and his past record for meeting obligations. As security, SBA will take whatever worthwhile collateral is available, including any fixed assets purchased with the loan. Paperwork and procedures under the plan are held to a minimum.

Opportunities for Very Small Businesses

The SBA assists and encourages very small businesses through loans and management training. Studies have shown that these businesses, while eager to expand and modernize and thus better serve their communities, generally are unable to obtain financing or management guidance. The SBA is helping to fill this need, and in this way to increase jobs and business activity. This program is especially helpful to areas that have long suffered from poverty, such as areas peopled by minorities.

Under this plan, the SBA may lend businessmen up to $6,000 for as long as six years. Here again, loan applicants are considered chiefly on the basis of character, integrity, and ability to repay a loan from earnings, rather than on collateral.

Closely coupled with the loans is management training. For example, as a condition of a loan, SBA may require an applicant to attend an evening management course taught by skilled businessmen and experienced educators. Other features of the program are workshops for prospective businessmen, to point out factors that weigh heavily in business success, and counseling of established businessmen on their management problems.

"Pool" Loans

These are loans to corporations formed by groups of small businesses. The SBA lends them money to obtain raw materials, equipment, inventory or supplies for use by the group members; to obtain the benefits of research and development for the members, or to establish facilities for these purposes. The SBA may lend as much as $250,000 multiplied by the number of pool members, either as the agency's share of a loan made jointly with a bank or as a loan made solely by the agency. The agency's interest rate is 5 per cent, and loans may be for as long as twenty years.

Special Help to Unemployment, Redevelopment Areas

To spur economic activity in areas of substantial unemployment or redevelopment (as designated by the Area Redevelopment Administration), SBA makes loans in these areas at 4 per cent interest. The agency also makes loans to firms in these areas which are up to 25 per cent larger than those businesses normally assisted.

Who Can Borrow?

Most small, independent businesses—manufacturing, wholesaling, retailing, service, construction, and other types—are eligible for SBA loans. However, because SBA has a unique responsibility as a lender of taxpayers' money, it will not make loans to a few types of businesses or for certain purposes. For example, it will not make a loan to a business that derives income from gambling activities. Nor will it make loans for speculation in any kind of real or personal property.

A business generally qualifies as "small" for SBA loan purposes on the basis of these yardsticks:

- Wholesale—annual sales of not more than $5 million.
- Retail or Service—annual sales or receipts of not more than $1 million.
- Manufacturing—small if it has no more than 250 employees, large if it has more than 1,000; within these breaking points are specific size standards for specific industries.

Because these standards are of a general nature—for example, a retailer of groceries and fresh meats may have sales of up to $2 million and still qualify—the businessman should ask the nearest SBA office whether a more specific standard has been established for his type of business.

Small Business Investment Companies

The SBA also helps finance small firms through the medium of small business investment companies, or SBIC's as they are commonly called. These are privately owned but SBA-licensed companies which supply small firms with long-term financing and equity capital so that they can develop and promote new products, modernize, or expand their operations in other ways. SBIC's also provide management assistance to firms they finance.

The SBA regulates operations of the SBIC's, and in some cases makes loans to them. However, since an SBIC is privately owned and operated, its transactions with small companies are private arrangements and have no connection with SBA.

The SBA has licensed more than 700 SBIC's. A list of the companies is available from SBA field offices.

Forming an SBIC

An SBIC may begin operations with a minimum of $300,000 of paid-in capital and surplus, of which half may be borrowed from SBA in exchange for the SBIC's subordinated debentures. If a company starts with more than the minimum, or subsequently increases its capitalization, SBA may lend it a matching amount up to $700,000.

An SBIC also may borrow operating funds from SBA. The agency may lend the company half as much as its paid-in capital and surplus, up to a maximum of $4 million. The SBIC also may borrow from private sources, the limit on these borrowing being four times its capital and surplus.

The SBA charges 5 per cent interest on funds supplied in exchange for subordinated debentures and on operating loans.

Congress has enacted liberal tax provisions to encourage SBIC's. The dividends an SBIC receives from investments in small businesses are tax-exempt. Losses may be applied againt ordinary income by both the SBIC and its stockholders. Profits can be taxed as capital gains. For owners of closely held SBIC's, there are certain exemptions from personal holding company taxes. SBIC's are permitted to establish tax-free bad debt reserves equal to 10 per cent of their outstanding loans.

How SBIC's Finance Small Firms

An SBIC has several methods of financing small firms. To cite a few: it may make long-term loans, purchase capital stock or debt securities of a business, or purchase debentures which are convertible into stock of a business. Financing provided by an SBIC must be for at least five years and may be for as long as twenty years.

An SBIC generally may invest no more than 20 per cent of its paid-in capital and surplus in a single small business. If a small firm needs more money than one SBIC may provide, several SBIC's may join in the financing.

Eligibility of Financing

As a rule, a business qualifies as a small business for purposes of SBIC financing if (a) it meets SBA's regular business loan size standards, or (b) its assets do not exceed $5 million, its net worth is not more than $2.5 million, and its average net income, after federal income taxes, for the preceding two years did not exceed $250,000.

Development Company Loans

A third way in which SBA helps small firms to begin business, expand, or modernize is through loans to state and local development companies for use in financing small business.

The agency has two development company lending programs.

In one, it lends money to state development companies for use in supplying long-term loans and equity capital to small businesses. The SBA may lend a state development company as much as the company's total outstanding borrowings from all other sources. The SBA loans may be for as long as twenty years. The interest rate is 5 per cent. However, SBA charges only 4 per cent when the development company uses the funds for long-term loans to small firms in areas of substantial unemployment, and passes along to small firms the benefit of the reduced interest rate.

In the other lending program, SBA makes loans to both state and local development companies for use in financing specific small firms. The SBA may lend up to $350,000 for each small business to be assisted. Funds may be used for plant construction, expansion, modernization, or conversion, including the purchase of land, buildings, equipment, and machinery. The SBA may participate with banks in these loans, or may make direct loans.

Loans under this second program may be for as long as 25 years.

The interest rate on a direct loan, or the SBA share of a bank participation loan, is 5½ per cent. If a participating bank will charge a lower rate, SBA will match it down to a minimum of 5 per cent. In addition, SBA charges only 4 per cent in areas of substantial unemployment.

To be eligible for financing under either program, a small business must meet the same size standards as for financing from SBIC's.

Disaster Loans

The SBA makes loans to victims of several types of disaster. In one lending program it helps to repair physical damage; in a second, it helps to overcome economic injury. The agency may make a disaster loan jointly with a bank or other private lending institution or may make the loan entirely on its own. The law places no limit on the dollar amount of disaster loans; the amount is determined by the loss and needs of an applicant and other factors. Loans may be for as long as twenty years.

Physical Damage Loans

Whenever a major disaster strikes—a storm, flood, or earthquake, for example—SBA moves quickly to help disaster victims restore or replace their property. The agency makes loans for this purpose to individuals, business concerns of any size, and non-profit organizations. Loans may be used to repair or replace damaged structures, and to replace lost or damaged furnishings or business machinery, equipment, and inventory.

The agency charges 3 per cent interest on its share of a loan made jointly with a bank, or on a loan made entirely by SBA. Where a bank-SBA loan is for repair of the borrower's home or construction of a replacement, a bank usually may charge no more than 3 per cent interest on its share. On other loans, the bank may establish the rate on its share within reasonable limits.

The SBA works closely with the American Red Cross in disaster areas, coordinating its loan program with the Red Cross grant program.

Economic Injury Loans

Major or Natural Disaster. Small firms which are located in an area where a major or natural disaster has occurred, as determined by the President or the Secretary of Agriculture, and which have suffered substantial economic injury because of the disaster, are eligible for SBA loans. SBA funds may be used to provide working capital, stock normal inventories, and pay financial obligations (except bank loans) which the borrower would have been able to meet had he not lost revenue because of the disaster.

The interest rate on SBA's share of a bank-SBA loan, or a loan made entirely by the agency, is 3 per cent. A participating bank may set the rate on its own share, within reasonable limits.

Product Disasters. SBA also makes loans to small firms which have suffered substantial economic injury through inability to process or market a product for human consumption because of disease or toxicity of the product. The disease or toxicity may result from either natural or undetermined causes.

The borrower is charged 3 per cent interest on SBA's share of a bank-SBA loan, or a loan made entirely by the agency. A participating bank may set the rate on its own share, within reasonable limits.

Displaced Businesses. Small firms that are forced to move by federally-aided urban renewal, highway, and other construction programs, and that suffer substantial economic injury as a result, are eligible for SBA loans to help them relocate. Reasonable upgrading of the business, in the course of reestablishment, is permitted.

The interest rate on the agency's share of a bank-SBA loan, or a loan made entirely by SBA, is established yearly according to a statutory formula. The usual rate is between $3\frac{1}{2}$ and 4 per cent. A bank may set the interest rate on its share of a bank-SBA loan, within reasonable limits.

PART TWO
SBA BUSINESS LOANS

Loan Purposes and Types

One of the principal ways in which the Small Business Administration serves small business concerns is by helping them obtain needed financing on reasonable terms.

As part of this service, SBA makes loans to small manufacturers, wholesalers, retailers, service concerns, and other businesses, provided they cannot obtain private financing on reasonable terms and are not eligible for financing from other government agencies.

Loans are made for business construction, conversion, or expansion; purchase of equipment, facilities, machinery, supplies, or materials; and for working capital.

The SBA's loans are of two types, "participation" and "direct." In a participation loan, the agency joins with a bank (or other private lending institution) in a loan to a small business concern. In a direct loan, there is no participation by a private lender—the loan is made entirely and directly by SBA to the borrower. By law, the agency may not make a direct loan if a participation loan can be arranged.

The agency's participation may be either under a loan guaranty plan or on an immediate basis. When it participates on a guaranty basis, SBA agrees that, on ninety days' default as to principal or interest, it will purchase its guaranteed portion of the outstanding balance of the loan. When SBA participates in a loan on an immediate basis, it purchases immediately from the bank a fixed percentage of the original principal balance of the loan. However, under the Small Business Act, the agency may not enter into an immediate participation if it can do so on a guaranty (deferred) basis.

Loan Policies

The general loan policies of the Small Business Administration are determined by a three-man Loan Policy Board created under the Small Business Act, which established the agency. The board is composed of the Administrator of the Small Business Administration, who serves as chairman, and the Secretaries of the Treasury and Commerce, or their designees. The board revises the loan policies of the agency whenever this is necessary to meet the changing needs of small business concerns and of the national economy as a whole.

Eligibility Requirements

To be eligible for consideration for a Small Business Administration loan, a business must qualify as a small business and must meet SBA's credit requirements.

What Is a Small Business?

For business loan purposes, SBA defines a small business as one that is independently owned and operated and nondominant in its field, and that meets more detailed standards developed by the agency. These generally are as follows:

A manufacturing concern is considered small if its average employment in the preceding four calendar quarters was 250 or fewer persons, including employees of affiliates, and is considered large if its average employment in this period was more than 1,000 persons. If its average employment was more than 250 but not more than 1,000 persons, it may be considered either small or large, depending on the employment size standard SBA has developed for its particular industry.

A wholesale concern is classified as small if its yearly sales are $5 million or less.

Most retail businesses and service trades are considered small if their annual receipts do not exceed $1 million.

Because these standards are of a general nature, the small business owner should consult the nearest SBA field office . . . to learn if a specific standard has been established for his type of business.

The form of organization of a business—that is, whether it is a proprietorship, partnership, corporation, or other form of business enterprise—has no bearing on the question of whether it qualifies as a small business.

Furthermore, the fact that a business is a subsidiary or affiliate of another concern or group of concerns or is itself a parent corporation having subsidiaries does not necessarily disqualify it from consideration for an SBA loan—the test is whether the entire group of businesses, considered as a unit, meets the small business standards.

A business which operates under a franchise or similar agreement must provide SBA a copy of the agreement or contract before submitting a loan application, so that the agency can first be certain the firm is not a large business through affiliation with the franchisor.

General Credit Requirements

In addition to qualifying as a small business, a loan applicant must meet the following general credit requirements established by SBA:

a. The applicant must be of good character.

b. There must be evidence he has the ability to operate his business successfully.

c. He must have enough capital in the business so that, with loan assistance from SBA, it will be possible for him to operate on a sound financial basis.

d. The proposed loan must be of such sound value or must be so secured that repayment will reasonably be assured.

e. The past earnings record and future prospects of the firm must indicate ability to repay the loan and other fixed debt, if any, out of income.

f. In the case of a new business venture, the applicant usually is expected to provide from his own resources approximately half of the total required funds.

Construction Loans

Applicants for all loans involving construction must agree to cooperate with SBA in fostering nondiscrimination in employment opportunities. The agreement is executed on SBA Form 601, "Applicant's Agreement of Compliance."

Ineligible Applications

As a public agency, using taxpayers' funds, the Small Business Administration has an unusual responsibility as a lender. The agency therefore will not make certain types of loans or loans under certain circumstances.

Loans will not be granted:

1. If the funds are otherwise available on reasonable terms (a) from a financial institution, (b) from the disposal at a fair price of assets not required by the applicant in the conduct of his business or not reasonably necessary to potential growth, (c) through use, without undue personal hardship, of the personal credit or resources of the owner, partners, management, or principal stockholders of the applicant, (d) through the public offering or private placing of securities of the applicant, (e) from other government agencies which provide credit specifically for the applicant's type of business or for the purpose of the required financing, or (f) from other known sources of credit.

2. If the direct or indirect purpose or result of granting a loan would be to (a) pay off a creditor or creditors of the applicant who are inadequately secured and in a position to sustain a loss, (b) provide funds for distribution or payment to the owner, partners, or shareholders of the applicant, or (c) replenish working capital funds previously used for either of such purposes.

3. If the applicant's purpose in applying for a loan is to effect a change in ownership of the business; however, under certain circumstances loans may be authorized for this purpose, if the result would be to aid in the sound development of a small business or to keep it in operation.

4. If the loan would provide or free funds for speculation in any kind of property, real or personal, tangible or intangible.

5. If the applicant is a charitable organization, social agency, society, or other nonprofit enterprise; however, a loan may be considered for a cooperative if it carries on a business activity and the purpse of the activity is to obtain financial benefit for its members in the operation of their otherwise eligible small business concerns.

6. If the purpose of the loan is to finance the construction, acquisition, conversion, or operation of recreational or amusement facilities, unless the facilities contribute to the health or general well-being of the public.

7. If the applicant is a newspaper, magazine, book publishing company, radio broadcasting or television broadcasting company, or similar enterprise.

8. If any substantial portion (50 per cent or more) of the net sales of the applicant is derived from the sale of alcoholic beverages.

9. If any of the gross income of the applicant (or of any of its principal owners) is derived from gambling activities.

10. If the loan is to provide funds to an enterprise primarily engaged in the business of lending or investments or to provide funds to any otherwise eligible enterprise for the purpose of financing investments not related or essential to the enterprise.

11. If the purpose of the loan is to finance the acquisition, construction, improvement, or operation of real property that is, or is to be, held for sale or investment; provided, however, that this prohibition shall not apply to loans for the remodeling or improvement of existing commercial and industrial structures held for rental where the applicant is performing substantial maintenance and operational services in connection with the structures; and provided further, that no loan may be made to build or acquire buildings for investments.

12. If the effect of granting of the financial assistance will be to encourage monopoly or will be inconsistent with the accepted standards of the American system of free competitive enterprise.

13. If the loan would be used to relocate a business for other than sound business purposes.

Amount of Loan

The amount that may be borrowed from the Small Business Administration depends upon how much is needed for the intended purpose of the loan. However, by law the maximum amount SBA may have outstanding to any one borrower is $350,000. The maximum applies to the agency's share of a participation loan and to a direct SBA loan.

On a percentage basis, the maximum SBA participation in a loan is 90 per cent.

An exception to the $350,000 limitation is the agency's program of "pool loans"—loans made to corporations formed by "pools" or groups of small business concerns (a) to obtain raw materials, equipment, inventory, or supplies for use by members of the group, or (b) to obtain the benefits of research and development for the members of the group, or (c) to establish facilities for the foregoing purposes. The maximum pool loan is $250,000 multiplied by the number of small businesses participating in the group corporation loan.

Loan Terms

Small Business Administration business loans generally are repayable in regular monthly installments, including interest on the unpaid balance. Interest is charged only on the actual amount borrowed, and for the actual time the money is outstanding. All or any part of a loan may be repaid without penalty before it is due.

The maximum maturity of a loan generally is ten years. However, loans for working capital usually are limited to six years; loans for construction purposes may have a maturity of ten years plus the estimated time required to complete construction, and loans made to small business pools for construction of facilities may have a maturity of up to twenty years.

The interest rate on SBA's direct business loans, and the maximum interest rate on the agency's share of a participation loan, is 5½ per cent. A private lending institution may set a higher rate than 5½ per cent on its share of a participation loan provided the rate is legal and reasonable. It also may set a higher rate than 5½ per cent on the SBA portion of a guaranteed loan, the higher rate on the SBA portion to apply until such time as SBA may purchase its guaranteed portion. If a private institution sets a rate lower than 5½ per cent per annum on its share of a loan, the interest rate on the SBA portion shall be the same as that of the private institution. However, the interest rate on SBA's portion may not be less than 5 per cent, except as provided below.

The interest rate on small business loans made to veterans and insured by the Veterans Administration may not exceed 5¼ per cent per annum. The interest rate on SBA's pool loans is 5 per cent per annum.

The SBA has reduced its interest rate to 4 per cent in redevelopment areas designated by the Area Redevelopment Administration, Department of Commerce, and in certain areas of substantial unemployment designated by the Department of Labor. This rate applies to a direct SBA loan and to SBA's share of an immediate participation loan. The agency also has modified its size standards to permit loans to firms in these areas which are up to 25 per cent larger than those normally assisted. SBA field offices can supply detailed information.

Terms and conditions of each loan depend on the particular circumstances present. It generally will be required that restrictions be imposed on salaries, dividends and expenditures for fixed assets and that individual guarantees be made by the owners of corporations, etc. Any such requirements are discussed with the applicant and incorporated in the loan authorization.

Collateral

By law, SBA's loans must be of such sound value or so secured that repayment will reasonably be assured. Accordingly, the proposed collateral for an SBA business loan must be of such a nature that, when considered with the integrity and ability of the applicant's management and the applicant's past and prospective earnings, repayment of the loan will reasonably be assured.

Collateral may consist of one or more of the following: A mortgage on land, building and/or equipment; assignment of warehouse receipts for marketable merchandise; assignment of certain types of contracts; a mortgage on chattels; guarantees or personal endorsements, and, in some instances, assignment of current receivables. As a rule, a pledge or mortgage on inventories is not considered satisfactory collateral unless the inventories are stored in a bonded or otherwise acceptable warehouse.

Is Other Financing Available?

By law, the Small Business Administration may make loans to small business concerns only when financing is not available to them on reasonable terms from other sources. An applicant for an SBA business loan therefore must be prepared to demonstrate to the satisfaction of the agency that funds are not available from the sources indicated in the paragraph numbered 1 under "Ineligible Applications."

In this connection, before applying to SBA for a loan, a businessman must first seek the needed funds from his local bank (or other local sources of financing). If the bank is unable or unwilling to make the loan, the businessman should learn whether it can or will do so if SBA agrees to participate in the loan.

If the bank will make the loan, provided SBA participates in it, the businessman may apply for a participation loan under SBA's Regular Participation Loan Plan.

If the bank will not make a loan to the small business, even with SBA's participation, the business may then apply to the agency for a direct government loan. (In some instances, as indicated in the following sections, two banks must decline to make or participate in the loan before the business may apply for a direct SBA loan.)

Regular Participation and Direct Loans

The maximum Small Business Administration share of a Regular Participation loan, on a percentage basis, is 90 per cent; on a dollar basis, $350,000.

Application for a Regular Participation loan is made on forms which are available from any agency field office.

To apply for a Regular Participation loan, the small business should file with the bank that proposes to participate in the loan three copies of the application and three copies of any supporting documents. The bank then should prepare a request to SBA for a participation agreement, using for this purpose space provided on the SBA form. The small business or the bank next should file two copies of the application and supporting documents with the SBA office serving the territory in which the applicant's home office is located. The third copy should be retained by the bank.

The maximum SBA direct loan to any one small business also is $350,000. To apply for a direct loan, a small business should file two copies of its application (using SBA forms) and supporting documents with the SBA office serving its area. The application must be accompanied by a letter from the small concern's bank stating it is unable to make or participate in the loan. Where the bank has declined the loan because the requested amount would exceed its legal lending limit or is greater than the bank normally lends to any one borrower, the applicant must be able to show also that the loan is not obtainable from a correspondent bank of his bank of account or from another lending institution whose lending capacity is adequate to cover the requested loan. In any event, if the small business is located in a city with a population of 200,000 or more, its application must be accompanied by letters from two banks stating that they cannot make or participate in the requested loan.

Small Loan Program

The Small Loan Program is designed specifically to meet the needs of very small businesses, including new enterprises, many of which have in the past been unable to obtain loans because of lack of adequate collateral. Under this program great stress is put on the character of the appplicant, his past record for handling obligations, and his future business prospects.

Who May Borrow

Any qualified small firm seeking financial assistance up to $15,000 for direct SBA loans, or bank participation loans where the SBA portion is not more than $15,000.

Maturity

Small loan maturities may not exceed six years plus time need for construction work when the loan will be used for building construction.

Interest

Small loans bear the same interest rate as prescribed for larger loans.

Collateral

As security SBA will require the pledge of available collateral, including any fixed assets purchased with the loan proceeds. However, the agency will not require mortgages on residences occupied by borrowers, or on furniture and fixtures used in the borrowers' homes. No assignment of life insurance or of leases or after-acquired property or lessor's agreements will be required. Automotive equipment will be taken as collateral only where it is the most important part of the collateral available. Exceptions to the foregoing will be made only in participation loans when the exceptions are desired by the participating institutions.

Other Assistance

When the need arises, SBA specialists will assist borrowers under the Small Loan program with such services as counseling in marketing, production, and management.

Loan Applications

Loan application forms may be obtained from any SBA office.

Loans for Very Small Businesses

The SBA assists and encourages very small businesses through loans and management training. Studies have shown that these businesses, while eager to expand and modernize and thus better serve their communities, generaly are unable to obtain financing or management guidance. The SBA is helping to fill this need, and in this way to increase jobs and business activity. This SBA program is especially helpful to areas that have long suffered from poverty, such as areas peopled by minorities.

Under this plan, the SBA may lend businessmen up to $6,000 for as long as six years. Here again, loan applicants are considered chiefly on the basis of character, integrity, and ability to repay a loan from earnings, rather than on collateral.

Closely coupled with the loans is management training. For example, as a condition of a loan, SBA may require an applicant to attend an evening management course taught by skilled businessmen and experienced educators. Other features of the program are workshops for prospective businessmen, to point out factors that weigh heavily in business success, and counseling of established businessmen on their management problems.

Of Special Interest to Banks

To encourage the widest possible bank cooperation in small business loans under the Regular Participation Program, the Small Business Administration has developed a simplified participation plan for banks. Of particular interest to banks is an early maturity feature of this plan which was developed jointly by SBA and the American Bankers Association.

The SBA's Decision

The time required for processing a specific application is affected by the care the businessman has taken in preparing his loan request, the completeness of the information he has furnished, and the amount of work required for full consideration by the SBA of all elements of the application.

Generally, the agency can act more quickly on an application for a participation loan than one for a direct loan, because the bank which proposes to share in the loan has completed most of the necessary credit investigation before the application is submitted to SBA.

The smaller loan requests frequently can be acted upon very quickly since in most cases the local SBA office has the authority to approve or decline the applications.

Compensation for Services

The SBA makes no charge for assistance in the preparation and filing of a loan application or for other assistance with financial management problems.

Subject to the agency's approval, a loan applicant may pay reasonable costs incurred for services rendered by attorneys, appraisers, and accountants in connection with the preparation of his loan application or the making of the loan.

However, a businessman may not pay, or agree to pay, a fee or commission contingent upon approval of a loan by SBA or by a lending institution which proposes to participate with SBA in making the loan, unless the amount of such fee bears a necessary and reasonable relationship to the services actually performed.

Loan Closing

If the Small Business Administration approves a small business concern's loan application, whether for a participation or a direct loan, a formal loan authorization is sent to the business by the SBA office in its area. This authorization is not in itself a contract to lend or a loan agreement. Instead, it states the conditions the borrower must meet before the loan funds will be disbursed.

When the borrower notifies the agency he is prepared to meet these conditions, SBA or the participating bank then arranges a date, time, and place for "closing" the loan. In most cases all notes, mortgages, and other required documents are executed at the closing. However, where the applicant is located at a distance from the SBA office and there is no participating institution, the SBA office may vary the closing procedure.

Once the loan has been closed, the agency or the participating institution disburses the funds by check, either immediately or as required by the applicant.

Prompt closing of a loan, after SBA has issued the loan authorization, depends laregly upon the borrower and the time he requires to comply with the terms and conditions of the authorization.

The SBA and participating banks are prepared to disburse loan funds simultaneously with loan closings.

Eugene P. Foley
Administrator

Small Business Administration

Washington, D. C. 20416

FACT SHEET

SMALL BUSINESS ADMINISTRATION'S SMALL LOAN PROGRAM

Purpose:

The Small Loan program is designed specifically to meet the needs of the very small business, including new enterprises, many of which have in the past been unable to obtain loans because of lack of adequate collateral. Under this program great stress is put on the character of the applicant, his past record for handling obligations, and his visible future business prospects.

Who May Borrow:

Any qualified small firm, including new businesses, seeking financial assistance up to $15,000 for direct loans, or bank participation loans where the SBA portion is not more than $15,000.

Maturity:

Small loan maturities will not exceed 6 years, plus time needed for construction work when the loan proceeds are used for building construction.

Interest:

Small Loans will bear interest at 5-1/2 per cent, except in areas of major, persistent unemployment when the rate will be reduced to 4 per cent. Banks participating in these loans will be permitted to charge their usual interest rates. If the bank's interest rate is below 5-1/2 per cent SBA will match the lower interest rate, down to 5 per cent.

Loan Conditions:

Loan conditions and requirements are to be kept at a minimum. A calculated risk will be assumed with respect to the adequacy of earnings, provided the earnings potential appears reasonably favorable.

Collateral:

As security SBA will take in the simplest way possible whatever worthwhile collateral is available, including any fixed assets purchased with loan proceeds. Title searches will not be made and no mortgages on residences occupied by the borrowers, no furniture and fixtures used in the borrowers' homes, will be taken. No assignment of life insurance, assignment of leases or after-acquired property or lessor's agreements will be required. No automotive equipment will be taken as collateral except where such equipment is the most important part of the collateral available. Exceptions to the foregoing will be made only in participation loans when such conditions are desired by the participating institution.

Other Assistance:

When the need arises, SBA experts will assist all borrowers under the Small Loan program with services such as counseling in marketing, production and management.

Proof of Non-Availability of Other Funds:

By law SBA may make loans to small firms only when financing is not available to then on reasonable terms from private sources. However, applicants for Small Loans need only furnish SBA the names of banks contacted and SBA will obtain verification that a bank loan was not available.

Loan Applications:

Loan application forms (6B) may be obtained from any SBA office.

(Fact Sheet No. _7_)

Prepared by Office of Public Information   May 1964

UNITED STATES OF AMERICA
SMALL BUSINESS ADMINISTRATION

APPLICATION FOR LOAN

SBA LOAN NO.

This form is to be used in applying for either a direct loan of not in excess of $15,000 or a participation loan in which the SBA share will not exceed $15,000.

(For Instructions See Page 4)

1. APPLICANT (Show official name without abbreviations unless an abbreviation is a part of the official name. For proprietor or partnership, show name(s) followed by d/b/a and trade name used, if any)		Date of Application
Name		
Street		Amount of Loan Requested
City & Zone		$
County	Telephone No.	Maturity Requested
State		
Type of Business (Attach history of business using separate sheet if necessary)	Date Established	Number of Employees (Including subsidiaries and affiliates).

Marital Status (If not a corporation, give name of spouse for each married partner or owner):

2. AMOUNT AND PURPOSES OF LOAN - GENERAL STATEMENT (Why you need the loan):

Purposes (How you will use the loan, i.e., purchase inventory, purchase machinery, retire mortgages, etc.)	Amount
	$
Total (This should agree with amount of loan requested) . .	$

3. COLLATERAL OFFERED: (For DIRECT Loans, attach detailed list of collateral offered)

	Book Value (Net)	Present Liens Or Mortgage Balance, If Any
Business real estate	$	$
Business machinery and equipment.		
Business furniture and fixtures		
Autos and trucks		
Accounts receivable		
Inventory		
Farm or investment property		
Life insurance (not "G.I."), cash surrender value (less loans) .		
Endorsers, Comakers or Guarantors personal net worth		XXXXXXXXXXXXXXXXX
Other (specify)		

NOTE: If more space is needed use a separate sheet

4. NAMES OF ATTORNEYS, ACCOUNTANTS, AND OTHER PARTIES. The names of all attorneys, accountants, appraisers, agents, and all other parties (whether individuals, partnerships, associations or corporations) engaged by or on behalf of the applicant (whether on a salary, retainer or fee basis and regardless of the amount of compensation) for the purpose of rendering professional or other services of any nature whatever to applicant, in connection with the preparation or presentation of this application or with any loan to applicant which SBA may make, or in which SBA may participate, as a result of this application, or such loan or participation; and all fees or other charges or compensation paid or to be paid therefor or for any purpose in connection with this application whether in money or other property of any kind whatever, by or for the account of the applicant, together with a description of such services rendered or to be rendered, are as follows:

Name and Address	Description of Services Rendered and to be Rendered	*Total Compensation Agreed to be Paid	*Compensation Already Paid

*Subject to SBA approval. In the event of loan approval SBA form for describing services performed or to be performed must be executed by applicant, and the parties, if any, listed above. Applicant should immediately notify SBA of any change or addition to the information set forth above.

IT IS NOT REQUIRED THAT AN APPLICANT EMPLOY REPRESENTATIVES IN ORDER TO FILE A LOAN APPLICATION WITH SBA

5. DISCLOSURE OF SPECIAL INFORMATION REGARDING PRINCIPALS: (a) List on separate sheet the names of any SBA employees or SBA advisory board members who are related by blood, marriage or adoption to, or who have any present or have had any past, direct or indirect, financial interest in or in association with, the applicant, or any of its partners, officers, directors or principal stockholders (such interest to include any direct or indirect financial interest in any other business entity or enterprise); (b) When the proprietor, or any partner, officer, director, or person who holds 10 percent or more of the applicant's stock is an investor in a licensed Small Business Investment Company, or a proposed investor in an SBIC which has filed for a license, detailed information shall be submitted with this application; and (c) Likewise, if any person identified in (b) above is an employee of the U. S. Government (including members of the armed forces), detailed information shall be submitted with this application.

If none, check here: (a)☐ (b)☐ (c)☐

-1-

SBA Form 6B (4-64)

84

6. BALANCE SHEET AS OF _____ , 19____ , FISCAL YEAR ENDS _____

(Balance sheet must be dated within 60 days of the filing of this application. Omit $.00)

(The applicant may submit in lieu of the balance sheet prescribed below, a copy of his regularly prepared balance sheet dated within 60 days of the filing of this application provided he supplies (a) details on items marked with an asterisk; (b) aging of accounts receivable and accounts payable; (c) details of notes, contracts and mortages payable)

Assets		Liabilities	
Cash on hand and in banks	$_____	Notes payable for merchandise	$_____
Notes receivable		Notes payable to banks	
Accounts receivable . . . . $_____		Notes to officers, directors, and stockholders . .	
Less reserve for doubtful accounts _____		Notes to others	
Inventories (How valued)		Accounts payable for merchandise	
Finished . . . . $_____		*Accounts due officers or stockholders	
Stock in process . . . . _____		Income taxes	
Raw material. . . . . _____		Other accruals	
*Other current assets		*Other current liabilities	
Total current assets	$_____	Total current liabilities	$_____
*Due from affiliates or subsidiaries		Mortgage debts	
*Due from officers, directors, and stockholders . . .		*Other liabilities	
Life insurance (not "G.I."), cash surrender value .		Total liabilities	$_____
**Land			
**Buildings . . . . $_____			
**Machinery and equipment . . . . . _____		Net Worth:	
Business Furniture and fixtures . _____			
**Autos and trucks . . . . _____		Capital stock. . . . . $_____	
Less reserve for depreciation . . _____		Surplus and undivided profits _____	
*Other assets		Capital account (If individual or partnership) . . .	
Total assets.	$_____	Total liabilities and net worth	$_____

*Itemize on a separate sheet all items marked with a single asterisk.   **State name(s) in which title is held.

Contingent Liabilities: Accounts or notes receivable discounted or sold with endorsement or guarantee and all other contingent liabilities, including terms of any leases, should be explained on a separate sheet; also, describe any pending or imminent litigation. If none, check here ☐

Aging	Accounts Receivable	Accounts Payable
Under 30 days . . . . $_____	$_____	
30 - 60 days . . . . _____		_____
60 - 120 days . . . . _____		_____
Over 120 days . . . . _____		_____
Uncollectible . . . . _____		_____
Totals . . . . $_____	$_____	_____

Notes, Contracts and Mortgages Payable:

To Whom Payable	Original Amount	Original Date	Balance	Maturity	Monthly Payment	Security
	$		$		$	

7. CONDENSED COMPARATIVE STATEMENTS OF SALES, PROFIT OR LOSS, ETC. (Attach detailed profit and loss statements) (Your income tax returns should be of help to you in giving this information)

If a corporation, use this block:	19	19	Current Year - To Date
Net sales (Gross sales less returns and allowances)	$	$	$
Depreciation			
Income taxes			
Compensation of officers (Included in expenses)			
Net profit (After depreciation and income taxes)			
Dividends paid			

If a partnership or proprietorship, use this block:	19	19	Current Year - To Date
Net sales (Gross sales less returns and allowances)	$	$	$
Depreciation			
Withdrawals (For income taxes)			
Personal withdrawals by owner or partners			
Net profit (After depreciation and withdrawals)			

-2-   SBA Form 6B (4-64)

85

Net Worth Reconciliation

	19	19	Current Year - To Date
Net worth - beginning	$	$	$
Profit or loss			
Dividends			
Withdrawals			
Paid in			
Revaluation of assets			
Other additions (Explain)			
Other deductions (Explain)			
Net change (Increase or decrease)			
Ending net worth			

*Must agree with the net worth figure shown in the balance sheet above (Item 6)

8. INFORMATION TO BE FURNISHED AS TO THE PROPRIETOR OR EACH PARTNER OR EACH OFFICER, DIRECTOR AND HOLDER OF 20% OR MORE OF APPLICANT'S STOCK.

First and Middle Names in Full and Last Name	Date and Place of Birth (1)	U. S. Citizen? (2)	Percent Ownership (3)	Office Held (4)	Annual Compensation (5)	Net Worth Outside of Applicant* (6)	Life Insurance Which Is Assignable** (7)

*Signed and dated personal balance sheets must be submitted except for shareholders who own less than 20% of applicant's stock. If applicant is a proprietorship or partnership, and the proprietor or partners own assets that are not included in the applicant's balance sheet, the proprietor or partners must submit signed personal balance sheets which coincide with net worth shown in Item 8, Column (6) above.

**Attach separate sheet giving details.

9. AGREEMENT ON NONEMPLOYMENT OF SBA PERSONNEL. In consideration of the making by SBA to applicant of all or any part of the loan applied for in this application, applicant hereby agrees with SBA that applicant will not, for a period of two years after disbursement by SBA to applicant of said loan, or any part thereof, employ or tender any office or employment to, or retain for professional services, any person who, on the date of such disbursement, or within one year prior to said date, (a) shall have served as an officer, attorney, agent, or employee of SBA and (b) as such, shall have occupied a position or engaged in activities which SBA shall have determined, or may determine, involve discretion with respect to the granting of assistance under the Small Business Act, or said Act as it may be amended from time to time.

10. CREDIT INFORMATION. Applicant expressly authorizes disclosure of all information submitted in connection with this application and any resulting loan to the financial institution agreeing below to participate in such loan or, if none, to its bank(s) of account and (Insert name of other financial institution if desired) _____.

11. CERTIFICATION. I hereby certify that:

(a) The applicant has received and read SBA Form 394, and has not paid or incurred any obligation to pay, directly or indirectly, any fee or other compensation for obtaining the loan hereby applied for.

(b) The loan herein requested is not readily available from my personal assets nor from the personal assets of any officer or partner of the applicant and that the banks or other financial institutions listed below have declined to make this loan and have declined to participate, in any manner, with SBA in making this loan: (Attach decline letters from banks, if available. If bank letter(s) not supplied complete information below).

Name of your bank of deposit or bank contacted	Address of bank	Name of person seen at bank

Date of contact	Amount of loan requested	Terms of repayment requested

Other bank contacted (if any)	Address of bank	Name of person seen at bank

Date of contact	Amount of loan requested	Terms of repayment requested

(c) SBA is authorized to contact the bank(s) listed above to verify the information given.

(d) The applicant or any officer of the applicant or affiliates or any other concern with which such officer has been connected has never been in receivership or adjudicated a bankrupt. (Any reservations, qualifications or exceptions to this certification are set forth by statement attached hereto).

All information contained above and in exhibits attached hereto are true and complete to the best knowledge and belief of the applicant and are submitted for the purpose of inducing SBA to grant a loan to applicant. Whether or not the loan herein applied for is approved, applicant agrees to pay or reimburse SBA for the cost of any surveys, title or mortgage examinations, appraisals, etc., performed by non-SBA personnel with consent of applicant.

_____
(Individual, general partner, trade name or corporation)

(SEAL)

By _____

Attest _____ Title _____
         (Title)

Date _____

Whoever makes any statement knowing it to be false, or whoever willfully overvalues any security, for the purpose of obtaining for himself or for any applicant any loan, or extension thereof by renewal, deferment of action, or otherwise, or the acceptance, release, or substitution of security therefor, or for the purpose of influencing in any way the action of the SBA, or for the purpose of obtaining money, property, or anything of value, under the Small Business Act, as amended, shall be punished under section 16(a) of the Small Business Act by a fine of not more than $5,000 or by imprisonment for not more than two years, or both. Whoever, with intent to defraud, knowingly conceals, removes, disposes of, or converts to his own use or to that of another, any property mortgaged or pledged to, or held by, the Administration, shall be fined not more than $5,000 or imprisoned not more than five years, or both; but if the value of such property does not exceed $100, he shall be fined not more than $1,000 or imprisoned not more than one year, or both.

SBA Form 6B (4-64)

INSTRUCTIONS TO APPLICANT

1. The application must be completed in full and signed; if more space is needed, use separate sheet. Failure to submit all required information will delay processing of this loan application.
2. Submit 3 copies of application and 3 copies of each supporting document to participating bank. For a direct loan submit only 2 copies of application and supporting documents to SBA office.

INSTRUCTIONS TO BANK
(FOR PARTICIPATION LOANS ONLY)

1. Be sure application is filled out completely and signed and balance sheet items detailed.
2. Official of bank to sign application for participation in space provided below.
3. Confidential report in letter form to be submitted in duplicate containing the following:
   - a. Opinion as to need for loan;
   - b. Bank's opinion of character and ability of applicant's management;
   - c. Future business prospects of applicant;
   - d. Repayment ability;
   - e. Opinion of adequacy of security for the loan;
   - f. Bank's previous credit experience with borrower.
4. Attach copy of any commercial credit report bank may have available.
5. Submit 2 copies of application and 2 copies of each supporting document to nearest SBA office.
6. Submit 2 copies of signed personal financial statement of proprietor, partners or principal stockholders, as of the same date of applicant's balance sheet, and date of signature indicated.

Note: Loan terms should show maturity, repayment requirements and any special conditions considered appropriate, as well as security to be obtained for the loan. Security may include, but shall not be limited to, mortgage on real or personal property, assignment of accounts receivable or moneys due on contracts, pledge of warehouse receipts, negative pledge agreements and corporate guaranties or personal endorsements.

(For use only by bank or other financial institution)

APPLICATION FOR PARTICIPATION OR GUARANTY

We propose to make a (check one):

☐ Guaranteed Loan: Bank Share _____%; SBA Share _____%.

☐ Immediate Participation Loan: Bank Share _____%; SBA Share _____%.

to the Applicant named on page 1 of this application, provided SBA will participate in or guarantee the loan to the extent of _____ percent. We hereby make application for the type of participation or guaranty checked above subject to the following loan conditions (use separate sheet if necessary):

Interest to be payable monthly at the annual rate of _____ percent on the unpaid principal amount of the loan advanced by the bank.

Without the participation or guaranty of SBA to the extent applied for we would not be willing to make this loan. In our opinion, the financial assistance applied for is not otherwise available on reasonable terms.

_____
(Name and address of bank)

Date _____, 19 _____

_____
(Authorized officer)

-4-   SBA Form 6B (4-64)

GPO-874-403

87

PART FOUR

THE GOVERNMENT AS A CUSTOMER

PRI and The National Aeronautics Space Agency[1]

PRI is an engineering firm specializing in telecommunications systems consulting and engineering. Established in 1952 to provide engineering services for the then emerging microwave communications market, PRI has since expanded its service offerings to include virtually all types of communications systems engineering. While PRI maintained its forte in microwave communications engineering, its new applications included communications requirement surveys; basic system design studies; procurement specification preparation; system surveys and appraisals; system equipment procurement services; system installation, construction and testing supervision for all types of communications systems. From 1952 to 1962 PRI had steadily built its business in all markets, including international markets, except the United States governmental market. In 1959, an extremely large contract was received from one of the two largest United States common carrier communications corporations. The contract was for the engineering of a transcontinental microwave system. Since this contract absorbed all available PRI talent and then some, PRI literally suspended its marketing and promotional program from 1959 to 1962. In mid-1962, one year before the large common carrier microwave systems contract was due to run out, PRI initiated a very limited marketing program. It was felt that since PRI was still quite well known by commercial firms, this limited marketing effort should be directed to developing governmental business, being content to act as subcontractor on such work which was performed for commercial contractors for the

[1] This case was prepared by Mr. Frank E. Ceglowski under the direction of Professor Donald Grunewald.

government. The strategy was to write the appropriate communications representatives in the various governmental agencies including the defense establishment and the National Aeronautics Space Agency (NASA). Although it was realized governmental policy did not encourage replies to general inquiries from vendors, it was hoped such letters would apprise the contact of PRI's potential and soften him for a future personal visit. Wherever possible, PRI applied for NASA bidders' lists. PRI also exhibited at the annual Armed Forces Communications and Electronics Association (AFCEA) convention, which was attended by representatives of all governmental agencies including NASA.

Personal visits were arranged, and PRI began visiting NASA. In June, 1962, just after it had been placed on the various NASA bidder lists, PRI visited the NASA Goddard Air Space Flight Center, at Greenbelt, Maryland. Goddard is the NASA Center most responsible for NASA communications. After much visiting PRI found a communications supervisor who was interested in having a comparison made of the best ways to furnish communications from a NASA launch point to Goddard. The NASA official stated that the project was just in the offing and PRI should "keep in touch." After several months of "keeping in touch," NASA reported that NASA, on its own, had decided to use Bell System facilities to provide the communications link between the Launch Center and Greenbelt, Maryland.

In early December, 1962, PRI received a "Request For Quote" (RFQ) from NASA at Greenbelt, Maryland. The RFQ had been sent to many other firms as well. The RFQ had to do with the provision of engineering in terms of personnel to work in residence at Goddard. PRI assembled a representative group, quoted a man-month rate, and delivered its bid to Greenbelt. PRI lost the bid as the result of a high man-month rate.

In an effort to improve its NASA promotional program, PRI decided to query certain officials at NASA to determine how its proposal could have been improved. A discussion with NASA officials indicated that PRI had submitted resumes of individuals who were too "high powered" for the job. They felt that perhaps this was one of the reasons why PRI's man-month rate was high. The NASA representative stated that this in turn showed a lack of appreciation for the parameters of the project. The job went to a large electronics firm with an extensive Washington, D.C., office. The NASA representative stated that a new procurement for high-quality technical assistance was being prepared. They promised that PRI would receive copies of this RFQ when it was distributed.

During March 1963, PRI received a "Request for Proposal" (RFP) covering an extensive survey, an appraisal of the entire NASA communications complex. The quote was to be made in terms of two factors, a man-month rate and the number of men involved. NASA had specified the time to be spent on each phase of the project. In addition to the quote, the RFP required a statement concerning company background, facilities, technical approach and the resumes of the individuals who would be utilized on this project. PRI assembled an extremely well-qualified team for this project. It was felt that it would be in the best interests of the government to utilize a small number of highly qualified engineers at a medium man-month rate rather than a large number of technicians at a low man-month rate. PRI reasoned that this way the job could be done at a lower over-all cost to the government and with a higher-quality performance. PRI submitted its proposal in accordance with the requirements of the RFP. In June, 1963, an award was made to a large systems engineering firm headquartered in Washington, D.C. Once again, PRI contacted NASA officials in an effort to determine why PRI did not receive this award. NASA stated the reasons were (1) poor technical approach and (2) lack of experience in related government work. PRI felt its technical approach was very sound, realizing, however, that this was a matter of judgment. PRI could only agree that it lacked experience in government work.

After such a poor and frustrating performance record in bidding on NASA projects which were well within PRI's performance capability, Mr. Preston, president of PRI, asked Mr. Renault, marketing manager of PRI, to set up a meeting to discuss the past NASA marketing program. He asked Mr. Renault to be prepared to recommend either continuing or discontinuing the program and the reason for the particular recommendation. In the event that continuation was recommended, he was to suggest what steps could be taken to improve it.

Renault decided that, in order to interpret successfuly and bid on NASA procurements, it would be almost an absolute requirement to have an office in Washington, D.C., since the record seemed to show that significant NASA procurements went only to firms with such offices.

PRI expected to earn a net profit of about 10 per cent on any NASA business generated. A Washington office would probably cost approximately $35,000 per year staffed by one Washington representative and a secretary. Costs would include supplies, rent, and overhead. The office could be used to solicit other possible government business as well as NASA orders.

A friend of Mr. Renault's suggested another possibility to him. The friend, an administrative assistant to a United States Senator, thought that if a little political pressure were applied, PRI might well get some NASA work. Renault was somewhat dubious about this approach, since PRI was a professional firm and had always maintained high ethical standards.

A third alternative was open to PRI. This was to abandon any further solicitation of NASA work.

The Precision Company

The experience of a small firm with government

The Precision Company is a small manufacturer of quality phthalomine. Phthalomine is the generic name for an industrial chemical product that varies considerably according to the needs of the customer. The general public is not aware of the existence of phthalomine, although it is used in connection with the manufacture of many consumer products.

Sales of the Precision Company have averaged in the vicinity of $5 million per year in recent years. The company has fewer than one hundred employees. Precision is located in the Ironbound section of Newark, New Jersey, where it has been in business for forty years. Before this time, the company had been located in New York City for more than thirty years. The chief executive of the company is Harry Tiffany, age 75. Mr. Tiffany started with the company as a laborer. Through his drive and interest, he educated himself in the business, both through formal study at night and informal attendance at industry clubs and meetings. As he became more educated, he advanced in the company and was elected an officer. At the time he began with the company (more than fifty years earlier), there were only ten employees. The firm had its greatest growth during his tenure as chief executive over the past thirty years. Mr. Tiffany owns 80 per cent of the common stock of Precision; the balance is held by relatives of the firm's original founder and by long-term employees.

Second in command of Precision is Martin Charles, the stepson of the founder's only daughter. Mr. Charles is the second largest stockholder. Mr. Charles worked for the company part time and summers during his schooling. He has worked in all departments and is the designated "heir apparent."

Precision manufactures in two locations. The main production facilities are in Newark, New Jersey, along with the laboratory and general offices. Despite its small size, the Precision Company maintains a nationwide distribution system through branch offices, controlled by the company but operated by individuals who run their own operations independently. The company also distributes its product through franchised dealers. These dealers sell related products as well as phthalomine. Both the branches and franchised dealers sell to individuals who use phthalomine in their manufacturing operations and then sell the manufactured products to the ultimate consumer.

Precision received notices of government bid requests from many different government agencies. One particular agency accounts for 75 per cent of Precision's government business. Hans Holger, the head of the government agency, is a progressive individual who is not satisfied with the normal method of buying phthalomine. Mr. Holger wants to avoid the widespread practice of using physical standards. At present, a small quantity of a satisfactory shipment is retained and is used as a standard for subsequent shipments. The difficulty with this procedure is that retained samples deteriorate with time, and allowances must be made when testing a fresh batch. Because of this change it is necessary for the tester to make a judgment on every test as to the change that has taken place.

Mr. Holger has made a project of eliminating the human factor from the tests. After much work and experimentation and discouragement, he developed a series of tests that reduced the human factor to one of technique rather than judgment. When he had gone to large phthalomine manufacturers, Mr. Holger had met with a cool reception. The manager of Precision's Washington branch heard about Mr. Holger's project and, learning of the cool reception, went to see if Precision could do the job. Convinced that it could after talking to Holger, he persuaded Mr. Charles and Mr. Tiffany that the account would be worthwhile, and so Precision agreed to cooperate with the agency on this project.

From the company's point of view, it meant a significant investment in equipment and a tremendous amount of time spent on a project that was producing no revenue. For almost a year, one man, who was one third of the technical staff, spent virtually all his time on this one project. Precision worked very closely with Mr. Holger and his staff getting the flaws out of the system.

Eventually, at the end of one year, the system worked well and bids could be made and filled in a routine fashion, although production was supervised more closely than normal. Precision did not have the business to itself, despite its close contact with the agency. Because of government regulations, bids had to be solicited from all interested parties, and the agency had been directed to establish at least three producers as "primary" suppliers, whenever possible. Precision submitted bids for all items solicited and had succeeded in capturing more than 60 per cent of the possible business. According to private information, volunteered by members of the agency staff, Precision has the best record of all suppliers for meeting specifications. Precision has had one shipment rejected in four years; the next best record was reported as ten rejections. In many cases Precision has supplied phthalomine, despite higher bids, when the low bidder was unable to meet specifications. Whenever the agency needs material in a rush they order from Precision without a bid, under emergency release-from-bidding procedure. Recently, the agency has accepted shipments from Precision and sent reports showing results for the simple tests and the following inscription, "Shipment accepted on the basis of supplier's record of successful submissions."

The company has mixed emotions about this government agency account. On the one hand, it is a "good" account which orders in large quantities at more or less regular intervals. The agency orders more phthalomine at one time than almost any other account. Also, the agency discounts its bills.[1] On the other hand, Mr. Tiffany emphasizes that the initial investment necessary to get the account was excessive. He points out also, that the orders are still treated with extra care and a technician must shepherd the batches through production. Thus, the company is not sure at all whether, despite the success they have had, the government agency account is worthwhile.

Precision also submits bids to other government agencies. Government agencies send specifications to the company and "invite" bids. Most often, the invitations demand a sample to accompany the bid; this sample must be equal or superior to a standard sample supplied with the invitation. Normally, this standard sample is from the production batch of the previous, successful bidder. The specifications are established on the basis of this sample. The government procedure is to test the sample from the lowest bidder. If this sample fails to meet specifications then the next lowest bidder's sample is tested until a satisfactory sample is found. The company has not been very successful in securing this type of bid. The next cause is failure to meet specifications. One complaint the company has about these bids is that a report on the unsuccessful samples is rarely published. Also, information about the successful bids is difficult to obtain in many cases.

The company submits bids on these invitations only when there is plenty of time to work on them. Mr. Charles feels that the bids that must be submitted are too "close" to be worth while. The company believes the government is not a reasonable customer. In a recent case, a shipment of phthalomine was accepted by the government and used for

---

[1] An important factor Precision has found when accepting government orders!

some three or four weeks. Then workmen complained about the "working properties" and the balance of the shipment was returned to Precision for adjustment. (The shipment was returned on the basis of a general clause in the bid.) This happened twice more before the government was satisfied. The shipments were all transported at Precision's expense. Mr. Tiffany's comment at this situation was that this one batch more than covered any profit, if any, that had been made on all the government bids for the last three years.

During the week of December 1, 1963, the *New York Times* reported that the United States government was suspending the most-favored nation clause for tariffs on certain commodities imported from Western Europe; one of these commodities was tendlichin.[2] The *Times* reported that the suspension was due to the rejection by the Common Market of United States demands for adjustment of their poultry tariffs. The increase in the tariff on tendlichin was 20 per cent.

Precision has begun to use tendlichin increasingly in the past six months as a basic raw material for a special line of phthalomine where price is significant but not the only factor. Both Mr. Tiffany and Mr. Charles were doubtful about adding this particular line in the first place, because of the price factor and because the competition is strong and not likely to weaken. However, since the branches and dealers were anxious to be able to supply this line to their customers it was decided to manufacture the product.

The increase in the tariff makes the situation more undesirable. It is unlikely that any producer will be able to increase his price; thus, the increased cost must be absorbed. The increased tariff, therefore, makes the new product less profitable than before. However, it is not clear what the company can do now. Precision has told its dealers and branches to market the new phthalomine and they have done so. Mr. Tiffany and Mr. Charles are conscious of the bad effect discontinuation of the product would have. The decision at the present time is to be sure the tariff stands, and see how the new phthalomine sells. If the tariff remains in effect and sales are not significant, then the company may drop the product at a later date.

The industry supplies phthalomine for certain applications where the product is likely to come in contact with food. In many cases, the product is separated from the food by barriers of paper or plastic. The industry has been concerned about the recent increase in activity by the FDA in connection with contamination of foodstuffs that come in contact with various materials. It was agreed by everyone within the industry that the amount of contamination that could result from the normal or even excessive contact with products using phthalomine was very small.

There have been no cases as yet where contamination has been

[2] Name disguised.

traced to any product using phthalomine. The FDA promulgated an order where the burden of proof was placed upon the manufacturer to show that his product would not contaminate food and cause injury to the consumer. Very few companies have gone through the lengthy and expensive procedure that has been set up for these tests. A further deterrent to action on testing by the companies has been the policy laid down by the FDA, as represented by the following statement attributed to the assistant general counsel at the FDA in charge of enforcement, to the effect that:

> The holder of a guaranty for a food additive cannot escape criminal prosecution under the Food, Drug, and Cosmetic Act for interstate shipments of adulterated food resulting from the use of the additive in the finished product. A chemical manufacturer cannot legally guarantee that food containing his product will not be adulterated. His guarantee can apply only to the additive itself.[3]

The company has come to the conclusion that the only course available is to refuse orders that are intended for food applications. The requests for this type of product are not numerous, but several important customers have made inquiries. The company has explained that the risk is much too great to supply products for this purpose. It is not possible to guarantee that product X, using phthalomine, would not contaminate the food it contacts. Also, even this disclaimer would not be enough to free the company of responsibility if the food were to become tainted. In any case, the company has no control whatsoever as to the use of its product. It is common practice for users to put materials into the product before using it, for instance. It is clear, in a case where the product has been altered in this way, that it is not the same as when it was supplied to the customer. Precision recommends, strongly, as do the other companies in the industry, that the user design his package so that there is an effective barrier between the company's product and the food. Thus, in any case where the company is aware that the product will be used with food, the order is not accepted. In 1961, the company sent a general letter to its branches and distributors stating its position on the law and the stand of the FDA. The position can be summarized as follows:

> Phthalomine is not a food additive. The company has no control over the use of the product; therefore, it cannot guarantee anything regarding toxicity. A barrier should be used to separate phthalomine from the food. Precision cannot offer any product which can be used in direct contact with food.

The latest statement (1963) that the industry has had from an official of the government is as follows:

[3] From the notes of the industry trade association secretary as reported in the January 1960 issue of its trade magazine.

. . . We are of the opinion that phthalomine used in accordance with the principles of good manufacturing practice for (common end product) is not a food additive within the meaning of the Act in that there is no reasonable expectation of a significant migration of any of its constituents to the food. Should, at any time, information be brought to our attention that the components of such phthalomine do contribute foreign substances to such food, we would of course reconsider our decision.[4]

The Precision Company moved to New Jersey in the 1920's and by the middle 1930's had expanded its business to the extent that additional working facilities were needed. The area in which the plant stood was industrial, with a number of tanneries (which was the business carried on in the building Precision purchased originally), metal-working processes, a hat maker, etc. However, there were also residential dwellings in the area. Many of these were rented by owners who had moved to the suburbs.

Precision had acquired property on either side of its original plant. It had purchased a metal-working factory that was not contiguous with its present plant but was separated by two lots on which stood two one-family dwellings, owned by the company. In 1935, the company proposed to build an addition that would connect the two plant buildings to create a C-shaped building with a yard. The plans were drawn for a two-story-and-basement addition that would serve as a storage area between the two buildings in which the production processes would take place.

When the plans were drawn, the company sent out notices, as prescribed in law, to every property owner within 200 feet of the plant. A notice is reproduced below:

PLEASE TAKE NOTICE:

That an application has been made by the undersigned for a variation from the requirements of the Zoning Ordinance so as to permit an addition to a phthalomine factory on the premises _____, and this notice is sent to you as an owner of property in the immediate vicinity. This application is now No. _____ on the Clerk's Calendar, and a public hearing has been ordered for Wednesday, _____, at 2 p.m. in the Commissioners' Chamber, 2nd Floor City Hall; and when the calendar is called you may appear either in person or by agent or attorney and present any objections which you may have to the granting of this application. This notice is sent to you by the applicant by order of the Board of Adjustment.

At the hearing a number of people living in the area raised objections to the new construction. One objection was that the company was not a good neighbor; that the production process caused excess noise,

---

[4] From the notes of the trade association secretary, reporting a letter from the Food and Drug Officer, Department of Health, Education and Welfare.

odor and dirt. Another objection was that the new building would reduce the light and air in the surrounding property. Objections were also raised on the basis that the company was unhealthy. The board put off final decision concerning the addition, in view of the neighbors' complaints and to give both sides opportunity to organize their cases.

Before the next meeting of the board, the company had many talks with the people in the neighborhood. Most of the people did not object to the addition, but there was a definite group that felt that the addition was to its disadvantage. The company found also that a few of its neighbors were willing to support the company, out of dislike of the neighbors who objected or because the company had treated them well.

At the next meeting, the company pointed out that the company was less odoriferous than the tanneries in the neighborhood, and that the present heating fuel was hard coal; in addition, the new building was to be heated by oil. The production procedure was not as noisy as that of the metal-working firm which had occupied the other building. The company also had pictures taken which showed that the properties adjoining the company's buildings were in terrible condition, with debris in the yards, window panes broken, fences unrepaired, etc. The company had the testimony of one neighbor who stated that the company had maintained its original building quite a lot better than the previous owner had done.

To strengthen its case further, Mr. Tiffany pointed out the following facts about the company: (1) The labor force was made up of "good" men, mostly homeowners, (2) raw materials were purchased locally, (3) the company had a good financial record and (4) that Precision's health and safety records were outstanding. Then he pointed out that, since the company needed the additional space the new building would provide, the company would be forced to move its operations to a more convenient location if the request were denied. This new location would not be in Newark, or even New Jersey, since only 5 per cent of the company's business was in New Jersey.

The company forestalled the argument that the new building was a fire danger by pointing out that the plant was fully sprinklered, protected by ADT, and that there was a watchman on duty during non-working hours.

After this meeting of the board, the company received permission to go ahead and put up the addition. A copy of the letter from the Board of Adjustment is reproduced below:

Gentlemen:

At a meeting of the Board of Commissioners held this day resolutions were adopted concurring in the recommendations of the Board of Adjustment and granting your application of an addition to your phthalomine factory on the above premises, on the condition that there be no increase in odors or noise.

The following paragraph was in a letter from the attorney who had handled the case for the company.

> I have this day been served with an application for a Writ of Certiorari in which I. and C. B_____ are appealing the Zoning Board and Newark Commissioners' decision on your application which was granted. I might add that the City of Newark and other persons were made defendants.

The next five months were spent negotiating with these neighbors about the addition, the ownership of a very small piece of land that belonged to no one but was a "jog" in the company's property, and the removal of a shed that extended onto the company's property. The upshot of these negotiations was that the company revised its plans and agreed to build a basement-and-one-story building only. For $200 and an agreement not to put up a second story for ten years, the company was able to have all objections dropped so the building could be started.

At the present time, there is still no second story on the addition. Also, the lawyer who handled the case for the company was, at the time of the decision, a Commissioner of the City of Newark.

The Precision Company is one of the founding members of the industry trade association. The activities of the association are quite limited when compared to those of major industries, but the association is active among its members. The only full-time employee is the secretary who handles all facets of the association's activities, from "watchdogging" in Washington, D.C., to checking and arranging for the annual convention. This man, an attorney, keeps track of legislation affecting the industry. He is responsible for the active interest the association has taken in the food additives amendment. He has followed the GATT negotiations quite closely in his column in the industry magazine. The tariff on imports of phthalomine is 4 per cent and will probably be removed entirely before long. The secretary's article sounded pessimistic as to the effect of this change. The editor of the magazine, in the same issue, had the following to say: "The likely lifting of the present token tariff on phthalomine should have no appreciable bearing on imports and little hope is held out for increasing phthalomine exports which have been a dying field for some time."

The activities of the secretary in connection with legislation are small and ineffectual. This is so because the industry is small and specialized and does not affect substantially any segment of the company. The secretary testified against the IRS ruling on business expenses, and, as the secretary said himself ". . . it is unlikely that my testimony had any effect on the lawmakers, but we were part of a general business protest and every little bit helps."

An important confrontation between the company and government is in the field of taxes and reports to all types of government—federal, state, county, and city. One requirement made by all the states in which the company maintains any investment in goods or property is domestication. This is necessary in all states except the state where the company is incorporated. This requirement is handled for the company by the Corporation Trust Company. For a fee, Precision can designate the local office of CTC as its official agent in a state. CTC keeps the company abreast of tax and legal developments in a state, through annual reports. Many of these reports cover the requirements and changes relating to a particular tax in a particular state. The cost of this service is $35 per state plus extras for any filing or form filling that is necessary.

Most of the taxes the company pays and the reports it makes are to the state governments. Of the total of all such taxes and reports, 69 are for state governments, 24 are for city governments, and nine are for county and school district governments. The amounts of the taxes cover a wide range, from $1 for a number of information reports to four-figure taxes for personal property or franchise taxes. A simple breakdown of the figures shows that of 63 taxes, 24 are for amounts less than $50 and 39 are for amounts in excess of $50.

The company does not handle any of the calculations in connection with any taxes. This chore is handled by an outside accounting firm. The accountants compute all the taxes to be paid and inform Precision of the amounts. The check is drawn by the company secretary and paid as directed. The biggest job the accountants handle is the federal income tax. This task is left to the accountants entirely. A team of three men spends about three months a year at the company main office, after the first of the year, on a more or less steady basis. Of course, much of the information required by the federal government in reports is required by the other governments as well.

The staff of the company itself takes care of the reports required when there are no figures to be computed or entered. These reports are generally of the type such as "List of Resident Stockholders and Bondholders" (Kentucky) or "Report of Issuance of Shares, Increases in Stated Capital and Paid in Surplus" (Illinois) or "New Jersey Application to Pay Wages by Check."

The reports and taxes demanded by various governments occupy a considerable portion of office time in the company. Each tax represents at least two sets of correspondence between the accountants and the company—in many cases, even more. In many instances, it is necessary to file an estimated tax, and the process of collecting excesses or paying deficiencies involves time. For instance, in 1961 the company received payment for an excess paid on an estimated tax for 1958. In addition, the company collects taxes for the federal government in the form of withholding taxes. This work is time consuming, especially when added to it is the necessity of withholding wages for various state taxes as well as the federal taxes. An added chore is the completion of tax-exemption certificates for customers.

In a number of states the company has stated that if certain taxes are enforced it will withdraw its offices from the state. At the present time, in one state there is a threat that the state will try to collect taxes from the company as a whole based on the per cent of sales made in that state. Mr. Tiffany has stated that if this tax is upheld, the company would consider closing the branch there.

The actual amount of the taxes is only the beginning of the costs involved with these dealings with government, according to Mr. Charles. In many ways, Precision is at the mercy of a capricious government, with no way to get its side heard. The company feels that, in most cases, government does not appreciate or understand the problems of business. The company does not see where many of the taxes and reports are of any benefit to it. Besides the taxes themselves, the company feels that the preparation of the forms and reports takes an inordinate amount of time. There has not been any effort to quantify this cost. The cost of the accountants is high also. Their fee exceeds the salaries of all but three men in the company. The attitude of the company is well expressed in the following letter from Mr. Tiffany to one of the branch managers. The letter is more than thirty years old, but it expresses the present attitude quite well.

December 2, 1935

AIRMAIL

Gentlemen:

Social Security Act:—Your airmail letter of November 29th received. I wish what you say was true so that we didn't have to worry or do anything about Los Angeles or any of our other branches in connection with this act, but unfortunately we are advised by our accountants and counsel that we must be prepared to give the government the data requested in our general letter of November 22nd and we ask you, therefore, to send it along by return mail.

We have been trying hard to have our branch offices that operate on a commission basis take care of their own social security act reports, but have been advised that that cannot be done. There is considerable vague language used in this act and departmental interpretation and even court interpretations may be necessary before we will understand what it is all about. The government are just feeling their way through. In the meantime it is as you say, harrassing business and making us all feel very uneasy. You know what disturbances the N.R.A. caused until finally it was ruled unconstitutional by the Supreme Court and you haven't the slightest idea all the many tax laws that we at the home office have to look into. We have had to fight sales tax in Illinois, Michigan, Kentucky, New Jersey and Ohio and have been successful in every state with the exception of Ohio, but the tax paid there is very small. Last month it was only 3 cents but it is costing us many dollars worth of additional work in our office, so we ask that you kindly give us the information as requested.

With very kindest personal regards, I am,

Safety Lines Marking Inc.

One of the many new fields of business enterprise which have expanded rapidly in recent years is municipal service. More and more cities and towns are turning to contractors to perform specific, standard, repetitive functions which they have traditionally carried on themselves, because they have found that it is cheaper and more efficient to do so. While it is true that an occasional career, professional employee is both able and willing to manage a government service so that costs are minimized even though he does not have the spur of the profit motive to help him, the normal human response under such circumstances is to do as well as you can without upsetting too many applecarts.

The government administrator is faced with several other handicaps as well. He may have limited hiring and firing authority over his staff because of civil service regulations, and to some degree, political considerations; without a profit and loss statement, his yardsticks of efficiency are vague; his supervision, subject to frequent elections, is constantly shifting; and he may well have trouble convincing the community to make the capital outlays necessary to improve efficiency.

Typical of the many companies which have entered this new field is Safety Lines Marking, Inc. of Boston, Mass. Safety Lines was established in 1955 by Terrence White, a young resident of suburban Boston. After a few years spent working in an administrative capacity with a fund-raising concern, White began to look around for a business he could undertake on his own. In the course of his investigations, he learned that the suburban town of Needham was about to contract out the job of painting the traffic and safety markings on its streets and municipal parking lots.

Examining the situation further, he discovered that the contractor was a man who had entered the business only a few months before and already had more work than he could handle. The possibilities appealed to White, because the capital investment was small, the opportunities growing. The only outlay required was for the trucks and painting equipment, which would cost him about $1,500. He could employ his labor as he needed it, and the supply of manpower which could be trained to do this work was plentiful. His lifelong association with politics and municipal government—he came from a family of active, successful politicians—convinced him that he knew enough about the people to whom he would be selling and the problems they faced to be more effective than someone who had been brought up in another kind of environment. Finally, the amount of work of this kind being done was increasing and municipal governments were beginning to look for a better way to handle it.

Originally, the police department and the public works staff painted safety lines on request of the citizens of an area. It was a part-time occupation, even when a city had advanced to the point where it was doing particular sections regularly. It was a two-to-three month job. Cambridge, Mass., for example, used only about 250 gallons of paint a year in 1945, although it was a city of 111,000 population. But with the increased number of vehicles, development of new roads and housing areas, and growing pedestrian traffic, more than 4,000 gallons were required annually by 1965. Furthermore, the number of men required grew considerably, and, since the work was seasonal, (April-October) the enlarged labor force which was usable for only half a year represented an expensive and troublesome management problem.

An additional complication developed as a result of the new type of equipment which was introduced in the 1950's. The old hand or gravity-feed units were replaced by far more sophisticated machines which required trained manpower. A city could no longer simply hire part-time unskilled labor; it needed semi-skilled operators who had to be trained, and thus could not be inexpensively replaced on a seasonal basis.

By the time White was considering going into business, some citizen pressure was beginning to be felt. Newspaper editorials and neighborhood groups were protesting the failure to repaint worn crosswalk markings and safety signs, claiming that increased accident rates were due to poor maintenance. Motorists became annoyed at being held up during rush hour by line-painting crews who blocked off half a highway in order to do their work.

To cities faced with growing problems in this area, White offered a full line of service. He pointed out that his specialization in this one field enabled him to provide "prompter service, competent supervision and more efficient programing. Trained crews, scientifically planned markings and a complete line of modern equipment guarantee the customer maximum production, safer operation and better quality control," he pointed out in his brochure. He was able to perform the work at hours when it would not interfere with traffic, and could save cities as much as 33 per cent on a standard job.

The City of Boston, the Massachusetts Turnpike Authority, and communities like Hartford, Conn. and Needham, Walpole and Waltham, Mass., became his customers, in addition to a number of companies, department stores and drive-in restaurants.

For five years he concentrated on line-painting, but in 1960 an opportunity developed for an additional type of municipal service. The Hertz Corporation had developed an electronic coin-collecting process which collected, sorted, and counted change. The company saw real possibilities for sales to cities with parking meters and was looking for a firm to serve as agent. Hertz wanted a firm with experience in selling to municipalities and contacts with a range of communities of different sizes in a fairly large region. White's operation appealed to Hertz, so he reached an agreement under which he leased and operated the equipment with personnel trained by Hertz.

He looked forward to substantial opportunities in this new line. Collection methods then in use demanded time-consuming and expensive manual procedures; meters had to be opened and emptied, slugs and foreign coins had to be removed by hand; coins had to be sorted and counted and prepared for deposit. ECP—Electronic Coin Processing—as Hertz called its product, moves the coins from the meter into a truck through an air hose, conveyor or blower system. Concentric drums spin the coins into different channels, distributing them by denomination; electronic sorters remove slugs and foreign money; and counters tabulate them. By the time the truck arrives at the bank, the deposit slip is made out and the coins are packaged and marked, all automatically.

Though this item was slow moving at first, because it required the displacement of full-time municipal employees (often members of the police force) and was subject to intense competition from local money-collection services, White was confident that it was a sound plan and would ultimately be highly successful. By 1965, it represented $150,000 annual revenue to his company, as opposed to $550,000 for the line-painting operation and $40,000 for sign maintenance, a sideline which he had taken on fairly recently.

As White had expected, selling his two services to municipalities proved to be a very different proposition from selling to private companies. From conversations with White and a number of other businessmen in similar enterprises, the casewriter identified a number of these differences.

In the first place, contracting for municipal services represents a relatively new approach to governmental activities. Like the managers of any established organization, government officials are hesitant to try something different and are not easy to convince that it is wise to depart from their customary methods. Elected officials and long-term career personnel who live in a community may be reluctant to professionalize services which they have been able to make available on a combination of a regular and a personal basis. It is satisfying for a mayor, a councilor, or the head of a public works department to respond to a friend's request, if it is a legitimate one. By the same token, it can be extremely embarrassing for any of these men to have to say "No" when a neighbor calls, operating on the assumption that putting up a stop sign or repainting a crosswalk is a task that falls under his direct supervision. Citizens generally regard both elected officials and top permanent employees as their personal property and do not easily accept what appears to them to be "bureaucratic excuses" for failure to respond favorably and quickly to a request. More than one municipal official has lost a friend or a supporter when he has had to say, "I'm sorry, Charlie, but I can't get the grass cut on that park opposite your house; we do that on contract now, and the work schedule doesn't call for that patch to be done until next month."

Furthermore, there is always a considerable amount of pressure to have local jobs done by local people. The idea of a professional, outside contractor does violence to this tradition. People often feel that they have a vested right to be given government jobs in their own areas, and many communities are convinced that they will get better service from "someone who lives here in town" because he knows the area and because he will be more responsive.

In most cases, an individual's reactions to specific situations in which he is involved are far more important in determining his attitudes toward municipal officials than his general, philosophical pronouncements—which everyone accepts in the abstract—that "we want our city run efficiently and as inexpensively as possible on a businesslike basis so we get the most from our tax dollar and eliminate waste and politics."

Significant changes of procedure may have effects which prove to be far-reaching in ways which no one had anticipated. In the park and parkway sections of the Greater Boston area under the control of the Metropolitan District Commission, for example, the principal governmental responsibility used to be patrolling for safety and order keeping purposes. The district was divided up into seven autonomous administrative areas to manage this task. Now, however, the main job is maintenance, and what was once essentially a police force has become about half a public works department. Modern equipment for maintenance functions like line painting would be uneconomical for an individual sector, but highly useful for the district as a whole. However, the tradition of sector control over its own area and employment of "locals" is imbedded, and anyone seeking to change the entire administrative structure of the district in order to take advantage of more efficient techniques of maintenance would be accepting a management challenge of very sizable dimensions.

Dislocation of personnel is always an unpleasant task for managers, and governmental officials find it no less difficult than do those in private enterprise. Aside from the human factors involved—no one likes to fire anyone—there is usually a whole network of personal connections and relationships which have to be considered. In government, with its system of elected officials dependent on the good will of the public for their present jobs and future prospects, these relationships become even more important than they do in business. It is true that public works departments, the ones most often affected by the change to contracted services, are not a particularly desirable source of patronage any longer. An affluent society has reduced the number of people interested in such jobs. The ones you can put on are not likely to feel especially grateful nor to be particularly effective supporters, and many of them know they can find other similar positions if they look for them. But the ones already there often maintain their earlier political contacts and, while they may not be of much help, can be a source of constant irritation if not a danger if anyone tampers with their jobs. Most elected officials, unequipped with scientific methods of measuring the precise damage an aroused individual can cause, find it necessary to play it as safe as possible and seek to keep everyone as contented as they possibly can.

Another problem of municipal selling is the location of the decision maker. He may be the top career employee in the public works department, he may be a city manager or town clerk and treasurer, he may be the mayor or a key city councilor, or he may, occasionally, be the leader of the dominant political organization. He may be the person who actually signs the contract, or in reality the power may be somewhere else in an "informal organization" that controls the formal structure as presented on an organization chart. Each community is different, and the would-be contractor has to be extremely careful and perceptive, sensitive to the feelings of local officials who may be touchy about their prerogatives, and alert to the actual sources of power. In many ways, according to businessmen experienced in selling services to municipalities, it is easier if there is a well-established political organization, especially if the contract is a large one. The power is centralized and recognized and the sale can be made without a lot of wasted effort and delicate negotiations.

The problem of payoffs is not a minor one, several midwestern contractors explained to the casewriter. Some businessmen claimed that the question came up in 50 per cent of their contacts. The career employee almost never asks for a "fee," but elected officials or political organization leaders often do. For the businessman, such a demand poses both moral and practical problems. He may well have scruples against the practice, even though it may be disguised in one way or another (it can, for instance, be associated with insurance policies or bonding). He knows he faces the possibility of prosecution if he is caught. And he never knows for sure whether the official soliciting the bribe really has the leverage to get the project sold. After all, if he is going to pay, he wants to be sure he will get something in return. People who can block a contract are often unable to get it approved. Almost always, the individual involved will greatly exaggerate his power.

The few contractors who were even willing to discuss this topic with the casewriter said that they much prefer to deal with political organizations. Political organizations demand less, since they are in business over a long period of time, and the gift can usually be in the form of a campaign contribution. The elected official, on the other hand, is generally underpaid and usually feels himself threatened by the next election. Consequently, he tends to want more money and want it faster. When asked about the added cost represented by such payoffs, all the businessmen involved made plain that this represents no problem: it is well understood by all parties concerned that the price is simply to be tacked on to the agreed-upon figure for the contract and thus, ultimately, comes from city revenues.

The larger a governmental agency, the more difficult it is to sell it on a new approach such as contracting. The further removed the contracting is from the elected official, the less likely one is to secure a contract. The political figure is usually much more willing to make changes, to do things differently, to try new ideas and to make a record for himself than the career official who has a stake in things as they are. The elected official, who tends by definition to be an activist, was not responsible for setting up existing procedures and is often impatient with the argument that "we've never done it that way before." He has none of the prior associations of the long-term employee who has his own constituencies, loyalties and commitments to the established ways of operating. He wants to feel that he is "the boss," in fact, not just on paper and in the eyes of the public, and he seeks for ways to assert his leadership. Thus, with all the constraints on him mentioned above, he is still a better potential customer than the career employee.

Finally—and many businessmen claim this is the most difficult problem of all almost all governmental units have open public bidding procedures. Legislatures and city councils have established and maintained this system, which requires that invitations to bid be available to all qualified suppliers and that the contract be awarded to the lowest bidder. These rules were established in response to public pressure; generally, Americans distrust government officials and suround them with safeguards which are designed to keep them honest but, in the process, greatly increase the "red tape" and reduce the efficiency of government managment and decision making.

Terrence White ran into precisely this situation in one city in upper New York State recently. A bright young businessman had just been elected mayor of the city on a reform ticket. He was looking for ways to improve the community, to increase efficiency, and to establish his reputation as an able, imaginative administrator. Hearing about White's Electronic Coin Processing service, he wrote and asked for details. White came out and demonstrated the equipment, and a verbal agrement was reached. The mayor seemed to have handled any possible objections within his official family and the career staff.

However, shortly after White returned to Boston the project began to run into difficulties. One of the necessary preconditions for the successful operation of the equipment in this particular town was the adjustment of the meters, an expense which the municipal government was to assume. Apparently, someone had heard about the impending contract and objected to it, and a group started to raise questions about the cost of the changes. So the mayor decided to mount a large public demonstration of the equipment which, he hoped, would both quell any potential opposition to the plan and also help to establish his image. White was asked to return for a full-dress performance which would be widely publicized. He agreed to do so, but only reluctantly, because he would have to pay for the necessary adjustments to the 200 meters which were to be used.

The demonstration was a great success, but from White's standpoint the publicity was a mixed blessing. As a result of the widespread awareness of and interest in the contract, the mayor and the city council decided that they would have to abandon their original plan of a negotiated contract, allowable only under severely restricted conditions, and go to open bidding. In their view, the public suspicion of any other system, though misguided, was just too strong. However, they assured White that he would ultimately receive the contract.

In public bidding, the specifications for the job can be written in such a way as to make it virtually impossible for anyone but a preselected contractor to secure the work. This practice, a perfectly legitimate method of securing the kind of performance which the contracting authority desires, is also generally suspect with the public. Consequently, when the advertisement for bids was published, it included no special features or requirements but simply called for bids on the collection of coins from the city's parking meters. Immediately, much to White's surprise, a local detective agency submitted a proposal. White's price had been widely advertised in connection with the earlier publicity, so it was a simple matter for the agency to come up with a lower figure. His service, in no way similar to White's electronic operation, was far inferior but he did meet the very general specifications listed by the city.

At this point, White did not know what he should do. He was aware of the fact that local ordinances required contracts to be awarded to the lowest bidder; at the same time, he knew the mayor had the right to reject all the bids and readvertise, with new specifications if he wished. Back in Boston, he watched his local competitor build up political pressure against him as an "outsider," and wondered what his next step should be.

Batesville School Department

John A. Hanley, a 42-year-old engineer, succeeded in 1964 to the ownership of Hancock Associates, a manufacturers' agent in the state of Illiana dealing in electrical fixtures. Hanley, the son of a missionary, had joined Hancock shortly after his graduation from college and return from the service. Gradually he had worked his way up in the organization, which was made up of some fifteen sales engineers, until he became the heir apparent to Quincy Hancock, founder of the company. During the early 1960's, Hancock slowly withdrew from active participation in the affairs of the firm; in July, 1964, he announced his formal retirement and sold out his interest to Hanley.

The company was organized as a solely owned enterprise. Hanley paid each of his salesmen a salary plus a bonus based on the amount of business the man developed. His own pay depended on the over-all financial well-being of the firm. Judging from Hancock's income, Hanley estimated that it would run from $18,000 to $37,000 during the years immediately ahead.

Hancock Associates sold a variety of electrical fixtures, largely to the commercial and institutional trade. They commonly made their sales to the electrical contractor on major building projects. He himself was hired by the general contractor. Hancock Associates' equipment covered everything from desk and table lamps to fluorescent office and factory lighting.

During the last years of Mr. Hancock's association with the firm, Hanley has been discussing the possibility of merger with another concern in an allied business. This company, New Trier Sales Corp., sold a range of fixtures which would augment the Hancock lines. In addition, New Trier was the agent for large fluorescent lights made by the Bright-lite Co., one of the companies serviced by Hancock. This meant that Brightlite had two agents in the area, although each handled different products, and it had long been evident that one of them would eventually have to take over the other. The question of which agent would emerge as the principal one gave rise to a great amount of tension and concern among the employees of both companies.

After extended discussions with the principals of New Trier, Han-ley decided he could proceed with the deal in the early winter of 1964. Since Hancock was so much larger and better established than New Trier, he was able to work out an arrangement which called for an ab-sorption of the New Trier personnel into Hancock, along with the products which New Trier sold.

As might be expected, this process was not an easy one. The New Trier personnel, who were somewhat suspicious of the change, feared that the Hancock staff would take over their accounts. They also sus-pected that Hanley would tend to favor his own people at their expense in the assignment of potential customers. Hanley did the best he could to bring the new men into the organization and reassure them, but the first months proved difficult, with more tension and mistrust than he had anticipated.

It was during the course of these early weeks of the merger that a school contract came up in Hanley's home town of Batesville.

Batesville is a community located about fifteen miles from the capital city of Illiana. A suburban town, it has grown rapidly in the postwar years until it reached a population of 30,000 by 1964. Like all such communities, the school population has increased dramatically each year, and new school construction is needed constantly.

In Illiana, the school districts are coterminus with the municipal areas. Local school boards, elected by the community, are charged with the responsibility of administering the educational system. They are finan-cially autonomous in that their operating budgets are not subject to control by any other town governing body. On the other hand, they have to turn constantly to the Town Council for approval of bond issues neces-sary to build schools.

For many years, the School Board itself served as the committee in charge of building schools. However, with the rash of new schoolhouses in the postwar period and the increasing complexity of building, the town began to establish special committees for each school project. These citizen's groups included people in the town who were knowledgeable about education, construction, maintenance and financing. At least one member of the School Board was on the committee.

During the course of planning and constructing a school, the members of the committee developed a great deal of experience and knowledge. At some stages they would meet several times a week, selecting architects, developing specifications, conferring with the school authorities, working with contractors, and so on. However, once the school was built and "accepted" by the town, these people were absolved of any further responsibility.

In the middle 1950's, it occurred to several members of the School Board that a great deal of talent and experience was going to waste because each new committee had to start pretty much from the beginning in accumulating knowhow about the educational program, its relationship to the proposed building, the planning and construction process of a school, the town's finances, the politics of selling the bond issue to the community, and so on. Consequently, they suggested that the town establish a Standing School Building Committee made up of people who would serve terms of three years, on a staggered basis. This committee would be assigned the job of building each new school as it came along, if the town so desired. The community approved this idea and the committee was set up, with full legal authority to construct whatever schools were assigned to it.

Hanley was very active in Batesville, where he had lived for more than fifteen years, and he knew all the principal figures in the town government as well as the professional administrative leadership in the school system. An active church member, president of several cultural and athletic groups, and increasingly involved in local politics, he was a significant figure in town. In the spring of 1962, at the urging of his friends, he had run for a post on the town Zoning Board, which was responsible for developing and implementing a master plan for land use in the community. He was easily elected and immediately became very active in the board's policies. Because of this association and because of his participation in the general life of the town, all the members of the School Board were his close friends, and several people on the Standing School Building Committee—including the chairman—had been his friends or acquaintances for some time.

Though there were no legal conflict-of-interest questions involved, since he had no control over any school department contracts as a member of the Zoning Board, he had long since decided not to try to sell any of his products to the officials of his own town. However, he did not impose this same restriction on his salesmen. If they wanted to go after a contract in Batesville, he felt he could not prevent them from doing so. He did not feel that it was fair to limit his sales force in this way, particularly since he himself had no conceivable authority over the letting of contracts, and in view of the fact that, in reality, the contracting on jobs was done by the electrical firm, a subcontractor, and not directly by any town official.

In January, 1965, Batesville was in the throes of planning another junior high school. The Town Council had turned the job over to the

Standing School Building Committee, which had chosen an architect, drawn up the detailed specifications for every aspect of the building, and advertised for bids. The specifications for classroom and hall electric lighting called specifically for either *Brightlite* fixtures—the product once handled by New Trier Sales Corporation—or a competing line, marketed under the brand name of *Moonshine*. The other schools in town were equipped with either Brightlite or Moonshine, and the school department wanted to standardize the fixtures throughout the system.

Late in January one of Hanley's salesmen, a man named Arthur Fisher who had been with New Trier, informed him that he was working on the Batesville contract. "I know you live out there and have a lot of friends in high places who could be helpful," he said. "Would you talk to them and see if we can get that job?" Hanley explained his policy on Batesville projects, including his concern about trading on his personal friendships and his official town position to swing deals for his company. Though Fisher accepted the decision, he did not seem to be pleased nor to understand fully why Hanley felt as he did. His reservations were strengthened when he found out later that the Moonshine salesman who was also trying to get the contract lived in Batesville as well and was apparently using his friendship with local people with no hesitation whatsoever.

Fisher spent a great deal of time with the architect, the general contractor and the electrical contractor—especially the latter. By late February, he had secured the order, for $12,500. As finally drawn, the sale meant a profit of some $1,250 to Hancock Associates, which would be divided between Fisher and Hanley on a 90 to 10 basis.

A month later Fisher burst into Hanley's office. "Have you heard what has happened on that Batesville order?" he demanded.

"No, what?" asked Hanley.

"The Assistant Superintendent for Business Affairs of the school department has written a letter to the contractor saying that Batesville officially prefers the Moonshine equipment. Consequently, the contractor is withdrawing our order and giving the job to Moonshine. In effect, they are changing the specifications on us. If you ask me, I'll bet this is the result of some pretty fast footwork by that Moonshine salesman who lives in Batesville and knows all these people. So what do *we* do now?"

Allis-Chalmers
and The TVA [1]

Milwaukee Journal.—11-24-58.

A strong protest to the proposed purchase of Swiss-made generators by the Tennessee Valley Authority (TVA) was made Monday in Knoxville, Tennessee. J. L. Singleton, group vice president of Allis-Chalmers Company, appeared before the TVA Board.

Allis-Chalmers was the lowest of three United States companies bidding to provide the generators to be installed at Wilson Dam near Sheffield, Alabama, but three foreign manufacturers underbid the American firms. The TVA engineers have approved the $2,639,000 bid of Brown-Boveri & Co. Ltd. of Switzerland, and the Authority's purchasing department has recommended that the Board accept it. For the three 60,000-kilowatt generators, the bids were: American Elin of Austria, $2,542,500; Brown-Boveri, $2,639,000; English Electric, $3,103,974; Allis-Chalmers, $4,290,180; Westinghouse Electric Corp., $4,495,300; and Elliott Corp., $4,654,929.

Singleton told the TVA Board that the direct loss to the Allis-Chalmers generator shops in Milwaukee was estimated at 400,000 man-hours of work, or approximately 1.2 million dollars in payroll. He continued, "Our purpose in appearing here today is to make certain the Board realizes the serious effect of this decision upon American workers. It takes just as many man-hours to engineer and produce a generator in the United States as it does in Switzerland. Including fringes, we pay

[1] This case was prepared by Professor Howard T. Healy of The Robert A. Johnston College of Business Administration of Marquette University. Reprinted with the permission of Marquette University. The quoted articles are reproduced in abbreviated form. In each instance the meaning has been retained as originally presented.

about $3 an hour for skilled production labor, as against $1 an hour for the same type of labor employed in Switzerland."

In addition to the A-C loss of man-hours, hundreds of thousands of other man-hours will be lost to the United States because purchase from a foreign country transfers work from American steel mills, forge shops and so forth to those of another country, he said.

"If decisions such as this are permitted to stand, it will have a serious effect upon our own living standard and upon taxes our government is able to collect. This and other actions like it will kill the goose that laid the golden egg."

He noted that by government regulation, his company must purchase materials for government orders such as this from firms in the United States. Furthermore, "TVA's specifications dictate to the American manufacturer the minimum wage that must be paid."

"How can a government agency have the right to waive these wage specifications for a foreign bidder to the detriment of the American workers?" Singleton recalled that Allis-Chalmers had provided 10 hydraulic turbine-generator units for the same Wilson dam, six in 1942-'43 and four more in 1950, and that all were still operating satisfactorily.

He told the directors that "Most of the money which comes from government institutions, such as the TVA, is wrung out of American taxpayers, both corporate and individual, in the form of taxes. The only reason that our government can set tax rates so high is due to the high-level economy which we have developed in this country. Your purchasing in this case is ignoring your responsibility to play fair by spending money our government collects in the same kind of an economy from which it gets it."

Milwaukee Sentinel.—11-26-58.

A congressional investigation into the TVA acceptance of a foreign firm's low bid in a multimillion dollar project was demanded Tuesday by Local 248, AFL-CIO United Auto Workers. The UAW local, which represents about 9,000 Allis-Chalmers workers (including some 2,300 on layoff) made the demand in telegrams sent to Sens. Proxmire and Wiley, and Congressmen Reuss and Zablocki.

Edward J. Merten, president of Local 248, urged the legislators to investigate the spending of the American taxpayers' money in foreign countries while our own economy is in jeopardy and unemployment is at a high level. He said, "Serious consideration should be given to this matter to protect the American taxpayers' money from being used to undermine the American people. We of labor believe the time has come for labor, management and the government to pull together to preserve our American heritage."

Tuesday night, Local 663, International Brotherhood of Electrical Workers, which bargains for about ninety Allis-Chalmers electricians, fired off another protest by wire—this one to President Eisenhower. It termed the TVA action "shocking" and asked the President to overrule it.

Mark W. Ryan, Local 663 president and business manager, said in the IBEW wire:

"It need hardly be pointed out that in this era of short work weeks and unemployment, an order of this size—4¼ million dollars— would be a welcome shot in the arm to taxpaying American industry and workers."

A TVA spokesman said Tuesday that although the Swiss firm's bid has been accepted, no final decision has been reached on the matter.

Milwaukee Journal.—11-26-58.

The board of directors of the TVA, Tuesday denied that it was discriminating against American manufacturing firms. The board issued a statement from its Knoxville (Tenn.) headquarters after receiving a protest from the Allis-Chalmers Manufacturing Co. The possible purchase of Swiss-made generators from the Swiss concern of Brown-Bovari & Co., Ltd., offers TVA a saving of between $1,400,000 and $1,700,000 or between 35 to 40 per cent under the Allis-Chalmers bid.

The TVA board said, "Economy and efficiency are of primary importance in all of TVA's operations. Foreign bids are considered and purchases made when they would contribute to economical operation. Such purchases are in conformance with the national policy of the United States with respect to international trade."

It was the Allis-Chalmers company's understanding that the Authority's purchasing department had recommended that the board accept the Brown-Boveri bid of $2,639,000 for three 60,000-kilowatt hydroelectric generators to be installed at Wilson dam near Sheffield, Ala. A TVA spokesman said, however, that the purchasing department had not yet made a recommendation. Allis-Chalmers' bid, the lowest of the three American manufacturers', contains an escalator clause to guard against increases in the prices of labor and material. The Swiss bid was a "firm" bid, the TVA said.

The TVA board said that "Allis-Chalmers is totally in error in asserting that funds for the proposed three generators would come from American taxpayers. The generators," the board said, "would be paid for from revenue of the power system and thus the electric power consumers of the TVA would pay every penny of the cost. Competitive bidding, as required in the TVA act, is one of the most effective instruments of cost control. This attention to economical operation has been an important factor in enabling the power system to provide low-cost electricity for its customers, among whom the federal government is the largest."

The board said that there are a number of provisions of law and policy that operate to protect American labor and industrial interests.

In order to receive a federal government contract, foreign bidders must be at least 6 per cent lower in price than the lowest bid of a domestic manufacturer and 12 per cent lower where the domestic manufacturer is in a substantial surplus labor area. Milwaukee was classified an area of substantial labor surplus by the Department of Labor last July. In addition, the prices quoted by foreign bidders must include the prevailing import duty as well as transportation costs.

The board said, "Over a 25-year period, TVA purchases have totaled slightly over $2.1 billion, of which only about one-quarter of the total has been spent abroad."

A TVA spokesman said that he did not know when the Authority's purchasing department would make a recommendation and the board would act on it. The board's next regularly scheduled meeting will be on December 4.

Milwaukee Sentinel.—11-27-58 (Editorial)

It's time for the Tennessee Valley Authority, a government agency, to live by the government's set of standards. The case in point is the TVA's proposed purchase of three generators at a bid price of $2,639,000 from a Swiss firm, second lowest bidder for the work. The Allis-Chalmers Manufacturing Co. here was the lowest U. S. bidder at $4,290,180, ranking fourth in the bidding. Since labor is a big factor in production, the TVA's plans set up U.S. workers against foreign labor. A-C estimates its skilled production labor costs, including fringes, at $3 on the project, as against $1 an hour for Swiss workers. Since the TVA passed up the low bidder, it would not be improper for TVA to favor the American low bidder in its decision.

From all the workers and firms involved, the U.S. would receive a return in taxes—and the economy another lift.

Our United States Senators and Representatives in Congress would do well to check up immediately on TVA's policies in matters like this.

Milwaukee Journal.—11-27-58.

The Milwaukee County Board was asked in a resolution Tuesday to help the Allis-Chalmers Manufacturing Co. get a big generator contract from the TVA. The resolution by Supervisors Bert B. Busby, John P. Murphy and Robert Schmidt asked the board to petition the Authority to award the contract to the West Allis Co. instead of a Swiss firm. Pointing out that loss of the contract might result in more layoffs at Allis-Chalmers, the resolution said that resulting unemployment and loss of tax revenues would have a direct bearing on county public assistance budgets and tax revenues.

The resolution also declared that the board should have in mind "the fact that the people of these United States of America cannot continue to disburse large sums in financial aids to various nations of the world if the source of such revenues—taxation—is dried up by economic disasters here at home."

Supervisor John L. Doyne, acting board chairman, questioned whether the resolution was in order, but after conferring with C. Stanley Perry, corporation counsel, said he would recognize it. Supervisor William F. O'Donnell, however, objected to suspending the rules to adopt immediately. He said he did not think the board should get into such matters. Supervisor Edward F. Mertz contended that "we should not stick our neck out on this" because an American firm might sometime be low bidder on a European project and suffer by similar treatment then. After some discussion, it was decided to refer the measure to the institutions committee, of which Busby is chairman. Busby said he planned to invite labor leaders to the meeting.

Milwaukee Sentinel.—11-27-58.

Rep. Reuss (Democrat, 5th Milwaukee Congressional District) said Friday he has asked the Tennessee Valley Authority to explain its decision to award a huge contract to a Swiss firm in preference to the Allis-Chalmers Manufacturing Co. Reuss said he wanted to find out whether the contract would comply with the "Buy American" law. Reuss would decide whether to take further action after he hears from TVA.

Rep. Zablocki (Democrat, 4th Congressional District) said he was also awaiting a reply from TVA, while Sen. Wiley (R-Wis.) said TVA's action may result in a thorough study of such contract awards. Wiley said the award might "pry open" a thorough study of the whole question of U.S. export-import policy in the next congress.

Milwaukee Sentinel.—11-28-58.

The TVA has not yet awarded a multimillion dollar generator contract to a Swiss firm and will undoubtedly review the situation in view of vigorous protests from the Allis-Chalmers Manufacturing Co. and its UAW local, Rep. Zablocki (Democrat, 4th Congressional District) declared here Thursday. Zablocki expressed strong confidence that all the factors involved would persuade the TVA board to make the award to an American company. Zablocki said American agencies had both authority and precedent for awarding contracts to American firms even though underbid by foreign companies. Maintenance and repair parts must be readily available and certainly a prime consideration must be the needs of depressed areas in the American economy, he declared. Even within this country, Congress has made it clear that hard-pressed areas should be given first consideration, Zablocki said. He was against an extreme policy of "Buy American" only, thus crippling foreign trade, but, he said, there is a danger in inviting competition into areas where depressed conditions prevail.

Reps. Zablocki and Reuss (D-5th) said on their return to Washington Friday they would make the TVA contract their "first order of business." Reuss said he would ask TVA for the "exact facts" and if they indicated TVA had not followed the "Buy American" act, then he would ask the Government Operations Committee, of which he is a member, to look into the situation.

In a telegram to Herbert D. Vogel, TVA chairman, Sen. Proxmire (D-Wis.) asked that TVA give consideration to the layoff situation at Allis-Chalmers in considering the generator bids. He also asked Vogel to advise him on the status of the negotiations.

Milwaukee Journal.[2]—*11-28-58.*

Senator Wiley (Rep., Wis.) Friday conditionally supported the effort of the Allis-Chalmers Manufacturing Co. to get a contract from the TVA. Wiley is one of four Wisconsin legislators who are looking into the possibility that the TVA board may award the contract for the manufacture of the hydroelectric generators to a Swiss firm. Wiley said that he would not act as "judge and jury." He said, however, that "it would appear to me, in view of the unemployment situation, that the contract might well be let to Allis-Chalmers." Wiley is the ranking Republican member of the Senate Foreign Relations Committee and a former chairman of the committee.

The situation, he said, "is but one of many instances that call for re-examination into our commercial arrangements with other nations."

The loss of the contract to Allis-Chalmers, Wiley said, would undoubtedly mean loss of wages to Milwaukee area workers, loss of profits to the company and loss to the government of taxes on those profits.

"These are all factors that have to be considered in the over-all picture," he said.

If the Authority has complied with the provision of the "Buy American" law, Rep. Reuss said, "I would be inclined to think that it would be in the interests of the taxpayers and world trade that a government agency would buy—in compliance with law—where it can get products the cheapest and the best." Reuss said that he felt that the problems of areas with a labor surplus should be solved by a vigorous area development program "such as the Democrats espoused, but was defeated through Republican opposition in the last session of Congress." Purchase by government agencies of foreign manufactures, Reuss said, is "simply one means of getting to foreign countries the dollars with which the foreign nations pay for the United States' annual 15 billion dollars in imports, which includes Allis-Chalmers' products."

In another development, the West Allis Chamber of Commerce added its voice to the protest against awarding the generator contract to a foreign firm.

2 The Milwaukee Sentinel is a morning paper. The Milwaukee Journal is an evening paper.

In telegrams to Wiley, Proxmire and Zablocki, Herbert P. Velser, president of the Chamber, said that his organization "views with the greatest alarm the growing wave of foreign sales. Companies across the face of our nation are hamstrung with a maze of governmental red tape and regulation," Velser said. "Wage scales are established through national union organizations. How, then, can any American company really be free to compete in an international market where low bids are accepted without consideration for living standards, wages or serious effects to our workers?"

Milwaukee Journal.—11-30-58. (Editorial)

The happy, relatively carefree days for American exporters are about over, John J. McCloy, chairman of the Chase Manhattan Bank, warned the other day. He was talking before the convention of the National Foreign Trade Association in New York.

McCloy told how the end of World War II found the United States the preeminent trading nation. Only this country among the great industrial powers was spared vast property devastation. Great Britain, which had dominated world trade for decades, was down and nearly out. German and Japanese industry were in ruins. As world trade reached new highs, this country was prime benefactor. Exports more than doubled over prewar figures, adding significantly to postwar prosperity.

Now the picture is changing, McCloy advised his audience. Western European nations, with American aid, have reconstructed economies and rebuilt industries and are competing more and more with our exporters. Japan is again active in world trade. The Russians are making tremendous strides in industrial development and are beginning, with the satellites, to compete for markets. Formation of the Common Market in Europe, along with various free trade moves and attempts to integrate regional trade in the Middle East and Latin America, poses new problems for American exporters.

McCloy minced no words about the outlook. "We have to face the fact," he said, "that we in many lines are pricing ourselves right out of the world market. It is up to us to make it clear to all that we have to keep prices and costs down. We have to make better products and we have to work longer and harder to make them. There are a disconcertingly large number of people in the world who are working harder and they are rapidly achieving a competitive know-how."

The United States, advised the head of the nation's second biggest bank, "is in a testing period of its political and economic institutions." In this period, he added, all Americans must accept increased responsibility for leadership and "for resisting pressure groups which disturb our political and economic balance."

"We are in an increasingly complex and interdependent world," McCloy declared, "and the challenge it induces demands more, rather than less, of our energy and character, even if it entails some work on Saturday or a later train to suburbia."

Figures emphasize the importance of McCloy's warnings and counsel. In 1957 the United States exported $19.5 billion worth of goods to foreign countries. Foreign trade accounted for 4½ million American jobs. Here in Wisconsin, seven major manufacturing groups contributed $403 million to the 1957 export total.

Milwaukee Sentinel.—12-1-58.

Loss of a multimillion dollar generator contract to the Allis-Chalmers Manufacturing Co. "would be reflected adversely in our city's economy," Mayor Arnold H. Klentz of West Allis said in letters sent to Wisconsin representatives in Congress Sunday. Klentz joined the company Local 248 of the United Automobile Workers (AFL-CIO) and the Milwaukee Association of Commerce in protesting a possible award by the Tennessee Valley Authority (TVA) to a Swiss firm.

In letters to Sens. Proxmire (D-Wis.) and Wiley (R-Wis.) and Rep. Zablocki (D-4th), Klentz said: "A summary of the benefits which would accrue in the way of employment and wages to the company's workers residing in this city, in addition to tax revenue, would go a long way toward off-setting the bid of the manufacturer located in a foreign nation."

Milwaukee Journal.—12-4-58.

The Milwaukee County CIO council balanced skillfully on a tight-rope Wednesday night, with the yawning chasm of its parent AFL-CIO's policy on one side and the sharp rocks of the position of its largest affiliate on the other, a resolution contained a lengthy excerpt from AFL-CIO policy statements on foreign trade and noted that the "national AFL-CIO position on international trade policy calls for gradual reduction of trade barriers and expansion of international trade and commerce."

The County CIO, the resolution said, "concurs with the international trade policy position of national AFL-CIO, but wishes to point out that special consideration to international trade policies should be given in situations where an American industry has prolonged lay-offs of workers, which seriously curtail the American economy." The resolution urged Wisconsin's senators and Milwaukee County's congressmen "to investigate" the matter "to the end that all avenues be explored to have the contract awarded to the American firm."

Milwaukee Sentinel.—12-5-58.

Over the protests of Milwaukee industry and labor spokesmen, directors of the Tennessee Valley Authority Thursday awarded a $2,637,135 contract to a Swiss firm for the manufacture of three generators. The action brought forth an immediate prediction by the Allis-Chalmers Manufacturing Co. that other government agencies are likely to bypass American manufacturers in favor of foreign industries and a telegram to President Eisenhower by an Allis-Chalmers union president demanding the ouster of the TVA board of directors.

In a statement Thursday night, Allis-Chalmers expressed disappointment at the TVA decision. "For many years," the company statement said, "we have watched various government agencies pursue the policy as set forth in the "Buy American Act" as interpreted by an executive order. However, in appearing before the (TVA) board, we did so because we wanted to plead a cause and principle regarding the heavy power equipment import problem. We thought that the people of Milwaukee and the citizens of the U.S. should be aware of what was happening. We felt they had a right to know how their tax moneys were being used abroad and by so doing taking work from our American wage earner. It is quite evident that no American firm can compete in the heavy electrical equipment market with foreign bidders whose labor costs are one-third of those of the U.S."

In a telegram to President Eisenhower, Mark W. Ryan, president and business manager of Local 663, International Brotherhood of Electrical Workers (AFL-CIO) called for "the immediate discharge of the directors of the TVA for their unprincipled awarding of the Wilson Dam generator contract to a Swiss firm." Ryan accused the TVA directors of being "calloused and indifferent to the plight of unemployed Milwaukee workers and an ailing Milwaukee firm. After the spectacle of their unilateral handling of this matter," he said, "they have surely lost the confidence and respect of the American public and should be replaced immediately by men who can regain it."

Edward J. Merten, president of the United Auto Workers, Local 248 (AFL-CIO), which represents the bulk of Allis-Chalmers employees, declared on being informed of the TVA action: "It seems to me the TVA should have given the legislators a chance to talk this matter over before making their decision." Sens. Proxmire and Wiley and Reps. Reuss and Zablocki had been asked to confer with the TVA on the contract situation.

Milwaukee Journal.—12-5-58.

The Tennessee Valley Authority board of directors late Thursday awarded a contract for three hydroelectric generators to a Swiss firm. National policy, the TVA board said, is set forth in the "Buy American" act as interpreted by an executive order and further modified in practice by the council on foreign economic policy.

The generators are for a 24 million dollar project at Wilson Dam at Muscle Shoals, Ala. Construction is to start early in 1959 and completion is scheduled for the fall of 1961.

The board also awarded a contract for three 74,600 horse-power hydraulic turbines to the S. Morgan Smith Co. of York, Pa. Allis-Chalmers is scheduled to assume control of the Smith firm around Jan. 1.

The TVA board said that the Smith firm's bid for the turbines was $2,815,950 and $261,000 lower than the next lowest bid from three other domestic firms and one foreign firm.

Allis-Chalmers also bid on the turbines.

Milwaukee Journal.—12-7-58. (Picture Caption)

Some of the 1,080 engines shipped recently by Wisconsin Motor Corp. of Milwaukee to Portugal and North Africa were readied for loading aboard the Suderholm at the Milwaukee harbor. The consignment was the second largest engine shipment ever to leave the Milwaukee port, the record having been set by Wisconsin Motor in 1955 with a shipment of 1,383 engines.

Wall Street Journal.—1-22-59.

In a report issued today, the General Accounting Office in Washington renewed its recommendation that TVA be required to pay interest on the Federal investment in the power agency, and that Congress have the authority to approve any new power units installed in the system.

Milwaukee Sentinel.—1-24-59.

Rep. Reuss Friday requested President Eisenhower to explain his administration's "double standard" in awarding contracts involving competitive bidding by domestic and foreign companies. Reuss reminded that a Swiss firm received a contract for TVA generators because its bid was more than 12 per cent below the lowest domestic bid submitted by Allis-Chalmers Manufacturing Co., Milwaukee. But Reuss said the "exact opposite procedure" was followed when the Baldwin-Lima-Hamilton Corp. of Pennsylvania was awarded a contract for hydraulic turbines although a bid by the English Electric Co. of London was 19 per cent lower. Reuss made his request in a telegram, which was referred to the office of Civil Defense and Mobilization.

U.S. News and World Report.—1-30-59.

Another and tougher way of keeping down imports was used by Washington on January 20. Low bid of a British manufacturer on two turbines for an Arkansas dam project was passed over by Washington for "national security" reasons. Baldwin-Lima-Hamilton got the contract, despite a bid 20 per cent higher than the one submitted by the English Electric Export Corporation.

From time to time in recent years, British and European firms have won similar federal contracts on the basis of the lowest bid. At other times, their bids have been rejected because of national-security considerations. Now, big U.S. manufacturers in the heavy electrical field are trying to get Washington to stop all buying of turbines and generators from foreigners, on Federal projects, such as the Arkansas dam. The claim is that foreign purchases threaten national security, since in the event of breakdown, service and spare parts would not be readily available. An official ruling on the proposed embargo is expected in a week or two.

Note this, however: The President is setting up an inter-agency government committee on prices and costs to examine, among other things, the upward pressure on domestic prices felt from excluding cheaper foreign goods.

Business Week.—2-14-59.

In spite of Britain's rising exchange reserves—calculated last month at $3.1 billion—the feeling is spreading in London that the government is slowing down its plans to liberalize restrictions on dollar imports. According to London observers, this is due partly to disappointment over Canadian trade, partly because of the jolt created by U.S. rejection of English Electric Co.'s turbine bid for Greer's Ferry Dam in Arkansas (BW-Jan. 31, '59, p. 32).

In London last week Board of Trade Pres. Sir David Eccles gave Canadians a sharp warning. He said that while the British government hopes to go further in liberalizing dollar import restrictions, it must have "some confidence that the Canadian market will make a sustained and exceptional effort to buy our goods." British-Canadian trade, Eccles said, is "terribly and uniquely lopsided."

Business Week.—2-14-59.

U.S. makers of heavy electrical equipment were protesting violently this week after the Tennessee Valley Authority awarded the contract for a 500,000-kw steam turbine-generator to Britain's C. A. Parsons & Co. Parson's bid of $12 million was $5.5 million lower than the lowest U.S. bid.

General Electric, one of the also-rans, called the award a "dangerous precedent" and cited national security in a plea to the government to make its agencies do the buying of such equipment at home. G. E. based its argument on the ground that foreign companies cannot repair and maintain equipment adequately in times of war or national emergency. Some U.S. companies contend that they cannot compete with foreign makers on a purely price basis, because of wage differentials.

Forbes Magazine.—2-15-59.

The U.S. may be pricing itself out of world markets, foreign trade experts fear. One straw-in-the-wind: estimates for the first nine months of last year show shipments of manufactured goods by the world's No. One exporter down 13 per cent (to $7,198 million), vs. a drop of only 3 per cent in the over-all total of manufactures exported. Meanwhile, West Germany for the first time took over the No. Two spot from Great Britain. The German exports: $5,657 million, or 18.4 per cent of total trade, vs. 18.2 per cent for Britain.

PART FIVE

ACCESS TO A LEGISLATURE

The Would-be Lobbyist

Matthew F. Cullen, a recent graduate of a business school who had been working as a trainee for the Daly Company of Chicago for about a year, had just received a new assignment. He had been told that he was to open a Washington office for the firm under the general direction of the vice president for public relations.

Cullen was surprised that he had been given this responsibility because he had no particular background in the workings of the federal government, nor did he know anyone of special importance in the nation's capital. However, he had majored in political science in college, had taken a course in business-government relations at business school, and had participated in local government in his home town to a minor extent.

Although the vice president was vague in spelling out the details of the job, Cullen gathered that the company had come to the conclusion that they needed both ears and a voice in Washington. The firm, which manufactured a range of consumer products mostly in the sports field, had expanded rapidly until it had plants in four small cities in two states. As the company grew, top management found itself engaged in a number of activities which might conceivably bring it into touch with the federal government. It was beginning to think about growth by merger. It was about to start a national magazine and TV advertising campaign. It was doing some importing of ice skates and baseball gloves for ultimate distribution under its own brand name. Its unionized labor force now numbered 1,200. It transported a number of its products by truck and rail over fairly long distances. It was seriously thinking of developing an international business by exporting, licensing, joint ventures, overseas investments, or a combination of devices.

Daly Company did not sell any of its products to the federal government, nor did it have any plans to do so. Cullen had been told that his new job was not going to involve any such activities. If the company did decide to try to develop government business, Cullen was instructed, the sales efforts would be conducted by its home office sales staff. But it was not anticipating any such project.

As Cullen thought over the conversation with Mr. O'Brien, the public relations vice president, he found himself more and more confused about exactly what he was to do. The discussion was full of phrases like "keep your eyes open and let us know what is going on," "get in touch with people who might be important to us," "we'll ask you for things from time to time," and "represent our interests and make sure those government guys understand our problems." Finally, Cullen asked O'Brien, "Yes, sir, but precisely what am I to do and why does the company feel we need a Washington office?" O'Brien dismissed the question lightly: "Oh you're the political scientist around here, so you work it out. Just keep us in touch." And the meeting ended.

Cullen decided that his first move would be to talk with an old Washington hand in his firm's trade association to see if he could find out what the nature of his new position would be and what he ought to do. So he made an appointment with Henry Desautels, a one-time Congressman from the Midwest who had served a short period with one of the executive departments and was now the government relations director for the association.

After welcoming him to the town and to "the business," Desautels began the briefing. "The first step is to register as a lobbyist," he said. "A lobbyist?" responded Cullen. "But I don't want to get involved in pressure and payoffs and all that." "Oh come now," said Desautels, "you don't really believe all that dime-novel nonsense that makes Washington look like a sort of Peyton Place on the Potomac, do you? That business of black bags and skeletons in Cabinet Officers' closets is very dramatic and all—it even happens every now and then—but it has little to do with the day-to-day business of developing and maintaining connections between your company and the key people here. Anyway, whether you like the term 'lobbyist' or not, you have to register. So go up to the House Clerk's office, fill out the forms, including the financial one, or you'll be in violation of the law right at the start.

"Next, find out which members of Congress have a potential interest in your particular company. You have to recognize that Daly Company as such—as a corporate entity—is not particularly important to them, except in the sense that they are generally concerned with the economic well-being of their districts. Further, Mr. Daly and Mr. O'Brien and Mr. Blumenthal and all those top-management people who are so significant to you are just individuals to them. But the Senators and the Congressmen —incidentally, you may have to explain the difference to some of your executives since they are constantly getting them mixed up—are extremely interested in the people whose fortunes depend on the health of your firm."

"You mean, our workers?" asked Cullen. "Yes, your employees and their families. So find out where your people live—you may discover they work in one city or even state and live in another—identify as precisely as you can the numbers in the several Congressional districts and states, and then start calling on the Congressmen and Senators who represent them."

"How do you mean, 'start calling'? Do I just go into their offices— and what do I say?" "Oh, just get acquainted, tell them you are there to be of help." "How about throwing a big cocktail party for all of them, and bringing some of our top management people down?" "Well," answered Desautels, "I know a lot of people do that. But I'm not much of a cocktail party man myself. They are all about the same, pretty routine and superficial, the members get almost limitless numbers of invitations, and no one really has a chance to meet anyone. Maybe later, after you get to know them a bit, but I think most of these parties are a waste of time and money.

"Of course," he continued, "you do have one problem, and that is convincing your people back home that you are doing something and meeting people. They have heard so much about Washington parties that they are likely to assume you are lying down on the job unless you throw one. But I think, instead of spending the company's money on those things, you will do better to increase the sophistication of your top management about this town."

"So for the first few months I should just get to know these men?" Cullen asked. "That's right—but don't stop just with your own Congressmen and Senators. Check the committees, find out which ones could be important to you, and drop in on the chairmen and ranking majority and minority members. And don't overlook the staffs, both of the committees and of the individual members. You will often find it hard to get through to a member, but if you know his administrative assistant really well and have rapport with him you may find he is just as good. You should remember, too, that committee staffs are often indistinguishable from the personal staffs of the key committee members. Some are professionals to start with, some become so, but they are virtually all beholden to a member. And they are very influential all over the town.

"But don't stop just with knowing the people. Find out all you can about their jobs, and how they view them, and about them personally. You have to understand that, by and large, these are intelligent and aggressive people who know their business—even if they may not know yours. They tend to be prima donnas. Many of them are sensitive about their status. They expect to be treated with respect and, for my money, they have earned it. Furthermore, they expect the office they hold to be treated with respect.

"Another generalization—here in Washington they are successful to the degree that they are able to accomplish what they want with their colleagues and with the executive branch, and at home in terms of their ability to get themselves reelected. Since they have specific executive power only over their own staffs, the impression that they make on others and their persuasive skills are their main tools. If they are embarrassed or made to look stupid and uninformed in front of their constituents or their colleagues because of an error you make, they will never forgive you."

"I don't think I understand what you mean," Cullen asked. "How could I ever put one of them on the spot?"

"Oh, it happens all the time," Desautels replied. "For example, suppose you announce that you are setting up a plant in Japan to make skis. Your delegation isn't informed in advance; a hometown reporter calls Congressman Sutton and asks for his comments and all he can say is 'This is the first I've heard of it.' Or a fellow committee member on a group considering balance-of-payments legislation needles him about it on the way to a session and your man looks blank because he hasn't had a chance to read the paper that morning. Never ever take a risk of leaving a Congressman or Senator looking as though he doesn't know what is going on in his own district.

"This leads me to another point. Washington—or any other political community for that matter—functions primarily by exchange. I don't mean bribery, God knows, and I certainly don't mean any precise tit-for-tat. Anyone who says outright 'I got that VA check for your constituent yesterday—now you get my friend Joe appointed to an honorary committee at the Defense Department' is dead before he starts. But there has to be a mutuality of service, of friendship if you like, with a flow both ways and honesty and cooperation both ways."

"But what could I possibly do for a member that would be useful?" Cullen asked.

"Two kinds of things: personal and professional. Taking the latter first, because I have just been talking along those lines: explore all the possibilities you can think of to help your members enhance their positions with their constituents and gain some publicity. Let him issue a release saying 'I have been informed by the Daly Company that they are about to build a new factory in Euphoria which will employ 150 skilled workers. I am delighted with this new addition to the economy of my district, etc., etc.' Invite him to speak at the company. Ask your top people to arrange appearances for him at their clubs and associations. Have him cut the ribbon when you open your new cafeteria. Let him give out the watches at retirement ceremonies. Just get him into the act whenever you can. And always warn him in advance of bad news so he can decide what he wants to say if he is asked for a comment.

"On the personal side, see what your members enjoy. Companies have everything from boxes at ball games to symphony tickets which they make available. Airlines have inaugural flights to which they invite members; you people must be involved in many sporting events which some of those men would like to attend. I know one firm that used a blimp to advertise their product; when they brought it into Washington, they invited Congressmen—and their families—to come aboard for dinner and go for a ride."

"All those services sound legitimate enough to me. But where do you draw the line between the acceptable and the unacceptable favors?" Cullen was plainly worried about the morality of the kind of give-and-take Desautels was discussing.

"That is a very difficult question. You can, of course, get some help from the statutes. There are some practices that are simply illegal, and any company that engages in them is asking for trouble. But so much of this is a matter of personal philosophy and standards—and the grey area is very large. Is it legitimate to throw some legal practice to a lawyer-Congressman? It's done all the time—yet a long-term Congressman was defeated recently and may go to jail because of it. Is it legitimate to organize your people to give him campaign contributions? Some companies go so far as to have executives trump up expense accounts in order to reimburse them for their contributions to designated candidates. Is it legitimate to give a Senator's son a summer job? Can you send his youngsters samples of your sporting equipment? At one level, it depends on the man with whom you are dealing and his standards as well as yours—this is the pragmatic approach. I know one government executive who was so insulted when an airline offered him a ride on one of their overseas inaugural flights that he blasted the firm from one end of the town to another. This gets back to knowing your man. But the ethics of it all—that's a different matter.

"I have one rule of thumb I use," Desautels continued. "First, I ask myself whether the action is illegal under the terms of legislation. Then I ask myself whether it violates the spirit of the act. And finally, I ask how it would look in the papers and whether or not I could justify it to the public if I had to. But you and your company will have to answer this question for yourself in terms of specific actions as they arise.

"Another point—and it is not unrelated because the lengths to which you will go depend on the significance of what you are after—it is vital that you learn to distinguish between those issues which are really important to your member, or your company, and those which are peripheral. Politicians, like businessmen, are always asking for things which they would like to have but don't absolutely require because they, in turn, are being pressed by others."

"You've lost me, I'm afraid," said Cullen. "I assume that if a Congressman asks that someone be given a job or that a constituent be given a Small Business loan, he means it."

"Oh no, not by a long shot. I have a friend in the White House who once told me that he waits for at least three letters and two telephone calls—and from the member himself, not the AA—before he begins to think that the man really cares. Don't forget, these people are besieged by requests, and they feel obligated to make a show of concern and do what they can for everyone who asks. But they aren't going to use up their brownie points trying to drive through favors that aren't really important to them—they know that their bank balance is limited because there is only just so much they can do in return. The trick in Washington is to keep as unobligated as you can while piling up as many IOUs as possible. Further, they know that it is inordinately difficult to accomplish most of what their constituents desire.

"Businesses are not that different—I know, because I am constantly testifying and issuing statements on behalf of you people. We kind of have to take general stands on reduced budgets and less government and labor legislation but every now and then something really important to our members comes along, like new trade practice rules at the Federal Trade Commission or an urban renewal grant to one of our companies or a technical tariff rate change that needs legislation. Then we really go to work.

"By the same token, don't forget you are sort of an honest broker between your firm and the government. When it is a case of 'I hope you can,' tell both the company and the member; when it is a 'must,' and it usually won't be, then make sure everyone concerned knows that too. It is up to you to make the company show it is a 'must' before you start drawing on your credit."

"You know, you have been talking as though the member's main function for us was that of liaison with the executive branch rather than legislation," observed Cullen. "Well, that is probably increasingly true," replied Desautels. "As business-government relations increase, and government gets ever more complicated, you'll find a guide and an ally around here very useful indeed."

"How about my dealings with the executive branch?" asked Cullen. "The same general rules apply; identify the agencies with which you may be involved, get to know them and their people, get really informed so you don't get them mixed up," answered Desautels. "But you must remember that there are fewer favors than you can or ought to do for them, that they are more likely to view the issues uncomplicated by the political implications—in fact, they pride themselves on doing so—and that the level of competence and concern for the public interest as they view it is very high.

"Well," Desautels continued, "that's about all I have to say. This business you learn by doing. Just remember that company representation in this town is a matter of human relationships. Don't act as if you own a Congressman, even if you do, because you do violence to his self image and this is bad human relations. Don't talk about people behind their backs. Don't assume that the member is just there for you—recognize his problems and how he sees his job. Don't ask him to do things for you which he just can't do—your company may be against the repeal of right-to-work laws, but your man may come from districts where his support for your position could cost him his seat. Remember that part of your job is to make sure your top-management people understand his problems; don't expect him to be with you 100 per cent of the time. You'll find that your teaching responsibilities run both ways—you have to educate the members about your problems, and you have to educate your management about the Congressman's. And above all, be honest and straightforward. Don't try to give anyone the swerve. If you do, you'll be spotted and marked, and you might as well go back home because no one will listen to you again. In this town, if you have lost your credibility, and thus your ability to persuade people, you have come to the end of your line of credit and you are all through."

Slumber Casket Corp

Since the publication of *The American Way of Death,* by Jessica Mitford in 1963, there has been considerable controversy over possible regulation of the funeral industry in the Pennsachusetts State Legislature. Pennsachusetts is a large industrial state similar to New Jersey or Pennsylvania.

Part of the difficulty in deciding what type of regulation of the funeral industry should be instituted, if any, was that the state legislature had split party control in 1964. The state Senate was elected on a county-wide basis, with one Senator for each of the state's 35 counties. Except for four years in the 1930's, at the depth of the depression, the Senate had been controlled by the Republican Party since Civil War days. Although recent U.S. Supreme Court decisions made reapportionment of the state Senate inevitable, no suit had yet been brought in Pennsachusetts. In the 1964 state Senate, there were twenty Republican members and fifteen Democrats. The other branch of the state legislature, the Assembly, was elected on a district basis with roughly equal population in each district. The Democrats held 77 of the 150 seats. One seat was vacant owing to the recent death of a Democratic Assemblyman; one seat was held by an Independent, and the rest were held by Republicans.

The year 1964 was an election year in Pennsachusetts for the governorship, the principal state officers, one half of the state Senate, and all seats in the Assembly. The present governor of the state, a Republican, was not running for re-election due to poor health. The Republican state attorney general was a "shoo-in" for the Republican nomination for governor. While the Democrats were, as usual in Pennsachusetts, squabbling among themselves, it seemed likely that their candidate for governor would be a young Congressman from the rural area of the state. The Democrats had the additional advantage that the incumbent President of the United States, a Democrat, was expected to run well in the state, thus hopefully helping the entire ticket.

The Republican state attorney general, in building up his reputation prior to running for governor, had conducted several investigations, including one of funeral homes. The funeral investigation revealed several instances of price padding, adding extra costs beyond those first promised, etc. Several newspapers and various labor and consumer groups in the state called for reforms.

Accordingly, early in 1964, a bill was introduced in the state legislature to require an itemized quotation for all funeral services to be rendered by the funeral home when its services were contracted for. This bill, introduced in both houses of the legislature by Republican members, was commonly known as the Attorney General's Bill. This bill was also supported by the incumbent Republican governor.

Several reform Democrats introduced a much broader bill in both houses of the legislature. The latter bill would establish the office of Burial Administrator. The Burial Administrator, who would be appointed by the governor and confirmed by the state Senate, would have the power to investigate the industry from time to time and to establish standards of ethical practices in such matters as advertising by funeral homes and the administration of eleemosynary cemeteries. In event of abuses, he could make recommendations to the attorney general for prosecution. Penalties involving fines, suspension of license to do business, and/or jail sentences were specified in the bill for certain specific abuses.

The various branches of the funeral industry were up in arms over the charges in Miss Mitford's book and over the proposed legislation. The Pennsachusetts Association of Funeral Directors and the Embalmers Union took stands opposed to both bills. Advertisements (such as that reproduced in exhibit one) were placed in all the major newspapers of the state by local funeral homes. The Pennsachusetts Association of Cemeteries voted to oppose the more drastic bill proposed by the Democrats, as did the Gravedigger's Union. The local Roman Catholic newspaper, which usually represented the views of the local Archbishop, took a stand against the Democrats' bill.

Much of organized labor, apart from the embalmers and gravediggers unions, backed the Democrats' bill. Some church groups as well as individual clergymen of all three major faiths and several liberal church publications (including one Catholic publication) also endorsed one or the other or both of the proposed bills.

Some business leaders and business interests backed the Attorney General's Bill as a logical compromise between taking no action and going "overboard" for excess regulation. The supporters of the attorney general were particularly anxious to get business backing for his bill, in the hopes that its passage would help his chances to become governor. The Pennsachusetts Women's Federation endorsed the Attorney General's Bill, as did several local Chambers of Commerce.

Mr. Charles Starr, president of the Slumber Casket Corp., was approached by his next-door neighbor, the Republican county chairman, and asked to head up a committee to work for the passage of the Attorney General's Bill. Mr. Starr, a Republican, was favorable to the attorney general's candidacy for governor. He was also very much opposed to a Democrat's being elected governor, as he believed the Democrats, in office, tended to raise taxes on business enterprises such as his. He also believed the Democrat, if elected, might support a drastic bill regulating the funeral industry. On the other hand, Mr. Starr was somewhat reluctant to take a stand opposed to that of his industry. Regardless of his stand, Starr did not believe his customers were likely to switch suppliers because of the transportation advantage held by Slumber Casket Corp., which was the only casket manufacturer located in the largest city in Pennsachusetts. Mr. Starr was well respected within his industry and in his community as a progressive, honest businessman.

Assuming Mr. Starr decided to support the Attorney General's Bill, there would be quite a task to get it passed. Both the cemetery industry and the funeral directors of the state maintained full-time lobbyists at the state capital. The labor lobbyist, who had close ties with the Democrats, would undoubtedly work for the passage of the more drastic bill sponsored by the Democrats rather than the Attorney General's Bill.

The only sure lobbying support the Attorney General's Bill could count on would come from the powerful Pennsachusetts Women's Federation and perhaps from the lobbyist for the Chamber of Commerce, who was a close friend of the attorney general. The lobbyist for the race tracks might be induced to support the bill as well. Mr. Starr would have to form his own *ad-hoc* group to push for the bill and seek widespread support.

Both formal and informal legislative channels are important in Pennsachusetts. In the state Senate, committees are relatively unimportant, particularly if the president of the state Senate and the majority leader support a bill. Starr believed that if the Assembly passed the Attorney General's Bill, the Senate leadership would go along with it. The Senate majority leader came from a "swing" county, so he might also favor the Democrats' bill if it passed the Assembly. In the latter case, the Senate action might go in any of three ways: pass the Attorney General's Bill, pass the Democrats' bill, bury both bills.

Consequently, it was probably important to push the bill through the Assembly first. The bills would first be heard by the Assembly Committee on Commerce and Industry. After hearings and debate, this committee would report one of the bills to the Assembly floor. A favorable committee vote might be helpful even if the Assembly substituted the Democrats' bill. The committee membership included five Democrats, three Republicans and the one Independent. However, two of the Democrats were hostile to the reform Democrat who introduced the more drastic bill in the Assembly. The Independent Assemblyman was very unpredictable in his voting. One of the Republicans was opposed to any regulation of business. However, he was a party man and if the governor "put on the pressure," he might well go along.

Once a bill was reported to the Assembly by the committee, there would be three readings. The first reading was purely perfunctory. After the second and third readings, there would be a debate and a vote on whichever bill was reported out of the committee. Another bill could be substituted for the committee bill at the time of either vote by vote of the members of the Assembly.

If sufficient Democratic support could be gained in the Assembly to pass the Attorney General's Bill, this bill would then go to the Senate and would probably be passed. If the more drastic bill were passed in the Assembly, anything might happen in the Senate. If the Senate passed a different bill, the legislation would be returned to the Assembly. If the Assembly did not accept the Senate substitute, a conference committee would be appointed to suggest a compromise bill. The conference committee would consist of four Senators (all of whom would presumably favor the Senate bill) and four Assemblymen (all of whom would presumably favor the Assembly bill).

If the compromise bill were favored by both houses of the legislature it would go to the governor for his signature or veto. If the compromise bill were not acceptable to one branch of the legislature or to the governor, no further action could be taken in 1964.

Although the Democrats controlled the Assembly, some of them might vote for the Attorney General's Bill. Some Democrats from the smaller "out-state" industrial cities were personally antipathetic to the big-city reform Democrats who were pushing the more drastic bill. Several machine Democrats from the largest city in the state were also out to thwart the reformers. Two Democrats were undertakers, who, although probably opposed to both bills, might go along with the Attorney General's Bill rather than take the more drastic bill.

The Republicans also were not completely united. Several were opposed to any government regulation of business. One Republican was strongly opposed personally to the attorney general and would probably not vote or would vote against his bill. Most, however, would go along with the wishes of the governor in order to insure party harmony.

Mr. Starr is uncertain as to whether he should get involved in this fight at all. If he does, he must decide on what tactics should be followed to secure passage of the Attorney General's Bill.

EXHIBIT ONE

Slumber Casket Corp.

(This is a full-page ad placed in a leading Pennsachusetts newspaper.)

FACTS ABOUT
FUNERAL SERVICE
EVERY FAMILY SHOULD KNOW

Everyone should know about funerals. It is a service which no one wants to buy, and one with which few people will be concerned except at infrequent intervals in a lifetime. Consequently, there is much ignorance about funeral service which tends to serve as a basis for much ill-formed criticism. This advertisement is, therefore, being published to gain better public understanding of funeral service and its religious significance.

THE MODERN AMERICAN FUNERAL

Comparisons are odious but this does not stop the critics from trying to compare American funeral customs with those in other lands. They suggest Americans adopt the funeral customs practiced in other countries which have little or no regard for the feelings of the bereaved or the religious rites attached to the funeral.

American funeral service is not a perfect institution. No such claim has ever been made that it is. But there is much to be said for it that is not even hinted at, much less mentioned by the critics. Instead, they prefer to make fun of the funeral rites practiced in this country and give big play to isolated, and not always completely founded instances in order to make their points.

They go beyond the limits of good taste to caricaturize the funeral directors as "profiteers of death", as "ghouls", suggesting that as a group they should be banished. They overlook the fact that there are thousands of funeral directors throughout the country who are leaders in their communities and highly respected by their fellow citizens. Such an admission would be too damaging to their case for it to be mentioned!

Thousands of letters are received every year by funeral directors from bereaved families they have served expressing their gratitude for the services rendered them in the time of their grief. Fewer than 1 per cent of those received are critical of the services rendered, or the costs of the funerals concerned.

An ostentatious funeral—a simple funeral—an open casket for viewing by the bereaved and their friends—the closed casket—all these are decisions for the family, often in consultation with their clergyman, to make—not the funeral director. A funeral director has an obligation to serve the public as they wish to be served as to the type of funeral, and the price they wish to pay.

MEANING OF FUNERAL SERVICE

Death in all its forms has been viewed with fear by men since time immemorial. Therefore, anything connected with death is avoided by most people until circumstances force them to face its realities. Some, but only a few, among close relatives and friends are able to weather the emotional crisis it creates. For most it takes time to face up to the finality of death, the acceptance of the fact that the loved one will no longer be part of familiar environment.

This is not a new concept. Pioneer work in this field was done by Freud in his "Mourning and Melancholia". Even more recently, Dr. Erich Lindemann, a noted psychiatrist, made further contributions to the subject as a result of his work with bereaved survivors of the tragic Coconut Grove fire in Boston some years ago.

The major role in easing the grief of survivors is played by their spiritual advisers. But the funeral director, no less than the clergyman or rabbi, has his role to play, too. The wisely-selected funeral director assumes the myriad of responsibilities in setting up the necessary arrangements on behalf of the family. His counsel can be depended upon to assist from the hour of passing to the final disposition. Everything he does is planned to ease the suffering and sorrow of the bereaved, and to help them pass through the difficult period during the immediate days after death strikes.

SERVING FAMILIES

Professional critics of funeral directors like to bolster their case with this charge that the bereaved are subjected to high pressure sales tactics when the time comes for them to arrange a funeral. Most families who have been served by established and reputable funeral firms know from experience that such is not the case. Instead, they have a free choice as to the kind of service they wish to select—earth burial, cremation, or giving the body for medical research—at the price they wish to pay. Many firms offer a wide range of prices beginning as low as $200, from which families can select a complete funeral service.

The fact is that in common with many other professions and businesses, funeral directors must adhere to strict codes of ethics in the conduct of their operations. They must obey the laws of the various states under which they operate. They must respect all creeds, religions and customs of those they serve. They must adhere to the highest standards of moral responsibility, character and business integrity in maintaining the goodwill of the families they serve, and the respect of the communities in which they live and perform their duties.

FUNERAL ESTABLISHMENTS

It would be possible for a funeral director to operate his mortuary out of a tent. BUT, no family would wish to patronize such a firm.

The American public demands that facilities available to them should be properly housed in appropriate surroundings such as the churches or synagogues they attend. They want convenience, comfort and dignity. In these days when living space is less spacious than it was fifty years ago, the bereaved looks to the funeral director to provide family rooms where they can greet relatives and friends who come to pay last respects. Private chapels maintained by funeral firms have also been developed in response to many persons who are not related to churches, or to meet the needs of those who do not choose to schedule their services in church. However, should the family wish to receive their friends at home or have the religious services conducted in the church or synagogue of their choice, this is a matter for their decision.

FUNERAL PRICES

No one denies that more money is being spent on funerals today. But this is because the public wants to spend more. This is the case in almost every line of service or merchandise being offered to the American public today. The individual determines what he is going to spend. No one else makes this decision for him.

U.S. Department of Commerce figures show that funeral sales lag behind income increases, and behind the price increases of retail and service trades. They show further that operating costs of funeral establishments have risen substantially at the same rate as the rise in costs of other business.

In a national survey covering 358,489 adult funerals held last year which was conducted among members of National Selected Morticians, it was revealed that the national average cost was:

$0—$374—18.2%
$375—$749—39.2%
$750—$999—30.3%
$1,000—over—12.3%

These prices do not include cemetery charges, or shipping charges for funerals in distant cities.

Unpublicized, and completely ignored by the critics, are the many funerals conducted by firms without charge each year because the families have no funds.

FUNERAL SERVICE

This is another myth being foisted upon the public by the professional critics who are advocating the quick disposal of the dead without benefit of religious services. Surveys show that far from making big profits, as alleged, most firms make less than 10% before taxes, and their average net profit is in the area of 4%. Few other business enterprises enjoy such a low profit margin compared with the total amount of investment required to equip, maintain and operate a modern funeral firm.

Capital investment comes high today compared with a few years ago. The funeral coach which cost $5,000 a comparatively short while ago, today costs $13,000. Taxes, supplies, wages, repairs, and all other costs of doing business have steadily increased, yet families may still buy a funeral for about the same price they could in 1943.

Profits have not increased in that period, but the cost of doing business has multiplied many times over.

CLERGY RELATIONS

Critics try to drive a cleavage between the funeral director and the clergyman, priest, or rabbi by suggesting that the former is usurping their role as counselors in time of grief and need, and distorting the solemn religious rite. Religious leaders who accept this thesis put forward by the critics are in the minority. Experience shows that there is a deep and close relationship which exists between clergy of all faiths and the funeral director. The latter recognizes his contribution is chiefly in the realm of material services for the deceased and in serving the living. Many families arranging funeral services are found to have no church affiliation. Sometimes they ask, and sometimes it is the funeral director who makes the suggestion to put them in touch with a clergyman of their own faith.

But, no responsible funeral director would wish to assume the responsibilities of the clergyman in this important religious rite. Instead, he works with the clergyman to help and counsel the family in all possible ways. Together, they cooperate in many different ways in making the funeral A MEANINGFUL AND SIGNIFICANT RELIGIOUS RITE for the bereaved.

Thus the roles played by the clergyman and the funeral director are a blending of the practical aspects of the service, as rendered by the latter, and the religious rituals performed by the church or synagogue.

EMBALMING

Much has been made of the fact that embalming is a universal practice in the United States, and as such it is not necessary. The discrediting procedure followed by the critics is simply to undermine the claims of embalming, allegedly based upon considerations of hygiene and mental health. Embalming is important, particularly if there is to be a delay between the time of death and actual interment. Medical experts will testify that embalming is a sanitary precaution not inconsistent with the rules of good health. Further, on the part of many survivors, there is a natural desire to look upon the deceased for the last time. This is not morbid curiosity. Rather, there is psychological support for the idea that it helps survivors to face the reality of their loss. In presenting the embalmed body for viewing—sometimes only in private or a family situation —the mortician must employ his skill in cosmetology. This is particularly true in instances where the deceased has suffered a violent death.

The practice of embalming is spreading and many countries, led by England, are adopting it.

FUNERAL DIRECTORS

In a few short years, there will not be enough funeral directors to serve in this country. Each community, big or small, needs a mortuary. Mortuaries have to be accessible to citizens—within reasonable reach. Whether a mortuary handles a large number or just a few cases each year, the differential in cost in running operations is not so great as some might think. While the average cost per case will decline with volume—there is a point below which they will not go.

Only in some major metropolitan centers will there be found what is apparently an over-supply of mortuaries. But, it should not be forgotten that many of these are established to serve special religious or nationality groups.

MORE FACTS

Expensive clothing is sold to survivors to dress the person to be buried, is another of the charges made by critics of American funeral customs. The truth is that more than 80% of the dead are buried in their own clothing. It is rare, indeed, that it is necessary to purchase special clothing to bury the deceased.

* * *

Early American settlers buried their dead in a simple pine box attended by a small group of family and friends, so it has been written, in an attempt to destroy the idea of a traditional funeral service. The truth is that this may have been a frontier tradition when sometimes the dead were buried without even benefit of a pine box. But this was not true of settled sections of earlier American society. Early Americans observed some rather elaborate and expensive funeral customs, as careful research will show.

* * *

Funerals represent a new status symbol in America, it has been claimed. True—in some instances. Some people view the funeral as a means to gain new status among their neighbors and friends. Status conscious Americans also find expression in other symbols as well as in funerals. Such institutions may be to a funeral director's advantage, but they are not of his making. He is obligated to provide the type of funeral service demanded. On the other hand, there are many times when funeral directors counsel families against making unnecessary expenditures.

* * *

"Funeral directors provide and charge for all that the traffic will bear," is a criticism which has been repeated so often that few people heed it. Actually, most funeral firms have been in existence for several generations. Many are family owned and operated. They could not continue on a "one time" basis—and they could not attract families, time and time again, to use their services if they charged on an "all that the traffic will bear" basis.

FREEDOM OF CHOICE

It is the inalienable right of every American to have freedom of choice whether it involves the election of a candidate for political office, the kind of clothes he wants to wear, the kind of schools to which he wants to send his children, the kind of a wedding he wants his daughter to have. So it is when it comes to the selection of a funeral. The right remains that of the individual or family to purchase a funeral service of THEIR OWN CHOICE, at the price THEY WISH TO PAY, from the funeral director of THEIR CHOICE. No reputable funeral director would presume it should be otherwise.

Reputable firms urge you to select in advance of any emergency the funeral director in whom you have confidence. Contact him, tell him about the kind of service you desire for yourself or your family, and the price you want to pay. He will respect your wishes and those of your loved ones. This is the wise way to handle such matters without committing yourself to paying membership fees in an organization over which you have no control or in which you are denied discretion or decision.

PRESENTED IN THE PUBLIC INTEREST
FRIENDLY FUNERAL HOME
100 Greenforest Avenue
Friendly, Pennsachusetts

Branch Banking in Pennsachusetts

For several years, some of the larger banks in the state of Pennsachusetts have been advocating an expansion in the size of banking districts. Under the present banking laws in the state of Pennsachusetts (a large industrial state similar to New Jersey or Pennsylvania) banks were prohibited from having offices or branches in more than one county in the state. Within the one county in which a bank was permitted to operate, the bank could establish as many branch offices as it wished within its home office city or town, provided there was not more than one branch or home office for every 2,000 in population. In towns or cities within the county but outside the town or city where the home office was maintained, a bank could establish branch offices with the permission of the state banking commissioner (and federal authorities when necessary) provided no other bank maintained its home office in that city or town. Banks could also expand by merger with or acquisition of other banks in the same county, provided the banking authorities (state and/or federal) approved the merger or acquisition. Expansion by merger or acquisition was the only way banks could move into a town which was the home office of another bank. In fact, from time to time there had been allegations that "big-city" banks in Pennsachusetts would help establish new banks under friendly management in suburban towns where suburban banks maintained home offices. Then, several years later, these friendly banks would be acquired by the "big-city" banks and the big-city banks could then do business in the suburban towns.

Three of the five largest banks in Pennsachusetts all had their home offices in the largest city of the state, located in Eisenhower County. Eisenhower County included several suburban areas in addition to the large city. The three large banks had managed to establish branches in most of the suburban areas of the county as a result of mergers with and acquisi-tions of smaller banks. The total population of Eisenhower County was more than two million in 1964. Beginning in the early 1950's, the popu-lation growth in Eisenhower County slowed to a small rate. Rapid growth in population was occurring mainly in neighboring Jefferson County, which increased its population from 250,000 in 1950 to over 450,000 in 1964. Present growth trends are expected to continue in much the same fashion at least until 1970.

The population expansion in Jefferson County and the gradual evolution of a single trading area composed of Eisenhower County and much of neighboring Jefferson County was hindering the competitive position of the three large Eisenhower County banks. Commercial cus-tomers who moved their plants or stores from Eisenhower County to Jef-ferson County or established branch operations in Jefferson County were often forced to seek local bank connections to service payrolls and other operations in Jefferson County. The Eisenhower County banks were even losing some loan business from these concerns to Jefferson County institu-tions. Relatively speaking, the generally small banks in Jefferson County were much less sophisticated than the larger and more adequately staffed Eisenhower County banks in the types of services performed for their cus-tomers. Furthermore, individual customers who lived in Jefferson County and worked in Eisenhower County often had to maintain accounts in two banks (one in each county) to get the services they needed at home and office. Customers of the Eisenhower County banks who shopped in some of the new shopping centers just across the county line in Jefferson County could not be served with branch offices of Eisenhower County banks for check cashing and other purposes.

Finally, the competitive position of the big three Eisenhower County banks was worsening with respect to other large banks throughout the nation because of the limitation on expansion to within the one county. Since the loan limits of any bank are based on the amount of its deposits, an expanding base of depositors and deposit expansion are im-portant to a bank's competitive position, since large corporations often like to be able to borrow large amounts from one large bank. New York State recently has recognized this problem by expanding the size of its bank districts. For example, New York City banks were put in the same district with Westchester and Nassau County banks. Thus, the big-city banks could expand to the more rapidly growing suburbs. Other states have gone even further. California, for example, permits banks to establish branches anywhere in the state.

Because of these competitive disadvantages, Mr. C. T. Rin, the president of the Pennsachusetts State National Bank, one of the "big three" Eisenhower County banks, decided to seek legislation to expand the size of the banking districts in Pennsachusetts. Mr. Rin decided that there would be too much opposition to statewide branch banking at this time. He decided to push for a more modest contiguous county law, which would permit banks to operate in any two contiguous counties in the state, such as Eisenhower and Jefferson Counties, under the same rules as they now operated in any one county. The presidents of the other two large Eisenhower County banks promised to support Mr. Rin in his efforts.

Mr. Rin asked Dominik Farmacetti, who represented Eisenhower County in the state Senate, to introduce the bill in the state Senate. Senator Farmacetti, a Republican serving his first term, accordingly introduced the bill in the 1963 session of the state legislature. The bill was also introduced in the Assembly by a local Republican Assemblyman. The Senate bill was referred to the Banking and Finance Committee, which was chaired by the Republican Senator from Jefferson County. Ordinarily, committees are not too important in the state Senate, particularly if the Senate president and the Senate majority leader favor a bill. In effect, the Senate majority party leaders appoint the members of all committees for a two-year term (i.e., 1963-1964). The leaders also, by virtue of controlling the Committee on Committees, decide which committee bills will be referred to. The decisions of the party leaders in these matters are seldom overturned by the members of the Senate. Mr. Rin decided not to talk directly to the Senate leaders, because they represented rural counties and thus might be hostile to the urban county banks. Rin decided instead to work through his local Senator and the ordinary committee process.

Hearings were held by the Senate committee on the Farmacetti-sponsored bill. Mr. Rin, the two other large bank presidents, a professor from the state university, several local citizens, and officers of prominent Eisenhower County firms testified in favor of the bill. Several bankers from South County, in which the state's second largest city is located, also testified in favor of the bill. Testimony in opposition to the bill was presented by bankers from 21 counties throughout the state. These counties were mostly small, rural counties. Bankers from Jefferson County were among those who testified against the bill. Officers from the Pennsachusetts Savings and Loan League, representing the state savings and loan associations and the Pennsachusetts Mutual Savings Bank Association, representing savings banks in the state, opposed the bill in their testimony. Both savings and loan associations and mutual savings banks in the more urban counties were faced with problems similar to those faced by the commercial banks, since they also could do business only in one county. However, these financial institutions were traditionally hostile to the commercial banks, since they competed on real estate loans and for savings deposits with the commercial banks. The Farmacetti-sponsored bill applied solely to commercial banks.

After the hearings were concluded, the committee voted to reject the Farmacetti bill by a vote of 3-2. The Republican chairman from Jefferson County and a rural Republican Senator voted against sending the bill to the floor and they were joined by a Democrat from a rural county. The other Democrat, from South County, and a Republican from a semi-urban county in the center of the state, voted in favor of reporting the bill. With the failure to bring the bill to the floor in 1963 in the Senate, the Republican Assemblyman who agreed to sponsor the bill in the Assembly told Mr. Rin that there was no point in taking further action in the Assembly in 1963.

In 1964, one-half of the state Senate and all of the state Assembly were to come up for re-election. The composition of the Pennsachusetts legislature as of January, 1964 was as follows: state Senate (one Senator elected by each county) twenty Republicans and fifteen Democrats; state Assembly(elected by districts of roughly equal population) 77 Democrats, one vacancy, one Independent, and 71 Republicans. Of the Senators up for re-election in 1964, twelve were Republicans and five were Democrats. The state Senate, with the exception of a few years in the depression, had always been controlled by the Republican Party. One of the Republicans up for re-election in 1964 was the Senator from Jefferson County, which often is a "swing county" in a close election. The majority leader of the Senate was also up for re-election in 1964—his county had not returned a Democrat to the state Senate since the Bull Moose revolt in the Republican Party in 1912.

The incumbent Republican governor, who had taken no stand on the banking bill, was not running for re-election. Neither of the prospective candidates for governor, the Republican (big-city background) attorney general or the rural Democratic U.S. Congressman has taken any stand on the banking legislation.

The composition of the state Assembly usually reflects the over-all attitudes of the majority of the residents of Pennsachusetts as the Assembly is elected on a popular basis. Since the state is a highly industrialized urban state, urban interests tend to dominate in the state Assembly. The state Senate greatly overrepresents the rural areas of the state. For example, Eisenhower County, with a population of over 2,000,000 (about 20 per cent of the population of the state) has one state Senator; rural Tesumpsah County has a population of only 55,000 and also has one state Senator. Although the U.S. Supreme Court has ruled against similar disparities in population and representation in other states, no court cases or legislative reapportionment have yet occurred in Pennsachusetts.

Mr. Rin must decide whether to make a new effort in the 1964 legislative session or wait until after the election of a new legislature. He must also decide on the specific strategy and tactics that should be followed.

The Photographic Equipment Industry and Tariffs[1]

United States tariff policy since 1934 has been based upon the Trade Agreements Act, passed in that year as an amendment to the highly protectionist Hawley-Smoot Tariff Act of 1930. The program, begun in 1934, has been continued by Congressional action every one to three years, when the original act has been extended. The original act, although somewhat modified, gave the President authority to negotiate trade agreements which provide for mutual tariff reductions with foreign countries. These agreements are bilateral agreements, involving the United States and one other country, but, when made, are extended to virtually all other countries.

A substantial number of trade agreements have been negotiated, and the general trend of tariffs has been downward, but substantial protection for domestic industries which might be exposed to foreign competition still exists. This has been assured by a number of devices which limit the authority of the President in negotiating agreements, and which call upon him to revise tariffs if competition develops at a later date. In 1943, an

[1] The statements by Mr. Percy and Mr. Lewis of the photographic manufacturing industry are taken from hearings on the 1955 extension of the Trade Agreements Act, found in 84th Congress, 1st Session, House of Representatives, Committee on Ways and Means, "Hearing on H. R. 1, Trade Agreements Extension," pp. 621-652, 2397-2424. Excerpts from these statements have been rearranged to place contrasting points of view together.

Northwestern University cases are reports of concrete events and behavior, prepared for class discussion. They are not intended as examples of "good" or "bad" administrative or technical practices.

Copyright 1958, Northwestern University. This case is reprinted with the permission of Northwestern University.

"escape clause" was added, first by Executive Order and subsequently by writing it into the act; this clause permits either country to back out of an agreement if unforeseen developments seriously hurt domestic industry. In 1946, a "peril-point" clause was added; this requires the Tariff Commission to establish a specific rate of duty below which, in the Commission's judgment, tariffs could not be lowered without damage to United States industry or business. Presidential action in lowering any such rate below the peril point would require an official explanation to Congress.

Extensions of the basic act in 1953 and 1954 were for one year each, and hearings were held early in 1955 to consider a three-year extension of the act (to June 30, 1958) and possible changes in specific powers of the President, including the "escape" and "peril-point" clauses and the clause which would permit additional decreases in duties not exceeding 15 per cent over three years, or 5 per cent in any one year. Representatives of industries which had been or might be affected by trade agreements testified before the House Committee on Ways and Means. The following leaders in the photographic equipment industry gave oral testimony:

1. Charles H. Percy, president of Bell & Howell Co., Chicago, Illinois, the leading domestic producer of motion-picture cameras, testified on January 24, 1955, and submitted a written reply to Mr. Lewis' testimony later. Mr. Percy identified himself to the committee as vice chairman of the board of a committee for a national trade policy.
2. Robert E. Lewis, President of Argus Cameras, Inc., Ann Arbor, Michigan, the leading domestic producer of 35 mm. cameras, testified on February 7, 1955. Mr. Lewis identified himself as an officer and former president of the National Association of Photographic Manufacturers. (Argus was subsequently acquired by Sylvania.) . . .

Testimony concerned the essential nature of the photographic industry for defense, the effects of the present level of tariffs and of possible reductions in existing rates, and the movement of the photographic industry abroad.

The Present Position of the American Photographic Industry

MR. PERCY: Rather than deal in generalities I should like to be as specific as possible. May I, therefore, focus your attention for a moment upon the American photographic industry—an industry vitally concerned with and directly affected by any foreign-trade policy the Congress adopts.

We compete with photographic manufacturers all over the world, our greatest competition coming from Germany, Japan, England, Switzerland, Austria, and Belgium. Germany alone sells the United States 150 different models and brands of still cameras. It is estimated that approximately three million cameras were produced in Germany in the year 1954.

Imports to the United States last year of cameras in the under $5 unit import classification were 200 per cent of our domestic production of such cameras. In addition, these countries ship huge quantities of photographic lenses to the United States. A total of 16,000 lenses was imported in 1949. By 1953, the figure had risen to 205,000 lenses, 38 per cent of them coming from Japan. The photographic industry competes with so-called cheap foreign labor. I have personally visited most major photographic plants abroad. I have seen skilled German workers who are paid an average of 37 cents an hour, skilled Italian workers who receive 34 cents an hour, and Japanese workers who earn only 27 cents. In contrast, the average hourly wage paid to American workers by the photographic industry is better than $2 an hour, eight times the rate in Japan. The photographic industry is essential to our national defense; the Defense Department considers it one of the most critical in the national-defense program.

Nor are we without protection. A tariff wall of 20 per cent on cameras, 25 per cent on camera lenses and up to 45 per cent on other photographic products shelters us from foreign competition.[2]

MR. PERCY: Permit me also to focus closer attention on Bell & Howell Co.'s position within the industry. We employ better than 3,000 workers; our annual sales, almost exclusively in photographic products, are in excess of $40 million. Of this volume, approximately 94 per cent is sold within the United States, only about six per cent going to the export field.

Bell & Howell is an essential company in the national-defense structure. During World War II, we converted 100 per cent to war work, manufacturing $90 million of defense products for the Army, Navy, and Air Force.

[2] This statement by Mr. Percy, as he admitted in his written reply, omitted certain rates under 20 per cent. Mr. Lewis, in his testimony, commented on the situation in these words:

Does this statement give the impression that the lowest rate on photographic products is 20 per cent and that the rates on other photographic products range from 25 to 45 per cent? If so, the statement is very misleading. There are 27 customs classifications involving photographic products; 24 of these are on an ad valorem basis, as follows:

Two at 2.25 per cent, sensitized paper; seven at 6.25 per cent, unsensitized paper and film; three at 10 per cent to 12.5 per cent, paper items; two at 15 per cent, includes cameras over $10; four at 20 per cent, includes cameras under $10 and motion-picture cameras; four at 25 per cent; two at more than 25 per cent.

Motion-picture cameras are 20 per cent regardless of value. The most generally used tariff for still cameras is 15 per cent which applies to cameras over $10, where the lens is not the chief component of value.

The 25 per cent for still cameras applies only to cameras whose lenses are the chief component of value and is of no significance because very few cameras fall in this category. The 45 per cent rate does not apply to cameras, but only to parts of lenses, and two projectors, and incidentally, it does apply to motion-picture projectors which protects Mr. Percy's company.

The tariff on still cameras with a value of over $10 was reduced on October 1, 1951, as a result of the Torquay protocol, from 20 per cent to 15 per cent. Imports jumped very sharply after this reduction.

All the evidence indicates that Germany and Japan have been extremely successful in the United States still-camera market even with the present tariff.

The photographic industry as a whole has no wish to lose its tariff protection. On the contrary, it would probably like to have that wall strengthened. I appear before you today as a member of American industry and as a private citizen. I do not represent the photographic industry, for its views are not my views. No one desires more than I the health, vigor, and growth of the photographic industry. Yet I do not believe we must gain these things through artificial trade restrictions. I think we can, and we will, win them for ourselves in a freer and, therefore, more competitive market.

The free nations of the world want and need the products we manufacture. But they cannot buy from us unless we buy from them. To be able to trade with the United States would raise the standard of living of millions of free peoples.

For our part, to refuse to trade with the world—and tariff and customs barriers are in practice a refusal—in no way serves our own self-interest. Ultimately, the refusal will isolate us from the free world and the friendship of free nations, as it will surely aid the cause of world communism. . . .

Let us not think in terms of manufacturers alone. Importers and exporters live on foreign trade, as do people in transportation, shipping, and other closely related industries. Wholesalers, distributors, thousands of retailers, and hundreds of thousands of their employees, would find opportunities for increased business if tariff barriers were lowered. And that "forgotten man" the consumer . . . shall he be forbidden to buy imports because they compete with the products of American manufacturers? Or, if he buys them, shall he pay a premium because an American manufacturer cannot produce that particular product as economically as his foreign competitor?

I do not believe he should . . . and my belief has been severely tested. Just prior to the war, our company decided to enter the high-priced 35-millimeter still-camera field. Our camera was an exceptionally fine instrument and today it is used by some of the world's leading photographers. It could not be mass produced; it required many hand operations. In competing with foreign camera manufacturers, we lost one and a quarter million dollars. It was at this time that Bell & Howell first began to appraise its attitude toward our national foreign-trade policy. The temptation, of course, was great to seek higher tariff protection. We were forced to face the question: "Shall national interests be subordinated to special interests?" We decided they should not be. We felt we had no right to ask the American people to pay a higher price for foreign cameras simply because we had decided to go into this particular field. In 1952, we discontinued production of the camera.

Mr. Lewis: . . . I appreciate the opportunity to speak for my own company. At the same time, I believe that I reflect the interest of most of the photographic industry because my story parallels the brief filed with the Tariff Commission by the National Association of Photographic Manufacturers. In presenting the problem with which my company is faced I also wish to correct what I believe are false impressions created by Mr. Charles H. Percy, president of the Bell & Howell Co., who appeared recently before this committee. . . .

Mr. Percy stated he was speaking only for himself in rendering his testimony in favor of a reduction in tariffs.

But actually his testimony was concerned principally with the photographic industry. . . .

A matter of considerable importance that I wish to point out is that the only cameras made by the Bell & Howell Co. are motion-picture cameras. These are not subject to real competition from foreign sources. The reason for that is quite simple:

Amateur motion-picture photography has been too expensive a hobby for people in other countries, with the result that the manufacturer of such equipment never reached any substantial proportions outside the United States.

This is not true of still cameras. The still-camera industry in Germany and Japan is well developed and very substantial. In fact, today its competition is such that every still-camera manufacturer in the United States is importing complete cameras or parts for cameras.

There is actually a movement of our still-camera industry from the United States to Germany. I know of only one industry which parallels this, and that happens to be the watch industry. . . .

The problems of the photographic industry cannot be understood when reviewed in the light of the motion-picture-camera business the manufacturers of motion-picture cameras and projectors have never been seriously threatened by foreign competition. The opposite is true in the case of still cameras.

I should like to quote to you, if I may, an excerpt from a speech made by Mr. Percy before the New York Society of Security Analysts on April 30, 1953, when apparently he did not feel quite the same as he did when he testified before the committee. I quote Mr. Percy:

> Foreign competition, especially from Japan and Germany, is a real threat to the industry, especially to the still-camera field. It is not yet a threat to movies. We are considering buying some of our lenses from Japan and maybe even from Germany. While in Chicago at the photographic show two weeks ago, I talked with many of the 35 Japanese and 20 German representatives. All of them told me that they did not intend to enter the moving-picture field. They posed, however, a very real threat to the still-camera field. . . .

> In other words, the United States still-camera industry has a real problem. The Japanese are obviously not worried about competing with United States manufacturers. It is the Germans they are concerned with.

> I have here with me an advertisement from the *New York Times* photographic section which shows a German camera which is offered for sale for $29.95, including a leather case and flash gun. This camera has a 2.8 lens, a good shutter, and a metal body. Here is the camera. I purchased it after I saw the advertisement. The only still camera of American make that has a 2.8 lens is the Argus C4 which retails at $84.50, also including a flash case and a gun. . . .

> In the field of still precision cameras the prewar imports from Germany actually exceeded our domestic production in spite of a 20 percent duty on cameras in general, and a 45 percent duty on cameras where the lens was the chief component of value.

The 1954 German production of still cameras hit a new high—about 14 percent ahead of 1953, when the Germans made 2,441,308 cameras valued at $47,979,848 at manufacturers' levels.

Our information is that there are about 113 different styles and brands of German cameras on the American market. The Japanese have at least 101 different styles of cameras on the American market. . . .

MR. PERCY: I respect Mr. Lewis's right to present his views and the views of other manufacturers within the photographic industry to the House Ways and Means Committee. I regret that he has chosen to attack the validity of my statement, but I do not reply for any personal reasons. Nor do I reply because the arguments presented by Mr. Lewis are the traditional arguments of the protectionist manufacturer. I take the time of this committee only because I believe that a clear view, from both sides, of the complex problems of foreign trade in specific terms of one industry will be helpful. . . .

Mr. Lewis may speak for one segment of the industry, 84 of the 85 members of the photographic manufacturers association. He does not, I believe, speak for the scores of photographic importers and exporters whose business depends upon keeping our trade lanes open. He does not speak for fifty photographic distributors, a significant portion of whose business is in foreign-made products. Nor does he speak on behalf of thousands of retail photographic dealers and their employees who sell imported products. . . .

Mr. Lewis stated "the only cameras made by Bell & Howell are motion-picture cameras; these have never been subject to real competition from foreign sources." While to date foreign competition in motion-picture cameras has not been as keen as in still cameras, we expect an ever-increasing degree of competition in the future, both at home and abroad. For example, 42 per cent more motion-picture cameras were imported into the United States in the first nine months of 1954 than in the same period in 1953.

It is not true that we manufacture motion-picture cameras only. We also make lenses, microfilm equipment, slide projectors, and tape recorders. We are the largest manufacturer in the world of 16-millimeter sound motion-picture projectors. There are competitive sound projector manufacturers in almost every major country of the world. . . .

In the past a tariff of 45 per cent has protected us in the United States from foreign sound projector competition. Within recent months, however, sound projectors have been reclassified and they are now subject to a tariff of only 13¾ per cent. As a result of this reclassification, foreign competition is preparing to make major inroads in the American market in the near future.

While I have long favored a gradual reduction in tariff barriers, I have always opposed any such drastic change that does not permit a reasonable time to make needed adjustments.

But regardless of tariff reductions, we expect to compete in the future, as we have in the past, by offering the consumer a relatively better value. If we find that we cannot successfully compete in any one product field, we will shift our capital, management, and labor to other fields in which we can use them more efficiently.

In the 1952 Annual Report of the Elgin Watch Company, Mr. J. G. Shennan, president, stated the case as well as I have ever seen it: "Our plight, and what we are doing about it, perhaps provides a perfect case history of a United States industry which has been caught up in the international trade problem and which has resolved boldly to extricate itself * * * by * * * a firm rejection of the classic idea that cheap foreign competition inevitably destroys a domestic industry and causes wholesale unemployment. We are substituting for that concept the principle of industrial evolution; we are hedging against foreign competition by diversifying, so that we can create new sources of income and new jobs to replace the old when needed."

THE PLACE OF THE PHOTOGRAPHIC INDUSTRY IN NATIONAL DEFENSE

MR. PERCY: Recently, in a meeting called by the Department of Commerce, I heard the head of one of our photographic optical manufacturing companies speak with a conviction that could only come from belief. He said that it takes ten years to train an optical worker and that for this reason the industry requires special tariff protection. If this is true of his company, I can only say that it is not true of all optical manufacturers. It is true that at the outbreak of World War II, we were vulnerable because of our dependence upon German optics. Bell & Howell, along with other firms, was asked by the War Production Board to produce lenses. We started with two optical workers in 1941, and by 1943 we had 500. We took housewives and insurance salesmen and bank clerks—and within six months we made trained optical workers of them. If we had to do it again, we think we could do it in three months.

Our industry points with alarm to the fact that because of foreign competition there are perhaps no more than 2,000 optical workers in the United States. This may be true, but the industry fails to mention the fact that in the process of learning the optical grinding business, we have radically changed and improved the methods used in Germany and other countries for hundreds of years. As a result the present unit productivity of our 2,000 workers is probably greater than the productivity of our optical grinding industry during the war.

In Bell & Howell's rough grinding department alone, we now turn out ten times as many lens surfaces with eleven workers using automatic diamond grinders than we did in 1943 with one hundred workers using the traditional "thumb and finger" technique.

I am willing to believe that in special instances there are industries so vital and strategic to our national-defense program that they must be kept alive whether or not the consumer in the commercial market is willing to purchase their products. But I believe statements on behalf of such industries should be made direct to the Defense Department rather than to the Tariff Commission, and I believe it is the responsibility of the Defense Department either to give preference in the placement of contracts to such industries, to maintain their facilities in a standby condition, or in some other way to subsidize them—on their own budget. . . .

MR. LEWIS: The photographic industry is essential to our national defense. The Defense Department considers it one of the most critical in the national-defense program. If the still-camera section of the photographic industry —and it is more than half the total—is driven out of the United States, where will the nucleus be for the precision optical instruments that are made by our industry in periods of national emergency?

As a matter of record, Argus was engaged 100 per cent in making military instruments during World War II and to a substantial degree during the Korean crisis. These instruments are of an extremely precise nature used for the control of gunfire, and are such that they can be made only by trained personnel and organizations.

I want to assure you gentlemen when I say trained personnel, I don't mean trained in six months. We have put them into individual operations when the heat was on and got them doing useful work in six months, but when you talk of a trained optical worker, you are not talking of three, six, or twelve months. You are talking at least of several years. . . .

Labor Costs and Labor Productivity

MR. PERCY: It has been said with great force that trade thrives when we exchange that which we make best for that which other nations make better than we. It must be recognized that where we still use handicraft methods, we do have difficulty in competing. I am sympathetic to such industries, and I recognize the problem they face. We had a million and a quarter dollar problem ourselves recently. But our present foreign-trade policy cannot be tailored to meet the needs of a handicraft industry any more than can our national economy.

The true criterion of cost is not dollars or cents per hour of labor, but rather total labor cost per unit produced. Years ago we sold a movie camera for $49.95, the lowest-priced camera we had ever made. At that time we paid our workers an average of forty cents an hour. After the war, we doubted we could ever again produce a camera at this price.

Yet today, with our average labor cost in excess of $2 an hour, we are again selling a movie camera for $49.95. And it is a finer camera, with more features and better workmanship than our previous model. The highly paid American worker has become the most efficient in the world, two to ten times as productive as his European counterpart.

In mapping our future program, we assume an ever-increasing hourly wage rate. In the final analysis, the combined effect of foreign competition and high American wage rates has been fortunate—it has forced us to find new and better ways of doing things.

Labor cost is by all odds the most important single element in my company's cost structure. I think that this can be most dramatically illustrated in lens manufacturing, where we have a great deal of foreign competition. Here is the raw glass required in the manufacture of a one-half inch f/1.9 Bell & Howell lens. Here is the aluminum required for the metal lens mount. The value of the glass and the metal required for the entire lens is only 43 cents. After molding, grinding, polishing, centering, cementing, coating and assembling, the finished lens has a value of $87. Yet despite the tremendous labor content of our lenses, we are able to compete with manufacturers in Japan, England, France, and Germany.

Recently our lens designers developed a greatly improved wide-angle lens for motion-picture cameras. To determine whether we should make it or buy it to our specifications, our purchasing division secured quotations from a number of foreign manufacturers as well as from our own lens-manufacturing division.

On a strictly competitive basis, our lens-manufacturing division secured the business. Despite the enormous disparity in hourly labor rates, the ingenious techniques developed by our staff produced so low a unit cost that even without tariff protection our bid would still have been below that of our foreign competition.

Without the spur of foreign competition, it is doubtful whether these techniques would ever have been developed.

MR. LEWIS: The chief problem that faces the still-camera industry in this country is the fact that labor costs in the United States are about seven times those of Germany and about ten times those of Japan. Average hourly earnings for camera workers in Western Germany are in the neighborhood of 37 cents an hour. In Japan earnings are about 26 cents an hour. This compares with the average wage in our plant in Ann Arbor of $2.24 an hour. In addition to this, we pay so-called fringe benefits amounting to 22.5 per cent of our total payroll.

In other words, instead of $2.24 an hour, we really pay $2.74 an hour. Some of these fringe benefits, such as social security, unemployment insurance, workmen's compensation insurance, are required by law, and others, such as vacation pay, holiday pay, health and life insurance, recreational activities, have become a standard part of the American scene. Benefits like these are substantially missing in the foreign countries that compete with us.

Still cameras, lenses, and shutters have trivial amounts of materials but a very high labor content, so that we are up against the problem of meeting wages. Using Germany as an example, they are 37 cents an hour as compared with $2.74 in this country.

Mr. Percy made the statement to this committee that American workers are two to ten times as efficient as those in foreign countries. This is not true. It is well known that workers in the industrial countries of Europe are just as efficient as workers in this country. As a matter of fact, the factory workers in Germany are highly efficient, since they usually start as apprentices when they are about fourteen years of age.

The Eastman Kodak Co., which has comparable camera plants in Rochester, N.Y. and Stuttgart, Germany, recently made a survey to determine the relative efficiency of their workers. They found that on a time basis, excluding all differences in wage rates, there was little to choose between the efficiency of the German and the American workers.

In cases where an industry in one country is technically superior to that in another country, it is true that the productivity of labor is greater through the use of expensive machinery and tooling. The automotive industry is an example of this situation. Germany is by no means inferior to the United States when it comes to technological progress in the optical and photographic fields, and Japan is rapidly catching up.

They have the volume to warrant complete mechanization identical to ours. It is interesting to note that German photographic technicians were sent to Japan during World War II when those two countries were allies in the war against us. I might add that in order to make Japan a more effective partner in war, that was done.

MR. PERCY: Mr. Lewis has pointed out, as did I, the wage differential existing between foreign and American labor. I also pointed out that the true criterion of cost is not dollars or cents per hour, but total labor cost per unit produced.

But Mr. Lewis said "Mr. Percy made the statement to this committee that American workers are two to ten times as efficient as those in foreign countries. This is not true."

The authority for my statement can be found on page 69 of the January, 1955, issue of *Fortune* magazine in an article entitled "The Engine: Rising Productivity." The article was written by Mr. Gilbert Burck, a member of the board of editors of *Fortune,* and I quote:

"Today the United States manufacturing worker turns out from two to ten times as much per hour as his European counterpart, and United States farm and service workers doubtless boast a similar margin over their European counterparts."

Mr. Burck's statement is confirmed by my own experience at Bell & Howell. Without greater productivity, we could not compete with foreign motion-picture camera lenses, where labor is the major component. But we do compete and compete successfully, as I showed by specific examples in my previous statement.

I know that our workers at Bell & Howell are more productive than foreign workers. I believe that this is also true of all American industry and the photographic industry as well. If it were not true, then I freely admit we could not meet foreign competition.

For despite the expressed concern of certain American photographic manufacturers, as an industry we have captured a substantial share of the world market, and our exports of photographic equipment exceed our imports by almost three times. In 1953 the United States exported $65 million of photographic goods and imported only $25 million. Authority for these figures may be found on pages 917 and 919 of the 1954 Statistical Abstract of the United States, published by the United States Department of Commerce.

Movement of the American Photographic Industry Abroad

MR. LEWIS: Every major manufacturer of still cameras in the United States has found it necessary to import either complete still cameras or important components and subassemblies for the still cameras they manufacture. In this manner, complete still cameras of foreign manufacture are now being offered in the United States market carrying some of our most famous American name brands. Included are Eastman Kodak, Bell & Howell, Ansco, Bolsey, and DeJur. . . .

The United States manufacturers all either have adequate plant facilities to manufacture their cameras themselves, or could purchase their component requirements domestically.

They would all like to do so, but cannot in the face of foreign competition.

Now that foreign cameras are carrying the United States brand names, it appears that further movement of camera manufacturing to foreign factories is almost certain in the immediate future.

Using my own company as an example, we have been able to compete successfully up until now under the present tariff for several reasons:

1. We are a very efficient manufacturing organization.
2. We have had the advantage of better merchandising, advertising, and service.

We have bought some of our components and parts in Germany.

Now, however, we are faced with two things that cause us concern: One is the possible lowering of tariffs, and the second is the increased distribution of German and Japanese still cameras by well-known American photographic brand names.

I assure you that Argus Cameras, Inc., will not be driven out of business. We will meet this competition. We are importing many camera parts from Germany now, and last month we established a wholly owned subsidiary in Stuttgart, Germany, where we will manufacture cameras, camera parts, and projectors.

I am not pleading for the survival of our company because I am confident that we can survive by manufacturing products abroad, if necessary. But that will not provide jobs for most of our skilled employees in Ann Arbor. If the skilled employees are not retained, what will happen to the photographic industry? . . .

MR. PERCY: Referring to the future Mr. Lewis had this to say: "We are confident * * * of our ability to maintain a competitive position in a growing industry and to grow with the industry by aggressive selling and merchandising."

Looking at the entire photographic industry, the Department of Commerce reports that sales increased 473 per cent from 1939 to 1953, a rate well in excess of all United States industry.

I cannot believe that this record bespeaks a retreat abroad of the photographic industry.

Assuming H. R. 1 is enacted, 15 per cent tariffs would be reduced to 14¼ per cent by 1956, to 13½ per cent by 1957, and finally to 12¾ per cent by 1958. Is it reasonable to assume that the American photographic industry hangs so precariously on its wall of protection that its sales would topple and its employment be jeopardized by such moderate and gradual tariff restrictions?

With or without tariff reductions, I predict with confidence the continued growth of the American photographic industry by any standards of measurement that can be devised—sales, earnings, or total employment. I believe that competition, both domestic and foreign, will keep the industry vigorous, will stimulate it to bring forth new products, lower its costs, and maintain it in a state of readiness in the event that it is needed in an all-out national-defense program.

I earnestly recommend that the members of this committee do not confine their study of this question to statements and evidence submitted by certain manufacturers and their trade associations. I recommend that they study the annual reports of these companies to get the complete picture and to restore their confidence in the true, underlying strength of our American economy.[3]

[3] In support of his statement about examining annual reports of companies, Mr. Percy spoke of the increase of Argus sales from $5,333,788 in 1950 to $22,409,132 in 1954, and earnings before taxes increasing from $778,054 to $3,131,179. The number of employees rose from 675 to 1,111.

Reciprocity and the Protection of Domestic Industry

MR. LEWIS: Do we have reciprocity? Those who make the strongest bid for free trade emphasize the advantages of obtaining increased export markets through reciprocity. If this were true, we would welcome it. But in practice reciprocity has not been made to work.

My company has found it virtually impossible to compete in the world market, for several reasons. We speak of reciprocity in the world trade, but I think it is important that you gentlemen note that it is almost impossible to get an import license. We talk of a two-way street, in this foreign trade, but the evidence indicates that it is a one-way street.

The record shows that imports of still cameras into the United States amount to 29 times the exports to those same countries. . . .

MR. PERCY: Mr. Lewis feels that while we talk of trade as a two-way street, the evidence indicates that it is a one-way street. "The record shows," he said, "that imports of still cameras (and parts and lenses) into the United States amount to 29 times the exports to those same countries." This statement is technically correct but actually misleading. By "those same countries" he means the eight nations which sell cameras to the United States. He fails to mention that our total exports of still cameras, parts, and lenses to all countries are greater than our imports from all countries. (In the first nine months of 1954 the figures were $9 million in imports compared with more than $11 million in exports in still cameras, parts, and lenses, according to United States Department of Commerce figures.) I think that this is a two-way street.

In the 1954 annual report of this company Mr. Lewis told stockholders that "Export of Argus cameras and projectors to civilian markets has been virtually impossible because of a dollar shortage and import restrictions in foreign countries." I can think of no better argument than this for the gradual and reciprocal reduction of tariffs and import restrictions.

Mr. Lewis, however, in an article in the August 15, 1954 issue of *Forbes* magazine seemed to feel that his company is successfully meeting foreign competition in the United States. The article reads: "Lewis, however, believes Argus is winning the battle against them (Japanese and German cameramakers with labor rates of thirty and fifty cents an hour), and in proof points to Argus commercial sales in calendar year 1953 of $16.5 million, 60% greater than the total imports of still cameras." . . .

(Mr. Percy in response to question on peril-point and escape clause):

There has to be compromise in government and business, I suppose. We try not to compromise very much in business, From what little I know about government, there is a great deal of area for compromise. In thinking about the escape-clause provision, I could not help but come to the same conclusion that probably the Commission did. This is an immoral point. There is really no morality to it. It is just another form of subsidy, and it is an immoral one at that.

But I can well recognize that many constituents would be maybe in favor of this gradual program, if they felt there was that stopgap. I hope eventually manufacturers themselves will realize that they are asking the American Congress to put provisions in our contracts that they themselves in all honesty would never ask their own lawyers to put in a contract, because American business people, essentially, I feel are honest and aboveboard. But they are doing it, and they are asking Congress to do it.

If the pressures are such that the escape clause and the peril-point provisions will allow this legislation to go through the Congress, I feel this is one of those areas where a practical compromise may be necessary. I am not wholeheartedly in favor of it by any means, but I am in favor of the President's program as it stands. It represents, I think, in my humble estimation, a brilliant set of compromises.

General Recommendations

Mr. Percy: I am in favor of the President's program for further developing the foreign economic policy of the United States as expressed in his message to Congress January 10, 1955, and as reflected in the bill now before this committee.

I believe that the proposed moderate and gradual reduction of 5 per cent a year in present tariff rates should apply to the imported products competing with Bell & Howell, as well as with the products of all other manufacturers.

The appeal of the President's tariff-reduction proposal is its moderation and the gradualness with which it becomes effective. It is not a giveaway program. The requirement of reciprocity provides American industry with an opportunity to participate in expanded foreign markets. As foreign nations increase their business in this country, they increase their ability to buy in this country. There is only one place that an American dollar can be spent, eventually, and that is in the United States. In this respect, the American eagle on the dollar ultimately becomes a homing pigeon. As our imports increase, so will our exports. I do not advocate any sudden or drastic tariff reductions, and I would not feel that any country should expect us to make such reductions. But I do believe that authority should be given the President to reduce any tariff rates in excess of 50 per cent to that level over a three-year period, and to reduce by not more than one-half in a three-year period tariff rates on articles which are not now being imported or which are being imported only in negligible quantities.

I believe that the President's power to lower our own tariffs should not be conditioned solely upon the grant of tariff concessions to us by foreign countries. The President should also be given the power to reduce tariffs in exchange for the removal of import restrictions inhibiting the flow of American products abroad.

I favor the curtailment of foreign aid, but I also believe that we should expand both directly and through the United Nations the export of American technical assistance to underdeveloped countries. Compared to direct financial aid, this can be done at relatively low cost. But even more important, it offers these nations an opportunity to help themselves become stronger and more self-reliant through their own ingenuity and effort. . . .

I believe our customs administration and procedure should be simplified and improved. We should do everything possible to encourage United

States investment abroad, and we should work unceasingly toward free convertibility of currencies throughout the world. We should act vigorously to prevent the dumping of foreign goods in our country and we should be careful not to engage in similar practices. I believe that the procurement offices of the federal government should be authorized to purchase goods at the lowest possible cost regardless of the origin of manufacture and I therefore favor repeal of the Buy American Act.

I recognize that I may be severely criticized for this stand by other manufacturers in the photographic industry. But because of the sincerity of my convictions I cheerfully submit myself to such criticism. I wish to make it clear, however, that I do not suggest that we assume the role of lambs led to slaughter, nor do I feel that it is our obligation or responsibility to relinquish our domestic markets to foreign competition. My own company recognizes that foreign competition in the years ahead will become an increasingly important factor. We intend to fight it with as strong an organization as we can possibly build—with the most brilliant research and development, the most ingenious manufacturing and vigorous merchandising and service organizations we can possibly command. But we will adjust ourselves to the tariff policy that is best for our country.

I recognize too that some shareowners of Bell & Howell Co. might well question the wisdom of these recommendations in the best interest of their company. To them I say that I am confident that we can adjust to increased foreign competition as effectively as we have adjusted to domestic competition throughout the years. We have demonstrated our ability to cope with changing conditions, as did all American industry, by rapid conversion from wartime to peacetime production in 1945 to 1946.

I believe that our corporate interests can be served by a program consistent with the national interest. If every company and industry were to request that our national policy be molded to fit its own interests, such action would spell ruin to our country and to its citizens. We must never forget that in addition to being producers with "special interests," we are also consumers and taxpayers. To gradually lose our allies because they find it necessary to turn eastward to keep open their own trade lanes, to become an isolated island in a sea of communism, to find our economy crushed under an intolerable national defense burden would serve the interests of neither group. The expansion of foreign trade, with its adjustments and hard work for those of us affected, represents the cost of insurance against this eventuality.

MR. LEWIS: Specifically, as to the provisions of H. R. 1, I believe that the provision which would permit the further reduction of existing duties by 15 per cent over a period of three years either should not be enacted, or should be modified to provide, one, that no rate can be reduced under this provision which has already been cut 50 per cent or more of its 1930 rate and, we have several in that category, incidentally, in our industry.

And, two, may not be used as a basis for reduction unless adequate foreign concessions are obtained in return.

Finally, I believe that there is a major deficiency in the act, namely, that today there is no agency in our government which has the duty or the authority to give adequate consideration to the needs of national security in connection with trade-agreement matters, nor is such consideration now required by the act. . . .

In suggesting a correction of this situation, I am stating what is also the recommendation of the National Association of Photographic Manufacturers; namely, that the act is suitably amended to guard against impairment of national security by requiring adequate consideration to be given to its needs at all steps in the process of reducing or increasing tariffs, or, if need be, in establishing import quotas. . . .

Further, it is suggested that the Tariff Commission be required to consider and give appropriate weight to the defense aspects in any of its studies, recommendations, or decisions, such as in connection with the escape-clause procedure, and the peril-point findings, and that its responsibility not be limited to situations where the industry as a whole has been seriously injured, but shall also include those in which the industry is in a particular product area only.

I sincerely hope that this suggestion will appeal to you as being highly meritorious and deserving of your favorable action.

Public Service Electric & Gas Company[1]

Company action on a municipal ordinance

In October, 1956, Public Service Electric & Gas Company commenced tower construction on a transmission line in the Borough of Roselle, a suburb of Elizabeth, located in Union County, New Jersey. The Roselle Borough authorities immediately directed the work to stop. They believed the transmission line would be detrimental to their community. The following paragraphs will explain why the construction of this line was necessary in the view of Public Service.

Public Service Electric & Gas Company is the largest of five major companies supplying power in the state of New Jersey. It furnishes electric service to the greater part of that portion of the state which is most densely populated and heavily industrialized. This fourteen-county territory, in which it supplies power to 1,400,000 customers, extends from Bergen County in the northeast, southwesterly to Camden County. This service area is about 106 miles long and its width varies from seven to approximately 24 miles. Production of electricity is by means of steam generating stations, which must be located where adequate supplies of condensing water are available and where satisfactory arrangements can be made for necessary fuel deliveries.

Public Service now has seven such generating stations. Those in the northern section are located in the eastern part, on waters in the general New York Bay area. Those in the south are situated adjacent to the Delaware River in the western part of the section. The electricity produced must, of course, be carried by bulk transmission lines from the points of

[1] This case was prepared by Mr. Robert W. Metcalfe under the direction of Professor Donald Grunewald.

generation to the places throughout the territory where it is required for use. The entire system is integrated within itself, as well as interconnected with the systems of other utilities in adjoining areas and states. Unusually heavy requirements or breakdown "outages" at a generating station or in a particular section may be immediately met by switching power from some other area. Also, these interconnections produce great economy for all concerned.

The entire territory has, in recent years, experienced a phenomenal growth in population, commercial and industrial activity, and home construction, as well as in new and increased uses for electricity. This growth has resulted in greatly increased demand for electricity and need for additional facilities to meet the demand. Predictions indicate a continuance of this expansion during the next several years. A utility must, in fulfillment of its obligation to furnish adequate service, construct facilities to be prepared to meet the present and prospective demand without fail. Such facilities must necessarily be geared, not to the average projected load, but to the possible peak load on the busiest day of the year. This time has changed in recent years from the winter months to the summer periods, due to the greatly increased use of electric cooling devices.

Public Service has predicted a 45 per cent increase in peak load by 1964 over that which actually existed in 1959. This, in turn, was substantially higher than the demand a few years earlier. An even larger increase in the next five-year period is predicted. It is estimated that, by 1970, generation capacity required to serve this load will double. Consequently, additional bulk transmission facilities, necessary to integrate the new capacity and deliver the energy in huge quantities to all parts of the service area, must be provided.

As part of the increased facilities necessary for current and expected future needs, Public Service by 1956 had put into operation a new generating station in Linden. This facility was capable of generating 465,000 kilowatts but was planned for expansion to meet additional demands. The location is about four or five miles southeast of Roselle. In order to connect with the integrated system, power generated at Linden must reach a switching station at Aldene in the Township of Cranford, just west of Roselle. This is necessary in order to serve the interior areas which even now are inadequately supplied.

The line in question through Roselle is part of this link. It is proposed to run within the 100-foot-wide private right-of-way of the Staten Island Railroad, an old, non-electric, freight railroad extending from Cranford to Staten Island. The right-of-way, some 9,000 feet of which is in the borough, runs through the southern part in a northwesterly-southwesterly direction. While the railroad right-of-way itself does not appear to be included in any zone of the borough zoning map, it is bordered by an industrial zone for some 1,900 feet, a business zone for 400 feet and residential zones for the remainder of the distance. The evidence discloses that considerable portions of the adjoining residential zones still remain vacant for some distance from the track. In other sections homes (many of recent construction) abut the right-of-way. It is to be noted that the community is substantially residential and for the most part fully developed.

Public Service first proposed to carry the line through the borough, as in the other municipalities through which it had to pass, on 150-foot steel lattice-work towers. The uninsulated line is designed for ultimate 220,000 volt 600 megawatt capacity, but at inception is to carry only 132,000 volts. The type of transmission is a familiar one, frequently seen throughout the state, especially in sections not heavily developed. Public Service last year had 405.4 circuit miles of such high voltage transmission lines supported by 1,852 steel towers in operation in some 79 municipalities within its fourteen-county territory.

After the borough authorities ordered the work on the transmission line to stop, Public Service immediately sought to resolve the controversy by offering to substitute H frame structures for the 150-foot steel towers. Such structures are 70 feet high, and each consists of a pair of columns connected by a rigid beam spanning the railroad trackage, to which the power lines would be attached. They are substantially the same in appearance and operation as those used on electrified railroads running through all types of land use areas in the state and would not differ from the construction necessary if the Staten Island Railroad were to be electrified through Roselle. The negotiations were unavailing.

The effort by the Borough of Roselle was pursued on two fronts. The first involved an amendment of the local zoning ordinance adopted after construction of the transmission line in question had been commenced. Before the amendment, the ordinance did not deal with the subject matter. The amendment required a utility to obtain a permit before erecting, in any zone in the borough, poles and towers for any transmission of electric current. The Board of Adjustment was vested with authority to hear the application and make recommendation to the governing body for issuance. Specifically, it provided that no permit should be issued unless both bodies found that in their judgment "The use in the case in question would not be detrimental to the health, safety and general welfare of the community and is reasonably necessary for the convenience of the community." Public Service Electric and Gas Company applied for exemption from this amendment before the Board of Public Utility Commissioners, and the board agreed to the exemption.

The borough, after the adoption of the zoning ordinance amendment and before the Public Service application for exemption, asked the board for an investigation to determine whether Public Service should not be required to attain its objective of service through the overhead line in question by some other means such as underground transmission or use of an alternate route. It also asked the board to determine whether the plans for the line contemplated provision for additional future service without appropriate consideration of future development of engineering methods. The board considered both applications (Public Service's and the Borough of Roselle's) at the same time and ruled that, since the factors involved in both cases were the same, only one decision was necessary. They ruled in favor of Public Service. The borough and the County of Union, in which it is situated, appealed the decision of the board, and the New Jersey State Supreme Court certified the appeal.

The second front of the borough's continuing attack took the form of a general police-power ordinance adopted after the final decision of the board and the taking of the appeal therefrom in February, 1960. This local legislation provided, in effect, that all electric power lines in Roselle carrying more than 33,000 volts must be installed underground. It went on to specify standards for such installation, as well as the requirement of filing plans and specifications, and the obtaining of a municipal permit before any such line could be lawfully constructed or maintained. The borough's objections to overhead transmission of bulk power and the basis of its claim of right to compel an undergrund method are founded on an alleged adverse effect upon the safety and welfare of its inhabitants in these respects:

1. A hazard and danger to persons and property, especially when near the route.
2. Depreciation of property values in the vicinity of such lines and destruction of the residential character of adjacent areas, which constitute as well a serious impediment to the further orderly development of the entire borough as a residential community.
3. Offensiveness of appearance of towers and lines.
4. Interference with family radio and television reception.

Public Service must decide what action to take with respect to the Roselle ordinance requiring, in effect, that the proposed transmission line be built underground. The costs of building an underground line would be approximately seven times more expensive than the overhead transmission line.

PART SIX

ACCESS TO THE EXECUTIVE BRANCH

Quality Mailing Company and Third Class Mailings at The Parsons Post Office [1]

Mr. Case, plant manager of the Quality Mailing Company, is trying to determine what further action, if any, should be taken in respect to its dealing with the Parsons, Metropolia, Post Office. Metropolia is a highly populated industrial state, similar to Connecticut.

Quality Mailing Company, known as QMC, specializes in the preparation and maintenance of mailing lists, and the addressing, sorting and insertion of mail. Most of QMC's clients use third-class mail, which is defined as "all matter which weighs up to but not including sixteen ounces and is not classified as personal correspondence or as a periodical." Postage for third-class mail is four cents for the first two ounces or fraction thereof, and two cents for each additional ounce or fraction. However, by fulfilling certain regulations, bulk mailing rates are two and five eighths cents per piece, or eighteen cents per pound of mail; whichever is more postage is applicable. The bulk rates are applicable to lots of at least fifty pounds or 200 identical mailing pieces which have been sorted, tied into bundles, and placed in mail sacks by the mailer. An annual fee of $30 per calendar year is charged for the privilege of mailing at bulk rates. Postage for third-class mail may be paid by use of precancelled stamps, meter stamps, precancelled government stamped envelopes or by permit imprint. The permit imprint, or indicia, as it is called, is the most common way of paying third-class postage. If postage is to be paid by use of an indicia, an additional fifteen-dollar fee is charged. This fee is paid only once and lasts indefinitely, providing that at least one mailing a

[1] This case was prepared by Mr. Gerald Joseph Katz under the direction of Professor Donald Grunewald.

year is made under this permit. All bulk rate indicias must contain the following information: U. S. Postage Paid, bulk rate, the post office where the mail originated and the permit number at that post office. The postage money for the mail must be deposited and credited to the permit number at the post office prior to the arrival of the mail.

The mail must be accompanied by a mailing statement in duplicate when delivered to the post office. The mailing statement requires the following information to be filled out by the mailer:

1. Post office.
2. Permit number.
3. Name and address of permit holder.
4. Date of mailing.
5. Name and address of firm preparing mailing if other than permit holder.
6. Number of sacks of mail delivered.
7. Weight of each piece of mail.
8. Number of pieces per pound of mail.
9. Total weight of mailing.
10. Postal rate applicable.
11. Total postage.

The post office, upon receipt of the mail and mailing statements, weighs the sacks of mail to verify the correctness of the mailing statement and to deduct the correct amount of postage from that previously credited to that permit number. The duplicate copy of the mailing statement is reurned to the mailer.

The post office that originally receives the mail from the mailer gets and keeps all the postage money deposited, even if none of the mail is to be delivered by that post office. Although third-class mail is sorted and sacked by city in order to qualify for bulk rates, the final sort into postal carrier routes is the responsibility of the post office making the delivery to the postal patron. Hence, a post office may receive a great deal of revenue for merely transshipping mail sacks, while the post office that must perform the sorting and delivery of the mail will receive no money for performing the greatest part of the work. This makes the postmaster anxious to receive all the mail that his post office is responsible for delivering.

Mr. Case's problem is that Parsons Post Office is continually revising the count of pieces mailed as reported on the mailing statement. Although QMC deals with thirty to fifty post offices weekly, the Parsons Post Office is the only one that consistently revises the count as reported on the mailing statement. The count revisions are usually quite large, usually amounting to about 10 per cent. QMC bills the customer on the basis of the number of pieces mailed as verified at the post office. These revisions have caused a considerable loss of billings. Mr. Case is also concerned that the customer may be dissatisfied because he is not being given the advertising coverage that he has requested.

Parsons is a suburban community located between Hoskins, the principal business and industrial city in Metropolia, and Center City, a very large city in an adjoining state. Parsons has become one of the fastest-growing suburban communities in the area because of its location at the hub of two major highways. Since World War II, its population has increased fivefold and nearly equals that of the older, established city of Hoskins. Suburban branches of Hoskins' and Center City's finest shops have located in the Highway Shopping Center in Parsons. The Fair and Square Supermarket chain has its largest, most modern supermarket in the state located in the Highway Shopping Center.

Fair and Square is one of the largest and fastest-growing supermarket chains in the state. It has taken a good share of its business from the older established chains such as A&P and Acme. Fair and Square has been able to compete with the older established chains by group buying, warehousing, distribution and advertisement of its own branded products while maintaining individual ownership for the stores within the chain. The mass purchasing and individual ownership have enabled Fair and Square to have the economic advantage of large organization purchasing power without the high overhead costs of rigid centralized control. The policy of passing these savings on to the consumer in the form of lower prices has helped Fair and Square grow from six small self-service grocery stores to its present size of more than 75 stores in Metropolia and neighboring states. Although there is individual ownership for the stores, an owner or combine may operate several stores within the chain. The store at Parsons is owned by a combine of the original founders of the chain.

A large proportion of Fair and Square's advertising budget is spent on direct-mail advertising. Originally, the chain was using direct mail only to announce new store openings. However, the use of coupons and food specials in circulars has given Fair and Square an accurate measurement of the better response for direct mail. It has been more effective than newspapers, because the advertising concentration is made in a store's trading area.

The mailings are usually made weekly, and the store owners prefer early-week postal delivery. This is done to induce a portion of the customers to shop early and also to attract shoppers who make one major trip on Friday or Saturday, but still make minor trips during the week. Because of the competitiveness of the business and the market variations in wholesale prices, the printing-to-mail-delivery schedule must be compressed as far as possible. Working back from the target delivery date to the consumer of Monday or Tuesday, the following schedule is used:

Monday .... Determination of the following week's specials

Tuesday .... Advertising format preparation with the exception of prices

Wednesday .... Calling in prices to printer

Thursday .... Printing and delivery of circulars to mailer

Friday .... Addressing circulars

Saturday .... Delivery of circulars to post offices

Monday and Tuesday.. Delivery of circulars to consumer

The time value of the circulars makes adherence to the schedule imperative.

QMC does the mailings for about 45 stores of the Fair and Square chain. Other mailing companies do other stores in the chain; none of QMC's competitors handle more than five or six stores. The mailing for the Fair and Square chain is made from QMC's occupant list, which contains the mailing addresses of approximately four million homes in Metropolia and adjacent states. Although not required by regulations, the list is filed in postal carrier route order to expedite handling at the post office. The list is maintained on metal plates, with each plate being embossed with one mailing address, such as:

OCCUPANT
23 MAIN STREET
PARSONS, METROPOLIA

The plates are specially designed to be used with a high speed addressing machine called a speedaumat. Addressing by speedaumat is a two-man operation, with an operator and a helper. The operator is required to select the correct file of plates, load them into the plate feed, load the circulars into the hopper and operate the feed switches for both. The addressed circulars are carried by conveyor to the helper, who must tie them into a bundle, place them in mail sacks and tag the sacks to assure routing to the proper post office. The number of pieces addressed by the speedaumat is determined by a counter which is actuated each time the speedaumat arm comes down to address a piece.

QMC completes its calculation for the mailing statement by dividing the number of pieces per pound into the number of pieces addressed as reported from the speedaumat's mechanical counter. The number of pieces per pound is determined by a very accurate scale. The postal authorities verify the mailing statement by weighing all sacks of mail, deduct the weight of the empty sacks and divide the net weight by the weight of a single piece of mail to determine the number of pieces mailed.

In considering why Parson changes the mailing statements and the other post offices do not, Mr. Case looked at the differences in the circulars for the Parsons store. Because of its excellent highway location, the trading area for the Parsons store is much larger than that of any other store. The mailings for the Parsons store are either 20,000 or 35,000 circulars, depending on whether the mailing is intended only for the primary trading area or whether it includes the secondary trading area of the store. The other Fair and Square stores have mailings of approximately 7,000 to 10,000 circulars. The Parsons store usually has more special items on sale and mails a ten-page circular compared to a six-page circular for the other stores. More circulars of greater weight would probably make more obvious the variations between the two methods of calculations. Mr. Case has attempted to minimize these variations by checking both the counters on the machines and the scale used to weigh the pieces. The counters and scale proved to be entirely accurate. Mr. Case has spoken to the Superintendent of Mails at Parsons, who reports his scales are checked monthly, without any great variations in accuracy between checkings. For a period of several weeks, Mr. Case assumed the time-consuming task of weighing the seventy or eighty sacks of mail prior to delivery to the Parsons Post Office. During this time, the Parsons Post Office still showed a much lower weight and a change in the count of pieces mailed. Mr. Chase has pointed out to the Postmaster at Parsons the pains taken at QMC to assure an accurate count, and the revenue lost by the Parsons Post Office by these continual revisions in count. The Postmaster feels that the post office cannot accept a mailing statement without strict verification and that the mailings for the Parsons Fair and Square is the only one that consistently shows variation.

Mr. Case is convinced that someone is short-counting him at the Parsons Post Office. His alternatives are:

1. Ask the postal inspectors from Washington to investigate.
2. Mail for the Parsons store out of the Hoskins Post Office.
3. Do nothing.

Each possible action has a possible turn of events that can affect QMC adversely. An investigation by the postal inspectors may determine that the Parsons Post Office has been right and many of the other post offices have not been verifying the mailing statement correctly. This would mean that QMC would have the same problem with about fifty post offices instead of Parsons alone.

Mailing out of the Hoskins Post Office would cause the Parsons Post Office to lose all the revenue for the Fair and Square mailings. The Parsons Post Office could retaliate by not delivering the circulars immediately. The post office can hold third-class mail as long as 72 hours.

Doing nothing would mean a continued loss of billings because of the count revisions. However, more important to Mr. Case is the customer dissatisfaction for inadequate advertising coverage. If QMC loses the Parsons store, with its influential owners, it could precipitate the loss of other stores to its competitors. Up until this date the owners of Parsons Fair and Square have not complained to QMC, but Mr. Case has to solve this problem before they do complain.

Apple Valley
Farmers' Market[1]

The Lincolnia state milk board had summoned the management of Apple Valley Farmers' Market to appear at a hearing to show the board reason why its dairy license should not be revoked. The milk board had declared that Apple Valley was selling milk without a proper profit in violation of the Lincolnia milk code. Lincolnia is a state with a population of about 5 million.

APPLE VALLEY　Apple Valley Farmers' Market is a discount house
FARMERS' MARKET　in a growing suburban community near a major
metropolitan area. The market had undergone three stages of growth from its rural beginnings to its modern discount unit format. Under its present management, Apple Valley pursued a vigorous policy of deriving profit through moving huge volumes of merchandise at low profit margins.

Apple Valley consisted of individual units leased to independent merchants. The merchants were limited to specific merchandise lines, and they had to follow a discount method of operation. Advertising was institutional and also consisted of weekly "loss leaders" designed to attract customers to the market. An additional assessment in the form of a percentage of the gross receipts was taken for advertising. All merchants paid this assessment. Ads were solicited by the management, and the final decision for advertisement composition lay with the management. Al-

---

[1] This case was prepared by Mr. Michael Kalbs under the direction of Professor Donald Grunewald.

though each merchant paid his advertising money, he was not necessarily guaranteed a space in the advertisement.

On the other hand, if a merchant had a particularly good loss leader, but if the cost were a little too much for that individual to handle, the market would underwrite part of the cost. This was done only in unusual cases, and the merchandise was sold at the merchant's location.

On very special occasions the market would underwrite an entire "giveaway." One example of this was the purchase of an entire boxcar of Prestone Anti-freeze in gallon cans, to be sold at a fantastically low price of $1.19 or even 99 cents. The loss was written off to advertising.

It was this seeking for a special promotional item that led to the action of the Lincolnia Milk Board.

LINCOLNIA MILK BOARD   The Lincolnia Milk Board has several duties. Among the major duties are:

1. *Grant licenses to sell dairy goods.*

    This establishes the power of the commission. In order to sell dairy goods in Lincolnia, one must have a dairy license. The commission has the power to revoke a license when a violation of the milk control law or sanitation code takes place.

2. *Control retail and wholesale price of milk.*

    This was done with the object of protecting the Lincolnia farmer and wholesaler to insure him of a proper price. When a milk war ensues, retailers tend to go to other states to save a penny or two, and milk would back up on Lincolnia farms. The establishment of a minimum retail price eliminates this.

3. *Record minimum price.*

    When a retailer applies for a dairy license in Lincolnia, he records the price at which he is going to sell milk. He is limited to this price from that time on.

APPLE VALLEY VERSUS   Apple Valley Farmers' Market's troubles with
THE MILK BOARD   the milk board actually began in the neighboring state of Urbania. The large metropolitan area to which Apple Valley catered was in Urbania. After enjoying a long period of little competition and prosperity, a large, family-owned cheese-manufacturing company located in Urbania found itself in a bitter struggle with a major dairy for the local cheese business. In retaliation, the cheese-manufacturing company went into the milk business.

Actually there was no hope of hurting the major dairy, but the cheese manufacturer did find itself in the milk business, which made up for the losses in cheese. The milk was a quality product sold for resale in local groceries.

The cheese manufacturer attempted to extend its dairy sales. When it tried to break into the lucrative Lincolnia market, the large dairies froze the family out. A period of backroom maneuvering began, as the family tried to break the powerful influence of the large dairies. It was during this time that the cheese-manufacturer-turned-dairyman learned that the governor of Lincolnia was considering dropping milk price controls and letting the retailers re-establish new minimum milk prices, hopefully lower ones. This was to be done quietly and was not common knowledge.

After learning of this, the cheese manufacturer contacted the Apple Valley management and offered to sell them milk at a very low price if Apple Valley would resell the milk at a very low price. The cheese-manufacturing family wished to do this to point out the unreasonable power wielded by the large Lincolnia dairies and supermarket chains and to show how they artificially inflated retail milk prices far above a true minimum.

By careful maneuvering and waiting for the last possible moment to post prices, Apple Valley Farmers' Market posted a 79-cent-per-gallon price while the major chains posted a $1.09-per-gallon minimum. This tremendous gap resulted from the large dairies' practice of paying a 10-cent-per-gallon rebate to the retailers who used their milk. The inflated price plus the dime rebate insured the retailer of a good profit, and the dairies effectively froze out competition. The retailer could not declare the illegal rebate, so it made for a large source of profit.

The Urbania cheese maker had, in addition, agreed to pay for a major portion of the Apple Valley advertising program. Large ads were taken in most prominent Lincolnia papers in the area, and milk sales at Apple Valley Farmers' Market shortly rose to 3,000 gallons per week.

When the mistake was realized and the threat to their business recognized, the large dairies and supermarket chains began to apply pressure on Apple Valley to raise its prices. When this failed, an offer to purchase Apple Valley Farmers' Market was made. The discount house's management turned the offer down. When all pressure and offers by the retailers and dairies failed, the Lincolnia Milk Board began action on revoking Apple Valley's license. By this time, so much interest had been raised over Apple Valley Farmers' Market prices that both national wire services, the metropolitan newspapers, and most local Lincolnia papers attended the hearings.

The Lincolnia Milk Board presented contentions that Apple Valley did not make a fair profit on its milk and told how this endangered the Lincolnia dairy farmers. The milk board also showed that this milk control was not only justifiable economically but legal and constitutional.

Apple Valley countered with its argument. Apple Valley quite agreed that the milk controls were legal and necessary, but Apple Valley also felt that a price of 79 cents was also legal. Proof was submitted that the cost of the milk to Apple Valley from the Urbania dairy was 70 cents per gallon. The milk board then contended that nine cents was not a true profit, for Apple Valley did not include any overhead. Apple Valley then submitted further proof that the direct cost of help and transportation was between three and four cents a gallon, leaving a margin of five cents per gallon. The market said that any other costs would be incurred whether or not the market sold milk and should not be included in the cost of the milk. Furthermore, Apple Valley Farmers' Market argued, it was a discount house, and five cents per gallon is a good margin when one considers it was selling 3,000 gallons of milk a week. The milk board retorted that this was not a "true" profit, and Apple Valley's action threatened the farmers.

Meanwhile, as the hearings dragged on, the newspapers played up the public's interest and questioned how an Urbania dairy could sell milk at 70 cents per gallon while Lincolnia dairies demanded more. The situation threatened to spread from a local issue around Apple Valley to the entire state of Lincolnia.

As a resolution, the milk board asked Apple Valley Farmers' Market to raise its price to 87 cents per gallon, and this became the Lincolnia minimum price for a gallon of milk.

EXHIBIT ONE

An Apple Valley Discount Special

—————

PUREST NAME IN
MILK
79¢
Per Gallon
In 2, One-Half Gallon Containers

In Our New   Lincolnia's Finest
Modern Discount   Family *Savings* Center
Supermarket

10 A.M. to 10 P.M.   APPLE VALLEY
Sunday Noon to 6 P.M.   FARMERS' MARKET

                                    Apple Valley, Lincolnia
                                    Between Rts. 90 and 37

NOTE: This first ad was run in local newspapers to probe for public reaction to the 79¢ price.

EXHIBIT TWO

IS YOUR MILKMAN MILKING YOU?

COMPARE

Check Your Home
Delivery Price!

PUREST NAME IN

MILK

79¢

Per Gallon

In 2, one-half gallon containers

In Our New Modern
Supermarket

Lincolnia's Finest
Family *Savings* Center

(Picture	FOR THE GOOD	APPLE	FARMERS'
of	HEALTH OF OUR	VALLEY	MARKET
Baby)	FUTURE CUSTOMERS		

"DRINK MILK FOR   APPLE VALLEY, LINCOLNIA
BETTER HEALTH"   Between Rts. 90 and 37

Daily 10 a.m. to 10 p.m.
Sunday Noon to 6 p.m.

NOTE: When public reaction to the first ad indicated a smashing success, and the initial supplies of milk ran behind demand, Apple Valley Farmers' Market ran another type of ad. This ad brought immediate reaction from the local teamsters union which represented the milk deliverymen in the area. The union asked deletion of the phrase, "Is Your Milkman Milking You?," because the deliverymen worked for the dairy which set the price, not the deliverymen. The ad implied that the deliverymen did set the price, and the men were receiving abuse from their customers. Apple Valley agreed and discontinued this series of ads.

EXHIBIT THREE

THANK   YOU
GOVERNOR
BASS!

To The Milk Buyers of Lincolnia:

We take this opportunity to thank Governor Bass for eliminating price
controls on milk.

We believe in giving the consumer every possible break in the price of
a necessary food item such as milk.

We shall continue to bring you the "Purest Name in Milk" at greatly
reduced prices.

Look for the "Purest Name in Milk" in the dairy case at the Apple
Valley Farmers' Market—Giant Supermarket.

Apple Valley Farmers' Market
Between Routes 90 and 37
Apple Valley, Lincolnia

PUREST NAME IN
MILK

79¢
Per Gallon
In 2, One-Half Gallon Containers

NOTE: After ads of the type shown in exhibit two were discontinued, Apple
Valley switched to ads of the type shown above. All ads stressed the low price
and quality of the milk and showed the price in very large type (two inches
high).

EXHIBIT FOUR

PUBLIC NOTICE!

To The Milk Buyers of Lincolnia:

We regret that on Monday, (date) , the Apple Valley Farmers' Market price on MILK was increased from 79¢ to 87¢ a gallon. (No deposit)

We want to sell you *MILK* at the lowest possible price, but the *State Milk Board* has ordered us to charge you *8¢ more per gallon* than our business judgment tells us to charge.

We will continue to fight for LOWER MILK PRICES. Won't you help us in our fight by telling your State Senator and Representative to throw out this board and the minimum price law.

Apple Valley Farmers' Market
Between Routes 90 and 37
Apple Valley, Lincolnia

"PUREST NAME IN MILK"　　87¢　　　Lincolnia's Finest
　　　　　　　　　　　　Per Gallon　　Family Savings Center

In 2, One-Half Gallon Plastic Containers.　APPLE　　FARMERS'
　　　　　　　　　　　　　　　　　　　　VALLEY　　MARKET

NOTE: After the milk board ordered Apple Valley to raise its prices, it ran this ad. The price is now shown in smaller type (approximately one inch high).

Island Super Markets

Earily on the morning of July 2, 1957, Harold Westport, Island Super Markets vice president for sales, met at the company's main office with Martin J. Samson, supervisor of the dairy and frozen foods departments, and Alvin Harris, the chain's grocery supervisor. The meeting was called at Mr. Westport's request to discuss a problem arising out of a letter the company had received from the New York State Agriculture Department.

Arthur Dunlap, Agriculture Department agent, covers that area of Long Island where most of the company's 28 supermarket units are located. On one of his regular inspection tours he noted that the grocery department carried a brand of mayonnaise with label instructions, "Keep Refrigerated."

Paraphrased excerpts of Mr. Dunlap's letter follow:

"In accordance with the manufacturer's directions for freshness maintenance, the Department of Agriculture directs Island Super Markets, Inc. to either move Saxon brand mayonnaise to a refrigerated location or remove it from sale within ten days of the above date."

Westport emphasized his desire to avoid any problem which would raise public question of Island's freshness control and opened the meeting to suggestions. Al Harris immediately noted that removal from sale was out of the question, since Saxon was a nationally known

1 This case was prepared by Mr. Bernard H. Segal under the direction of Professor Donald Grunewald.

brand and Island's biggest seller. He suggested that the dairy department allow enough space for the product. Samson was completely
opposed to this idea. His position was based on three arguments:

1. Moving one brand of mayonnaise to a new location (Island
   carries four other brands) would effect a net drop in sales,
   since people expect to find and buy mayonnaise in the condi-
   ment aisle.
2. Cubic footage of dairy case space is much more valuable than
   grocery shelf space, and the small profit percentage of mayonnaise did not warrant taking space from high-profit sellers.
3. The mayonnaise package design did not lend itself to display
   in dairy cases; therefore, it would be space wasted.

Samson continued that in his opinion the only action was to get Saxon
to clarify the label statement, since the packaging process they used
required refrigeration only after the jar had been opened for the first
time. He also suggested that if such a statement did not satisfy the Agriculture Department, they should get Saxon to change the label.

Saxon is the brand name used for mayonnaise, salad dressing, by
the North American Foods Products Company, which also packages
dairy items carried by Island. Therefore, Samson suggested that he contact NAFP's vice president, John Grant, with whom he had cooperated
on numerous sales programs during the past several years, and get the
necessary statements. Both Westport and Harris agreed and the meeting
was adjourned.

A phone call to the NAFP office was enough to set up a luncheon
appointment with the vice president for that very afternoon. During
lunch, Samson explained the problem and the decisions reached at the
morning meeting. Grant agreed to have a statement prepared for the
Department of Agriculture, but indicated that it would be necessary
to consult with other officials of the company on the cost of changing
the label.

NAFP's statement, with a request by Island for reconsideration
of the Agriculture Department's directive, was sent by special delivery
to Arthur Dunlap at his department office. During the rest of the day
and the day following, Samson personally contacted officials of competitive food chains on Long Island to determine how they were affected
by the problem. He found that they, too, had received orders from the
Agriculture Department and for the most part were not sure what
course they would pursue. Samson explained what he was doing and
asked for their cooperation. They all agreed that the problem did not
affect their competition with Island and on an off-the-record basis (no
public statements) would cooperate.

On July 5, an answer from the Agriculture Department arrived. The Department recognized the problem faced by Island Super Markets, and, on the strength of NAFP's statement, agreed to extend the time period for action to thirty days. While the packaging process did allow non-refrigeration shelving, the consumer's only information was that stated on the label: that the product required continuous refrigeration.

At this point, Mr. Samson is now faced with the problem of deciding what action he should take during the next thirty days.

FHA Standards

The domestic hardwood plywood industry received word that the Federal Housing Administration was considering requiring hardwood plywood used in FHA-insured homes to be either:

1. ½" or thicker rather than ¼" thick and
2. installed over a noncombustible backup material rather than on studs or firring, or
3. chemically treated to be fire resistant.

The purpose for the proposal was said to be to reduce loss of life due to fire. There had recently been two fires in the San Francisco area in FHA-insured homes. Although nonflammability of hardwood plywood would not have prevented loss of life in those fires, the local code authority had imposed restrictions in the use of hardwood plywood along the lines contemplated by FHA.

The managing director of the Hardwood Plywood Manufacturers Association was quite concerned about this development because, if imposed, these requirements would substantially increase the cost of hardwood plywood used in private dwellings and reduce usage by a considerable volume.

New homes insured under FHA programs accounted for approximately 19 per cent of new-home construction in 1963. While this is not a major portion of the construction industry, the association was quite concerned with the requirement the FHA was considering because the VA and local building code authorities frequently followed

FHA provisions in establishing their own construction codes. Imposition of the proposed FHA requirements would mean the virtual elimination of hardwood plywood wall paneling from medium- and low-cost housing, and reduce usage in high-cost housing. The proposed FHA requirement would also have applied to other laminated products used for wall coverings or for walls in private homes. Because of the magnitude of the problem, and because this was a situation in which interests would be compatible, the Hardwood Plywood Manufacturers Association (HPMA) decided to work with other trade associations. In mid-December, the managing director of HPMA, Clark McDonald, wrote a letter to the Federal Housing Administration stating the position of his industry on the proposals and, in essence, advised the FHA that it was his feeling that the FHA, in its desire to prevent loss of life in home fires, was not reaching the basic problem. McDonald proposed other courses of action which would have more effect in preventing loss of life: namely, the requirement that each room in a home have two means of ingress and egress, that windows in homes be required to be within three feet of the floor, and that homes have fire or smoke warning systems. McDonald also pointed out in his letter that the major cause of loss of life in home fires was the burning not of the building but of the contents. Just before Christmas, McDonald and the counsel for the Hardwood Plywood Manufacturers Association met with personnel of the Federal Housing Administration to discuss these proposals. At that time, the FHA indicated that it would not take immediate action and that the letter was merely sent to get the feeling of the industry concerning the proposal. During the course of the meeting, Federal Housing Administration personnel advised that they would certainly take no action until after the holiday season, when their standards personnel would be back from leave. Rumors which people in the industry had heard led McDonald to believe that the FHA had already laid plans to issue revisions to the building code requirements for FHA homes which would lead to, or substantially require, compliance with the FHA proposal outlined in FHA's initial letter to McDonald. Some time earlier, the FHA had advised the domestic hardwood plywood industry that it was considering revisions to its standards which would have substantial effect upon the industry. It was later found that the FHA had already had printed and prepared for distribution "interim" revisions to its specifications which would *require* what the FHA had said that it was only considering. McDonald did not want a repetition of that. Accordingly, he expressed a desire to head off any proposed revisions before they were ever in print. One leading member of the industry was advised by its man in Washington that FHA would not do anything on this matter for a long time and that, therefore, the industry should do nothing. No one else in this industry or related industries shared that opinion.

The domestic industry recognized the problem of fire in private homes, and had already indicated to the FHA its concern with action which would reduce the flame-spread rating of hardwood plywood. In fact, during the previous summer, the Hardwood Plywood Manufacturers Association had written FHA asking what tests would be recognized by FHA as constituting valid measure of flame-spread rating. In December, McDonald had not yet received a reply to that letter. The domestic industry, however, had decided to buy radiant panel test equipment for measuring the flame-spread rating of hardwood plywood panels. This test consisted basically of radiating heat against panels and measuring the charring which resulted. The other recognized method of measuring flame-spread rating was to have a controlled fire in a tunnel and measure the time it took for flame to spread on a material placed inside the tunnel.

Equipment for the radiant panel test would cost between $5,000 and $6,000. Equipment for a tunnel would cost substantially more, and estimates were approximately $35,000. However, there was some indication that FHA would not recognize the radiant panel test. The Forest Products Laboratory, a division of the Department of Agriculture, had indicated, however, that radiant panel testing was compatible and as valid for test purposes as tunnel tests. After the December meeting with FHA personnel, McDonald and his attorney considered that it would be appropriate to take action necessary to prevent precipitous action by the FHA before the affected industries had an opportunity to study the problem further, to propose alternatives, and to determine whether any further action was necessary on the part of FHA. Alternatives available to the industry were to take no action at all; to exert, through Congress, political pressure on the FHA to take no further action; to request FHA to hold industry-wide hearings; to have an industry-wide meeting with FHA to discuss the matter further; to exert Congressional pressure to have FHA delay enactment of standards changes until the industry had studied the matter further, or to rely upon a combination of these alternatives.

At the time that the plywood industry and other associations were considering what action they should take, McDonald was wondering where the pressure for the change was coming from. Personnel at FHA advised McDonald that the code authorities in San Francisco were urging that the FHA make the standard applicable there universal throughout the nation. When McDonald mentioned this to other members of the industry, some expressed doubt, stating that there had been pressure of this type for fire-retardant standards for quite some time. Mr. Adams of the Abercrombie Plywood Company said he had observed that FHA had been trying to impose testing standards upon plywood used for decorative purposes for a long time, and that this could be one way of attempting to set standards for decorative materials in an FHA-insured home. Mr.

Brown of Baker Plywood Company expressed the thought that perhaps the pressure for this change was coming not from the fire code people in San Francisco upon the head of FHA, but was coming rather from the gypsum people and others who made wall paneling which was competitive with hardwood plywood and was losing its market to hardwood plywood and similar laminated material. Mr. Charles, from a related trade association, mentioned to the group that there were some Congressmen who had been exerting pressures upon the Federal Housing Administration to impose tighter standards concerning fire-retardant factors. Mr. Baker said "this proves my point that perhaps the gypsum people or somebody else with whom we are competing are trying to do this to get us out of this market." These conversations took place at a meeting where both related and dissimilar associations, industries and companies were discussing what should be done. These industries and associations were concerned because they felt that while the FHA's motives—to reduce loss of life in home fires—were appropriate, it was not attacking the basic problem: namely the cause of fires, warnings, and means of exit from buildings.

The Federal Government and the Sale of Cranberries [1]

On Monday, November 9, 1959 Arthur S. Flemming, Secretary of Health, Education, and Welfare, held a special press conference in Washington, D.C., at which he "urged that no further sales be made of cranberries and cranberry products produced in Washington and Oregon in 1958 and 1959 because of their possible contamination. . . ." (See Appendix A.) This action was taken at the request of the Food and Drug Administration, a division of Dr. Flemming's department, because of the discovery of residual quantities of aminotriazole, a chemical weed killer alleged to cause cancer in rats, in some berries from that area.

In the question period which followed the reading of his prepared statement, the Secretary stated that he appreciated the seriousness of the step he had taken, but that the Pure Food and Drug Act required him to disseminate such information whenever there was an imminent danger to health. When asked how a buyer of cranberries, canned or fresh, is to tell whether or not they came from the Pacific Northwest and were grown in the years in question, the Secretary stated that the industry and his department would try to work out a coding system, but that at the moment there was no way to tell. "If you can't get the information about where and when the berries were grown, don't buy them," he said.

Later in the question period, the Secretary was asked whether one could eat cranberries for Thanksgiving, about two weeks away. In reply he said, "Probably." The reporter then asked if that answer did not contradict his whole statement, and he said: "We take risks every day,

[1] Copyright 1961 by the President and Fellows of Harvard College.

185

such as being hit by a car. On the basis of our evidence, this is a risk, and we are obligated to say so to the American people."

The press conference, and particularly the comments made by Secretary Flemming in the question period, came as a great shock to the officers and members of Ocean Spray Cranberries, Inc., the newly adopted corporate name of the National Cranberries Association. Mr. Ambrose E. Stevens, executive vice president and general manager of the company, had received a call from a press officer in the department late the week before, asking whether Ocean Spray would cooperate in developing a plan to identify and segregate contaminated berries, and he replied that they had been doing so for some time. Late Sunday night, November 8, he received another call saying that the Secretary had called a special press conference for the next morning to inform the public about the danger from contaminated berries.

Mr. Stevens, who was attending a conference in New York, asked if he might be permitted to attend the session with the press, but was told that only newspapermen would be allowed. (He later discovered that his own Washington counsel was present, as well as representatives of the companies making the chemical.) He asked for a delay, but this too was denied. He immediately called Mr. George C. P. Olsson of Plymouth, Massachusetts, the elected president of Ocean Spray. Mr. Olsson, an attorney and for many years active in Massachusetts Republican politics and former Clerk of Plymouth County, called Congressman Hastings Keith, a first-term Representative whose district included the main cranberry growing area, and Senator Leverett Saltonstall. He urged them to telephone Secretary Flemming and try to persuade him to call off, or at least to delay, the conference.

In addition, Mr. Olsson himself talked to the Secretary and FDA Commissioner George Larrick outlining to them the potential damage the impending announcement could do and reminding them that Ocean Spray, which accounted for more than 75 per cent of the cranberries processed and sold in the country, had been cooperating fully with the department in this problem for some time. Though he talked for half an hour, he was unable to convince Dr. Flemming to delay the announcement for the 48 hours he requested—the Secretary felt it was too late since all the arrangements had been made for complete TV and press coverage—but he did secure an agreement that the Secretary would limit his warning to West Coast berries, which represent about 10 per cent of Ocean Spray's supply, if Mr. Olsson would impound all the 1959 West Coast crop at once for further testing. This Mr. Olsson agreed to do. Neither Senator Saltonstall nor Congressman Keith were any more successful in their efforts to dissuade Dr. Flemming from proceeding with his plan.

Mr. Olsson and Mr. Stevens were especially apprehensive about the impact of the Secretary's statement, even with the proviso that he discuss only berries grown in Washington and Oregon, because they recognized that about two-thirds of their total annual sales would be made during the next six weeks. Though Ocean Spray had attempted to create more of a year-round market for their product, and had been making some progress in their efforts, they were still heavily dependent on the holiday season for their annual income. Up until the time of the press conference, they had reason to be much encouraged; their production was completed on all 1958 berries and September and October had both represented record months for shipments with 1.2 million cans going out in September alone.

They further recognized that retail grocers at 275,000 outlets and 4,000 wholesale warehouses had approximately four million cases of their merchandise on hand, the largest stock of their goods the trade had ever had on their shelves. The fresh fruit sales, also, were doing extremely well; the 1959 sales were between 25 per cent and 30 per cent ahead of the 1958 shipments for the same period. It appeared that their aggressive two-year marketing program and the $1.3 million they had spent in advertising during 1959, and the $35 million spent since 1952, was about to pay off. Consequently, when they read the reports of the press conference on Monday afternoon and saw the newspaper and television reaction to Secretary Flemming's sensational announcement, they were extremely concerned about the future of their $50 million industry and the 1,400 growers and their families who depended upon it.

The cranberry industry goes back to the early 1600's in the United States. By the middle of the last century, it was firmly established in the five states where the berries can be grown: Massachusetts, New Jersey, Wisconsin, Washington and Oregon. By 1959, the annual crop was 125,-300,000 pounds, with a value to growers of about $15 million.

The 1,400 cranberry growers in the country have an investment of about $80 million in their land and equipment; the investment in processing facilities, usually grower-owned through cooperative marketing associations, is about $7 million. Net sales for the year ending May 31, 1959, were some $35 million, thus averaging about $1 for every $3 of fixed investment. These growers faced the usual agricultural risks, plus the fact that their perishable fruit had a highly seasonal market.

Nearly 50 per cent of the berries grown in the country come from Massachusetts; Wisconsin accounts for about 30 per cent, New Jersey for 10 per cent, and Oregon and Washington together for about 10 per cent.

About 40 per cent of any given crop is sold as fresh berries in the year in which they are harvested; the balance is used primarily as canned cranberry sauce, although other products including juice, relish, a cordial and syrup account for some of its sales.

In 1959 the 1,400 individuals, companies or partnerships raising cranberries had holdings ranging from under an acre to 700 acres. This group is a fairly stable one, with an average time in the industry of some twenty years. A large majority of all the growers were members of cooperatives, as defined by the U. S. Department of Agriculture as follows:

> An agricultural cooperative association is a business organization, usually incorporated, owned and controlled by member agricultural producers, which operates for the mutual benefit of its members or stockholders, as producers or patrons, on a cost basis after allowing for the expenses of operation and maintenance and any other authorized deductions for expansions and necessary reserves.

In 1959 Ocean Spray was the largest cooperative and handled 75 per cent of the total production and 75 per cent or more of the sales. The remaining growers marketed their products through smaller cooperatives, independent cooperatives, independent sales agencies and in some instances, directly to commercial canners. The membership in the Ocean Spray cooperative was on the basis of 100 per cent Marketing Agreement signed for or entered into for a period of one year. At the end of any given contract year, the grower was free to market his crop through any available outlet.

Ocean Spray was organized in 1930 under the Capper-Volstead Law, which authorized the formation of agricultural cooperatives and gave them certain exemptions from the general provisions of the antitrust laws. It had marketing, research and processing facilities and devoted a considerable amount of its attention to promoting the use of cranberries throughout the year.

The Use of Aminotriazole

The controversy over the use of aminotriazole as a weed killer for cranberries and other agricultural products has a long history, as do the efforts of Ocean Spray to control and police it.

Aminotriazole is a synthetic chemical developed by the Amchem Company of Ambler, Pennsylvania and licensed by them to the American Cyanamid Company of New York. Together, these two companies hold an exclusive patent on the chemical. At the time of Secretary Flemming's press conference, the herbicide was widely used on a number of crops including cranberries, and was readily available at garden shops. In Massachusetts, only 25 per cent of the total sales of aminotriazole were made to the cranberry growers. In addition to its use as a weed killer by agricultural enterprises, the chemical was frequently employed as a spray to kill poison ivy, brambles, or grass along public roads.

From the standpoint of the cranberry growers, the chemical was highly desirable. In the first place, it was extremely selective and killed weeds which they had found particularly difficult to eliminate. Secondly, it was inexpensive; instead of $150 an acre which they had to pay for petroleum products, aminotriazole did a better job for $15 an acre.

Apparently it first came to general notice in 1955, when Amchem proposed to the Pesticides Regulation Branch of the Department of Agriculture, which must approve such preparations along with appropriate instructions for their use, that it be registered for use in controlling perennial weeds in pastures and noncrop areas. The department examined available research, and accepted a label for registration in March 1956 for use on noncrop lands but not on pastures.

A year later (March 1957), after it had conducted further research, Amchem asked that it be given a label which would allow use of aminotriazole on cranberries, corn, soybeans, and in apple orchards. The USDA then wrote the FDA asking it to comment on the data submitted by the companies in support of this application, which was on a nonresidue basis (that is, none of the chemical was to be left on the fruit itself). FDA responded that the chronic toxicity data presented were too meager to warrant conclusions, and counseled against the registration of the chemical. In December, 1957, however, aminotriazole was given a label for corn only. A month later, January, 1958, representatives of the Pesticides Regulation Branch met with representatives of both Amchem and American Cyanamid to discuss the proposed use of the chemical in cranberry bogs and to examine research data bearing on that possibility. On January 28, 1958 the department received letters from the companies submitting a proposed label which provided for the use of the material in bogs—but only in the period of from seven to ten days after the berries were picked. Since the weed killer is mixed with water and soaks into the ground, it gains access to the roots of the cranberry vines. Immediately after the harvest, cranberry vine roots are dormant and do not absorb the water with its herbicidal chemical; after this period of dormancy, the roots become activated and do take up water, which is absorbed into the sap stream of the bog and subsequently reaches the fruit itself.

On January 30, 1958, the Department of Agriculture approved the proposed use of aminotriazole on cranberry bogs, and notified the Food and Drug Administration of its action. A week later, FDA sent a memorandum concurring in the evaluation of the data upon which the approval was based. Later—in October, 1959, or just a month before Secretary Flemming's announcement—USDA accepted a label covering the use of the chemical in apple and pear orchards, so long as the application was made before the fruit forms in the spring and after the harvest.

Both FDA and USDA have responsibilities in the field of pesticides, herbicides, and the purity of foodstuffs. In the case of aminotriazole, as with all other similar chemicals, USDA compiled and reviewed research data from many sources including industry, state experiment stations and the Agricultural Research Service to check on the effectiveness of the material as a weed killer. Its pharmacologists studied the toxicological characteristics, the medical history of the workers that produced it, and anything else which might bear on the need for protection of the consumer. They also considered the matter of possible residue on crops.

The Department of Health, Education and Welfare, operating through the Food and Drug Administration, has the responsibility for taking action if contaminated food is moved in interstate commerce. They make some 1,000 or more seizures a year, which are recorded in official government journals but are not widely publicized. Further, they are charged with the examination of some 40,000 food and drug products, and their 500 field inspectors must keep surveillance over the proper labeling of these items. If illegal or contaminated food or drugs are found, they may ask the Department of Justice to take the steps necessary to make the actual seizures and to prosecute.

Under the provisions of federal legislation, the FDA is required to determine what degree of residue of a pesticide or herbicide is allowable as nontoxic for humans on fruits and vegetables. This amendment to the Food, Drug, and Cosmetic Act was passed in 1954 and is known as the Miller Act. It applies to cranberries as well as to any other agricultural product. To tighten up the Act still further, Congress passed the so-called Delaney Cancer Amendment in 1958 which went into effect fourteen months before Secretary Flemming's announcement. Under the provisions of this legislation, FDA could permit no tolerance whatsoever—in other words, no residue—of any chemical proven to cause cancer in man or animals, regardless of the amount which was necessary to do so. FDA scientists supported this bill because they felt since so little is known about the sources of cancer they would be unable to determine what a safe tolerance of a so-called carcinogen or cancer-producing agent might be.

Thus, when the USDA approves a chemical for use with specific directions, it does so only on the basis that no residue will remain on crops beyond the amount accepted by the FDA. In fact, from a practical standpoint, it makes sure that the residue will be well within the limits set by the Food and Drug Administration. Since no application for the setting of a tolerance had been made to FDA by the companies manufacturing aminotriazole, no acceptable residue had been established; consequently, USDA directions for the use of the chemical were so designed as to prohibit the existence of any residue whatsoever.

Although no formal representations had been made to the Department of Agriculture, the cranberry growers believed that aminotriazole was available for purchase in retail stores at least as early as 1954. In January, 1956, the Food and Drug Administration first learned of the possible use of the chemical on cranberry bogs in New England. Though they had little data on the material, they did know that the plant could absorb it and deposit it on the fruit.

In May of the same year, Ocean Spray printed an extensive article in its publication, the NCA News, explaining the Miller amendment and making clear that it made illegal the use of any insecticide, fungicide, weed killer and rodenticide not approved by the Department of Agriculture. It further described the provisions pertaining to the establishment of tolerances by HEW and the responsibility of the FDA to inspect commodities to make sure that no foodstuffs move into interstate commerce carrying more than the approved tolerance. It also pointed out that test cases had firmly established the liability of the grower, as the user of the chemical, for compliance with the law.

During April and May of 1957, Ocean Spray and the industry journal *Cranberries Magazine* warned growers generally that aminotriazole had not been approved. "If such approval is forthcoming," the articles said, "the authors urge every grower to follow closely the recommendations of the manufacturer and those of the Cranberry Experiment Station both as to the time and amount of the treatments." The experiment station was run and supported by the United States Department of Agriculture, the Commonwealth of Massachusetts and the County of Plymouth, for the research of local agriculture. Ocean Spray officials were very explicit on the illegality of the use of the chemical.

However, it came to the attention of the Ocean Spray authorities that some growers, especially in Washington and Oregon, were, in fact, using the chemical even though it had not yet been approved. Consequently, under date of July 2, 1957, it sent a formal letter to all its members saying that the board of directors had instructed the management to "advise the membership that such application will be at their own risk and that the Association cannot receive berries from vines which have been treated with this product." At the same time FDA investigated a report that the material was being used on New England bogs but discovered that it was only being put on bogs that were not yet bearing or old weedy bogs that would not be harvested.

By September, 1957, Ocean Spray established specific procedures for dealing with the problem. They instructed all plant managers to segregate any berries harvested from vines treated with the chemical, and pay for them. But if they were tested and found to have a residue of aminotriazole, the owner would be expected to reimburse Ocean Spray and the berries were to be destroyed. Under no circumstances were these suspected berries to be made available to the general market.

Investigations by FDA officials of the same reports indicated that 650 acres, or 40 per cent of the total northwest crop under the control of Ocean Spray, had been treated with the chemical. They further learned that some three million pounds of suspected cranberries had been segregated by Ocean Spray plant managers and were being tested. Cranberry association officials were confident that this was the extent of the problem, at least insofar as their growers were concerned. "This industry is so tightly knit," said one official later, "that everyone in it knows what I am going to do tomorrow, never mind today." Furthermore, they were encouraged by the report from one of the west coast managers that an FDA representative had complimented the association on its handling of the problem after a thorough study of the whole situation.

Still another stiff warning went out in the NCA News to all growers in December, 1957, which quoted George P. Larrick, Commissioner of Food and Drugs, as pointing out that any amount of aminotriazole found on cranberries makes them illegal and subject to seizure.

In January, 1958, Ocean Spray conducted a thorough study of the entire situation. They discovered that some 100 growers in Oregon, 150 in Washington, six in Wisconsin, one in New Jersey, and possibly 100 in Massachusetts purchased the material in 1957—or a total of about 20 per cent of their growers, though it did seem possible that only fifty of the Massachusetts people and none of the Wisconsin and New Jersey farmers (where, for some reason, the chemical was ineffective) had actually used aminotriazole. They estimated that some seven million pounds of berries might be involved. In the face of this finding, Mr. Stevens issued a directive that "all berries now in freezers, whether after chemical analyses show traces or no traces, are to be impounded in our freezers and under no circumstances are to be used in any manner, shape or form until further clearance is given." Ultimately, three million pounds out of a total crop of 110 million pounds were held.

Later in the same month, the Department of Agriculture issued its no-residue approved use of the chemical for cranberries, but Ocean Spray took great care to remind its members that this was for the immediate post-harvest period *only*. During March, FDA was similarly reminding growers who inquired that no tolerance had been established so any berries with residue were illegal and subject to seizure. Throughout this whole period, the Cranberry Experiment Station in Wareham, Massachusetts, and Ocean Spray, through its newsletter *Scoop* were constantly warning growers against the unauthorized use of the material. In May and August, for example, the statement was explicitly made that the organization would not accept any berries from vines treated in any way other than that approved by the USDA.

In April, 1958, American Chemical Paint Company applied for a tolerance of 0.7 parts per million for cranberries to the FDA under the Miller Act. The FDA returned the petition, however, saying that it was incomplete and the petitioner acknowledged the fact, requesting suspension of the petition pending completion of toxicity studies.

In a September, 1958, memorandum to Ocean Spray personnel, they were flatly told not to accept any berries from vines where the chemical had been used illegally; if the grower insisted, they were to segregate them for testing and tell him that if any residue was found, he was liable for the costs of storage and testing.

Amchem Products, Inc., (successor to the American Chemical

Paint Company) and American Cyanamid jointly petitioned for a tolerance of one part per million of aminotriazole on apples, pears, and cranberries in February, 1959, and the USDA told the FDA that the requested usage (eight to sixteen pounds per acre during a limited growing time) would reasonably result in the residues as requested. Throughout this spring, Ocean Spray officials felt confident that the requested tolerance would be established and the problem solved.

Much to everyone's surprise, the FDA's Division of Pharmacology concluded as follows in May, 1959: "The requested tolerance of one part per million of aminotriazole on apples, pears, and cranberries should not be established, as the pathological study shows undoubtedly that this compound is a carcinogen." The official FDA summary of the evidence on which this conclusion was based can be found in Appendix B.

Though the companies involved could have disagreed with the decision and asked that the matter be referred to an advisory committee to be selected by the National Research Council, they decided to withdraw the petition, and thus no tolerance was ever officially established.

Ocean Spray officials paid a visit to FDA and, as a result of those conversations, decided that other warnings should be issued to growers in view of the upcoming 1959 crop. Furthermore, during the summer of 1959, association personnel decided that the impounded berries from the 1957 crop would have to be destroyed, and made plans for bulldozing them under the approval of the FDA. By this time, given the findings in regard to the cancer-producing possibilities of the material FDA officials were extremely upset. According to one top official, "this is about as bad a substance as I have ever encountered."

During the ensuing summer and fall, FDA stepped up its efforts to develop a truly sensitive test for the presence of residue, and investigated to find out whether it had been used in 1958 and 1959. By September, they were convinced that a good deal had, in fact, been used in Oregon. In October they accelerated their studies and found what they called "growing evidence of widespread use of aminotriazole in both areas (Washington and Oregon) post-harvest in 1958 and during the 1959 growing season."

In the meantime, Ocean Spray had been developing its own protective procedures. A testing program had been activated, and a special letter went out from Mr. Stevens and Mr. Olsson in September stating that every grower must sign an affidavit under penalties of perjury that he either had not used aminotriazole at all or had used it under the approved conditions. All of their 1,100 growers did sign the statement. The rest of the industry followed Ocean Spray in establishing this procedure. During this period they had been in touch with FDA, explaining their control program and discussing the segregation of suspected lots and the destruction of the impounded 1957 berries. On October 8, Messrs. Stevens and Olsson met with FDA officials in Washington offering their full cooperation, describing the steps taken so far, asking if FDA wanted anything more done, and requesting them to notify Ocean Spray before any further action was taken.

Ultimately, Ocean Spray voluntarily withheld five million pounds of berries from the 1959 crop because of suspected contamination. Actually, when tested, the bulk of these berries proved to be all right. Likewise, 75 per cent of the berries from the impounded 1957 crop showed either no residue or an infinitesimal amount.

However, Ocean Spray was well aware of the accelerated testing program underway by the FDA, and of the provisions of the Delaney Act. Furthermore, they had reason to believe that there might be some friction between USDA and HEW over the matter, though this was subsequently denied by USDA authorities. To Ocean Spray, it appeared that the jurisdictional lines on matters of this kind tended to overlap and they saw this as a potential cause of tension between the two departments. Consequently, wanting to avoid trouble, they sent out a firm directive to all their growers on September 19, 1959, forbidding them to use aminotriazole in any way at any time as a herbicide in cranberry bogs. It seemed that the best way to sidestep any possible difficulty was to eliminate the chemical altogether. The rest of the industry followed suit shortly thereafter.

Given this background, Mr. Stevens and Mr. Olsson were especially upset by Secretary Flemming's action. They were convinced that they had managed to impound virtually all the segregated berries from the 1957 crop. They were further convinced that this fact, well known to their growers, coupled with their repeated warnings had been enough to discourage growers from using the chemical incorrectly during the 1958 growing season (although they had not taken any special action during that year). Therefore, they felt sure that none of the processed goods then on the shelves (the bulk of which came from that crop) had any residue whatsoever. Finally, they doubted that any berries with residue had slipped through their screen from the current harvest.

They were further irritated by the fact that, in effect, the Secretary had cast doubt on all cranberries rather than simply those grown in the Pacific Northwest as he had promised before his press conference. Although the statement was sufficient, he had indicated during the question period that there was no way of telling where berries had been grown whereas, in fact, no Ocean Spray west coast products are ever shipped east of Salt Lake City because of the high costs of freight. Furthermore, every can of processed berries is identified with a code so the year and the location of the plant where they were handled can be ascertained. Ocean Spray officials were angry with Secretary Flemming over this misstatement. They felt that if he had only taken the trouble to consult with them before making his announcement, these and other points could have been cleared up with him and perhaps the TV conference need never have been held.

The press conference set off a flurry of charges and counter-charges, press releases and TV appearances that lasted for a number of weeks, to the intense confusion of the American public. Experts of all kinds lined themselves up on one side or the other of the argument. Everyone from local health authorities and doctors to nationally known figures participated in the argument.

Ocean Spray moved promptly to try to lessen the damage it felt had been done by Secretary Flemming's original statements. Mr. Stevens, who was in New York for a convention of the food industry, issued a press release immediately (see Appendix C) insisting that "to the best of our knowledge all cranberries then available for purchase were free of any dangerous substance." In the next two days, he appeared on six television shows including Dave Garroway's, held a press conference at the offices of Ocean Spray's advertising agency (Batten, Barton, Durstine and Osborne) which was attended by 65 newsmen, sent off a telegram to Secretary Flemming (see Appendix D), and worked with his staff in Ocean Spray and BBD&O personnel to counteract the effect of Flemming's comments.

In addition, he talked over the telephone extensively with FDA Commissioner Larrick and requested a conference with Secretary Flemming, which was set for early the week of November 16. In the meantime, Mr. Olsson was talking to the Senators and Representatives from the five cranberry-producing states in an attempt to see what could be done. This group proved to be extremely cooperative, and soon formed themselves into a committee headed by Congressman Keith to study the situation and search out remedies. On November 11, an offer to help came from another quarter: Agriculture Secretary Ezra Benson issued a statement offering all the assistance possible from his department to the cranberry growers. Ocean Spray officials had reports that Benson, who apparently knew of Flemming's plans in advance, had been trying to get hold of him to discuss it for several days before the announcement as well as afterward, but met with no success.

From the standpoint of the cranberry growers, events moved from bad to worse during the days that followed. City and state health authorities were banning cranberries or warning against them all over the country. The states of Ohio, Illinois, and Washington actually forbade the sale of fresh or processed berries. Cities like Chicago and San Francisco took similar action; Michigan and Kentucky issued stern warnings to housewives against their use. Retailers by the thousands were removing them from the shelves. Departing from usual practice, the Department of Health, Education and Welfare maintained a steady drumfire of news releases about the situation, including the announcement of additional seizures as they occurred. (In the final analysis, about fifteen lots were condemned of the thousands tested, representing less than 1 per cent of the crop which the FDA examined.)

On November 12, Vice President Nixon and Senator John Kennedy, campaigning in Wisconsin with an eye to the spring primary there, made a point of eating cranberries. On November 15, 10,000 citizens of Massachusetts congregated in Plymouth to down 1,000 gallons of cranberry juice as an expression of protest of Flemming's announcement.

Medical specialists on the side of the cranberry growers claimed that one would have to eat up to 15,000 pounds of cranberries a day for many years before any harm could come to them (the average American consumes about one pound a year); that the compound in aminotriazole that was causing the trouble was used medically for treatment of thyroid conditions; that there was no evidence it would cause illness in humans and, in fact, had not done so in the dogs tested by American Cyanamid in connection with their tolerance petition; that a similar compound occurs in many other vegetables, including turnips. (See Appendix E.) For his part, Secretary Flemming got the support of the Associate Director of the National Cancer Institute, of the National Institute of Health, who declared that there was no way of knowing how much of the compound might cause cancer in human beings. In his public statements the Secretary re-emphasized his responsibility to the American public to make the facts known in cases of "imminent danger." He explained that he had been getting questions about the situation for several weeks prior to his press conference, and stories were appearing in west coast newspapers about the situation. Until the seizure of two shipments from the first seven of the 1959 Ocean Spray crop, he was simply planning to commend the industry for the destruction of the contaminated berries and point out the relationship between this action and the Delaney Amendment; however, when he learned of the first seizures and heard from the Seattle FDA office that samples from twelve additional lots showed probable contamination, he decided that Ocean Spray's program was not effective enough and he would have to issue his warning.

The nation as a whole, apparently already somewhat on edge because of public discussions of the dangers in cigarettes, additives of various kinds, and even atomic radiation, indicated that it preferred to be safe rather than sorry, and sales dropped to an appalling extent. The first week of the scare, consumer purchases of processed cranberry products were down 63 per cent, fresh cranberries down 71 per cent and cranberry sauce from Ocean Spray specifically was off 53 per cent from the same week the year before.

Ocean Spray directors and officers met almost immediately after the announcement and decided to reactivate the Cranberry Institute, an organization representing all producers and handlers whose president, Orin Colley, lived in Duxbury, Massachusetts. The organization, which had been relatively dormant for some time, was housed at Ocean Spray offices, the records were kept there, and the secretary-treasurer was an Ocean Spray employee. Contributions were sought, and some $100,000 was made available by the growers to finance the effort to recoup.

On November 16, a delegation from the institute, including Mr. Olsson, visited with HEW and FDA officials and sought to have the Secretary retract his statement which, to their view, condemned and threatened to destroy the entire industry on the basis of a very minor and well-controlled danger. They again traced the efforts made by the industry to police itself; reiterated their conviction that only the smallest percentage of berries, either fresh or processed, then on the market were contaminated and that this degree of contamination could not possibly harm anyone; pointed to the damage that was being done to the industry, especially because of the timing of the announcement; and again urged that a clarifying comment be issued which would restore public confidence in cranberries in time for the Thanksgiving market.

A press conference was then scheduled for November 18 at which the entire problem would be discussed, and the industry was asked to suggest a plan which would protect the public by segregating contaminated from uncontaminated berries. Subsequently, the Secretary decided to substitute an open, public, televised hearing for the press conference, at which anyone could participate. On the morning of the 18th, industry representatives discussed the matter, and the format for the hearing, with Flemming and the meeting itself got underway at 9:30 a.m.

On behalf of the cranberry growers, Mr. Stevens presented a five-point program. (See Appendix F.) He suggested that the industry's current ban on aminotriazole be continued, that their existing segregation plan be continued, that all 1959 berries then in the hands of the primary handlers be tested, that all berries with residue be destroyed, and that the industry continue to do research and cooperate with the government on the problem. On this basis, he asked the Secretary to state that cranberries on the market were safe.

A number of witnesses representing independent producers as well as Ocean Spray endorsed the plan. Following this group, Senators, Congressmen or their representatives appeared or submitted statements urging the Secretary to take steps as quickly as possible to repair the damage. The final participants in the hearings were representatives of various conservationist, homemaking, and wild-life organizations (known to some as the "bird and bunny people") who generally backed the Secretary in his stand. According to the Secretary's office, this latter group felt the same as the majority of the American people; his mail, the office reported, was running 10 to 1 in support of his position.

Unfortunately from the standpoint of the industry, Secretary Flemming ruled that its proposal did not go far enough. Instead, he said that his department would make available special "Approved" seals which could be placed on all processed and fresh berries once the lots from which they came had been tested by approved methods, either by the government or by the processors or distributors.

Since each test cost $25 and took, at that time, some 14 hours, the industry was disappointed, for it did not see any real headway could be made by Thanksgiving time. In effect, the Secretary was requiring that tests be made of goods on hand at every one of the 275,000 retail and 4,000 wholesale locations. Ocean Spray then asked Arthur D. Little, Inc., for an opinion on how long it would take to clear the berries under this plan and how much it would cost. They stated that the expense would run in the neighborhood of $15 million and the project would take some six months.

Following up on Secretary Benson's offer of help, the industry then had an interview with Undersecretary of Agriculture True D. Morse, who expressed interest and concern but could produce no particular program with the exception of an offer to buy up some of the now surplus berries for the school lunch program. In the weeks since the original announcement, a number of similar moves had been made by Mr. Olsson. (See Appendix G.)

During this period and the weeks that followed, the sales situation continued to be catastrophic. The week of November 15, consumer purchases of cranberry sauce were off 79 per cent from the year before, fresh berries were down 83 per cent, and Ocean Spray sauce was down 78 per cent. The next week, the figures were —63 per cent, —64 per cent, and —61 per cent. December 5 showed —56 per cent, —65 per cent, and —54 per cent; December 12: —58 per cent, —75 per cent, and —46 per cent. It was evident that the 1959 crop was going to back up, and the 1958 processed berries were going to clog the market for the 1960 season even if public confidence was restored.

Ocean Spray called on Trendex to find out how extensive the damage caused to public confidence had been. They discovered that:

> 51 per cent of the respondents did not serve cranberry sauce at Thankgiving
>
> Of this group, 91 per cent had served cranberry sauce on previous Thanksgivings
>
> Of the 91 per cent, 55 per cent voluntarily mentioned the cancer scare as the reason for not eating cranberries in 1959
>
> Of this 55 per cent, 47 per cent said they would never serve it again

In a last-ditch effort to save the Christmas business, Ocean Spray launched a crash testing program of their own under the supervision of Arthur D. Little, Inc. After about 845 assays on processed berries taken from all parts of the country and made by independent laboratories had turned up no lots whatsoever of contaminated berries, and 2,111 similar assays by FDA had uncovered only nine lots (representing about 250,000 pounds out of 19 million tested) with any evidence of contamination, Ocean Spray presented another proposal to Secretary Flemming on December 8, 1959. These tests represented at least one assay for 95 per cent of all Ocean Spray produce from all plants from July 10, 1959, through November 1, 1959. (See Appendix H.) They pointed out that this represented less than one-third of 1 per cent and asked that the Secretary permit the "Approved" stamps to be attached to all processed berries. They did not seek clearance for fresh berries pending further testing.

To the industry's great disappointment, their request was rejected, apparently on the basis that there were still some processed goods on shelves which had not been tested, and that so long as any remained the Secretary would not issue a clearance.

This decision, coming about two weeks before Christmas, posed a number of questions for Ocean Spray Cranberries, Inc. The sales losses continued: December 13-19 showed processed berries off 51 per cent from 1958, fresh off 67 per cent, and Ocean Spray sauce down 46 per cent. In the face of these figures, Ocean Spray officials asked themselves:

Is it too late to do something about the Christmas business, or should we make another effort to work out some kind of statement that Flemming would be willing to make? How could we go about getting him to do so? On the other hand, would that simply serve to stir up the scare again, even if it were an essentially positive comment?

Could we use our political influence to get some statement from the White House? How? What kind of statement?

Should we hire a public relations counsel (Mr. Stevens had been exploring this possibility with Ivy Lee and others since the beginning of the scare)? If so, should Ocean Spray or the Cranberry Institute do it?

Should we launch an advertising campaign? Should it be done on behalf of Ocean Spray or the whole industry? What approach should it take?

Should the cranberry industry seek relief from the Federal Government in some way? Should this be through Congressional action, administrative action, or how? What kind of relief can and should we seek?

Should the cranberry industry hire Washington counsel to help with this effort? Their attorney in Washington was competent to handle routine matters but had never had experience with this kind of question before. How should we find the right man?

Are there any allies in terms of trade associations with whom the industry could work on this program?

Up to now we have been fairly gentle with Mr. Flemming. Should we launch an all-out effort to discredit him and get him fired?

Is there some way in which the industry could get real help from the Department of Agriculture who did, after all, bear some of the responsibility here since they had cleared the chemical. What kind of help?

What should we do about retailers and wholesalers who were now insisting upon returning cranberries and cranberry products to Ocean Spray?

Should the industry demand a Congressional investigation of the whole affair in order to air our side of the story? Suppose individual Congressmen show signs of initiating such an investigation, what should our stand be?

In a cooperative of this sort, where members can sell their products to the group or not as they see fit, how might we control the actions of growers more effectively in the future than we have in the past?

Should we push ahead with research on aminotriazole and seek to get it cleared sometime in the future, given its effectiveness and low cost, or should we forget about it permanently?

Is there some program which could be developed to make sure that the industry has the maximum support among press people, columnists, and so on? The industry was disturbed when Drew Pearson referred to "cancer-producing cranberries."

What kind of long-range marketing strategy could we work out to recoup our losses?

How could the industry's relations with the government be improved to guard against this kind of catastrophe befalling us again?

APPENDIX A

For Release at Conclusion
of News Conference

Statement[1]
by
Arthur S. Flemming
Secretary of Health, Education, and Welfare

The Food and Drug Administration today urged that no further sales be made of cranberries and cranberry products produced in Washington and Oregon in 1958 and 1959 because of their possible contamination by a chemical weed killer, aminotriazole, which causes cancer in the thyroid of rats when it is contained in their diet, until the cranberry industry has submitted a workable plan to separate the contaminated berries from those that are not contaminated.

The Food and Drug Administration has already discovered contamination of some of the 1959 crop and is undertaking a check of the 1958 crop.

The Food and Drug Administration will use its normal procedures of investigation and seizure in coping with this problem. In addition, we have the pledge of the national cranberry association (known as Ocean Spray Cranberries, Inc.), to cooperate in every way it can with the Food and Drug Administration to protect consumers. This organization controls about 75 per cent of the crop.

Over three million pounds of cranberries from the 1957 Northwest crop and a small amount from the 1957 Massachusetts crop are now being destroyed because of contamination by the weed killer. This action is being taken voluntarily by the national cranberry association, with the supervisory cooperation of the Food and Drug Administration.

These contaminated berries, about one-third of the Northwestern crop for 1957, are being buried with the use of bulldozers at Albany and Coquille, Oregon, and Centralia and Markham, Washington. It will take until about Christmas to complete the job.

Commissioner Larrick tells me that so far there is no information to implicate 1958 and 1959 cranberries grown in Wisconsin, New Jersey, and Massachusetts, the other principal growing areas. An investigation is nevertheless underway in these areas, Mr. Larrick said, and if evidence of contamination is found, appropriate action will be taken.

In view of what has resulted from the improper use of aminotriazole on cranberry bogs, it is obviously imperative that this chemical *not* be used on any other crops in a way that will leave a residue in or on the produce. Growers should follow meticulously the directions for use on the pesticide label registered with the Department of Agriculture.

The Food and Drug Administration is looking into the situation to determine whether any other crops are contaminated. If residues are found, the information will immediately be made public and appropriate legal action will be taken.

The story on cranberries from the beginning is as follows:

[1] Released at News Conference, Washington, D.C., Monday, November 9, 1959.

The weed killer, aminotriazole, in 1958 was registered by the Department of Agriculture for use on cranberry bogs a few days *after* harvest. Unfortunately, many cranberry growers used the weed killer *prior* to harvest of the 1957 crop. As a matter of fact, I understand that some growers used the pesticide even before the Department of Agriculture had approved directions for its use on cranberry bogs. As a result of the misuse of the chemical, plants took up the aminotriazole and some of it got into the berries.

The contaminated production from the 1957 cranberry crop was voluntarily withheld from the market by the growers, after the Food and Drug Administration refused to establish a tolerance for residues of the weed killer because no tests had been conducted to show what, if any, amount of the chemical would be safe.

Very little checking has been done by the Food and Drug Administration on the 1958 crop, and we are informed that the cranberry association also did little or no checking of that crop. It was believed that the withholding of three million pounds of the 1957 crop from the market, plus the warnings being issued by the association to its members, would prevent any further misuse of the weed killer unless and until a tolerance was established. The 1958 crop was grown, harvested, and marketed while the toxicity studies on the chemical were being conducted by the American Cyanamid Company and the Amchem Company.

In May of this year evaluation of experimental data submitted by the manufacturers was completed, and the conclusion was reached that aminotriazole is a carcinogen. The Food and Drug Administration then began checking on grower spray practices and perfecting the analytical method for detecting residues of the chemical. The national cranberry association likewise again instituted its own system of inspecting growers and holding for analysis all lots from growers where there was any reason to suspect misuse of the weed killer.

Commendable though the association's program is, it is apparently not fully effective.

Examination of the first series of samples from the newly harvested 1959 Northwestern crop has just been completed. Two inter-state shipments out of seven examined so far have been found definitely contaminated. Seizure is being recommended to the Department of Justice on one of these shipments. The other lot containing residues has already been distributed. Preliminary results on ten other lots not yet shipped, and evidence that some other growers have again failed to follow good agricultural practice in use of the weed killer, indicate that we are likely to find additional contaminated lots in the 1959 crop.

Both members and nonmembers of the cranberry association are involved in the lots in question.

In view of the findings on the 1959 Northwestern crop, and the previous history of the 1957 crop, we believe it reasonable to assume that the 1958 crop may also be contaminated.

Because of the implications of this incident in its relation to the safety of our food supply, I am prompted to make the following additional comment.

As the cranberry episode illustrates, the Food and Drug Administration has declined to set any tolerance for any amount of a chemical in foods if the chemical produces cancer when fed to test animals. This principle is set down in the Food Additives Amendment, enacted last year, in a specific provision prohibiting the Food and Drug Administration from setting any tolerance for any such chemical. Even though the earlier Pesticide Amendment, which is applicable to the cranberries, does not contain such a specific prohibition, the same principle has been applied.

The application of this principle is necessary in our opinion because while in theory there may be a minute quantity of a carcinogen which is safe in foods, in actuality our scientists do not know whether this is true or how to establish a safe tolerance.

Therefore, we would oppose any attempt to take the cancer clause out of the Food Additives Amendment, and we will support the inclusion of such a clause in the color bill which is now before the Congress.

Summary of Questions and Answers

During a pause in the reading of the statement, a woman reporter said, "I bought a can of Ocean Spray cranberries. Can there be any danger if they are canned?" To which Flemming replied that he would come back to that later after he finished his statement.

At the end of his prepared statement, Flemming said that he appreciates this is serious action to take but on the basis of evidence developed by Food and Drug, he has no alternative. The Act places responsibility on the Secretary to disseminate information when there is an imminent danger to health.

When asked how a buyer of Ocean Spray is to know which crop the cranberries are from, Larrick said they will try to work out a coding system and make it public. Now they can't tell. Flemming said it is part of the Government's plan to work out methods; they don't assume that it is all contaminated, but they have enough evidence to know that some of the 1959 Northwest crop is contaminated.

The question was then asked: "Won't this prevent people from buying Ocean Spray?" Flemming asked that the question be held until he finished his previous comment. He went on to say that he recognizes that a consumer will have a very real question in his mind about purchasing any of the 1958 or 1959 crop until the plan is submitted. The government may find only a small portion of the crop contaminated. There is a question whether he should have said anything before the plan is worked out, but he has a duty to the public and has no right to sit on information of this kind. He makes this information available to the public even when he knows the public may have difficulty, but if he waits, serious damage may be done.

A question was asked as to how the consumer can tell a northwestern cranberry from others, at which point Larrick mentioned that Ocean Spray is a cooperative controlling about 80 per cent to 85 per cent of the entire crop. Flemming said George C. P. Olsson, Clifford Road, Plymouth, Massachusetts, talked with him by phone and said he would take immediate action and come in with a plan.

He was then asked, Unless the can says Northwest how will any consumer know? and, Shouldn't the warning be: Don't buy any until you know the code? He replied that the government will try to work out a code and let the public know.

Asked about the investigation, he said their investigators are not out; they alerted them over the weekend. He said there is no evidence of contamination for New Jersey, Massachusetts, and Wisconsin. Flemming then asked if Northwest cranberries are rare, there is no other way to give information to the consumers as to where the berries come from, to which Larrick responded that they are not rare and must get that information from the industry.

Flemming then went on to say that if the industry presents a plan to show their origin and to distinguish between contaminated and uncontaminated berries, the government will release that information immediately, with their evaluation, and maybe call another press conference, but he feels he must get this information out to the press now, although their conclusions are not final.

Asked about 1957 berries, Larrick said they found 10 ppm. give rats cancer; the 1957 contaminated berries were destroyed; FDA destroyed about 3 per cent, about 3 million out of about 100 million, or about 12 per cent of the Northwest crop.

Asked whether fresh packaged cranberries are marked by state of origin, Flemming said he thinks some are. Asked whether they are all right if marked from Eastern states, he said HEW has no evidence that they are not all right.

Asked when he asked the industry for a plan, he said the industry has been working on this for some time, but apparently missed some contaminated berries.

Asked why no publicity in 1957 when this first came up, he said there was a lot of publicity on the West Coast criticizing Food and Drug for holding up berries.

As to other foods, he said his statement recognizes this possibility and Food and Drug is looking into it. The cranberry people say this is the case and asked why they got singled out, but if there is a health hazard, they can't wait until they look into other foods.

Asked if this is timed now because of Thanksgiving, he said no, they just got the information on the 1959 crop the last part of last week and they will try to get clean berries for Thanksgiving.

Asked how the consumer tells the difference between cans on the shelf and whether she is advised not to buy until this is worked out, Flemming said he stands by the first paragraph in his statement. If she can't get the information, to be on the safe side, don't buy. What the scientists say is, here is a chemical which under certain conditions produced cancer in rats. Can they establish a tolerance? They don't know, therefore can't establish one, so the only thing the government can do is prohibit the use of the chemical under certain circumstances. The label makes it clear to use it after harvest, but it has obviously been used before harvest because the evidence can be found in the cranberry crop. When the time comes that FDA scientists can set a tolerance they should go to Congress and ask for authority to do so. Meanwhile HEW will protect the public; they have the authority even without the Delaney Amendment and will apply it across the board.

He added that there are those who will debate that because cancer is found in a rat it will develop in man, but no one has proved that. When HEW has evidence that it has developed in animals, it can do no less than to inform the public.

As for the label on the chemical, he said that if HEW finds evidence the language on the label should be changed, it will be. Research has not brought them to a point where they can establish a tolerance. Asked whether there is a lack of coordination between HEW and Agriculture and about personal error by users, Larrick responded that there is no lack of coordination, that we will always have pesticides, for nonfood uses and in greenhouses, for example, and can't prohibit them but must educate people for their proper use. Flemming added the present label says, "don't use before harvest," which is completely consistent with the evidence, but new evidence may lead to a change in the label. This is not an admission that the label is not all it should have been, it was okay on the evidence then available.

Asked why growers in all these states made the same mistake, and whether they were advised by "the company" to use this chemical Larrick answered that no company advised it, but the growers learned it was an efficient weed killer. Flemming added that about 80 per cent to 85 per cent of total production belongs to the co-op.

One female reporter asked whether he is setting a precedent which could be applied to cigarettes. Flemming said cigarettes are not a food, so the reporter pointed out that lipstick is controlled. Flemming said the latest information on cigarettes is being incorporated into an article for a professional journal and will be released to the press.

Asked for more information on where HEW is investigating now for other crops, Flemming said they are going back to the office now and work out a program and some investigation is already underway.

Asked about 10 ppm. being toxic and the residue found in cranberries, he said 1/5 to 1/10 of that, and a member of his staff said 1/10 ppm.

Flemming was then asked whether you could eat cranberries safely for Thanksgiving and he said probably.

Then asked whether that doesn't contradict his whole statement, he said we take risks every day, such as that of being hit by a car, but on the basis of FDA evidence this is a risk, and they are obligated to say so to the American people.

He was finally asked about the system of voluntary compliance and whether this information wouldn't get to the people quicker if he had taken the matter into court before, to which he replied that the technique was just perfected and they couldn't have gone into court, but now they have a method to detect its presence and can take cases to court. There is evidence that the system is not 100 per cent foolproof.

APPENDIX B

U.S. Department of Health,
Education and Welfare

Food and Drug Administration

Scientific Background for Food and Drug Administration Action Against Aminotriazole in Cranberries

The Food and Drug Administration's action regarding aminotriazole in cranberries is based principally on research reported by the American Cyanamid Company in a petition for a one part per million tolerance for residues of this pesticide in cranberries.

The Food and Drug Administration found in its own laboratories on feeding high dosages of the weed killer to rats for 19 weeks that there was stimulation of abnormal growth of the thyroid gland. FDA scientists therefore suggested to research workers of the American Cyanamid Company that particular attention be given to the effect of the chemical on the thyroid. FDA scientists consulted with the American Cyanamid Company researchers as the studies progressed. When the studies were completed results were submitted to the Food and Drug Administration along with the petition for a tolerance. Food and Drug Administration scientists reviewed all the data carefully, and examined some of the tissue slides made from the thyroid of the treated rats and of the untreated control rats in order to confirm the type of injury reported.

Following is a brief resume of the research done by the American Cyanamid Company as submitted in its petition for a tolerance:

Acute toxicity studies were done in rats and cats. The lethal dose by mouth for half of the experimental animals (rats) was found to be 25 grams per kilo of body weight.

Subacute toxicity studies on rats showed an increase in size of the thyroid after feeding at 50, 250, and 1,250 parts per million in the drinking water for 106 days.

Chronic feeding studies were conducted on rats and dogs but tests were terminated on dogs at the end of one year. No effects on the thyroid in dogs were reported. Rats were fed for two years at 100, 50, and 10 parts per million, thyroid tumors also appeared in decreasing number. A "no effect" level was not established. In the light of these findings, reported by the petitioner, aminotriazole is a carcinogen. In addition, it is a highly potent antithyroid drug.

It has not been determined scientifically whether it is possible to establish a safe level of use for a carcinogen in human food. This is reflected in the law which now requires safety of pesticides and food additives of all kinds to be scientifically established before they are introduced into the public food supply. In the food additive law, passed in 1958, Congress dealt specifically with carcinogens and prohibited their addition to foods.

It may be noted that without a no effect level, FDA could not scientifically establish a safe tolerance for any chemical, even one which was not a carcinogen.

APPENDIX C

Monday, November 9, 1959

Statement
by
Ambrose E. Stevens,
Executive Vice President and General Manager,
Ocean Spray Cranberries, Inc.

First, we can state that to the best of our knowledge all cranberries in groceries and super markets today are pure and wholesome and untainted by any dangerous substance.

Second, we are shocked that the United States Government has made public what we consider an inflammatory statement concerning possible contamination of cranberries by a weed killer approved by the Department of Agriculture. This comes surprisingly at a time when we had already taken precautionary measures to prevent any allegedly contaminated products from reaching the housewife.

This had been a matter of a cooperative discussion between the Food and Drug Administration and ourselves since midsummer. Any crop suspected of contamination has already been isolated from the market. Moreover, on September 18 all Ocean Spray growers were instructed to discontinue any use whatsoever of the aminotriazole compound.

The "Plan" referred to in the government statement to separate and destroy any contaminated crops has already been put into effect. We are just as much interested as the government in the welfare of the millions of people who eat cranberries.

Finally, we are prepared to destroy any part or all of our 1959 crop should research indicate the presence of any aminotriazole.

In view of our sincere actions in the public interest, we can only deplore this attempt to create headlines at the expense of the confidence of the American people.

AMBROSE E. STEVENS,
EXECUTIVE VICE PRESIDENT
AND GENERAL MANAGER,
OCEAN SPRAY CRANBERRIES, INC.

APPENDIX D

TELEGRAM

November 10, 1959

HONORABLE ARTHUR S. FLEMMING
SECRETARY OF HEALTH, EDUCATION, AND WELFARE
WASHINGTON, D. C.

IN JUSTICE TO THOUSANDS OF CRANBERRY GROWERS AND DIS-TRIBUTORS AND MILLIONS OF CONSUMERS, WE DEMAND THAT YOU TAKE IMMEDIATE STEPS TO RECTIFY THE INCALCULABLE DAMAGES CAUSED BY YOUR ILL-INFORMED AND ILL-ADVISED PRESS STATEMENT YESTERDAY.

UNLESS THIS IS DONE WITHOUT DELAY, YOU WILL CAUSE FINAN-CIAL DISTRESS TO MANY FARMERS AND GREAT DAMAGE TO A FINE AMERICAN INDUSTRY . . . AND ALL UNNECESSARILY.

YOU ARE KILLING A THOROUGHBRED IN ORDER TO DESTROY A SINGLE FLEA.

YOU MUST KNOW THERE IS NOT A SHRED OF EVIDENCE THAT A SINGLE HUMAN BEING HAS BEEN ADVERSELY AFFECTED BY EAT-ING ALLEGEDLY CONTAMINATED CRANBERRIES. YOU MUST KNOW THERE IS NOT A SINGLE BIT OF EVIDENCE THAT AMINOTRI-AZOLE CAUSES CANCER IN HUMAN BEINGS.

YOU MUST KNOW THERE IS NOTHING TO INDICATE THAT A CAN OR BOTTLE OR PACKAGE OF AMINOTRIAZOLE-CONTAMINATED CRANBERRIES IS ON ANY GROCER'S SHELF, IN ANY DISTRIBUTOR'S WAREHOUSE OR ANY PACKER'S PLANT.

YOU MUST KNOW THAT RESPONSIBLE PEOPLE IN THE CRAN-BERRY INDUSTRY, WORKING AND COOPERATING CLOSELY WITH THE FOOD AND DRUG ADMINISTRATION, HAVE ALREADY TAKEN EXTREME PRECAUTIONS TO PREVENT ANY CONTAMINATED BER-RIES FROM REACHING THE MARKET, AND THAT ALL BERRIES ABOUT WHICH THERE IS THE SLIGHTEST SUSPICION OF CON-TAMINATION HAVE BEEN AND ARE BEING SET ASIDE AND DE-STROYED.

> AMBROSE E. STEVENS
> EXECUTIVE VICE PRESIDENT
> AND GENERAL MANAGER
> OCEAN SPRAY CRANBERRIES, INC.
> HANSON, MASSACHUSETTS

APPENDIX E

Statements of Experts

Dr. Edwin B. Astwood, Senior Physician at New England Center Hospital and Professor of Medicine at Tufts College, stated "The weed killer (aminotriazole) contains a compound which affects the Thyroid gland, it inhibits its action, the remedy has been used in medicine for fifteen years and in no way causes cancer. The quantity of this chemical in cranberries would be minute and in no way cause any trouble . . . let alone cancer. A similar compound occurs naturally in vegetables, mustard, cabbage, turnips and broccoli, and no one refrains from eating these vegetables because of this compound."

Dr. Theodore R. Flanagan, University of Vermont scientist and an agronomist said it is practically impossible "short of suicidal intent" for a human to absorb a harmful dose of aminotriazole. "A person probably would have to eat between 75 and 100 pounds of the chemical to do serious damage," he said, adding, "one could not eat that much of anything in a short time without harmful effect."

Dr. Boyd Shaffer, toxicologist of New York, says, "even if the berries were badly tainted, they are not harmful to human beings. A person would have to eat 15,000 pounds of cranberries a day for many years before he would suffer any ill effects from the consumption of the residue."

Mr. H. C. E. Johnson, Editor-in-Chief of THE CHEMICAL WEEKLY, has this to say . . . "Mr. Flemming's statement may indicate the basic error in current administration of the Federal Food, Drug and Cosmetic Act. There is no question that the law gives Health, Education and the Food and Drug Administration the right to seize adulterated foods in interstate commerce, but this is not the worry for companies subject to FDA regulation. Their basic worry is the misuse of 'government by publicity.' Let's look at it specifically as it affects cranberries, and generally as it affects the safety of the nation's food supplies. On the specific level, of the 337 lots of cranberries on which test results had been announced on the day this column went to press, only four were shown to contain any aminotriazole. (And to get the actual weight of the herbicide that caused carcinogenic reactions in rats, a person would have to eat two quarts/day for 25 years; to get the same per cent of body weight, a person must eat more than 15,000 pounds of cranberries a day for a comparable period.)

"To us, the discovery that 80,000 pounds of the 4.8 million pounds of cranberries tested has even this low level of adulteration does not constitute a matter of wide public concern. The fact that Secretary Flemming and his publicity men created the uproar they did is most assuredly a misuse of 'government by publicity.'

"The general question of the safety of the nation's food supply is more complex. Unwarranted scares such as this makes it ever more difficult for food producers to keep the public's deserved confidence."

William L. Money of the Memorial Center for Cancer and Allied Diseases, affiliated with Memorial Hospital—James Ewing Hospital, Department of Hospitals, City of New York—Strang Cancer Prevention Clinic—Sloan-Kettering Institute for Cancer Research—Sloan-Kettering Division, Cornell University Medical College, writes . . .

"For the past fifteen years, we have been interested in the factors involved in growth and function of the thyroid gland. As part of this continued study, we have investigated some of the factors responsible for thyroid hypertrophy and tumor production. Along with several other investigators, we showed many years ago that compounds like thiouracil (generally called 'thiourea-like compounds') when given in adequate doses to rats for extended periods of time will induce tumors of the thyroid gland. We have never studied the response of the rat thyroid to aminotriazole. However, on the basis of chemical structure, one would predict that aminotriazole would act as an antithyroid agent, produce thyroid hypertrophy and ultimately result in the development of thyroid tumors. Examination of the slides Dr. Shaffer had supports this postulate.

"In our studies with thiouracil (a similar chemical), we have not felt that the thyroid tumors produced in the presence of the compound were true cancers. Moreover, we have not obtained evidence in our studies that they were malignant. Other investigators have concluded that their studies, similarly done, resulted in the formation of thyroid cancers. This in part becomes a question of terminology, definition or personal opinion. Whether our opinion is correct or that of others is a question which cannot be resolved at the present time.

"There are chemical compounds present naturally in many foods which will produce the development of thyroid tumors. For example, cabbage, turnips, kale and soy beans all contain compounds which act in a similar manner. Moreover, rats maintained on a diet low in iodine for long periods of time will also develop thyroid tumors similar to those induced by the so-called 'antithyroid' drugs. It is quite likely that any compound which interferes with thyroid hormone production would under proper conditions result in thyroid tumor production. It is also probable that the absence of any chemical needed for thyroid hormone synthesis would do the same thing. If this is true, and it certainly is in iodine deficient intake, it is difficult to understand how an absence of a substance could be 'carcinogenic.'

"The slides which Dr. Shaffer had did not show anything surprising. The types of tumors, if not identical, were similar to thyroid tumors which we have observed in many experimental animals treated with thiouracil. Although it is difficult to quantitiate with the limited amount of information available, I had the impression that aminotriazole was not as effective in inducing large tumors as is thiouracil. Furthermore, there appeared to be less follicular hypertrophy in the uninvolved thyroid tissue than would have occurred with thiouracil. In other words, I had the impression that aminotriazole is a weaker antithyroid drug and not as potent a goitrogen as thiouracil. This, however, could be a dosage difference and such a comparison would then be unfair. My opinion, based on our observations with thiouracil, is that these tumors are benign and are not true cancers. Again I should add that others would hold some of the thyroid lesions to be cancers. The question of interpretation probably could not be entirely resolved within the framework of our present knowledge."

APPENDIX F

Cranberry Industry Plan Submitted
November 18, 1959
(Excerpts from record of hearing conducted by Secretary Flemming)

MR. STEVENS: Good morning, Mr. Secretary.

SECRETARY FLEMMING: Mr. Stevens, delighted to hear from you.

MR. STEVENS: Good morning, Mr. Commissioner.

MR. LARRICK: Good morning.

MR. STEVENS: Thank you for making it possible to be here today.

By way of identification, I am Ambrose E. Stevens, Executive Vice President and General Manager of the Ocean Spray Cranberries, Inc., which is a wholly owned farmers' cooperative representing 75 per cent of the cranberry growers in America. In my capacity I have consistently told our farmers that our only function is to attempt to secure for them the best possible return for their efforts and investments consistent with the discharge of our duties to the public.

Among the most important of our duties to the public is the responsibility of providing them with the finest cranberries possible—pure, wholesome, and nutritious, at prices which represent a good value.

From this standpoint, Mr. Secretary, your views and our views and objectives join, in that we both share the responsibility of providing our American public with a product which they may buy with confidence, not only because it is enjoyable and a part of our great American tradition, but also, because this truly American fruit is nourishing and without defect. Cranberries contain fourteen valuable vitamins and minerals, and more pure fruit pectin than found in any other fruit, including apples, oranges and bananas.

These facts have been long established. Until November 9, now known as "Black Monday" in the cranberry industry, Americans have been regularly enjoying cranberry products ever since the Pilgrims arrived at Cape Cod.

Then out of the blue came a statement in the press which coupled cranberries with a bad disease. This created a wave of fear hysteria which swept America and has not yet subsided. Too many Americans like myself tend to believe too much of what we read in the newspapers, hear on the radio, see and hear on television. The fact that these statements reach the public through mass media from a well-regarded public servant, high in official government service, has lent them additional credence.

I am not here this morning, Mr. Secretary, to argue the merits of the statements made by you. I have consistently said, since that black day, though, that I thought the announcement was ill-advised.

Nevertheless, I realize and respect the duties that you, in your high office, have to perform. And I appreciate that perhaps the statements you made were in discharge of your consideration of your public responsibilities. With this I have no quarrel. Nor do I believe that you had any full realization of the wave of fear hysteria that your announcement was sure to cause.

This morning I am here on behalf of the cranberry industry to present to you a constructive plan for the solution of the problem. The challenge is this—how do the American people buy cranberries with confidence and enjoy them; not only for Thanksgiving this year, but for every month in succeeding years to come?

The plan I now propose is in a number of stages. Several steps in this plan have already been taken, as you will see. Whether you or your staff were aware of them I have no way of knowing. But I am happy to tell you what we have done, what we are doing, and what we propose to do.

Mr. Secretary, let me present you with a copy of the plan.

SECRETARY FLEMMING: Thank you very much.

MR. STEVENS: I should like to read the plan, Mr. Secretary, and then make some comments upon it.

The following plan submitted to the Secretary of Health, Education, and Welfare, on behalf of the cranberry producers and marketing agencies of the United States is designed to restore confidence in the buying public and to permit the normal movement of cranberries in the channels of commerce with full and complete protection to the public. It consists of five parts, some of which have already been put into effect in whole or in part, and the balance of which are to be made operative promptly upon approval by the Secretary. These steps are as follows:

1. Continuation of the ban on all use of aminotriazole until the pertinent facts concerning it, including its effects on human beings, have been determined. This does not imply that use of this chemical is harmful but only that as yet enough is not known about it, and until more is known, it seems wise to refrain from using it. The industry has already voluntarily adopted this ban.

2. Segregation by the primary handlers or marketing agencies under appropriate safeguards of all cranberries which there is any evidence to believe may contain any aminotriazole. This plan of segregation was put into effect at the beginning of the 1959 harvest and under it a total of approximately 4,800,000 pounds of cranberries have been impounded.

3. Testing of all cranberries of the 1959 crop now in the possession of the primary handlers of the major distributors by appropriate methods and sampling procedures, consistent with the methods and procedures used by the Pure Food and Drug Administration.

4. Destruction of all cranberries found by such tests to contain any residue of aminotriazole or the impounding thereof under appropriate safeguards until final determination as to their proper disposition.

5. Continuation of scientific research and cooperation with governmental agencies, national and local, to insure uninterrupted delivery to the public of an adequate supply of pure and wholesome cranberries and cranberry products.

Before taking each step in detail, may I again define the purpose of this plan. The purpose of this plan is to have cranberries on every American table for Thanksgiving by making it possible for everybody in America to buy cranberries with complete confidence.

The operation of the plan calls for continued close cooperation and collaboration between the cranberry industry and the Food and Drug Administration of your Department, which has been consistently in effect now for quite a long time.

I have, Mr. Secretary, the highest regard for the personnel of the Food and Drug Administration, and I regard them as dedicated public servants to the American people. I am in a unique position to appreciate and sympathize with their philosophy and their attitudes because I, myself, was once a public servant here in Washington.

Step No. 1. Because of the controversial nature of aminotriazole, approved for use on cranberries by the U.S. Department of Agriculture for postharvest application but denied tolerance of any degree of residue by the Food and Drug Administration, we wrote our farmer members on September 18, 1959, directing them never to use this chemical compound on their cranberry properties in any manner, shape or form, even though it had and still has the approval for postharvest use of the United States Department of Agriculture. This prohibition is still in effect and will continue in effect until a firm determination of the facts is made as to the absorption of this herbicide and its possible effect on human beings.

Before I present Step No. 2, let me explain again that cranberries are grown in Massachusetts, New Jersey, Wisconsin, Washington and Oregon. The harvest of the first berries usually occurs in Massachusetts about the middle of September. The harvest of berries in other areas takes place in October and the early part of November. Because some of our farmer members did use this herbicide in question, we notified all of them that they would be required to sign an affidavit under penalty of perjury as a condition of receipt of their berries by us that they had not used aminotriazole; or if they had used it, such use was only as prescribed by the United States Department of Agriculture's approved postharvest manner. By "postharvest" let me say again what we mean by that. It may be applied to cranberry bogs seven to nine days after completion of the harvest.

As Step No. 2, we did not stop there. Where we had reason to believe that any cranberry bogs had been exposed to this compound because of its use by highway departments on roadsides, as Mr. Olsson mentioned previously or any other manner, if we believed there had been such an exposure, we had the berries from these growing bogs set aside, and we still have them set aside. They are impounded with a rigid embargo until we have an opportunity to chemically test these berries for any residue of the herbicide. These berries are deferred before even placing them on the market. We have an aggregate at the moment of 4,800,000 pounds from the 1959 crop so set aside for the reasons stated.

We will be testing this supply, the set-aside berries, over a period of many, many months, to determine which ones should be destroyed and which ones should be offered to the public.

To do this, we have secured the assistance of a well-known authority on statistics, Dr. Fred Stephan of Princeton University, recommended to us by the Food and Drug Administration, to assist us in our sampling techniques of any questionable berries, so that, when assays are made, we and the Food and Drug Department will have full assurance that no questionable berries are ever offered to the public. The Food and Drug Administration has also very kindly offered us the benefit of their own sampling techniques.

In Step No. 3, because the Food and Drug Administration indicated serious concern over some of the berries grown in the States of Oregon and Washington, we have impounded the entire crops from those areas until we have a chance to study them further and they are still under embargo from these two States as well as others. Any berries containing any residue whatsoever of the herbicide will be destroyed.

Step No. 4. It should be explained that because of the traditional use of cranberries by American families at Thanksgiving and Christmas, a large part of the cranberry crop is enjoyed at this happy season. Because the harvest of cranberries comes so late in the year, cranberries harvested in the fall of one year are usually not consumed by the public until the subsequent fall; that is, of berries that are in canned goods form. This applies to the 65 million cans of cranberry sauce on grocery store shelves in America right now. At least they were there until Black Monday, November 9. These canned goods were made from cranberries from the 1958 crop. In addition to that, to them, there are fresh cranberries on the market packed in bags and boxes, totalling about 10 million pounds which came from the 1959 crop.

Neither the Food and Drug Administration nor ourselves have any reason to believe that the 1958 crop was improperly treated in any manner with the questionable herbicide, nor that cranberries from this crop now on the market in the form of canned cranberries and bottled cranberry juice are anything but wholesome and pure.

The very careful restrictions made by us on fresh berries also indicates that the 10 million pounds of fresh cranberries in grocery stores today are entirely pure.

The various tests made on the 1958 crop by the Food and Drug Administration and by us reveal not one single analysis showing that the cranberries differ from those of the past, pure, wholesome and nutritious.

Therefore, Mr. Secretary, as Part 4 of this plan, I request from you, sir, a declaration to the American people that cranberries now in grocery stores are completely wholesome and free from blemish of any sort, and I implore you, sir, to implement this statement by making a suitable announcement through the press, through the radio and the television, so as to reverse the trend of fear hysteria caused by the announcement of November 9.

Step No. 5 calls for further testing of the 1959 crop in full collaboration and cooperation with the Food and Drug Administration, and we will certainly be glad to see that this continues as long as it is necessary.

Mr. Secretary, I believe that you want the American people to have cranberries for Thanksgiving and, Mr. Secretary, we want the American people to have cranberries for Thanksgiving and in the months to come. In view of the thorough precautions voluntarily taken by us as enumerated above, I see no reason why our mutual desire for the American public cannot be achieved.

When you approve this plan, Mr. Secretary, we will be truly protecting the American food suppply and meeting the demand for a traditional American friut.

Respectfully submitted, sir.

SECRETARY FLEMMING: Thank you very much, Mr. Stevens.

Could I ask just one or two questions relative to your statement and your plan?

MR. STEVENS: Surely.

SECRETARY FLEMMING: I notice in Point No. 3 of the plan as you submitted, it reads: "Testing of all cranberries of the 1959 crop now in the possession of the major distributors by appropriate methods."

Do you have any suggestions to make relative to distributors that would not fall under the heading of "major distributors?"

MR. STEVENS: Yes, I think I could, first off, we have to define what major distrubtors are.

SECRETARY FLEMMING: That is right.

MR. STEVENS: Frequently, in the technique of sampling, which is a technical thing, and I am not a statistician, and when you take random samples, it is done in a pretty scientific manner. The Food and Drug Administration has a lot of techniques on that. They have their statisticians. I would apply whatever statistical methods were recommended from those two sources, and it would include some major distributors, minor distributors, medium distributors, whatever the sampling technique called for.

SECRETARY FLEMMING: You referred also to the fact that up to the present time you have set aside voluntarily 4,800,000 pounds of the 1959 crop. Do you have that broken down by states of origin, the states where the crop was grown?

MR. STEVENS: Yes, sir. I have it not only broken down by the states where it was grown, I can tell you precisely where those berries which we have set aside are located by warehouses. I could tell you how they are packed, every one of these lots of berries has a grower's name on it and we have a complete control upon those berries.

SECRETARY FLEMMING: I am wondering if you would be willing to give us a breakdown by states, not necessarily now.

MR. STEVENS: I would be delighted to give it to you, and give it to you right now.

SECRETARY FLEMMING: Fine.

MR. STEVENS: Let me go back and get my briefcase, and I will have it for you.

MR. QUARLES: Didn't you get that breakdown yesterday?

MR. LARRICK: Yes.

MR. STEVENS: This is like a man who is so proud of his little children, you know, I just happen to have a picture right in my pocket, so I just happen to have this document right on hand.

I might indicate, Mr. Secretary, that we gave this to the Commissioner and staff yesterday.

Now, we have stored and set aside these berries for further testing and will not reach the market place until they are. Undoubtedly some of them will have to be destroyed and should be destroyed. Some may be free and clean, and we will put them into the market place at some later date. In our warehouse at North Harwich, we have three, we call them barrels. They are three-sided containers. There are 290,000 pounds at North Harwich. We have the berries stored in 333-pound boxes. There is a grower's name on every box. There are no other berries except these particular berries in this building.

In Wisconsin, where we have no freezer facilities, we have shipped the questionable berries there to the Central Cold Storage in Chicago. We have there at the moment 1,683,000 pounds. These berries have been what we call in the cranberry industry, as screened, the chaff has been broken off, and they are packed in cloth bags, each bearing a tag with the grower's packing number. The lots are segregated and the location of each one is known, and the bags are set aside on a pedestal.

In Oregon, we have these berries of this nature stored in two warehouses, one at Albany, at the Albany Ice and Cold Storage Company, where we have 449,000 pounds in that warehouse, and in another warehouse at Coquilla, Oregon, we have 480,000 pounds.

In the Albany Ice and Cold Storage Company the berries are in cloth bags, each with a blue tag bearing grower packing number. The blue tag lots are in a separate room, all by themselves, separated from the bags which we have white tags on, which we know to be all right.

In Coquilla, in the warehouse there, it is about the same thing. Suspect lots will have blue tags and the white tags are okay. There is only one room in that warehouse, so both lots are in the same room. But blue tag ones are set aside for chemical testing and analysis.

In the State of Washington, we have 1,811,000 pounds, broken down— I don't know whether you want to get into the details. They are in four warehouses.

SECRETARY FLEMMING: Just the over-all total.

MR. STEVENS: Yes, sir.

SECRETARY FLEMMING: In other words, at the present time you have set aside portions of crops grown in Massachusetts, Wisconsin, Washington and Oregon?

MR. STEVENS: Yes.

SECRETARY FLEMMING: And that they total about 4,800,000.

MR. STEVENS: Yes, sir.

SECRETARY FLEMMING: Take the four states together.

MR. STEVENS: There may be more because, as the berries still come down from the growers, and we have more reason to suspect some more, there may be more than that before we are through.

SECRETARY FLEMMING: Can you indicate to us how you decide to set them aside, on the basis of what evidence do you set them aside? I mean generally, I don't expect a detailed answer on it, just generally.

MR. STEVENS: Mr. Secretary, the cranberry business is a little world unto itself. Everybody knows what is going on. They know what I did tomorrow. We have our own inspectors and service out in the cranberry bogs and these boys know what is going on. We instructed them way back in September before this harvest started, "Never mind the affidavits. That is pretty good. That is not good enough. If you have reason to suspect anything phony, different one way or another, when those berries come in, you tag them separately, and set them to one side," and that is what we did.

SECRETARY FLEMMING: Right.

You mentioned the fact that in September of this year you sent out, in effect, instructions not to use aminotriazole at all. As I understand it, the petition that was filed asking for a tolerance was turned down the latter part of May, and then, of course, the firm had the opportunity of deciding whether or not to appeal that, but on the first of July they withdrew their petition. In other words, they decided not to appeal this. Was this information made available to the growers at that time, the fact that the application had been turned down?

MR. STEVENS: Yes, sir. It certainly was made available to all the growers through our house organ. We call it *The Scoop*. In there appeared warning after warning before then, "Don't use this chemical in any other than a postharvest manner." And when the application was denied, the growers were immediately notified.

SECRETARY FLEMMING: So, is it fair to say that you have set aside the 4,800,000 because in at least some instances you have reason to believe that it was used other than in a postharvest manner?

MR. STEVENS: That is right.

SECRETARY FLEMMING: I notice that you have the feeling that maybe some of it finds its way in the crops because of spraying along highways, and so on.

MR. STEVENS: That is right.

SECRETARY FLEMMING: But then in addition to that, some of it was used other than in a postharvest manner as provided by the instructions approved by the Department of Agriculture.

MR. STEVENS: That is right. In addition to that, once in a while a grower may have sprayed his ditches or his dykes to clear them of weeds. He wasn't spraying the cranberry bog, but if there was possibly a drift due to the wind from that kind of spraying over on the bog, we regarded the bog as adjacent to that area and as suspect, in that we must test it further before putting it on the market.

SECRETARY FLEMMING: Thank you very much. I appreciate it.

MR. STEVENS: Thank you, sir.

APPENDIX G

Report of Activities
of
George C. P. Olsson,
President of Ocean Spray Cranberries, Inc.,
Since November 9, 1959.

Through Senator Saltonstall's office was able to effect clearance, through the Department of Defense, for the use of cranberries by the Armed Services for Thanksgiving.

Through Sumner G. Whittier, Director of Veterans Services, Washington, D.C., secured clearance for use of cranberry products in veterans' hospitals throughout the United States.

Attended Growers' Meeting in New Jersey with New Jersey Directors and Wisconsin director Bert J. Leasure on November 30, 1959.

Have worked daily with Cranberry Institute through Orrin Colley and Marcus M. Urann.

Have been in constant telephone communication with as many Directors as possible to keep them posted on developments.

Through my Congressman, Hastings L. Keith of the 9th Massachusetts District, have attempted to keep various Congressional Delegations informed.

Have made numerous radio appearances—wire recordings from Fresno, California, to WBZ-TV in Boston.

Communicated with the White House via Senator Saltonstall.

Have talked personally with many Congressmen from the growing areas.

Have talked with Vice President Nixon's Administrative Aide.

Answered hundreds of letters and made hundreds of telephone calls to establish our political war front and further good public relations.

Written a number of articles for farm publications; such as, *Capper's Farmer, Cooperative Digest,* etc., newspaper columns, etc.

Worked with Gilbert T. Beaton to set up and organize Massachusetts Growers' Meeting for December 15, 1959.

Made two trips to Washington, acting as spokesman for industry before the Food and Drug Administration and Secretary of Health, Education and Welfare—Flemming.

Made two visits to Department of Agriculture while in Washington, the last one with Orrin Colley before Under-Secretary True D. Morse.

Sent letters to all members of the Senate and House Agricultural Committees.

APPENDIX H

APPLICATION
CONCERNING THE CRANBERRY SITUATION
and
SUPPORTING MEMORANDUM

submitted to the

SECRETARY OF HEALTH, EDUCATION AND WELFARE

by

REPRESENTATIVES OF THE CRANBERRY GROWERS

December 8, 1959

Application and Supporting Memorandum

The representatives of the cranberry growers of the United States (the Applicants) submit the following request for action by the Secretary of Health, Education and Welfare and the following memorandum in support of such request.

Requested Action

The Applicants respectfully request that, on the basis of the results of extensive sampling and testing of cranberries and cranberry products conducted throughout the United States by the Food and Drug Administration and qualified independent public laboratories and of other facts now known to him, the Secretary determine and publicly announce the following:

1. That, through steps taken by the Food and Drug Administration and the cranberry industry in cooperation, all cranberry products now in the hands of the processors and the trade (distributors, wholesalers, chain stores and retailers) have been sampled and tested to the satisfaction of the Food and Drug Administration and found to be safe for public consumption, and therefore may be sold under the statement "certified under plan approved by the U.S. Government for cranberries. Signed ———————————————————————————
(name of company)."

2. That, with respect to all unprocessed cranberries now on hand, whether fresh or frozen, the procedure specified in the Secretary's news release of November 19, 1959, will continue in effect and all such cranberries will be tested by apppropriate methods and sampling procedures approved by the Food and Drug Administration before they are processed or offered for sale.

3. That, as a result of cooperative action of the cranberry industry and the Food and Drug Administration and of the continuing ban on the use of aminotriazole on cranberry bogs as heretofore self-imposed by the industry, this problem will not arise with respect to future crops.

Supporting Memorandum

The Original Plan. The Plan set forth in the Secretary's release of November 19, 1959, contemplated an extensive sampling and testing program to be carried out by the individual distributors, wholesalers, chain stores and retailers, and its success depended on their enthusiasm for it and active cooperation in implementing it. Despite the best efforts of the Applicants to promote the Plan, it soon became evident that it was almost totally unacceptable to the trade, primarily because it was too complicated and too expensive.

The situation was aggravated by misunderstandings between representatives of the Food and Drug Administration, the processors and the trade with respect both to the operation of the Plan itself and to the continuation of marketing of untested cranberries. These misunderstandings appear to have resulted, in part at least, from the Plan's having been hurriedly conceived and promulgated in an effort by the Government and the industry to salvage the Thanksgiving market without having sufficient time for preparation and explanation to those involved. Clearance by the Food and Drug Administration for some stores in a community while others failed to get similar treatment caused irritation and resentment against both the processors and the government. The market conditions became, and continue to be, badly disorganized and confused.

The present situation of the industry is indicated by the following figures: As of October 31, 1959, there was in the hands of the trade for the Thanksgiving and Christmas seasons an estimated aggregate of approximately 4,500,000 cases (24 one-pound cans to the case) or over 100,000,000 pounds of cranberry products. Based on the experience of recent years, it was anticipated that of this amount, approximately 4,000,000 cases would be purchased by consumers before the end of the calendar year, leaving 500,000 cases in trade hands on January 1, 1960, a normal inventory as of that date. About 70 per cent of all cranberries eaten by the public during the calendar year are eaten in October, November and December.

A specific and careful market research of what has happened to date, and may reasonably be expected to happen if present conditions remain unchanged, indicates that in reality, only about 1,000,000 cases will have been sold by December 31, 1959, leaving approximately 3,500,000 cases in the trade at the beginning of the year. (See annexed Appendix.)

Traditionally, under normal conditions, about 1,500,000 cases of replacement stocks are moved to the trade from January through August, representing consumer purchases during this period. Under present conditions, consumer purchases during this so-called "off season" will be comparatively very small, estimated at about 500,000 cases. This will leave in trade hands approximately 3,000,000 cases.

In addition, cranberries equivalent to 5,000,000 cases from the 1959 crop now in processors' hands will remain unsold, making a total carry-over surplus of more than 8,000,000 cases, when the 1960 crop comes in. This surplus, some of which by then will have begun to deteriorate in quality and saleability, will be a glut on the market, the effect of which can only be disastrous to the industry. The Applicants do not suggest that this condition of the industry should influence the Secretary's judgment on the merits of the case, but it obviously has an important bearing on the urgency of the action to be taken.

Possible Alternatives. Upon realizing that the plan was not going to accomplish its purpose, Ocean Spray Cranberries, Inc., (Ocean Spray), the farmers' cooperative representing the producers of approximately 75 per cent of the total national crop of cranberries, initiated two additional programs:

- A study of the feasibility (including cost, time and effectiveness) of its offering to provide the sampling and testing services for its customers; and,
- A broad sampling and testing of its cranberry products, picked at random from warehouses and stores throughout the United States, designed to determine in general the extent, if any, to which they contained any aminotriazole.

Since to be really reliable both of these inquiries required expert supervision and interpretation, Ocean Spray retained Arthur D. Little, Inc. of Boston, Massachusetts, to advise and assist with them. These programs have now reached the point at which the results can be evaluated and conclusions drawn.

It is found that any plan under which the processor undertakes responsibility for the testing of cranberry products for its customers or assumes the cost thereof is impractical. For example, Ocean Spray products are located in over 250,000 retail outlets throughout the United States. The expense of sampling and testing would be prohibitive and the time element would render the program of little value. Furthermore, the privilege could not properly be offered to any customer unless it could be offered simultaneously to all, and that is obviously impossible. In brief, the impasse resulting from the unwillingness of the trade to undertake the sampling and testing program cannot be circumvented by having a processor assume it.

Results of Tests. The testing program, however, has produced much more satisfactory and reassuring results. To date it has involved 845 assays, substantially all of which were of composite samples. On these assays, as reported by the independent laboratories making them, not one has produced positive proof of the presence of aminotriazole. Initially, about one per cent of them were reported as positive, but in every such case on further investigation this was shown to have resulted from a misinterpretation of the assay instructions (in some instances by competent and skilled personnel). Arthur D. Little, Inc. report that an analysis of the total program shows an excellent representative distribution of the tests over the entire outstanding stock of cranberry products and presents convincing statistical evidence that such products are free of aminotriazole.

Furthemore, we are informed by the Food and Drug Administration that it has conducted 2,111 assays of cranberry products of which only nine have shown the presence of aminotriazole. In view of the extremely difficult and delicate procedures involved in making the assays by the prescribed method, and the problems and uncertainties encounterd by Arthur D. Little, Inc., with laboratories of high repute, there may be a doubt as to the validity of some or all of these tests reported as positive, but we do not now press this point. The significant thing for our present purposes is that adding the two series of assays together gives a total of 2,956 assays of cranberry products of which only nine— less than one-third of one per cent—indicate the presence of any aminotriazole. It is respectfully submitted that the conclusion to be drawn from these facts is that the possibility of any individual can of cranberries containing aminotriazole is so remote as to be negligible; that the possibility of any individual person successively encountering cranberries containing any aminotriazole (necessary to produce a cumulative effect) is nonexistent; and that, since the possibility of repetition in the future is eliminated by other relevant provisions of this program the public can and should be promptly assured that the cranberry products now on the market are absolutely safe.

Unprocessed Cranberries. With respect to the unprocessed cranberries now on hand, fresh or frozen, the sampling and testing to date have been much less extensive. We are informed by the Food and Drug Administration that it has conducted 848 assays of unprocessed cranberries of which 16 have shown the presence of aminotriazole. Specific information is not immediately available concerning such tests conducted by others. Under these circumstances, the Applicants feel that the sampling and testing program should be continued on unprocessed cranberries and they are not requesting any blanket clearance of them. Pending further developments and any future modification of the program by the Secretary, none of these cranberries are to be processed or offered for sale until they have been sampled and tested and found to be free of aminotriazole, after which, of course, they may be sold, fresh or processed, under the certification of safety referred to above.

Future Crops. The aminotriazole problem is limited to the cranberries and cranberry products now on hand. No steps other than the continuation of the ban on the use of the compound are necessary or appropriate to prevent a recurrence affecting future crops.

Public Reaction. A special consumer research program has been conducted among a representative sample of American families. Some 51 per cent of those questioned stated that they did not serve cranberry sauce for Thanksgiving. Of these families, 91 per cent, over half voluntarily mentioned the cancer scare as their reason for not eating cranberries this year, and half of these indicated that they would never serve cranberries again.

As bearing on what is needed to clear up the confusion in the public's mind, the following figures are pertinent: In the research program just referred to, 64 per cent of those questioned stated that they would not buy cranberries again until they had confirmation of their safety from the Food and Drug Administration.

Conclusion

In brief, the position of the Applicant is that if and to the extent that there was any danger to the public health resulting from the presence of aminotriazole in cranberries, that danger has now been completely eliminated; that the time has come for clearing the industry of the cloud of fear which is rapidly destroying it; that this can be done, public confidence can be restored and normal marketing can be re-established only with the active help of the Food and Drug Administration and the Secretary; and that what is needed immediately is the action by the Secretary requested above. We hope that his statement will be given from the same forum and in the same manner as his public warning of November 9. If it could be made on Monday morning, December 14, the American public would still have nearly two weeks to purchase with confidence its traditional cranberry contribution to a Merry Christmas.

Respectfully submitted,

John R. Quarles, Counsel

December 8, 1959

APPENDIX

The following figures of purchases from stores, following the Secretary's warning to the public on November 9, concerning residues of aminotriazole in cranberries, as compared with the corresponding periods in 1958, are taken from the consumer panel data of Market Research Corporation of America.

Weeks	Cases Purchased (Processed)	Per Cent Change	Cases Purchased (Fresh)	Per Cent Change
Nov. 9-15, 1958	248,000		62,000	
Nov. 8-14, 1959	93,000	—63	18,000	—71
Nov. 16-22, 1958	534,000		212,000	
Nov. 15-21, 1959	115,000	—78	37,000	—83
Nov. 23-29, 1958	665,000		195,000	
Nov. 22-28, 1959	245,000	—63	73,000	—64
Total 1958	1,447,000		469,000	
1959	453,000	—67	128,000	—73

Trade Expansion Act
and Tariff Reduction

The Trade Expansion Act of 1962 gave the President of the United States the authority to reduce U.S. tariffs on certain items by 50 per cent. Among these items was hardwood plywood. Hardwood Plywood Manufacturers Association, a trade association composed of industry leaders, both large and small, had opposed passage of the legislation. Now that the law was passed, the president and directors of the association were considering whether the association should take any further action to stave off reduction of the tariff. Under provision of the law, the U.S. Tariff Commission was to conduct hearings at which interested parties would present testimony to the Tariff Commission on the effect that tariff reduction would have on the domestic industry. The Tariff Commission would then advise the President as to the probable economic effect of the modification of the duties. In addition, the Trade Information Committee in the Executive Offices of the President was to conduct hearings to receive suggestions on trade-barrier concessions which the U.S. might receive from other countries. After the two bodies conducted their hearings, they were to forward their recommendations to the President. The President's Special Representative for Trade Negotiations would then lead a team of negotiators in accordance with the President's determinations at the GATT (General Agreements on Tariffs and Trade) negotiations conducted in Geneva commencing in Spring of 1964.

The two agencies, in the autumn of 1963, announced in the *Federal Register* that hearings would commence in December, 1963. In early November, 1963, the Hardwood Plywood Manufacturers Association was having its board meeting and general membership meeting. At that time the president and managing director would have to recommend whether or not the association should participate in the hearings. On two previous occasions the association had asked for and been denied relief under the provisions of the U.S. Tariff Act called the "escape clause." To qualify for relief under that provision, domestic industry had to establish that increased imports as a result of trade concessions were causing injury to the domestic industry. If such claims were established as facts, then the tariff rates could be raised or other relief could be provided for the domestic industry. The last escape-clause hearing was held in 1959. The managing director of the association was disappointed that no relief was granted to his industry, since imports had risen from 8 per cent of the domestic market in 1951 (at which time the tariff was reduced) to about 57 per cent of the domestic market in 1959. The two escape-clause hearings had been quite expensive for the industry. Nonmembers of the association had contributed to help defray costs of the past hearings, and some nonmembers had indicated that they might contribute further if the association did make presentations to the Tariff Commission and Trade Information Committee. Some members of the association had begun importing hardwood plywood or turning to other products and processes in order to survive in the face of import increases. These members did not feel strongly about having a commitment by the association to the "tariff fight," nor did a few other members of the industry who considered the "tariff fight" a lost cause. However, some members considered work on the maintenance of tariffs the most important function of the association.

The Kennedy-Johnson Administration had committed itself heavily to relief of poverty-stricken areas and areas of unemployment. Most of the domestic production of hardwood plywood was in these areas. Against this background, the managing director was faced with the question of what to recommend at the board meeting. Some members of the association believed that opposition to tariff reduction should be expressed, but that the association should not and could not make a heavy financial commitment to its action because of its previous considerable expenditures in this area which were not fruitful. Accordingly, the association budget committee budgeted a nominal amount for the program, if approved by the board. Other industry had set aside large sums of money to oppose tariff reduction. One member at the board meeting said he hated to pour any more money into this fight. Another member stated that this would be, however, the last time for the foreseeable future that the industry could do anything with reference to tariffs and should not stand idle. The counsel pointed out that the recommendations of the Tariff Commission and Trade Information Committe would not be made public, so that the industry might never know how effective its presentation may have been. He believed, however, that since this industry was unique[1] in that imports accounted for more than 50 percent of domestic sales of hardwood plywood, efforts to oppose tariff reduction were justified and that the decision makers might be sympathetic to their domestic industry.

After some discussion at the board meeting, it was decided that the association had to oppose any further reduction in the tariff on hardwood plywood. The association declined, however, to take any position on reduction of the tariff on veneers (a component of the end product), since some of its members were importers of veneer as well as users. In addition, some members of the association were located in Canada and exported some veneer to the U.S. The Canadian members were lukewarm about any opposition to reduction of U.S. tariffs but indicated an understanding of the position of the U.S. members. In opposing reduction further, the first step was, of course, to make the presentations at the hearings. The managing director then began planning strategy for the hearings on wood products which would be held in the early part of 1964. Some of the tariff commissioners had been on the commission the last time the domestic industry had appeared before it seeking relief, and at least one of these men was sympathetic to the plight of the industry. The chairman of the commission had been a career employee of the commission, as chief economist, prior to being appointed chairman by President Kennedy. The two newest members of the commission were Kennedy appointees who had previously been on the faculty of a well-known business school in the East.

In preparing strategy, the industry was concerned about what would be compelling evidence for the members of the commission. The legal counsel for the association began preparing a brief for submission to the Tariff Commission and the Trade Information Committee. The brief traced the history of imports of hardwood plywood into the United States, and discussed the effects of previous tariff reductions on the industry; namely, increased imports. The brief also emphasized the fact that the industry was located primarily in areas of substantial and persistent unemployment. The association's managing director and counsel both felt that a detailed technical brief was not warranted, since the commission's technical staff had previously studied the hardwood plywood industry in detail. They were conscientious, competent individuals and would gather additional data from their own sources.

After the brief was submitted, the managing director and the counsel discussed the oral presentation to be made before the Tariff Commission and the Trade Information Committee. The counsel felt that since the managing director was well acquainted with the problems and had participated in a previous escape-clause hearing he should be

[1] For this reason the association felt that it should not work closely with other associations on the hearings presentations so that the severity of its plight would not be lost in total statistics.

the witness before the Tariff Commission for the industry. The two felt, however, that the witness before the Trade Information Committee should be one of the members of the association. The owner and president of a medium-sized company was selected to appear before the Trade Information Committee.

After the hearings were held, the director and the counsel believed that the Tariff Commission and the Trade Information Committee should be made aware of the interest of the legislative branch in the plight of the domestic industry. The members of the association and the industry were kept advised of the status of the hearings and were given copies of the briefs and presentations submitted. Many of the industry members wrote or visited their Senators or Representatives to express their concern about what might happen to the domestic industry if the tariffs on hardwood plywood were reduced. The association sought interest from the Philippines in expressing an interest in maintenance of the present U.S. tariff on hardwood plywood, since, due to trade agreements, the Philippines enjoyed a comparative competitive advantage over other countries exporting hardwood plywood to the U.S. under present tariffs. With a reduction in the U.S. tariff, the Philippines would lose its comparative advantage.

Since the Tariff Commission and Trade Information Committee were advisory agencies only, the association considered, prior to the actual negotiations in Geneva, whether it should concentrate its attention elsewhere. It was concerned about what else should be done to protect the interests of the members of the association.

EXHIBIT ONE

United States Consumption—Hardwood Plywood
(Square Feet—Surface Measure)

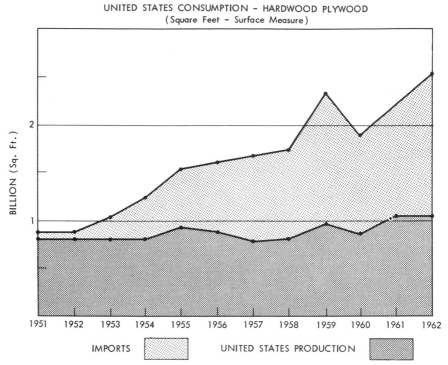

UNITED STATES CONSUMPTION - HARDWOOD PLYWOOD
(Square Feet – Surface Measure)

IMPORTS   UNITED STATES PRODUCTION

SOURCE: U. S. Bureau of Census—1962 Domestic Figures and Total Consumption Figures
are estimated.

EXHIBIT TWO

Number of Hardwood Plywood Plants by States

Number of Plants	State	Number of Plants	State
9	Alabama	1	Montana
3	Arkansas	4	New Hampshire
9	California	1	New Jersey
5	Florida	3	New York
10	Georgia	32	North Carolina
1	Idaho	1	Ohio
2	Illinois	10	Oregon
9	Indiana	6	Pennsylvania
1	Iowa	17	South Carolina
3	Kentucky	3	Tennessee
1	Louisiana	7	Texas
4	Maine	5	Vermont
6	Michigan	8	Virginia
4	Minnesota	15	Washington
7	Mississippi	1	West Virginia
		20	Wisconsin
	Total	208 Plants	31 States

EXHIBIT THREE

United States Bureau of Labor Statistics
Wholesale Price Index
(1957-59 = 100)

Year	Hardwood Plywood	Birch Plywood*	Gum Plywood**
1947	96.7	86.5	102.8
1948	100.9	90.3	107.5
1949	88.7	89.0	88.3
1950	96.7	96.4	96.7
1951	105.8	103.9	106.6
1952	96.6	102.0	92.9
1953	103.4	107.6	100.5
1954	95.7	101.9	91.5
1955	97.9	103.5	94.1
1956	99.9	103.6	97.4
1957	99.0	99.8	98.4
1958	99.7	100.0	99.6
1959	101.4	100.3	102.1
1960	102.8	101.2	103.8
1961	101.4	98.9	104.4
1962	97.8	94.7	103.8
1963 (1st quarter)	96.9	92.8	103.5

SOURCE: United States Department of Labor, Bureau of Labor Statistics.
  * Birch ¼" Standard Panel (Specifications as Below).
  ** Gum ¼" Standard Panel Grade 1-3 or 1-4, Type II Glue, 3-Ply, 48" x 96" car lots, manufacturer to wholesaler or dealer, fob factory, M per square foot.

EXHIBIT FOUR

Hardwood Plywood: U. S. Production, Imports, Exports,
and Apparent Consumption of Ordinary Hardwood Plywood, 1951-1962
(1,000 sq. ft. surface measure)

| | | | | | Ratio of Imports To— | |
| | | | | Apparent Consumption | Production (Percentage) | Consumption (Percentage) |
Year	Production	Imports	Exports	tion		
1951	805,249	66,761	553	871,457	8	8
1952	794,857	84,931	260	879,528	11	10
1953	819,107	218,862	463	1,037,506	27	21
1954	755,464	426,064	431	1,181,097	56	36
1955	933,948	617,936	325	1,551,559	66	40
1956	886,640	695,808	496	1,581,952	78	44
1957	791,431	841,470	393	1,632,508	106	52
1958	803,572	909,021	1,129	1,711,464	113	53
1959	976,717	1,318,035	1,951	2,292,801	135	57
1960	944,028	1,014,342	1,845	1,956,525	107	52
1961	1,099,277	1,097,387	1,556	2,195,108	100	50
1962	1,263,900	1,438,934	1,270	2,702,834	114	53

SOURCE: Compiled From Official Statistics of the United States Department of Commerce.

The Case of the Chinese Mushrooms

In July 1964, the Mushroom Canners Committee of the Pennsylvania Canners Association, an organization comprised of 21 canners in eight states who account for over 95 per cent of the domestic production of canned mushrooms, petitioned the United States Tariff Commission under the "escape-clause" provisions of the Trade Expansion Act of 1962—Section 301 (a) (1)—for the imposition of quotas or higher tariffs on mushrooms prepared or preserved (not including dried) provided for in item 144.20 of the Tariff Schedules of the United States (henceforth referred to as canned mushrooms). Relevant portions of the Trade Expansion Act of 1962 are reproduced in Appendix A of this case.

As a result of this petition, the Tariff Commission instituted an investigation. Public notice of the investigation and of a public hearing to be held in connection with the investigation was given by publication of the notice in *Federal Register*. All interested parties would be given the opportunity to be present, to produce evidence, and to be heard.

In addition to the evidence adduced at the hearing and contained in the formal briefs submitted by interested parties, the commission normally would obtain information from its files, from other government agencies, through fieldwork by members of the commission's staff, and from responses to questionnaires sent to the industry (in this case, domestic growers, canners, driers, and importers of mushrooms). In the case of canned mushrooms, it was necessary for the commission to compile statistical data on the basis of information supplied in response to the questionnaires sent to the industry, since no statistics concerning the output of mushrooms in the U.S. are published regularly by either governmental or private sources.

Commercial production of mushooms was first practiced on a significant scale in France during the reign of Louis XIV. While the commercial culture of mushrooms in the U.S. began in the late 19th century, the product attained widespread public acceptance only in recent years.

Fresh mushrooms are highly perishable and must be marketed within a few days after harvesting. About two-thirds of the domestic crop goes to canneries located chiefly in the growing areas (mainly southeastern Pennsylvania); most of the remainder is shipped to nearby population centers for sale to restaurants, hotels, and retail outlets. Canneries pack mushrooms whole, sliced, and in pieces; they also use fresh mushrooms to make canned soup.

Imported mushrooms have entered the U.S. primarily as a canned product and as a dried product. Canned mushrooms from France are generally deemed to be a prestige item.

Item 144.20 of the tariff schedules provides a rate of 3.2 cents per pound on the drained weight plus 10 per cent ad valorem on canned imported mushrooms, effective July 1, 1963. This represents the final stages of concessions negotiated under the GATT in 1960-1962; earlier concessions in 1936 and 1948 had reduced the basic rates set by the Smoot-Hawley Tariff Act of 1930 to four cents per pound on the drained weight plus $12\frac{1}{2}$ per cent ad valorem, effective June 6, 1951.

Consumption of mushrooms in the U.S. amounted to about 187 million pounds in 1962, compared with 100 million in 1958. Although increased purchasing power was a factor, the rise in consumer demand is attributed by the trade largely to an upgrading of diets, coupled with expanded advertising and promotion. The annual per capita consumption of mushrooms in the U.S. increased from seven ounces in 1946 to about sixteen ounces in 1962; this latter rate was somewhat higher than the per capita consumption in England or Denmark, but less than half that in France. Imports supplied 11 per cent of domestic consumption of mushrooms in 1962, compared with 9 per cent in 1958.

In the crop year 1961/62, there were about 800 commercial growers of mushrooms in the U.S. About three-quarters of the growers were located in Pennsylvania. Delaware and California were the only other states with more than 30 growers each. In 1961/62, the number of workers employed by the domestic growers ranged from 5,300 in the summer to 7,100 in the winter months; about a third of these employees were related to the growers.

For most growers, mushrooms are their only crop. The growing of a palatable mushroom is a long, arduous, labor-demanding process fraught with potential disaster and requiring consummate skill. Mushrooms are grown in cellars, caves, or specially constructed mushroom houses, under carefully controlled conditions of temperature and humidity. The growing medium is a specially prepared compost of horse manure.

Preparing the compost is a laborious job. Each mushroom house requires at least 60 or 70 tons of fresh horse manure per crop. The manure must be prepared by being completely turned or forked over and aerated three or four times at intervals of about a week. Even with the aid of a mechanical turner, the manure must be hand-forked into the turner.

When the compost has been prepared, it is placed in the growing beds. Each bed is filled to a uniform depth of five or six inches. A process of heating or pasturizing then is applied to improve the compost further. The spawn or mushroom "seed" is then planted at regular intervals to depths of about two inches. Mushrooms grow from spores, and the art of producing spawn from spores is highly technical and a separate business.

After the spawn has grown for about three weeks, each bed must be covered with an inch of fine soil slightly moistened with water. This process is called "casing." Four or five weeks after casing, the crop matures to full-grown mushrooms.

Picking is a laborious project. In picking, the grower goes through the aisleways and pulls the mature mushrooms by hand. Holes left in the beds where the mushrooms have been removed are filled with sterilized soil, and all loose roots, butts, and other dead tissue must also be removed by hand labor. This is essential to good yields. Picking mushrooms takes a lot of reaching and stooping to work the beds at various levels—knee-high, hip-high, and shoulder-high. When the crop is done, the entire mushroom house is cleaned out and reconditioned for the next crop.

Mushroom-growing is an intensive type of agriculture requiring a very small area, since the growing beds are placed in tiers. The average growing area per producer in 1961/62 was about 47,000 square feet (or about 1.1 acres). A grower usually harvests two crops per year, but with the use of airconditioning he may harvest three or even four crops a year. The average yield for a single crop was slightly more than two pounds per square foot in 1961/62.

In 1962, 22 canners of mushrooms accounted for 95 per cent of all the mushrooms canned in the U.S. U.S. production of fresh mushrooms has increased rapidly since World War II. Production rose from 63 million pounds in 1946 to 75 million in 1955, to 126 million in 1961 and to 166 million in 1962. Improved technology and new investment in production facilities have made it possible for growers to supply the rapid rise in demand. Successive record-breaking crops have been marketed in recent years without any serious break in prices. Published wholesale quotations in October, 1962, of 36 to 42 cents per pound at Philadelphia were about the same as in 1958, when the crop was 45 per cent smaller.

In 1962, about 30 per cent of the mushroom crop was sold to consumers who buy them as fresh mushrooms. Although the share of the crop which was canned declined from about 60 per cent in 1959 to 52 per cent in 1962, the estimated drained weight of the output of canned mushrooms rose from about 42 million pounds in 1959 to about 58 million pounds in 1962. The share of the total mushroom crop used in making soup has ranged from 15 to 17 per cent during the period 1958-62. Increasingly, canners are integrating backward, growing their own mushrooms and thus complicating the problems of the independent grower.

There are no separate U.S. statistics on exports of mushrooms. Canada is believed to be the major foreign outlet; Canadian statistics show that imports of fresh and canned mushrooms from the U.S. rose to about two million pounds (fresh equivalent) in 1957, but declined to less than one million pounds in 1962. Most of this trade consisted of fresh mushrooms.

Imports of canned mushrooms, the only type offering substantial competition to U.S. producers of fresh and canned mushrooms, averaged 2.4 million pounds annually during the years 1958-1960, rose to 4.7 million in 1961, and to 10.2 million in 1962. Imports in 1962 supplied 15 per cent of the domestic consumption of canned mushrooms and were equivalent to 8 per cent of the domestic production of fresh mushrooms that year. The bulk of the increase in imports from 1960 to 1962 came from China (Taiwan), which had not been a supplier until 1961. In 1962, China supplied 63 per cent of the U.S. imports of canned mushrooms, while the traditional suppliers, France and Japan, accounted for most of the remainder. The development of mushroom production and canning in Taiwan had been given assistance, chiefly of a technical nature, by the U.S. Agency for International Development (AID).

In April, 1963, the duty-paid costs of canned mushrooms from China (Taiwan) at West Coast ports were 25 to 40 per cent below the producers' prices to wholesalers f.o.b. Kennett Square, Penna., of similar domestic mushrooms. Recently, two large U.S. canners have contracted to have mushrooms packed by the Chinese. It is not known whether the imports by these canners will reduce their purchases of domestic mushrooms. Exhibit One shows the dramatic increase in the importation of Chinese canned mushrooms into the U.S. beginning in 1961.

The president of Brand X Company, a medium-sized manufacturer of toothpaste and toiletries, serves on the tariff advisory committee of the American Chamber of Industry (ACI). The ACI is a nationwide trade association of businessmen in a wide variety of industries. The ACI claims to be the voice of business in Washington. Since the ACI will undoubtedly take a stand on the position of the Mushroom Canners Committee before the U.S. Tariff Commission, the president of Brand X Company has asked his administrative assistant, Mr. Casimir Pilsudski, to prepare a report on the merits of the canners' petition and a recommended course of action for the president to recommend to the ACI.

In addition to the above information on the mushroom industry and its problems, which was gathered from trade association and government sources, Mr. Pilsudski, a recent recipient of the M.B.A. degree from a school of business at an Eastern state university, has talked with representatives of both the domestic canners and the importers of the Chinese mushrooms.

Both sides agreed that canned mushrooms are being imported in increased quantities from Taiwan. This, however, is all that both groups could agree on. The importers of the Chinese mushrooms pointed out that principal reductions in the duty on canned mushrooms were granted in 1936 and 1948; subsequent reductions have been minor. Quantitative increases in imports did not really become substantial until the 1961/62 crop year—13 years after the last major concession was granted. The rapid emergence of Nationalist China as a leading world producer and exporter of canned mushrooms, coupled with a U.S. demand that had already begun to expand before that development, have been much more significant than trade concessions, in the view of the importers, who therefore feel the commission should not advise the President to increase duties or impose quotas.

With the fall of the mainland of China to the Communists, the massive migration from the mainland greatly expanded Taiwan's population. Extensive programs were undertaken to provide the island and its people with a viable and expanding economy. It was logical that the production of mushrooms should be considered a promising venture; the necessary components of a successful industry were at hand. The modest U.S. assistance to Taiwan's mushroom-canning industry was extended primarily in the form of financial aid. China became a factor in world markets, but the success, and the very establishment, of its mushroom-exporting industry was but part of a broad program of the country's economic development, in the opinion of the importers.

The importers pointed out that the same circumstances that attracted increased imports to the U.S. also induced domestic producers to expand both their growing and canning operations. Imports and domestic production have both shared in supplying the increased quantities of mushrooms consumed in the U.S. Between the crop years 1960 and 1964, the U.S. annual consumption of mushrooms (fresh-weight basis) rose from 119 to 160 million pounds, while the domestic production of mushrooms increased from 108 to 131 million pounds.

The domestic canners pointed to the rapid increase of imports and the threat that this could cause the bankruptcy of the domestic in-

EXHIBIT ONE

U. S. Imports For Consumption of Canned Mushrooms By Principal Countries 1961-62 and January-October 1963

Country	Quantity in Pounds	Value in Dollars	Country	Quantity in Pounds	Value in Dollars
Year—1961			June		
France	1,940,437	1,308,917	Taiwan	1,104,357	542,292
Taiwan	679,707	361,726	Japan	179,509	92,867
Japan	2,000,424	1,166,257	France	34,310	26,296
Switzerland	27,647	29,024			
			July		
Year—1962			Taiwan	777,957	384,537
Taiwan	6,379,209	3,016,518	Japan	111,300	55,414
Japan	2,274,965	1,205,462	France	98,379	71,137
France	1,356,145	968,632			
Hong Kong	70,220	37,450	**August**		
			Taiwan	867,341	441,572
January—1963			Japan	219,958	101,946
Taiwan	156,173	75,640	France	69,257	51,377
France	38,593	29,480			
Japan	92,315	52,766	**September**		
			Taiwan	993,510	514,534
February			Japan	110,546	50,545
Taiwan	291,951	128,011	France	108,678	81,002
France	124,689	90,226			
Japan	170,708	94,691	**October**		
			Taiwan	1,384,455	692,806
March			Japan	61,761	33,615
Taiwan	787,491	383,487	France	143,458	92,813
Japan	143,260	72,698			
France	95,739	70,840	Total		
			Jan.-Oct. 1963		
April			Taiwan	10,242,703	5,089,234
Taiwan	2,603,016	1,297,273	Japan	1,339,169	676,184
Japan	148,337	20,514	France	902,660	656,219
France	88,424	65,182			
May					
Taiwan	1,296,462	629,082			
Japan	103,675	52,128			
France	111,133	77,866			

SOURCE: U.S. Department of Commerce, FT 110 Reports.

dustry. Mushrooms are a highly specialized product, and facilities used for mushroom growing could not be easily converted to other agricultural uses. Already, employment levels in the industry have declined compared with past years. (The importers claimed automation was responsible for the decline in the size of the labor force.) The domestic growers and canners stated that no matter how much they mechanized they could never compete with the low-cost Chinese labor supply unless tariff rates were raised.

Mr. Pilsudski wondered if he should consider any other factors in reaching his recommended course of action besides those strictly relevant to the mushroom industry. Mr. Pilsudski realizes that the testimony of the American Chamber of Industry at the public hearing might receive considerable weight by the Tariff Commission. Mr. Pilsudski must also recommend to the president of Brand X Company whether the ACI should take any other action with regard to the petition of the canners besides public testimony before the U.S. Tariff Commission.

APPENDIX A

Excerpts From Trade Expansion Act of 1962 (76 Stat. 872)

Sec. 201. Basic Authority for Trade Agreements

(a) Whenever the President determines that any existing duties or other import restrictions of any foreign country or the United States are unduly burdening and restricting the foreign trade of the United States and that any of the purposes stated in section 102 will be promoted thereby, the President may—

(1) after June 30, 1962, and before July 1, 1967, enter into trade agreements with foreign countries or instrumentalities thereof; and

(2) proclaim such modification or continuance of any existing duty or other import restriction, such continuance of existing duty-free or excise treatment, or such additional import restrictions, as he determines to be required or appropriate to carry out any such trade agreement.

(b) Except as otherwise provided in this title, no proclamation pursuant to subsection (a) shall be made—

(1) decreasing any rate of duty to a rate below 50 per cent of the rate existing on July 1, 1962; or

(2) increasing any rate of duty to (or imposing) a rate more than 50 per cent above the rate existing on July 1, 1934.

Sec. 221. Tariff Commission Advice

(a) In connection with any proposed trade agreement under this title, the President shall from time to time publish and furnish the Tariff Commission with lists of articles which may be considered for modification or continuance of United States duties or other import restrictions, or continuance of United States duty-free or excise treatment. In the case of any article with respect to which consideration may be given to reducing the rate of duty below the 50 per cent limitation contained in section 201 (b) (1), the list shall specify the section or sections of this title pursuant to which such consideration may be given.

(b) Within 6 months after receipt of such a list, the Tariff Commission shall advise the President with respect to each article of its judgment as to the probable economic effect of modifications of duties or other import restrictions on industries producing like or directly competitive articles, so as to assist the President in making an informed judgment as to the impact that might be caused by such modifications on United States industry, agriculture, and labor.

(c) In preparing its advice to the President, the Tariff Commission shall, to the extent practicable—

(1) investigate conditions, causes, and effects relating to competition between the foreign industries producing the articles in question and the domestic industries producing the like or directly competitive articles;

(2) analyze the production, trade, and consumption of each like or directly competitive article, taking into consideration employment, profit levels, and use of productive facilities with respect to the domestic industries concerned, and such other economic factors in such industries as it considers relevant, including prices, wages, sales, inventories, patterns of demand, capital investment, obsolescence of equipment, and diversification of production;

(3) describe the probable nature and extent of any significant change in

employment, profit levels, use of productive facilities and such other conditions as it deems relevant in the domestic industries concerned which it believes such modifications would cause; and

(4) make special studies (including studies of real wages paid in foreign supplying countries), whenever deemed to be warranted, of particular proposed modifications affecting United States industry, agriculture, and labor, utilizing to the fullest extent practicable the facilities of United States attaches abroad and other appropriate personnel of the United States.

(d) In preparing its advice to the President, the Tariff Commission shall, after reasonable notice, hold public hearings.

Sec. 301. *Tariff Commission Investigations and Reports*

(a) (1) A petition for tariff adjustment under section 351 may be filed with the Tariff Commission by a trade association, firm, certified or recognized union, or other representative of an industry.

(2) A petition for a determination of eligibility to apply for adjustment assistance under Chapter 2 may be filed with the Tariff Commission by a firm or its representative, and a petition for a determination of eligibility to apply for adjustment assistance under Chapter 3 may be filed with the Tariff Commission by a group of workers or by their certified or recognized union or other duly authorized representative.

(3) Whenever a petition is filed under this subsection, INVESTIGATION the Tariff Commission shall transmit a copy thereof to the BY TARIFF Secretary of Commerce. COMMISSION

(b) (1) Upon the request of the President upon resolution of either the Committee on Finance of the Senate or the Committee on Ways and Means of the House of Representatives, upon its own motion, or upon the filing of a petition under subsection (a) (1), the Tariff Commission shall promptly make an investigation to determine whether, as a result in major part of concessions granted under trade agreements, an article is being imported into the United States in such increased quantities as to cause, or threaten to cause, serious injury to the domestic industry producing an article which is like or directly competitive with the imported article.

(2) In making its determination under paragraph (1), the Tariff Commission shall take into account all economic factors which it considers relevant, including idling of productive facilities, inability to operate at a level of reasonable profit, and unemployment or underemployment.

(3) For purposes of paragraph (1), increased imports shall be considered to cause, or threaten to cause, serious injury to the domestic industry concerned when the Tariff Commission finds that such increased imports have been the major factor in causing, or threatening to cause, such injury.

(4) No investigation for the purpose of paragraph (1) shall be made, upon petition filed under subsection (a) (1), with respect to the same subject matter as a previous investigation under paragraph (1), unless one year has elapsed since the Tariff Commission made its report to the President of the results of such previous investigation.

(c) (1) In the case of a petition by a firm for a determina- ADJUSTED tion of eligibility to apply for adjustment assistance under Chapter ASSISTANCE. 2, the Tariff Commission shall promptly make an investigation to PETITION determine whether, as a result in major part of concessions granted BY A FIRM. under trade agreements, an article like or directly competitive with an article produced by the firm is being imported into the United States in such increased quantities as to cause, or threaten to cause, serious injury to such firm. In making its determination under this paragraph, the Tariff Commission shall take into account all economic factors which it considers relevant, including idling of productive facilities of the firm, inability of the firm to operate at a level of reasonable profit, and unemployment or underemployment in the firm.

(2) In the case of a petition by a group of workers for a determination of eligibility to apply for adjustment assistance under Chapter 3, the Tariff Commission shall promptly make an investigation to determine whether, as a result in major part of concessions granted under trade agreements, an article like or directly competitive with an article produced by such workers' firm, or an appropriate subdivision thereof, is being imported into the United States in such increased quantities as to cause, or threaten to cause, unemployment or underemployment of a significant number or proportion of the workers of such firm or subdivision. [PETITION BY GROUP OF WORKERS.]

(3) For purposes of paragraphs (1) and (2), increased imports shall be considered to cause, or threaten to cause, serious injury to a firm or unemployment or underemployment, as the case may be, when the Tariff Commission finds that such increased imports have been the major factor in causing, or threatening to cause, such injury or unemployment or underemployment.

(d) (1) In the course of any investigation under subsection (b) (1), the Tariff Commission shall, after reasonable notice, hold public hearings and shall afford interested parties opportunity to be present, to produce evidence, and to be heard at such hearings.

(2) In the course of any investigation under subsection (c) (1) or (c) (2) the Tariff Commission shall, after reasonable notice, hold public hearings if requested by the petitioner, or if, within 10 days after notice of the filing of the petition, a hearing is requested by any other party showing a proper interest in the subject matter of the investigation, and shall afford interested parties an opportunity to be present, to produce evidence, and to be heard at such hearings.

(e) Should the Tariff Commission find with respect to any article, as a result of its investigation, the serious injury or threat thereof described in subsection (b), it shall find the amount of the increase in, or imposition of, any duty or other import restriction on such article which is necessary to prevent or remedy such injury and shall include such finding in its report to the President.

(f) (1) The Tariff Commission shall report to the President the results of each investigation under this section and include in each report any dissenting or separate views. The Tariff Commission shall furnish to the President a transcript of the hearings and any briefs which may have been submitted in connection with each investigation. [REPORT TO PRESIDENT.]

(2) The report of the Tariff Commission of its determination under subsection (b) shall be made at the earliest practicable time, but not later than 6 months after the date on which the petition is filed (or the date on which the request or resolution is received or the motion is adopted, as the case may be). Upon making such report to the President, the Tariff Commission shall promptly make public such report, and shall cause a summary thereof to be published in the Federal Register. [PUBLICATION IN F.R.]

(3) The report of the Tariff Commission of its determination under subsection (c) (1) or (c) (2) with respect to any firm or group of workers shall be made at the earliest practicable time, but not later than sixty days after the date on which the petition is filed.

(g) Except as provided in section 257 (e) (3), no petition shall be filed under subsection (a), and no request, resolution, or motion shall be made under subsection (b), prior to the close of the 60th day after the date of the enactment of this Act.

Sec. 351. *Authority*

(a) (1) After receiving an affirmative finding of the Tariff Commission under section 301 (b) with respect to an industry, the President may proclaim such increase in, or imposition of, any duty or other import restriction on the article causing or threatening to cause serious injury to such industry as he determines to be necessary to prevent or remedy serious injury to such industry.

(2) If the President does not, within 60 days after the date on which he receives such affirmative finding, proclaim the increase in, or imposition of, any duty or other import restriction on such article found and reported by the Tariff Commission pursuant to section 301 (e)—

(A) he shall immediately submit a report to the House of Representatives and to the Senate stating why he has not proclaimed such increase or imposition, and PRESIDENTIAL REPORT TO CONGRESS

(B) such increase or imposition shall take effect (as provided in paragraph (3)) upon the adoption by both Houses of the Congress (within the 60-day period following the date on which the report referred to in subparagraph (A) is submitted to the House of Representatives and the Senate), by the yeas and nays by the affirmative vote of a majority of the authorized membership of each House, of a concurrent resolution stating in effect that the Senate and House of Representatives approve the increase in, or imposition of, any duty or other import restriction on the article found and reported by the Tariff Commission.

PART SEVEN

ANTITRUST PROBLEMS

Antitrust and the Twenty-nine Electrical Manufacturers

"Antitrusters Break-Through: What the Government Found in the Electrical Price-Fix case." (An article appearing in the Wall Street Journal, *Monday, January 9, 1961. Reproduced for educational use by permission of the publisher. Copyright* Wall Street Journal.)

Most of the legal questions in the government's antitrust suit against 29 electrical manufacturers were disposed of when the defendants entered a series of guilty and no contest pleas. But other questions remain. How did they conspire so widely? And why? What were the pressures by design and circumstance? This is the first in a series of articles prepared by John Bridge, assisted by Harlan Byrne in Philadelphia, Ames Smithers in Chicago and Stanley Penn and Scott Schmedel in New York.

Among the items of equipment in a big electrical power distributing installation are circuit breakers, power switchgear, power transformers and isolated phase buses. Some run to gigantic size and are priced in the hundreds of thousands of dollars. For example, some circuit breakers, which are not basically much different from similar controls for the flow of electricity in a home, stand as high as 26 feet, are forty feet long, twelve feet wide and weigh 85 tons. They are dramatic-appearing objects, looking as much as anything like huge basketballs with two great rabbit ears sprouting from the top. They function to help regulate the flow of large voltages of electricity; they literally keep the power station from blowing up.

In that job they are quite successful. But these gigantic circuit breakers, along with a dozen or so similar items, are at the heart of as big a blowup as has hit the world of industry in some years. The industry that makes them has been shaken from one end to the other, and repercussions are yet to come. For this equipment is sold, manufactured and distributed by men, and numbers of them from over a score of companies engaged in wide-ranging hanky-panky in the course of their work.

Secret Meetings

A government indictment charged them with conspiring to fix and maintain prices, with getting together in secret meetings and dividing up markets, and with submitting collusive and rigged bids to customers including the federal government. Of the 29 companies indicted, nineteen pleaded guilty on some charges and no contest on others while ten pleaded no contest. Most of the 46 individuals named in the indictments variously pleaded guilty or "no contest," while the indictment of one was dropped. Some of these defendants have complained they were pressured into these pleas by the cost of fighting a court case and by indications that the court would deal more rigorously with defendants found guilty by a jury. Says the attorney for one: "It is my opinion that at least one defendant in the industrial control equipment industry has, to my knowledge, actually perpetrated a falsehood in pleading guilty."

Be that as it may, the mass guilty and no contest pleas represent a milestone for the antitrusters. For many of the men involved, though, the cases are a personal tragedy. They could mean a jail sentence of up to a year and a $50,000 fine on each count. In some instances, careers have been shattered. There is bitterness at exile to corporate Siberias for, as some of the men see it, conforming to the corporate way of life in their industry.

Judge J. Cullen Ganey, hearing the twenty allied cases in the United States District Court for the Eastern District in Pennsylvania, raised a key question in the whole picture when he said: ". . . I have been struck . . . that if (the General Electric individuals involved) were doing this meeting, making these arrangements, rigging prices, and having these allotments made, certainly I am not naive enough to believe that General Electric didn't know about it and it didn't meet with their hearty approbation."

Some companies have denied their top officials knew. General Electric is one. It has dealt discipline to men involved, including loss of $30,000 in pay by one individual. Such meetings with competitors violate a written company policy. But generally the conspiratorial way of doing business was so widespread and so brazen as to raise the question why managements did not know. As antitrust Chief Robert A. Bicks, who personally handled parts of the government's case, put it: The conspiracies involved "a pattern of violations which can fairly be said to range among the most serious, the most flagrant, the most pervasive" in the history of the Sherman Antitrust Act.

The long list of defendants engaged in these activities in varying degrees, of course; some are bitter toward the government for painting them with much the same brush as the more flagrant violators. The government's cases were largely built on grand-jury testimony of people who had been involved and who won immunity from prosecution for their testimony, another source of bitterness. Jail sentences have seldom been the outcome of criminal antitrust cases, but when an Ohio judge in another case handed some out (and one defendant shot himself) there was a sudden flood of willing witnesses in the electrical case. "We could scarcely believe it ourselves," says one government attorney. "For years we had felt something illegal was going on but couldn't nail it down enough. Then all of a sudden we hit the jackpot."

The government's attorneys have put many details on the court record which alleged how the various and differing conspiracies operated.

Consider the circuit breaker case filed against General Electric and others. "The testimony," said Mr. Bicks, "is that (the conspiracy) was in effect for a quarter of a century." However, the clear evidence of the conspiracy begins in 1951. . . . Now just how did it work?

Inter-Company Memo

"In the early years there was a practice, a practice known as the inter-company memo. Once each week with quite regular precision the top executives responsible for the carrying-out of this conspiracy would communicate with each other via memo, which each executive initiated. At this stage bear in mind back in 1951 there were four companies . . . in this conspiracy, G.E., Westinghouse (Electric), Allis-Chalmers, and Federal Pacific. . . .

"There would be communications back and forth among the top people responsible for the conspiracy once a week. The initiator of the communication would change month to month, company to company; by communication known as the inter-company memo would deal generally with jobs that were coming up during the week, the price each would bid, and any comments that were to be offered on the general price level. Those communications, in short, dealt generally with the so-called private market, the $55 million to $60 million of non-sealed-bid business each year.

"The sealed-bid business . . . $15 million or so were dealt with at local-level, working-level meetings, where the sealed-bid business was rotated . . . among the four companies on a fixed-percentage basis. And here was the percentage: G.E. 45, Westinghouse 35, Allis-Chalmers 10, Federal Pacific 10. That was roughly the percentage that was agreed upon."

In another case involving power switchgear assemblies, a system was worked out apportioning the sealed-bid business without the need for meetings. At some undetermined time there came into being the so-called "phase of the moon" or "light of the moon" formula—so called because it permitted the bid winner to be rotated on a regular basis. "This formula was so calculated," the indictment charged, "that in submitting prices to these customers, the price spread would be sufficiently narrow so as to eliminate actual price competition among them, but sufficiently wide so as to give an appearance of competition. This formula was designed to permit each defendant corporation to know the exact price it and every other defendant corporation would quote on each prospective sale. . . ."

In one instance, the low-bid position was agreed on by drawing lots. "Names were put into a hat and slips of paper were drawn by a company representative from each company. Company X drew the lowest number and thereby acquired the low-bid position. The other companies drew their slips of paper which told them what position they would have above Company X."

This was part of the conspiracy charged by the government in the condenser case. Here Baddia Rashid, chief of the trial section of the antitrust division, drew a detailed picture.

"This conspiracy can be divided into three aspects," he said. "One is an alleged agreement to maintain market price levels on the product. The second are agreements to actually fix prices on condenser products. And the third is an agreement in a sense to allocate business among the companies.

Allocation of Jobs

"These three types of agreements were carried on by two levels of personnel. We have the high-level group and we have the working-level group. . . . The high-level group was concerned not so much with the fixing of actual prices or the allocation of specific condenser jobs. The high-level group rather was interested in maintaining a certain position, market-level position, so that the companies would always operate within a certain sphere of price-level.

"An example of the type of high-level meetings that were conducted is one in 1955 where the defendants in attendance . . . agreed that they would sell condensers at a price no lower than 5% below published book prices. In other words, they left the actual establishment of the book price to the working-level group, but they decided at the high-level group that in any sales there would be no price-cutting."

This, then, is the type of charge the government was prepared to take to trial in what it has called the largest group of criminal cases in antitrust law history. The no-contest plea by ten of the 29 companies involved, while not contesting the government's case nor affecting the possible sentence, cannot be used as evidence in a civil suit. Treble damages are possible for guilt under antitrust law, and a plea of guilty can be used as conclusive proof, though the plaintiff must prove his damages. Sentencing in all the cases is expected later this month.

TVA's Role

It was an argument between the industry and a leading customer, the Tennessee Valley Authority, that kicked off the case, at least by one authoritative account. For some time TVA had been noticing that bids from various companies were nearly identical. Partly because of this and rising prices for equipment, TVA issued invitations to foreign manufacturers to make bids. Enraged, the domestic industry called a press conference blasting TVA for looking overseas. Piqued, TVA put out a news release noting, among other things, the similarity of bids. This was printed by a Knoxville, Tenn., newspaper and came to the attention of the Kefauver investigating committee, which turned findings over to the Justice Department. This led to the impaneling of four grand juries in Philadelphia and they made the indictments. William L. Maher, chief of the antitrust division's Philadelphia office, directed much of the investigation.

Such charges of price fixing and market allocation have frequently been made both by Congress and the Justice Department, but, far more often than not, have gotten nowhere. Antitrust lawyers consider these cases a tremendous government victory, and some note that Robert Kennedy, the new Attorney General, is believed to favor price-fixing prosecution as the kind of antitrust action with the most impact on consumers.

But that aside, the question remains: How did these companies and individuals get into such a mess?

* * *

"Antitrust and Organization Man: A Climate and a Philosophy Brought Collision in Electric Case;" (An article appearing in the Wall Street Journal, *Tuesday, January 10, 1961. Reproduced for educational use by permission of the publisher. Copyright* Wall Street Journal.)

Most of the legal questions in the government's antitrust suit against 29 electrical manufacturers were disposed of when the defendants entered a series of guilty and "no contest" pleas. But other questions remain. How did they conspire so widely? And why? What were the pressures by design and circumstance? This is the second in a series of articles prepared by John Bridge, assisted by Harlan Byrne in Philadelphia, Ames Smithers in Chicago and Stanley Penn and Scott Schmedel in New York. The first appeared January 9, 1961.

The term "organization man" may well be looked on with suspicion as a too-simple, too-pat summation of a personality that is complex as any. But the term is meaningful. And while Judge Ganey and some of the attorneys involved in the government's criminal antitrust cases against various members of the electrical equipment industry sought to dodge the word, they found it a useful one in referring to some individual defendants.

Here were men of substance in their communities and in the business world who were pleading guilty or "no contest" to serious charges of conspiracy. From the court record and from some of the pleas it can hardly be argued that most of them did not know what they were doing. Yet the overwhelming impression is that these men hardly fit the stereotype of law evaders. Almost as pervasive as the almost undisputed evidence of wrong-doing was the question of why. And the simplest, if not the complete, answer goes back to the organization man.

It would seem that in these cases the term not only concerned solid and respectable businessmen, however, but also the whole mores—and what was taken for the mores—of an entire industry. One charge sometimes leveled against the organization man is that he is strong on conformity. If, in the case of the individuals in the electrical cases, what was to be conformed to was a large-scale system of law evasion, they evidently conformed to that, too.

Potentials for Trouble

Certainly the climate in which the individuals and companies in the heavy electrical equipment industry operated was loaded with potentials for trouble, and these may well have been the genesis of the legal difficulties which came to afflict a large segment.

The industry is a relatively compact one. Its members range from very large enterprises to relatively small ones. For example, among those indicted in the case were General Electric with $4 billion annual sales and Joslyn Manufacturing and Supply Co. of Chicago with annual sales of less than $2 million and only 45 production employees.

The industry is tightly knit, with many friendships among executives of competing firms; indeed, officials of smaller firms sometimes are former General Electric or Westinghouse Electric executives. The men involved oftentimes had similar educational backgrounds also—college graduates in engineering with a rise through technical ranks in the world of sales. There sometimes existed on the part of the men with the bigger companies an almost protective, big-brother attitude toward the smaller companies; this was reciprocated.

And the friendships were not only professional but often quite personal. Trade association meetings fostered these. It was perhaps easy in the camaraderie of these meetings at upper-bracket hotels, amid speeches typical of any association lauding the industry's members and "mission," to draw even closer than business and background indicated. It was perhaps easy, with wives and children present, and acquainted from past conventions, to drift into the belief that nothing could be very wrong in such an atmosphere.

Darkening Grays

Indeed, many of the meetings took place at the conventions of the National Electrical Manufacturers Association and other trade groups. Rather typically, after a conventional and perfectly lawful meeting of some kind, certain members would adjourn for a rump session and a few drinks in someone's suite. It seemed natural enough that mutual business problems would be discussed—specifications, for example—and like as not prices would come up. In time it was easy enough to drift from general talk about prices into what should be done about them—and finally into separate meetings to fix them for everyone's mutual benefit.

Thus purely legal gatherings might have drifted into ones with increasingly dark shades of gray and finally into ones that were pretty black; more than one moralist has noted that it isn't the blacks and whites of situations that get initially law-abiding citizens into trouble; rather it is a progressive inability to distinguish between shades of gray.

It was especially easy in this industry to get into price discussions.

The economic position of the various companies has often been one of feast or famine—large orders or none at all for the gigantic pieces of equipment manufactured. Widespread overcapacity after World War II brought intermittent price warring. In 1955, for example, there occurred a price war, known throughout the industry as the "white sale," which saw some prices cut as much as 50 per cent. Profit losses resulted and in some cases red ink. Again in 1957 there was a lesser wave of competitive cutting. At least during the "white sale" General Electric and Westinghouse wound up with most of the business. By reports then current, some smaller companies were seeking government intervention under the Sherman Act's antimonopoly provisions.

The case has a number of ironic aspects, but one of the great ones is that men in the large companies believed they had to protect the position of the smaller companies or run the risk of antitrust prosecution. Another is that much of the overcapacity underlying the "need" to fix prices was government spurred. Fast tax writeoffs, growing out of two wars in two decades, brought the greater capacity for defense that the government wanted, but they also left the manufacturers with an embarrassing amount of plant.

As a result of this industry makeup, the friendships, and the price-capacity situation, there evidently developed in wide segments the philosophy that collusive activity was ethical, illegal though it might be.

Perhaps an extreme exponent of this view, though expressing a widespread one, is F. F. Loock, president, general manager and sales manager of Allen-Bradley Co. of Milwaukee, who has pleaded guilty.

Looking back on what happened, he says: "No one attending the gatherings (in the electrical controls industry) was so stupid he didn't know (the meetings) were in violation of the law. But it is the only way a business can be run. It is free enterprise."

Price fixing is not usually associated with the idea of free enterprise, with the idea that the market mechanism is to be the ultimate controlling factor, and that this mechanism must remain unimpaired either by individuals or governments. But there is a rationale for the cartel system which permits the general type of collusive activity the electrical men were engaged in. According to it, markets are divided and prices fixed so that everyone involved can "get along." Even the consumer is supposed to benefit, because stable markets aid stable production and supposedly costs can thus be stabilized.

"Protection Against Buyers"

Price competition is anathema to such a setup. Mr. Loock says one reason for the gatherings in his industry was "we also need protection against buyers" and the "illegal meetings gave us such protection."

Elaborating on the need for "protection," Mr. Loock cites one instance in which the purchasing agent of a major Detroit manufacturer told one electrical manufacturer another one had offered a lower price. "By discussing the matter, which was not true, among ourselves, we were able to iron out the problems." He concludes: "I believe that in an industry where money is necessary to continue research and development of products we should have some protection against the crookedness of some buyers."

There was also a feeling in the industry that the antitrust laws were unjust. With a rationale developed of friendly live and let live among competitors, laws designed to force competition seemed "government interference." The question was also asked in the industry: If such getting together was all right under the old NRA, why isn't it all right now? Of course the NRA of the 1930's was declared unconstitutional by the Supreme Court, but some say the industry's philosophy of "getting together" has roots in that era.

But if illegal "stabilization" was an industry way of life, it should not be assumed that relations were continually rosy among competitors, or that all authority in the industry was bent on collusive activity.

Getting together to fix prices did not alter the basically competitive situation prevailing in the industry's markets. Indeed, it often seems some attendance at the collusive meetings was with tongue in cheek as to stabilizing prices, with a real reason of finding out what the rest of the industry was up to in order to get the jump in the next price cutting wave. Too, some of the conspirators pretty much inherited their roles from predecessors, older men who may have felt more of a tug from the industry's "way of life" than they did. In fact, there was personal dislike among some of the individual conspirators; perhaps an individual who did not like himself for conspiring had little respect for others also so engaged.

The question of how much top managements knew about the illegal activities is a thorny one; it probably has as many answers as there were companies involved. Most won't comment. But General Electric says its top officials had no part in the conspiracies. Indeed it won from the antitrusters a statement that "the government has not charged and does not claim" involvement of the company's directors, chairman and president.

General Electric offers a green-printed document entitled "Organization and Policy Guide 20.5" which it says was designed to keep just such illegal activities from taking place. This policy has to be signed annually by management people. Among other things it states:

"No employee shall enter into any understanding, agreement, plan or scheme, expressed or implied, formal or informal, with any competitor, in regard to prices, terms or conditions of sale, production, distribution, territories or customers; nor exchange or discuss with a competitor prices, terms or conditions of sale or any other competitive information; nor engage in any other conduct which in the opinion of the Company's counsel violates any of the antitrust laws."

It was because of violation of this policy that the company ladled out discipline involving loss of pay and grade to 48 employees. The employees disciplined were not always the same as those indicted. Some of those disciplined were not indicted because they had won immunity by testifying before the grand juries. And some indicted were not disciplined, G.E.'s reason being that their violations were prior to the three-year "statute of limitations" on policy "20.5." G.E. also told the employees involved, following an investigation of its own, that they would have to arrange and finance their own defense. This has been a source of bitterness; some other companies provided company lawyers.

Tarnished Images

The event has obviously been a disturbing one for all the companies. G.E., for one, is worried about a tarnished "corporate image." A favorable public impression is highly prized by a concern with the tremendous consumer goods business G.E. has. Because of a history of antitrust citations, mostly prior to 1950, the company has been particularly sensitive to, and aware of, the subject and its impact on that image.

This sensitivity has led to some questions about the widely publicized G.E. decentralization program.

Launched around 1950, pricing was left to each of the individual divisions, each designed to operate on its own and at a profit. But the violations of the law remained undetected at the higher company levels. Along with new auditing procedures the concern, while not changing its mind about decentralization, now believes some stronger checkrein must be devised to forestall such things.

Company spokesmen indicate other things—besides the "lesson" implicit in the discipline meted out—are in the works. These include communications studies and possibly some wider distribution of the directive, "20.5." G.E., along with Westinghouse and Allis-Chalmers, has said it will meet with customers to see if they feel they were overcharged, and try to work out some agreement.

The belief is widespread in the industry that some of G.E.'s top management was aware that hanky-panky had gone on in the past but thought it had stamped it out. President Robert Paxton spent many years in the heavy equipment end of the business. Evidently the word went out from time to time that "20.5" was to be followed strictly.

Conspiracy in a Cabin

What actually happened evidently was something else. Consider the odd activities of one G.E. defendant in the industrial controls case. The other conspirators held a meeting in August, 1956, in a cabin at an island resort in Canada. The G.E. man was not among those in the cabin. However, he rented one close by, the prosecutor's record states.

So an individual at the conspiratorial meeting was sent periodically to the G.E. man's cabin to consult with him. The G.E. man "agreed to the price increase and so notified the relay man who communicated this fact back to the remainder of the individuals in the first cabin."

It is plain that many of the individuals involved in the conspiracy were under, or felt they were under, heavy pressure to produce and basically believed their meetings, however clandestine, were ethically justifiable.

An attorney for one company sums it up: "Most of the businessmen and attorneys involved don't think there's a moral issue. This isn't a blind spot in American business. These people honestly think they were getting a fair profit and weren't hurting their customers. Under these circumstances they thought the meetings were justifiable. An unenforced law isn't respected. The government should have given the companies a warning before cracking down. Now either the companies will conform to the law or the law will be changed."

A look at some individual stories, and at some more of these meetings, illustrates the pressures and difficulties—the law aside—that these organization men ran into.

* * *

"The Problems of Price Fixing: Antitrust Violators Schemed to only Limited Success;" (An article appearing in the Wall Street Journal, *Thursday, January 12, 1961. Reproduced for educational use by permission of the publisher. Copyright* Wall Street Journal.)

For a number of years various electrical companies and individuals successfully evaded the antitrust laws. They periodically met to fix prices, divide up markets and otherwise cartelize their industry.

But examination of court records of the cases indicates the conspiracy was not a very successful one. Prices were not fixed except temporarily—some one of the conspirators was forever evading the intent of the conspiracy.

Markets were divided somewhat more successfully, but here again the planners of the market were always running afoul of new circumstances which did not fit into the master plan. Certainly the attempt to evade the give and take of the marketplace meant for the people and companies involved a good deal of unforeseen trouble—the law aside. Red tape flourished; bureaucracy, unofficial and perhaps illegal though it may have been, grew apace. The need for conspiratorial gatherings mounted, all as manmade rules were substituted for competition.

For example, the circuit breaker conspiracy involving General Electric, Westinghouse, Allis-Chalmers and Federal Pacific ran into this problem in 1958—what to do about the entrance onto the scene of a new company? While a new competitor is never an easy matter for an individual company, it was also quite complex for the conspirators.

What happened was that I-T-E Circuit Breaker Co., a factor in other aspects of the electrical equipment business, in 1958 bought out a small company and wanted to enter the circuit breaker field where prices were being fixed and markets allotted on a percentage basis.

"Now, room had to be made for I-T-E," Antitrust Chief Bicks noted in remarks at the arraignment of the defendants. "So a series of meetings began in January of 1958, at which I-T-E indicated its desire for some business. I-T-E had bought a company; it wanted to get into the business.

"The knowledge by I-T-E that it was entering into a pre-existing conspiracy is clear beyond doubt from the pattern of events in early 1958. I-T-E began meeting with the four conspirators that had been going, going more or less smoothly, it's true, with greater or less success, with greater or less mutual confidence that each of the conspirators was living up to his part of the deal, but, nonetheless, one constant conspiracy. I-T-E sought to get in.

Over-all Policy

"In early 1958 I-T-E secured an agreement as to the over-all pricing policy, leaving the allocation aside.

"The nature of that agreement arrived at in early 1958 at a series of meetings was roughly this, that general pricing would be tied to G.E.'s book price, that I-T-E in the southern part of California would be allowed 15 per cent off. . . . Remaining to be finalized was I-T-E's allocation share of the sealed-bid business. This was discussed . . . I-T-E was cut in for a share of 4 per cent following a series of conferences, and so from 1958 on everybody cut back a bit except Federal Pacific. . . .

"The three big companies, G.E., Westinghouse, Allis-Chalmers . . . cut down their percentage. Federal Pacific came up from 10 to 15. I-T-E was cut in for 4. That was roughly the pattern of the conspiracy that kept on until the date of the indictment."

I-T-E, seeking to plead no contest in this case, said among other things that it was charged with being only a small factor in the industry for a short period of time. It has told its men to stay away from competitors, that if they're caught in such activities again they'll be fired.

It was one thing, as in the circuit breaker case, to agree that a certain company would get a specific piece of sealed-bid business. It was something else again to see that the designated company actually got the job. Here, again according to Mr. Bicks' statement to the court, is how that worked, amid burgeoning red tape.

"At a working-level meeting where a particular big job was up for discussion, the percentages initially would be reviewed in light of what was known as the ledger list, which had on it recent sealed-bid jobs given to the other defendants. In light of that ledger list, it was decided which of the companies, to keep the percentages constant, would get the job. Now if that company was prepared to say the price at which it was going to bid, then the other companies could discuss among themselves what they would bid, add on for accessories, to make sure to give . . . the company . . . whose turn it was to get the job, the best shot at it."

Numbers Code

"If the company, whose job the particular rigged job was supposed to be, did not know the price, there would be later communication, either by phone to homes with just the first names used, or by letter to homes with just first names of senders, with no return address, and this wonderful code. . . . The numbers were 1, General Electric; 2, Westinghouse; 3, Allis-Chalmers; and 7, Federal Pacific. What happened to 4 or 5 and 6 until I-T-E came in remains a mystery."

One of the great ironies of the conspiracies was that no matter how hard the participants schemed, no matter how friendly their meetings and communications might be, there was an innate tendency to compete. Someone was always violating the agreements to get more business, and this continually called for new illegal plans. For example, price-cutting in sales of power-switching equipment to government agencies was getting out of hand in late 1958. This led to the "quadrant" system of dividing markets.

"So," declared Baddia Rashid, chief of the trial section of the antitrust division, "at a meeting in November of 1958 at Philadelphia . . . they decided that the best way to handle the sealed-bid market was to allocate the business; however, since there were sixteen companies involved in this particular conspiracy it would have been difficult to try to allocate the business as in other cases on a percentage basis, and therefore it was decided that it would be best to divide the country into four separate geographical areas which were called quadrants—the northwest quadrant, the southwest quadrant, the southeast quadrant, and the northeast quadrant.

"Four companies were assigned to participate in each quadrant, and one of the company representatives in that quadrant was designated as a secretary for the purpose of handling the allocation within the particular quadrant." For example, ". . . in the northeast quadrant . . . meetings were held and it was decided that the business within that quadrant would be allocated in an alphabetical rotation. . . ."

This plan did not work to everyone's satisfaction, but rather than fall back on the give and take of the marketplace which the law requires, the conspirators formulated another plan.

"In September of 1959, however, there were some complaints that had arisen because some companies felt they were not getting a sufficient share of the business . . . it appeared that certain of the quadrants were obtaining more sealed-bid business than other quadrants. Therefore, they held a meeting in Pittsburgh . . . in September, 1959 . . . and they discussed this situation. . . . After some discussion it was finally decided that perhaps the best way to do it would be to go back to a national allocation scheme at which each company would be allotted a certain percentage of the business. They all agreed to that plan and each company was then asked to indicate the percentage of the sealed-bid market it felt it should obtain. . . . An individual from one of the . . . companies was designated to act as secretary. . . ."

But the basic problem, in this industry where price fluctuations were sometimes drastic, was "stabilizing" prices and efforts to bring this about spawned many a difficulty.

Reviewing the Books

In one case one conspirator sneaked in a bid on a product below the price level which had been agreed upon, the government said. Discussions among the conspirators followed and the offending company was asked to bring in its books so they could be checked. The representatives of the other companies reviewed them and decided "that this company had deviated from the established prices. So the representative from this company indicated that henceforth he would try to control it a little better." Such meetings to keep the co-price-fixers in line were frequent in other cases.

In a case involving industrial controls, these meetings became quite numerous. The government characterizes this case as perhaps the most serious price fixing case encountered in the "past five or ten years." It counted 31 separate meetings from 1955 until the date of the indictment by the defendants, General Electric, Westinghouse, Square D Co., Cutler-Hammer Co., Clark Controller Co. and Allen-Bradley Co. Mr. Rashid spelled out some of the details for the court.

"The first (meeting) occurred in August of 1955, in Maine. At this meeting all of the defendants except a representative of General Electric were present . . . the individuals present agreed to increase the prices of industrial control equipment by 10 per cent and to put this price increase into effect the following September. They mutually agreed that Cutler-Hammer would be the first to announce the price change and that the rest would follow thereafter.

Mutual Complaints

"There was another meeting in November of 1955 at Atlantic City, New Jersey, in which again all the defendants except General Electric met to discuss the effect this recent price increase was having on the market.

"This was followed by a meeting in April of 1956 at Cleveland, Ohio. Between the November, 1955, meeting and the April, 1956, meeting, General Electric had unilaterally put into effect a price increase. The rest of the companies therefore met in April of 1956 to decide what they would do. . . . They had a discussion and decided that with respect to some products they would all follow G.E.'s prices; with respect to other products they would not follow it.

"When this was agreed upon General Electric thereafter retracted its price increase with respect to those products that the other companies did not agree to.

"There was another meeting in May of 1956 at Hot Springs, Va., which was a so-called price-cutting-discussion meeting at which the companies got together to complain against each other when they were cutting prices from those that had been agreed upon."

In a framework of fixing prices, there arose also the problem of how to price a new product. In some cases the pricing problem evidently stymied introduction of the product.

At a meeting in May of 1957 at Hot Springs, Mr. Rashid declared, there was discussion of the Double O starter that Cutler-Hammer wanted to market. After general discussion there was a "consensus" reached "that it should sell for about two-thirds of the price of the starter then in existence." They tentatively agreed that this new product should be put on the market . . . on or about January 1, 1960.

The following November some of the conspirators met in the suite of Allen-Bradley at the Traymore Hotel in Atlantic City, the government alleged.

"Cutler-Hammer at this meeting wanted to put on the market a low-quality starter; the other defendants (G.E. was not present) were complaining to Cutler-Hammer that that was a bad practice, that what Cutler-Hammer should do should be to put on the market a high-quality starter and that the price of that product should be comparable to the price of existing starters, so that as Cutler-Hammer was contemplating reducing the price of this new starter by about 20 per cent or 25 per cent, that would have cut into the market of the starter that was then being marketed."

Then at a meeting on January 9, 1958, the government said, ". . . they resumed a discussion of the Double O starter and they again criticized Cutler-Hammer for wanting a low-quality starter, and in the end the other companies won and it was agreed that Cutler-Hammer would put out a high-quality starter."

At the same meeting, "Square D Co. was criticized for having put out a new oil-type pushbutton enclosure. . . . The reason they were criticized . . . was the price . . . was lower than the prices of comparable products then in existence."

These then were some of the unexpected tangles that developed from the electrical equipment conspiracies. No matter how diligently plans and schemes were laid, they somehow could not defeat the basic economic factors, which insisted on responding to the inherent forces of the free market.

* * *

"The Road to Antitrust: How Three Executives Got Into Price-Fix Conspiracies;" (An article appearing in the Wall Street Journal, *Friday, January 13, 1961. Reproduced for educational use by permission of the publisher. Copyright* Wall Street Journal.)

The men in the heavy electric equipment industry who were involved in evading the antitrust law are understandably reluctant to tell their stories in public. But privately a few are willing to relate just what happened to them. Among these is Mr. A, a vigorous citizen with a philosophical turn of mind.

Says he: "One of the problems in business is what is normal practice, not what is the law. If it's normal practice, it's ethical, not legal, but ethical." He adds that if "an outsider" comes on the scene, failing to conform to the ethics though he alone may be conforming to the law (a price cutter, for example) he may well be "cut to pieces."

"I guess you'd say I believe in administered pricing," he avers. "I think it was and is wrong to allocate business. But I don't think it's unethical to eliminate prices as a main competitive factor in some goods. I believe the purchaser buys total value in which price is only one significant factor." He lists performance and service as the well-spring of "true competition."

Embracing as he does this philosophy, Mr. A suffered few of the pangs of conscience that came to afflict Mr. B, who often wondered if he should quit his job but found its financial rewards and fringe benefits too strong a pull. Nor did he lose sleep like Mr. C, who found that a stiff drink at three a.m. sometimes helped. Mr. B and C have also agreed to tell their stories, providing they remain anonymous.

The three men got into price fixing by different routes. A jumped in. B drifted in. C was trapped.

Mr. B became involved in price fixing without being aware at the time what was going on. He kept records for his company on competitive bids, and "I was amazed at how close together the bids were." At the time he tended to consider it evidence only of close competition. But now he says: "I don't know, but I'm certain that the prices were being discussed with competitors."

Later on, superiors introduced him to competitors, and it was implied he ought to talk with them. It was clear that this was part of the job, though not actually so stated, and it worried him. One time he went for a long walk with his superior and sought to bring the matter up but he couldn't. Finally he did bring it up at a later date. "The boss readily admitted there had been meetings to stabilize prices. But he said my predecessor had gone too far, and he didn't want me to go so far."

He adds: "When I was first convinced this was going on I thought it was very wrong. I thought of going to them and saying I didn't want the job. But by that time I had been doing the job for some weeks. And then I didn't know whether I was just being naive. I thought maybe this was the normal thing."

Thus B drifted. Finally he became convinced that this was rightly his job; he believed he had the "nod" from his superiors. Now he is somewhat bitter toward them. Speaking of one man high in his company, he declares: "He must have known. It burns me up to hear his damn hypocritical speeches now."

He adds: "The problem is, if I came up again knowing what I know now about how the business was conducted, I don't know what I'd do. Would I do it all again? Or would I lose my job?"

Mr. C, an articulate executive who has perhaps suffered the most personally, nonetheless has little self-pity. If he has any real criticism of his company it is a lack of guidance. "You need moral strength from a company, a sort of guideline on what to do." This, he says, was lacking in the past.

One thing C has learned is that it pays to ask questions. "I realize that in all the time I'd been with the company I simply did not ask enough questions in my job. One thing for sure, if I ever get in a real top position (he still has hopes) I'll hire people around me who'll be questioners. In this present mess, either the people at the top knew what was going on or were stupid for letting some key operations get out of hand."

When C first joined his company he accepted everything around him on blind faith. "I became aware it was accepted industry practice for competitors to get together and discuss price terms." As for the illegality of the practice, he doubts if it ever entered his mind.

He explains it this way: "A young guy comes into his first job. It's one of those things in business. My interests were to know what was this all about and why was it necessary." In the beginning he did not think to question the policy. "It was pointed out to me that this is the only way to run a heavy electrical goods business. This is the way of life. It was necessary, or so I thought, to prevent a chaotic market. There was a well-known high executive who had been fixing prices for years– it was latrine knowledge." You assumed, he says, that all this was the custom.

"These people above me were damn fine citizens and I had developed quite a respect for them. Why should I question them?" When he first took over the job of maintaining prices he "felt pride. I'd seen others doing it, and now they were entrusting it to me. Keeping the market stable —that was a big task."

He recalls that when he first started meeting with competitors to discuss price, "I told my wife there was a degree of risk involved. She accepted it as part of my job." He could not very well hide his activities from his wife. "Sometimes I'd be on the phone discussing prices with competitors from nine at night until one in the morning."

It began to upset him. "I'd be making calls from phone booths, and I'd get unsigned letters in the mails. There'd be calls for me at home." When he was feeling really down in the mouth, "I'd get up at three in the morning and go downstairs and get a drink. I'd have things to think over."

He admits he was aware that company policy stipulated you didn't talk to competitors. "At first, I probably thought, it's like going to school— you learn a lot of formulas but in business you never use them." Later on he began to wonder: What really was company policy? Did it consist of the dicta handed down by his immediate bosses, or of some verbiage that came out of headquarters? He leaves no doubt that at the time he believed policy was what his immediate bosses told him.

Disturbed Superiors

As time went on, however, new superiors came into the company "who became disturbed" about the price fixing. "Customers were irritated, too," he states. "You have a customer, and he likes you, and he says: 'Give me 2 per cent or 3 per cent off the market price, and I'll throw a good piece of business your way.' I had to say I cannot do this."

Why? He and his competitors had already laid down general price lines. "When I saw some company undercutting us and not living up to the ethics, or what you will, of the situation, it made me angry," he says.

He blames himself for not having said openly to top officials of the company that he didn't like what was going on. "But I never got together with the guys in the group and said this is not a good long-term thing for the company. We did not step up to the bar and do what was necessary.

"The tendency is for executives, who get stock options, big salaries, pensions and so on, to accept the facts of life going on around them." He adds: "It is very hard to quit when you get a big compensation, and it's also tough to be a nonconformist under such conditions."

Mr. C says he feels better now that the whole thing is over. "There's no question any more what the ground rules should be. I don't have to be coy with my people anymore. It affected my principles. When someone under me asked a question relating to price I often had to give a veiled answer."

C recalls some unpleasantness from the scrape. About a year ago he and three other colleagues, who were involved in the matter, were sitting in a bar having a drink. Along came a cocky young executive, looked at the four men whose careers were in jeopardy, and said: "Look who's here, the four displaced persons." Says C: "I could have socked him in the jaw."

Such are the stories of three of the many men who were involved in these antitrust law evasions. The pressures to which they succumbed were numerous and varied—the ever-present drive for sales, the makeup of their industry, its traditions, its problems were some. That they succumbed is perhaps best explained by the words of the poet Alexander Pope:

Vice is a monster of so frightful mien,
As to be hated needs but to be seen;
Yet seen too oft, familiar with her face,
We first endure, then pity, then embrace.

* * *

"Identical Bids on Materials Purchased by Governmental Agencies" (An excerpt of the Senate Report of the Committee on the Judiciary, Subcommittee on Antitrust and Monopoly, March 15, 1960.)

The subcommittee has had brought to its attention from time to time that governmental agencies are receiving a significant number of identical bids on materials bought on a bid basis. This situation appears to be especially true with respect to procurement by the Defense Department, General Services Administration (GSA), and the Tennessee Valley Authority (TVA). The Defense Department is the largest purchaser of materials in the Federal Government. GSA is second. TVA purchased in fiscal year 1958 materials valued at $125,936,788. Of this amount, $67 million was spent for manufactured products, practically all of which were bought on a bid basis. According to estimates, the Defense Department purchases on a bid basis approximately $3⅓ billion worth of products per year and GSA approximately $1 billion.

Some city governments had also called to the attention of the subcommittee their experiences in receiving identical bids, particularly in the purchase of electrical products.

In order to escape from identical domestic bids and to keep down its costs, TVA has been forced to seek bids from foreign companies. This was highlighted in February, 1959, when it was able to purchase a 500,000 kilowatt turbogenerator from an English firm at a delivered price of $12,095,800, whereas the lowest bid by an American manufacturer was $17,563,000. Even after adjusting the English bid for efficiency and escalation, it was more than $6 million below the lowest American bid. Since about one-half of the power from TVA goes to federal defense installations, such contributions to TVA's economical operation are important in the national defense budget.

Under the resolution of the Senate empowering the subcommittee to make continuing studies and investigations to determine the adequacy of existing antitrust laws to assure the benefits of free competition, the need for further antitrust legislation and the effectiveness of the enforcement of those laws, it was obviously appropriate to inquire into the facts of identical bidding. Beyond being appropriate, such an investigation is especially necessary since it is generally recognized that substantial accomplishments in this field may not be expected under existing antitrust laws, because mere identity of prices without other evidence of collusion or agreement is not sufficient to establish a violation.

Accordingly, the subcommitee held hearings at Knoxville, Tenn., on identical bid prices received by TVA and the cities of Chattanooga, Knoxville, Memphis, and Nashville, Tenn., and Hopkinsville, Ky. TVA products included cement, steel, such electrical products as tubing, cable, transformers, insulators, lightning arrestors, carrier current equipment, and others. City purchases were limited to products procured by the electrical departments or boards.

These hearings were held on September 28, 29, and 30, 1959. The evidence from TVA was presented by Mr. Paul Fahey, director, Division of Materials. Appearing for the named cities were representatives of the Electric Power Board of Chattanooga; Memphis Light, Gas, and Water Department; Knoxville Utility Board; Nashville Electric Service; and Mayor F. E. Lackey of Hopkinsville. The record of hearings consists of 311 pages and is in process of being printed.

After this series of hearings, members of the staff held conferences with a committee composed of representatives from the Departments of the Army, Navy, and Air Force with respect to the production of their records which would give to the subcommittee an understanding of the prevalence, nature, and other aspects of identical bids received in the Defense Department. Similar conferences have been held with representatives of GSA. The Defense Department has undertaken to furnish its material to the subcommittee by February 1, 1960, subject to any impossibility of meeting that date which may arise.

It is anticipated that when the information from these branches of the government is received and prepared for presentation, further hearings will be held to record the facts and to afford to bidders an opportunity to express their views on identical bidding and to explain them if they wish to do so.

Although the hearings already held indicate an extremely high percentage of identical bids, no report by the subcommittee on this subject is believed proper until the further hearings have been held and a more complete understanding of the problem is attained.

APPENDIX A[1]

Seven Electrical Officials Get Jail Terms in Trust Case
G.E. and Westinghouse Vice Presidents Must Serve 30
Days—$931,500 in Fines Imposed in Bid Rigging.

by Anthony Lewis
Special to *The New York Times*

Philadelphia, Feb. 6.—Seven executives of the country's leading electrical manufacturing companies received jail sentences today for violating the antitrust laws. Federal District Judge J. Cullen Ganey sent each to prison for thirty days.

In addition, Judge Ganey imposed fines totaling $931,500 on individuals and corporations in what the Government has called the largest of all criminal antitrust cases.

It was a long day in Judge Ganey's court room. It took from 10 a.m. to 4:30 p.m. to pass sentence in six of twenty pending indictments. The fourteen others are scheduled to be disposed of tomorrow.

Among those drawing prison terms were vice presidents of the General Electric Company and the Westinghouse Electric Corporation—the two largest companies in the industry. Aside from those going to jail, twenty men drew suspended prison sentences.

All the defendants had pleaded guilty or no defense to charges of fixing prices and rigging bids on heavy electrical equipment, such as power transformers. Sales of the products involved totaled $1,750,000 a year.

But the real drama in the courtroom today arose not from the money or the corporations involved. It lay with the men who stood before Judge Ganey to hear their fate.

They were middle-class men in Ivy League suits—typical business men in appearance, men who would never be taken for lawbreakers. Over and over their lawyers described them as pillars of their communities.

Several were deacons or vestrymen of their churches. One was president of his local Chamber of Commerce, another a hospital board member, another chief fund raiser for the Community Chest, another a bank director, another director of the taxpayers' association, another an organizer of the local Little League.

Lawyer after lawyer said his client was "an honorable man,"—a victim of corporate morality, not its creator. To a degree Judge Ganey agreed.

"The real blame," the judge said in an opening statement, "is to be laid at the doorstep of the corporate defendants and those who guide and direct their policy."

Judge Ganey said the typical individual defendant was "the organization or the company man, the conformist, who goes along with his superiors and finds balm for his conscience in additional comforts and the security of his place in the corporate set-up."

Policy Makers Singled Out

Judge Ganey imposed jail sentences only on men he thought were high enough in their companies to make policy. Jail sentences of any kind are unusual, though not unprecedented, in antitrust cases.

These sentences were below the statutory maximums—a $50,000 fine on each count and a year in jail for the individual defendants. Most were also below Justice Department recommendations, which were for the most part short of the maximums.

The recommendations were sent to Judge Ganey Jan. 19, the day before the new Administration took office. But the acting chief of the department's antitrust division, W. Wallace Kirkpatrick, read the court a statement by the new Attorney General, Robert F. Kennedy.

Mr. Kennedy said he had reviewed the cases and considered the crimes "so willful and flagrant that even more severe sentences would have been appropriate." He suggested, "under the circumstances," that "sentences at least as severe as those recommended be imposed."

Forty-five individuals and twenty-nine corporations were named as defendants, in the package of twenty indictments.

Today sentence was imposed on the thirty-six men and twenty-one companies. Some of the same defendants figure in the cases to be handled tomorrow.

The corporate defendants today drew a total of $822,500 in fines. The largest figures were $185,000 for General Electric, in five cases, and $180,000 for Westinghouse, in six.

All of the individual defendants also drew fines, ranging from $1,000 to $12,500. The total for them was $109,000.

Seven Get Jail Terms

These were the seven men who drew prison terms, listed in the order they were sentenced:

J. H. Chiles, Jr., Westinghouse vice president and division manager.
W. S. Ginn, General Electric vice president and division manager.
Lewis J. Burger, General Electric division manager.
George E. Burens, General Electric vice president and division manager.
C. I. Mauntel, Westinghouse division sales manager.
J. M. Cook, vice president of Cutler-Hammer, Inc.
E. R. Jung, vice president, Clark Controller Company.

Judge Ganey said he had suspended the sentences of some other defendants "reluctantly", and only because of their age or bad health.

He repeatedly rejected pleas by counsel to the effect that their clients were not deeply involved. He would cut in crisply to remark that the defendant had been an "aggressive competitor" in a shocking case.

The formal charge in all the cases was violation of the Sherman Antitrust Act, which prohibits conspiracies in restraint of trade. That is a common charge, but the Government said these conspiracies were unusually elaborate and damaging.

The defendants were said to have held frequent secret meetings, and used codes. They allegedly parceled out Government contracts among each other, submitting low bids in rotation under a scheme called "the phase of the moon."

Some of the customers for this heavy electrical machinery are now expected to bring civil suits for treble damages. The Justice Department has prepared such suits for overcharges to the Federal Government, and states and municipalities and utilities may be next to sue.

The six indictments were handled in turn today, and the drama built slowly in the court room. Government lawyers read their recommendations aloud in each case, and then counsel for the defendants had a chance to plead for mercy, as some called it, or leniency.

Gerhard A. Gesell of Washington, counsel for G. E., took vigorous exception to Judge Ganey's comment about corporate responsibility for the violations.

He noted that G. E. had a company rule, known as Regulation 20.5, directing strict obedience to the antitrust laws. And he observed that the company had demoted all officials involved before any indictments were brought.

"Simply Not a Fact"

"It is simply not a fact that there was a way of life at General Electric that permitted, tolerated or winked at these violations," Mr. Gesell said. "The company abhors, sought to prevent and punished this conduct."

But Judge Ganey disagreed with Mr. Gesell. He said he thought General Electric's Rule 20.5 "was honored in its breach rather than its observance."

Mr. Chiles was the first individual defendant called. A small man with gold-rimmed glasses, he stood with head slightly bowed as his attorney, Philip H. Strubing of Philadelphia, sought leniency.

"No further punishment is needed to keep these men from doing what they have done, again," Mr. Strubing said.

"These men are not grasping, greedy, cut-throat competitors. They devote much of their time and substance to their communities."

Mr. Strubing listed Mr. Chiles' activities—senior warden of his church, benefactor of charities for crippled children and cancer victims, fellow of an engineering society.

Led Off by Marshal

When Judge Ganey imposed the jail sentence, Mr. Chiles turned to go back to his seat in the courtroom. Then, suddenly, a marshal appeared, grabbed him by the elbow and led him off.

Next was Mr. Ginn, tall and distinguished in appearance. His attorney, Henry T. Reath of Philadelphia, also made a general attack on the Government's demand for jail terms.

He said Government lawyers were "cold-blooded" and did not understand what it would do to a man like Mr. Ginn to "put him behind bars" with "common criminals who have been convicted of embezzlement and other serious crimes."

In contrast to Mr. Gesell, Mr. Reath insisted that Mr. Ginn had only followed long-established company policy by getting together with supposed competitors to arrange their business.

Mr. Reath said Mr. Ginn was chairman of the building fund for a new Jesuit novitiate in Lenox, Mass., a director of the Schenectady, N.Y. boy's club and a member of Governor Rockefeller's Temporary State Committee on Economic Expansion.

"It would be a great personal tragedy for this fine man" to go to jail, Mr. Reath concluded. Judge Ganey took only a few seconds to mark Mr. Ginn down for thirty days in prison.

And so it went. Lawyers spoke of their clients' long years with one company, of their daughters in prominent colleges, of the shame that publicity had already caused.

Judge Ganey ordered the seven who were given jail sentences to begin their terms Monday at 10 a.m.

APPENDIX B[1]

Judge's Statement in the Electrical Antitrust Case

Philadelphia, Feb. 6 (AP)—Following is the text of a pre-sentence statement made today by Chief Judge J. Cullen Ganey in United States District Court in the electrical antitrust case:

Before imposing sentence, I want to make certain observations concerning the bills of indictment here involved.

They cover some forty-eight individual defendants and thirty-two corporations which comprise virtually every large manufacturer of electrical equipment in the industry. This is a shocking indictment of a vast section of our economy, for what is really at stake here is the survival of the kind of economy under which America has grown to greatness, the free enterprise system.

The conduct of the corporate and individual defendants alike, in the words of the distinguished assistant attorney general who headed the Antitrust Division of the Department of Justice, has flagrantly mocked the image of that economic system of free enterprise which we profess to the country and destroyed the model which we offer today as a free world alternative to state control and eventual dictatorship. Some extent of the vastness of the scheme for price fixing, bid rigging and job allocations can be gleaned from the fact that the annual corporate sales covered by these bills of indictment represent a billion and three-quarter dollars.

Pervasiveness likewise may be judged by the fact that the sales herewith are concerned with a wide variety of products and were made not only to private utilities throughout the country, but by sealed bids to Federal, state and municipal governments.

Company Officials Scored

This court has spent long hours in what it hopes is a fair appraisal of a most difficult task. In reaching that judgment, it is not at all unmindful that the real blame is to be laid at the doorstep of the corporate defendants and those who guide and direct their policy. While the Department of Justice has acknowledged that they were unable to uncover probative evidence which could secure a conviction beyond a reasonable doubt, of those in the highest echelons of the corporations here involved, in a broader sense they bear a grave responsibility for the present situation, for one would be most naive indeed to believe that these violations of the law, so long persisted in, affecting so large a segment of the industry and finally, involving so many millions upon millions of dollars, were facts unknown to those responsible for the conduct of the corporation and, accordingly, under their various pleas, heavy fines will be imposed.

As to the individual defendants, the Attorney General who secured the indictments and the present Attorney General who has, by letter, wholeheartedly agreed with the Government's recommendation that in the great majority of cases in well documented briefs strongly insisted on the individual defendants serving prison sentences due to the serious nature of their violations.

[1] An article appearing in the *New York Times*, February 7, 1961. Copyright © 1961 by the New York Times Company. Reprinted by permission.

It is not to be taken as disparaging of the long and arduous effort the Government has made, and even more, the highly efficient and competent manner of its doing, that only in these instances where ultimate responsibility for corporate conduct among those indicted, vested, are prison sentences to be imposed. Rather am I convinced that in a great number of these defendants' cases, they were torn between conscience and an approved corporate policy, with the rewarding objectives of promotion, comfortable security and large salaries—in short, the organization or the company man, the conformist, who goes along with his superiors and finds balm for his conscience in additional comforts and the security of his place in the corporate set-up. In that this can in any wise be a defense to their misconduct is conceded but long probationary periods where a watchful eye can be kept on their activities, fines will suffice for their first offense.

The Bright Side

But this is the sordid, greedy side of the situation and yet there is a bright side. Each and every one of those indicted, both corporations and individuals, faced up to the situation realistically and readily admitted by pleas of guilty and nolo contendere, their violations. For this much must be said, not alone in the saving of great time and expense to the Government, in preparing and trying these indictments which would have covered two or three years, but above and beyond that it would cause to point up and emphasize an already unsavory past which these admissions of guilt, it is hoped, will quickly move this great industry to a thorough reappraisal of their various competitive systems and help move the nation's economy forward under the banner of free enterprise.

Finally, I want to thank, as well as compliment, although they need no accolade from me, all counsel here involved. For the Government, the Attorney General, and especially Mr. (Robert A.) Bicks (head of the antitrust division), who spearheaded and coordinated in a highly competent fashion, the action which resulted in these bills of indictments, as well as Mr. (Charles L.) Whittinghill and Mr. (Baddia J.) Rashid, and likewise Mr. (William L.) Maher (all of the Justice Department's antitrust staff), whose unfailing courtesy to the Court was most helpful. To all of counsel for defense, I am likewise very appreciative, since at every turn they have given the Court the utmost cooperation and both orally and in written brief, have, with deep conviction, pleaded their various clients' causes, and if they were not persuasive in their arguments, it was not for any lack of industry on their behalf nor for enthusiasm in its presentation.

APPENDIX C[1]

Electric Firms Face Series of Suits from Government, Private Buyers.

Antitrust Violators May Get Triple, Double Damage Claims from Customers.

A *Wall Street Journal* News Roundup

The Federal Government and a number of the nation's largest cities are preparing a salvo of civil damage suits against leading manufacturers of heavy electrical equipment who pleaded guilty or no defense to charges of price fixing and bid rigging.

Other cities, states and private utilities said they were studying similar actions against the 29 equipment companies sentenced Monday and Tuesday in Philadelphia for violations of antitrust laws. The companies were fined $1,787,000 for illegally fixing prices and rigging bids on heavy apparatus.

In addition, 44 executives of the electrical concerns paid $137,500 in fines. Seven received 30-day jail sentences, which start Monday. Pleas to suspend these jail sentences were denied yesterday.

In Washington, Justice Department attorneys and economists are studying the mass of material developed during the recent criminal prosecution in Philadelphia in preparing lawsuits aimed at recovering millions of dollars the Government believes it was overcharged.

Agency Aids States, Cities

Federal trustbusters said they are feeding considerable information to state and municipal authorities to aid them in their damage suits. They are not extending such assistance, however, to private companies contemplating actions.

Among the major cities which planned to file suits against the equipment makers are New York, which said it would sue General Electric Co. for triple damages for alleged overcharges, Chicago, Los Angeles, San Francisco and Milwaukee.

In adidtion, the National Institute of Municipal Law Officers, made up of city attorneys around the country, disclosed it is considering a giant consolidated triple damage suit on behalf of about 180 cities which may have been overcharged as a result of the price-fixing conspiracy.

Baddia J. Rashid, chief of the Justice Department's antitrust division trial section, estimated that about 20% of the $7 billion of sales covered by the indictments were to Federal, state and local governmental agencies. He said he could not yet break down this estimate.

To Seek Double Damages

Mr. Rashid said the Justice Department is contemplating suits seeking double damages. Ordinarily the Federal Government is empowered to seek only

---

[1] An article appearing in the *Wall Street Journal,* February 9, 1961. © 1961 by the *Wall Street Journal.* Reprinted by permission.

straight damages in most civil antitrust suits, even though all other parties may seek triple damages. Under the False Claims Act, however, it may ask double damages when there is a conspiracy to defraud the Government.

There is a possibility, Mr. Rashid said, that some of the Government's suits will include alternative pleadings for either straight damages or double damages—allowing the judges before whom the cases are tried to choose the proper penalty.

Nineteen of the 29 companies in the Philadelphia case entered guilty pleas; the others were allowed to plead "no defense." A guilty plea constitutes an admission of the charge, thus freeing the suing party from having to first prove that the law was violated and enabling it to concentrate on establishing the extent to which it may have been damaged by the illegal activity. But on a no contest plea, the plaintiff in a damage suit must first prove violation of the laws, as well as proving damages.

Government officials did not indicate, however, whether they would restrict their lawsuits to the 19 companies who admitted the conspiracy, or whether all of the 29 would be sued.

Mayor Wagner of New York said City Corporation Counsel Charles Tenney notified GE chairman Ralph J. Cordiner of the city's intention to sue in the Federal courts.

"It is my intention," the mayor said in a statement, "to have the city act similarly with any and all of the companies which sold to the city and which have pleaded guilty or offered no defense to charges of conspiracy to violate the anti-price rigging provisions of the Sherman Act."

"Substantial Damages"

- Mr. Tenney, in a letter to Mr. Cordiner, said the city "has sustained substantial damages" and that he had instructed his staff to begin action.

A spokesman in New York's Corporation Counsel office said the amount of equipment bought by the city during the years covered by the indictments has not been determined. An inventory of these purchases is underway by city agencies including The Board of Water Supply, Department of Public Works, Transit Authority, Department of Water Supply, Gas and Electricity, Board of Education, Board of Higher Education and Department of Purchase.

Corporation Counsel Tenney appeared to hold out the possibility of a private, out-of-court settlement with GE, if the company was willing to work the matter out with city attorneys.

Mr. Tenney said in the letter to GE: "If you wish to enter into preliminary discussion with me relative to this claim of the City of New York please so advise me, and I shall hold in abeyance the issuance of process."

GE said New York's threatened damage suit will be "vigorously defended."

GE recalled it announced December 14 it would voluntarily sit down with customers to see if financial losses were incurred as a result of the antitrust violations. The company said this includes New York City.

General Electric noted an "exhaustive audit of most of the transactions involved" in the cases "confirms that the purchasers of electrical apparatus have received fair value by any reasonable standards."

"We haven't heard from GE yet," a spokesman in the city's Corporation Counsel's office said.

One advantage to the heavy electrical equipment makers of out-of-court settlements is they would avoid costly, triple damage suits.

Officials of Lansing, Mich., said they believe the city may be entitled to triple damages if overcharges can be proved against GE. Otto Eckert, chairman of the Board of Water and Light, said a $1,700,000 turbine generator recently was bought from GE.

Worth the Effort

Wisconsin officials said the state probably will file a triple damage civil suit in about a month for itself, its agencies, cities and counties. Attorney General John W. Reynolds said he does not know who the defendants will be or the amount to be sought.

Likely to be involved in the state suit is more than $500,000 of electrical water works equipment bought by Milwaukee, on bid, from Allis-Chalmers Manufacturing Co. Milwaukee also has started an investigation of that purchase.

Chicago is checking into all its purchases from the convicted electrical manufacturers and may sue for up to $5 million. John F. Ward, purchasing agent, said the city has purchased substantial amounts of electrical equipment in recent years for a multimillion dollar street lighting program, two large water filtration plants and pumping stations.

San Francisco is negotiating out of court with four electrical companies for alleged excess charges for hydroelectric equipment. Dion R. Holm, San Francisco city attorney, said the alleged overcharge is in the neighborhood of $400,000. He said since triple damages are involved he is asking for approximately three times that sum.

Mr. Holm said he is working toward an out-of-court settlement to avoid a "long, involved and expensive suit." The companies San Francisco is negotiating with are GE, Westinghouse Electric Corp., Allis-Chalmers Manufacturing Co., and Federal Pacific Corp.

In Los Angeles, city officials said their claim would "run into millions," United Press International said.

California has invited cities, counties, and utility districts to join in a single court action against all companies involved. Mr. Holm said he would consider such a move after he saw how well negotiations with the concerns worked out.

The Oakland City Council voted to investigate prices for electrical equipment it has purchased in recent years. The council asked the city manager and city attorney to determine whether it should seek damages.

In Cleveland, Ralph Locher, law director for the city, said Cleveland is currently making a survey to try to determine how much it may have bought from the convicted companies for Cleveland's municipal light plant. Mr. Locher said that the findings will be submitted to the National Institute of Municipal Law Officers.

The mayor of Pittsburgh, Joseph M. Barr, has asked City Solicitor David Stahl to check with the city's department of supplies whether any "stable pieces of electrical equipment" were purchased in the past four years from any of the convicted manufacturers. A spokesman said "once the check has been made, we will decide where to go from there."

In Syracuse, N.Y., Niagara Mohawk Power Corp. said it is studying the possibility of launching a civil suit to recover alleged overcharges. A question the utility must consider, a spokesman said, was whether the amount of money it might collect in court would be worth the effort of undertaking the complicated civil action.

Officials of two Wisconsin utilities, Wisconsin Electric Power Co. and Wisconsin Public Service Corp., said they are studying possible action.

Four major California electric utilities hired a Los Angeles law firm to

270 ANTITRUST AND THE TWENTY-NINE ELECTRICAL MANUFACTURERS

help them determine whether there have been overcharges for electrical equipment and whether the utilities should sue if overcharges are found. The utilities are Southern California Edison Co., Los Angeles, Pacific Gas & Electric Co., San Francisco, San Diego Gas & Electric Co., San Diego, and California Electric Power Co., Riverside.

The companies hired the Los Angeles law firm of Lawyer, Felix & Hall to investigate purchases of generating equipment, dating back to 1956. A spokesman for one of the utilities said it will probably be several weeks at least before the special counsel will make a recommendation on litigation.

Oz Bakery

In 1960 the bread and related products industry shipped more than $4 billion worth of goods at wholesale prices. By nature, the bread industry is a stronghold of small business, because of the freshness problem and the cost of transportation. The 1958 Census of Manufacturers lists 5,300 separate wholesale bakeries. Four firms controlled about 22 per cent of the market in 1960, despite the large numbers of firms in the industry, and the eight largest firms held about 37 per cent of sales. The large companies have been growing and the number of failures of the small companies have been increasing in recent years.

The advantage of the large bakeries is that they spread their operations out over many local markets. This enables them to keep prices high in some areas where there is little competition and use the extra margin to help finance price wars and other competitive practices in areas where competition is intense. The independent bakery, operating from one location, does not have much protection from this type of competition.

In 1948, Mr. Lemuel Purkess took over a bakery in Oz, Kansas, from his stepfather. Sales in 1948 were about $150,000 per year. By 1954, Mr. Purkess had increased sales to about $750,000 per year. The growth in the Oz market and the growth of the Oz Bakery attracted the attention of several large nationwide bakery companies. Two of these large companies served the greater Oz market from plants located in the city of Sasnak, Kansas, about 52 miles from Oz.

One of these nationwide firms made inquiries about purchasing the Oz Bakery in 1955. Mr. Purkess set a price of $250,000 and had the impression that the large firm was agreeable. Accordingly, he forwarded to the large firm information on his routes, customers, and costs. After receiving this vital competitive information, the large firm informed Mr. Purkess that the price would be only $140,000. Purkess refused to accept, despite hints that there was more than one way for the large firm to acquire the bakery.

Beginning in 1955, competition became more and more intense in the greater Oz market. The wholesale price of bread baked in Sasnak rose several times, reaching 16.4 cents per pound in 1965, in Sasnak and most localities served from the Sasnak bakeries of the large companies. However, in the greater Oz area, the two large nationwide firms maintained their prices, in 1965, at the 14.2 cents per pound wholesale price that had existed since 1953. Mr. Purkess estimated that it cost the large bakeries about a third of a cent to ship the bread from Sasnak to Oz. Purkess believed that the Sasnak bakeries were no more efficient than his own and he doubted that the 14.2 cents per pound wholesale price fully covered the costs of the Sasnak bakeries.

In addition to low wholesale prices, the large bread companies used other competitive tactics to enlarge their share of the market at the expense of the Oz Bakery. New bread racks, new store signs, and paint for the store fronts were sometimes provided by the large bakeries in exchange for prominent shelf space. Thousands of loaves of bread were even given away as a promotional device. It was difficult for Oz Bakery to compete with these tactics.

The large bakeries also began to flood the market with more merchandise than could be sold. The purpose of this tactic was to fill up shelf space (thus leaving less where Oz Bakery could display its product). Since, in the baking industry, unsold stale bread is returned to the baker for credit, such tactics tended to increased the number of stale returns. Oz Bakery, of course, had to fight fire with fire. As a result, the percentage of stale returns of the Oz Bakery almost doubled from 5.1 per cent in 1955 to 9.8 per cent in 1965.

As if all this were not enough, one of the large bakeries had recently introduced a "secondary loaf," also referred to as a "fighting loaf" to the greater Oz area. The secondary loaf is made from a leaner formula (more air and less dough) and is sold under a different brand name at a lower price.

Mr. Purkess knows that Oz Bakery cannot stay in business much longer if these competitive tactics continue, as operations are running at a loss. He can still sell out to one of the large bakeries for a fairly moderate price. He wonders if there are any other possible ways of solving his competitive problems.

APPENDIX A

Sherman Antitrust Act [1]

Sec. I. Contracts, Combinations, etc., in Restraint of Trade Illegal—Penalty

Section 1. Every contract, combination in the form of trust or otherwise, or conspiracy, in restraint of trade or commerce among the several States, or with foreign nations, is hereby declared to be illegal: Provided, That nothing herein contained shall render illegal, contracts or agreements prescribing minimum prices for the resale of a commodity which bears, or the label or container of which bears, the trade mark, brand, or name of the producer or distributor of such commodity and which is in free and open competition with commodities of the same general class produced or distributed by others, when contracts or agreements of that description are lawful as applied to intrastate transactions, under any statute, law, or public policy now or hereafter in effect in any State, Territory, or the District of Columbia in which such resale is to be made, or to which the commodity is to be transported for such resale, and the making of such contracts or agreements shall not be an unfair method of competition under section 5, as amended and supplemented, of the act entitled "An act to create a Federal Trade Commission, to define its powers and duties, and for other purposes," approved September 26, 1914: Provided further, That the preceding proviso shall not make lawful any contract or agreement, providing for the establishment or maintenance of minimum resale prices on any commodity herein involved, between manufacturers, or between producers, or between wholesalers, or between brokers, or between factors, or between retailers, or between persons, firms, or corporations in competition with each other. Every person who shall make any contract or engage in any combination or conspiracy hereby declared to be illegal shall be deemed guilty of a misdemeanor, and, on conviction thereof, shall be punished by fine not exceeding $5,000, or by imprisonment not exceeding one year, or by both said punishments, in the discretion of the court.

Sec. 2. Persons Monopolizing Trade Guilty of Misdemeanor—Penalty

Section 2. Every person who shall monopolize, or attempt to monopolize, or combine or conspire with any other person or persons, to monopolize any part of the trade or commerce among the several States, or with foreign nations, shall be deemed guilty of a misdemeanor, and, on conviction thereof, shall be punished by fine not exceeding five thousand dollars, or by imprisonment not exceeding one year, or by both said punishments, in the discretion of the court.

Sec. 3. Contracts, etc., Affecting Territories or District of Columbia Illegal—Penalty

Section 3. Every contract, combination in form of trust or otherwise, or conspiracy, in restraint of trade or commerce in any Territory of the United

[1] As amended by Miller-Tydings Act (Pub., No. 314, 75th Cong., H.R. 7472, approved Aug. 17, 1937).

States or of the District of Columbia, or in restraint of trade or commerce between any such Territory and another, or between any such Territory or Territories and any State or States or the District of Columbia, or with foreign nations, is hereby declared illegal. Every person who shall make any such contract or engage in any such combination or conspiracy, shall be deemed guilty of a misdemeanor, and, on conviction thereof, shall be punished by fine not exceeding five thousand dollars, or by imprisonment not exceeding one year, or by both said punishments, in the discretion of the court.

Sec. 4. Enforcement

Section 4. The several circuit courts[2] of the United States are hereby invested with jurisdiction to prevent and restrain violations of this act; and it shall be the duty of the several district attorneys of the United States, in their respective districts, under the direction of the Attorney General, to institute proceedings in equity to prevent and restrain such violations. Such proceedings may be by way of petition setting forth the case and praying that such violation shall be enjoined or otherwise prohibited. When the parties complained of shall have been duly notified of such petition the court shall proceed, as soon as may be, to the hearing and determination of the case; and pending such petition and before final decree, the court may at any time make such temporary restraining order or prohibition as shall be deemed just in the premises.

Sec. 5. Additional Parties

Section 5. Whenever it shall appear to the court before which any proceeding under section four of this act may be pending, that the ends of justice require that other parties should be brought before the court, the court may cause them to be summoned, whether they reside in the district in which the court is held or not; and subpoenas to that end may be served in any district by the marshal thereof.

Sec. 6. Forfeiture of Property

Section 6. Any property owned under any contract or by any combination, or pursuant to any conspiracy (and being the subject thereof) mentioned in section one of this act, and being in the course of transportation from one State to another, or to a foreign country, shall be forfeited to the United States, and may be seized and condemned by like proceedings as those provided by law for the forfeiture, seizure, and condemnation of property imported into the United States contrary to law.

Sec. 7. Suits—Recovery

Section 7. Any person who shall be injured in his business or property by any other person or corporation by reason of anything forbidden or declared to be unlawful by this act, may sue therefor in any circuit court of the United States in the district in which the defendant resides or is found, without respect to the amount in controversy, and shall recover threefold the damages by him sustained, and the costs of suit, including a reasonable attorney's fee.

---

[2] Act of Mar. 3, 1911, c. 231, 36 Stat. 1167, abolishes the courts referred to and confers their powers upon the district courts.

Sec. 8. "Person" or "Persons" Defined

Section 8. That the word "person" or "persons," wherever used in this act shall be deemed to include corporations and associations existing under or authorized by the laws of either the United States, the laws of any of the Territories, the laws of any State, or the laws of any foreign country.

Approved, July 2, 1890.

APPENDIX B

Clayton Act [1]

Definitions

Sec. 1. "Antitrust laws," as used herein, includes the Act entitled "An Act to protect trade and commerce against unlawful restraints and monopolies," approved July second, eighteen hundred and ninety; sections seventy-three to seventy-seven, inclusive, of an Act entitled "An Act to reduce taxation, to provide revenue for the Government, and for other purposes," of August twenty-seventh, eighteen hundred and ninety-four; an Act entitled "An Act to amend sections seventy-three and seventy-six of the Act of August twenty-seventh, eighteen hundrd and ninety-four, entitled 'An Act to reduce taxation, to provide revenue for the Government, and for other purposes,'" approved February twelfth, nineteen hundred and thirteen; and also this Act.

"Commerce," as used herein means trade or commerce among the several States and with foreign nations, or between the District of Columbia or any Territory of the United States and any State, Territory, or foreign nation, or between any insular possessions or other places under the jurisdiction of the United States, or between any such possession or place and any State or Territory of the United States or the District of Columbia or any foreign nation, or within the District of Columbia or any Territory or any insular possession or other place under the jurisdiction of the United States: *Provided,* That nothing in this Act contained shall apply to the Philippine Islands.

The word "person" or "persons" wherever used in this Act shall be deemed to include corporations and associations existing under or authorized by the laws of either the United States, the laws of any of the Territories, the laws of any State, or the laws of any foreign country.

Price Discrimination Unlawful

Sec. 2.[2] (a) It shall be unlawful for any person engaged in commerce, in the course of such commerce, either directly or indirectly, to discriminate in price between different purchasers of commodities of like grade and quality, where either or any of the purchases involved in such discrimination are in commerce, where such commodities are sold for use, consumption, or resale within the United States or any territory thereof or the District of Columbia or any insular possession or other place under the jurisdiction of the United States, and where the effect of such discrimination may be substantially to lessen competition or tend to create a monopoly in any line of commerce, or to injure, destroy, or prevent competition with any person who either grants or knowingly receives the benefit of such discrimination, or with customers of either of them: *Provided,* That nothing herein contained shall prevent differentials which make only due allowance for differences in the cost of manufacture, sale, or delivery resulting from the differing methods or quantities in which such commodities are to such purchasers sold or delivered: *Provided, however,* That the Federal Trade Commission may, after due investigation and hearing to all interested parties fix and establish quantity limits, and revise the same as it finds necessary,

---

[1] Act of October 15, 1914, as amended.
[2] As amended by Robinson-Patman Act of June 19, 1936.

as to particular commodities or classes of commodities, where it finds that available purchasers in greater quantities are so few as to render differentials on account thereof unjustly discriminatory or promotive of monopoly in any line of commerce; and the foregoing shall then not be construed to permit differentials based on differences in quantities greater than those so fixed and established: *And provided further,* That nothing herein contained shall prevent persons engaged in selling goods, wares, or merchandise in commerce from selecting their own customers in bona fide transactions and not in restraint of trade: *And provided further,* That nothing herein contained shall prevent price changes from time to time where in response to changing conditions affecting the market for or the marketability of the goods concerned, such as but not limited to actual or imminent deterioration of perishable goods, obsolescence of seasonal goods, distress sales under court process, or sales in good faith in discontinuance of business in the goods concerned.

Burden of Rebutting Price Discrimination on Accused

(b) Upon proof being made, at any hearing on a complaint under this section, that there has been discrimination in price or services or facilities furnished, the burden of rebutting the prima-facie case thus made by showing justification shall be upon the person charged with a violation of this section, and unless justification shall be affirmatively shown, the Commission is authorized to issue an order terminating the discrimination: *Provided, however,* That nothing herein contained shall prevent a seller rebutting the prima-facie case thus made by showing that his lower price or the furnishing of services or facilities to any purchaser or purchasers was made in good faith to meet an equally low price of a competitor, or the services or facilities furnished by a competitor.

Commission on Sales or Purchases Forbidden Except for Services Rendered

(c) It shall be unlawful for any person engaged in commerce, in the course of such commerce, to pay or grant, or to receive or accept, anything of value as a commission, brokerage, or other compensation, or any allowance or discount in lieu thereof, except for services rendered in connection with the sale or purchase of goods, wares, or merchandise, either to the other party to such transaction or to an agent, representative, or other intermediary therein where such intermediary is acting in fact for or in behalf, or is subject to the direct or indirect control, of any party to such transaction other than the person by whom such compensation is so granted or paid.

Payment for Services or Facilities for Processing or Sale must be Equal

(d) It shall be unlawful for any person engaged in commerce to pay or contract for the payment of anything of value to or for the benefit of a customer of such person in the course of such commerce as compensation or in consideration for any services or facilities furnished by or through such customer in connection with the processing, handling, sale, or offering for sale of any products or commodities manufactured, sold, or offered for sale by such person, unless such payment or consideration is available on proportionately equal terms to all other customers competing in the distribution of such products or commodities.

Equality of Services or Facilities of Processing, Handling or Sale

(e) It shall be unlawful for any person to discriminate in favor of one purchaser against another purchaser or purchasers of a commodity bought for resale, with or without processing, by contracting to furnish or furnishing, or by contributing to the furnishing of, any services or facilities connected with the processing, handling, sale, or offering for sale of such commodity so purchased upon terms not accorded to all purchasers on proportionally equal terms.

Inducing or Receiving Discriminatory Price Unlawful

(f) That it shall be unlawful for any person engaged in commerce, in the course of such commerce, knowingly to induce or receive a discrimination in price which is prohibited by this section.

Lease or Sale on Agreement Not to Use Goods of Competitor Forbidden

Sec. 3. It shall be unlawful for any person engaged in commerce, in the course of such commerce, to lease or make a sale or contract for sale of goods, wares, merchandise, machinery, supplies or other commodities, whether patented or unpatented, for use, consumption or resale within the United States or any Territory thereof or the District of Columbia or any insular possession or other place under the jurisdiction of the United States, or fix a price charged therefor, or discount from, or rebate upon, such price, on the condition, agreement or understanding that the lessee or purchaser thereof shall not use or deal in the goods, wares, merchandise, machinery, supplies or other commodities of a competitor or competitors of the lessor or seller, where the effect of such lease, sale, or contract for sale or such condition, agreement or understanding may be to substantially lessen competition or tend to create a monopoly in any line of commerce.

Treble Damage Suits

Sec. 4. Any person who shall be injured in his business or property by reason of anything forbidden in the antitrust laws may sue therefor in any district court of the United States in the district in which the defendant resides or is found or has an agent, without respect to the amount in controversy, and shall recover threefold the damages by him sustained, and the cost of suit, including a reasonable attorney's fee.

* * *

Act Inapplicable to Legitimate Activities of Labor

Sec. 6. The labor of a human being is not a commodity or article of commerce. Nothing contained in the antitrust laws shall be construed to forbid the existence and operation of labor, agricultural, or horticultural organizations, instituted for the purposes of mutual help, and not having capital stock or conducted for profit, or to forbid or restrain individual members of such organizations from lawfully carrying out the legitimate objects thereof: nor shall such organizations, or the members thereof, be held or construed to be illegal combinations or conspiracies in restraint of trade, under the antitrust laws.

Restriction on One Corporation Acquiring Stock or Assets of Another

Sec. 7.[3] That no corporation engaged in commerce shall acquire, directly or indirectly, the whole or any part of the stock or other share capital and no corporation subject to the jurisdiction of the Federal Trade Commission shall acquire the whole or any part of the assets of another corporation engaged also in commerce, where in any line of commerce in any section of the country, the effect of such acquisition may be substantially to lessen competition, or to tend to create a monopoly.

No corporation shall acquire, directly or indirectly, the whole or any part of the stock or other share capital and no corporation subject to the jurisdiction of the Federal Trade Commission shall acquire the whole or any part of the assets of one or more corporations engaged in commerce, where in any line of commerce in any section of the country, the effect of such acquisition, of such stocks or assets, or of the use of such stock by the voting or granting of proxies or otherwise, may be substantially to lessen competition, or tend to create a monopoly.

This section shall not apply to corporations purchasing such stock solely for investment and not using the same by voting or otherwise to bring about, or in attempting to bring about, the substantial lessening of competition. Nor shall anything contained in this section prevent a corporation engaged in commerce from causing the formation of subsidiary corporations for the actual carrying on of their immediate lawful business, or the natural and legitimate branches or extensions thereof, or from owning and holding all or a part of the stock of such subsidiary corporations, when the effect of such formation is not to substantially lessen competition.

Nor shall anything herein contained be construed to prohibit any common carrier subject to the laws to regulate commerce from aiding in the construction of branches or short lines so located as to become feeders to the main line of the company so aiding in such construction or from acquiring or owning all or any part of the stock of such branch lines, nor to prevent any such common carrier from acquiring and owning all or any part of the stock of a branch or short line constructed by an independent company where there is no substantial competition between the company owning the branch line so constructed and the company owning the main line acquiring the property or an interest therein, nor to prevent such common carrier from extending any of its lines through the medium of the acquisition of stock or otherwise of any other common carrier where there is no substantial competition between the company extending its lines and the company whose stock, property, or an interest therein is so acquired.

Nothing contained in this section shall be held to affect or impair any right heretofore legally acquired: *Provided,* That nothing in this section shall be held or construed to authorize or make lawful anything heretofore prohibited or made illegal by the antitrust laws, nor to exempt any person from the penal provisions thereof or the civil remedies therein provided.

Nothing contained in this section shall apply to transactions duly consummated pursuant to authority given by the Civil Aeronautics Board, Federal Communications Commission, Federal Power Commission, Interstate Commerce Commission, the Securities and Exchange Commission in the exercise of its jurisdiction under section 10 of the Public Utility Holding Company Act of

[3] As amended by the Antimerger Act of 1950.

1935,[4] the United States Maritime Commission, or the Secretary of Agriculture under any statutory provision vesting such power in such Commission, Secretary, or Board.

*   *   *

When Interlocking Directorates Forbidden

Sec. 8.[5] From and after two years from the date of the approval of this Act no person at the same time shall be a director in any two or more corporations, any one of which has capital, surplus, and undivided profits aggregating more than $1,000,000, engaged in whole or in part in commerce, other than banks, banking associations, trust companies and common carriers subject to the Act to regulate commerce, approved February fourth, eighteen hundred and eighty-seven, if such corporations are or shall have been theretofore, by virtue of their business and location of operation, competitors, so that the elimination of competition by agreement between them would constitute a violation of any of the provisions of any of the antitrust laws. The eligibility of a director under the foregoing provision shall be determined by the aggregate amount of the capital, surplus, and undivided profits, exclusive of dividends declared but not paid to stockholders, at the end of the fiscal year of said corporation next preceding the election of directors, and when a director has been elected in accordance with the provisions of this Act it shall be lawful for him to continue as such for one year thereafter.

When any person elected or chosen as a director or officer or selected as an employee of any bank or other corporation subject to the provisions of this Act is eligible at the time of his election or selection to act for such bank or other corporation in such capacity his eligibility to act in such capacity shall not be affected and he shall not become or be deemed amenable to any of the provisions hereof by reason of any change in the affairs of such bank or other corporation from whatsoever cause, whether specifically expected by any of the provisions hereof or not, until the expiration of one year from the date of his election or employment.

*   *   *

Liability of Directors, Officers or Agents for Violation by Corporation of Criminal Provisions of Act; Penalty

Sec. 14. Whenever a corporation shall violate any of the penal provisions of the antitrust laws, such violation shall be deemed to be also that of the individual directors, officers, or agents of such corporation who shall have authorized, ordered, or done any of the acts constituting in whole or in part such violation, and such violation shall be deemed a misdemeanor, and upon conviction therefor of any such director, officer, or agent he shall be punished by a fine of not exceeding $5,000 or by imprisonment for not exceeding one year, or by both, in the discretion of the court.

[4] 15 U.S.C.A. Sec. 79j.
[5] Sections relating to bank directors under the jurisdiction of the Board of Governors of the Federal Reserve System have been omitted.

Equity Cases: Jurisdiction and Procedure

Sec. 15. The several district courts of the United States are hereby invested with jurisdiction to prevent and restrain violations of this Act, and it shall be the duty of the several district attorneys of the United States, in their respective districts, under the direction of the Attorney General, to institute proceedings in equity to prevent and restrain such violations. Such proceedings may be by way of petition setting forth the case and praying that such violation shall be enjoined or otherwise prohibited. When the parties complained (38 Stat. 737) of shall have been duly notified of such petition, the court shall proceed, as soon as may be, to the hearing and determination of the case; and pending such petition, and before final decree, the court may at any time make such temporary restraining order or prohibition as shall be deemed just in the premises. Whenever it shall appear to the court before which any such proceeding may be pending that the ends of justice require that other parties should be brought before the court, the court may cause them to be summoned, whether they reside in the district in which the court is held or not, and subpoenas to that end may be served in any district by the marshal thereof.

* * *

When Injunctions Prohibited in Labor Disputes

Sec. 20.[6] No restraining order or injunction shall be granted by any court of the United States, or a judge or the judges thereof, in any case between an employer and employees, or between employers and employees, or between employees, or between persons employed and persons seeking employment, involving, or growing out of, a dispute concerning terms or conditions of employment, unless necessary to prevent irreparable injury to property, or to a property right, of the party making the application, for which injury there is no adequate remedy at law, and such property or property right must be described with particularity in the application, which must be in writing and sworn to by the applicant or by his agent or attorney.

And no such restraining order or injunction shall prohibit any person or persons, whether singly or in concert, from terminating any relation of employment, or from ceasing to perform any work or labor, or from recommending, advising, or persuading others by peaceful means so to do; or from attending at any place where any such person or persons may lawfully be, for the purpose of peacefully obtaining or communicating information, or from peacefully persuading any person to work or to abstain from working; or from ceasing to patronize or to employ any party to such dispute, or from recommending, advising, or persuading others by peaceful and lawful means so to do; or from paying or giving to, or withholding from, any person engaged in such dispute, any strike benefits or other moneys or things of value; or from peaceably assembling in a lawful manner, and for lawful purposes; or from doing any act or thing which might lawfully be done in the absence of such dispute by any party thereto; nor shall any of the acts specified in this paragraph be considered or held to be violations of any law of the United States.

[6] As amended by Norris-LaGuardia Act of Mar. 23, 1932.

Mohawk Republican Town Committee [1]

In March of 1958, the Republican Town Committee in the town of Mohawk, Illiana, found itself torn apart by internal bickering and personality conflicts. Because of this dissension, it had lost the respect of the town's citizenry and was unable to carry out effectively its responsibilities either as an arm of the party in the community or as a participant in the municipal government.

This condition of near paralysis was a matter of grave concern to many of the townspeople, and especially to local Republicans. One member of this group was Mr. Francis H. Bruno, a top executive in a well-known firm which had its headquarters in a nearby city. In an effort to exercise some constructive influence, Mr. Bruno talked with a few of his friends who were members of the 36-person committee and urged them to look for someone—perhaps from outside the group itself—who would be willing to undertake the job of chairman and, standing aloof from any particular faction, build a functioning team out of what currently was a disorganized group of angry individuals.

Since the committee was then in the process of electing a chairman, this suggestion had a great deal of appeal to some of the most frustrated of the committee members. After some consideration of the idea among themselves, they called on Mr. Bruno in a body which included his friends and a number of people he did not know, and asked if they could use his name as a candidate for the job. In so doing, they assured him that

[1] This case was made possible by the cooperation of a businessman who remains anonymous. It was prepared by Mr. Dan H. Fenn, Jr. Copyright, 1958, by the President and Fellows of Harvard College.

he would have at least 27 out of the 36 members "in his pocket" if he decided to become a formal candidate for the post.

Mr. Bruno had given no thought to this possibility when he made his initial suggestion. As a matter of fact, he had refused on a number of occasions to participate in local politics and had turned down several tentative bids from various groups to serve in local public office. His rejection of these various proffers of support had been based on two considerations: first, he had been deeply involved in politics when he had first moved to town some eight years before, and had found it taxing and time consuming; and, secondly, his business responsibilities were very heavy so he did not see how he could spare the time. As a matter of fact, he had earlier turned down a suggestion that he serve on the committee on the grounds that he was too busy and traveled too much. Furthermore, he was not at all sure how his superiors in his company would look on active participation in party politics.

However, he was concerned about the state of the Town Committee and impressed by the sincerity and vigor with which his fellow citizens were asking him to serve, so he agreed to think the situation over further and give the group his answer in several days.

Mohawk is an attractive, semirural suburban community not far from the principal business and industrial city of Illiana. An old town, it was a farming area during most of the nineteenth century, when it experienced considerable growth. During the nineteenth century a few small industries and commercial enterprises moved in, but the population began to decrease until it hit a low of 2,500 just after World War I.

About forty years ago the population curve turned upward, with a sharply increasing percentage of growth all the time. Beginning just before World War II, Mohawk became one of the fastest growing towns in the area because of its attractiveness and excellent commuter transportation lines to the neighboring city. With the great postwar exodus to the suburbs and decentralization of industry, Mohawk mushroomed. Since 1940 its population had increased 300 per cent, so that in 1958 local authorities set the figure at nearly 15,000.

The population breaks about evenly between people 35 and under and those over that age. It is nearly 90 per cent American born and white, with a handful of Negro families and about 1,500 foreign born. The state of Illiana, though comparatively homogeneous, includes three times as many Negroes proportionately and half again as many foreign born as Mohawk.

Only a quarter of the people in Mohawk work in town; another quarter commute to the city, and the rest either work in other cities in the county or are retired. The old-time residents tend to be relatively liberal in their political thinking; in this they are joined by a good-sized group of the newcomers. On the other hand, there is a sizable group of commuters who have moved in fairly recently and are conservative.

These variations in political attitude are, however, worked out within the framework of the Republican party; of the 8,500 registered voters in Mohawk, 6,000 regularly vote Republican and about 2,000 are Democrats. This proportion has held very constant despite the growth and changing nature of the town.

The town government of Mohawk has altered little since it was first established nearly 100 years ago. Patterned after New England communities, its central legislative body is a general meeting of taxpayers which is assembled annually in March and on other occasions as necessary. Though a gathering of all 8,000 voters would obviously be unwieldy, Mohawk has managed to preserve the system intact because only a few townspeople actually participate in the annual and special meetings. As a matter of fact, the town's affairs have been determined by as few as 25 voters, and Town Assemblies are rarely attended by more than 500.

The Town Assembly is the authorizing and appropriating body for the town budget, which now runs something over $2 million per year including school costs. By far the largest percentage of these funds is spent on public education: 65 per cent of the budget is spent in this area, while about 7 per cent goes into highway building and maintenance, and just under 7 per cent into general charges. School bonds and interest, apart from the cost of operating the school system, are nearly 10 per cent in Mohawk and are likely to rise even higher as more buildings are needed.

Two elected groups carry the major executive responsibility for the management of Mohawk, although there are a large number of elective and appointive posts in the town government. The Town Council is generally responsible for everything but the school department; the School Committee has exclusive and complete authority over the operation and maintenance of the town's public education, subject only to some loose controls by the state.

The Town Council, made up of three persons, meets weekly. The chairman, elected as such by the voters, is on the job more or less full time, and receives a salary of $7,500 plus an allowance for the use of his car; the other two members are paid $1,000 apiece. Under their jurisdiction fall the public works, fire, police, and park departments; they appoint the personnel, including department heads. In addition, they either appoint directly or influence heavily the appointment of a host of town officials and employees, including the town counsel, the fire commissioners, assessors, Board of Health, Recreation Committee, Finance Committee, special study and action committees charged with specific projects like salary studies or the construction of public buildings, plumbing inspector, building inspector, and so on. Some of these offices are compensated—among them the sealer of weights and measures and the animal inspectors—but most of them are voluntary. Some jobs are politically sensitive—such as wardens and vote counters for election day, and the

Board of Appeals, which passes on variances from the zoning bylaws—while others are virtually unknown to the public—such as the fence viewers, measurers of wood and bark, and field drivers.

The School Committee appoints all school personnel, though mostly on the recommendation of the superintendent; selects textbooks, sets salaries, determines building needs, approves (or disapproves) major matters of educational and administrative policy, serves as public relations board for the school department, and builds and approves the annual budget. They meet regularly twice a month, although in practice they hold many special meetings.

In addition to these major elected committees, there are a large number of positions in town filled by ballot. Included are the town treasurer, the town clerk, the tax collector, justices of the peace, constables, Planning Board, trustees of public trusts, Board of Tax Review, and cemetery commissioners. In all, there are over 150 regular appointed and elected officers in town; when ad hoc groups are included, the total in any given year may run as high as 225. In one recent year, for example, there were fifteen special committees, including an "Additional Fire Station Committee," "Library Addition Building Committee," "Committee on Lectures Under the Will of Mary and George Griswold," "Historic Document Committee," "Hospital Needs Study Committee," and "Oak Street School Building Committee."

Unlike many communities, Mohawk is governed on a partisan basis. Each party puts up a slate of officers for each elective post in town, and names of candidates are printed on the ballot with party designations. However, careful provisions have been established to protect the minority party. Of the three members of the Town Council, for instance, no more than two can be from a single party, and the nine-man School Committee cannot be more heavily weighted than six to three in favor of one group. In making appointments to various committees, the council has consistently appointed large minority representation, but in the case of single offices—like town counsel—they have invariably followed party lines and appointed a member of the party which held a majority on the board. With the exception of two brief periods in the town's history, the Republicans have held control, so almost all key officials in town are Republicans.

Some citizens in town had begun to complain that the municipal structure was outmoded. "It was perfectly adequate when this was a stable community," they said, "but we have enormous new problems today. We are growing very fast, and the town will change its character unless someone does some real planning. Our tax base is very narrow; almost all our revenue comes from residential property taxes, since we have no industry in town. We are going to be faced with tremendous problems in providing street, sewer and water facilities. We have virtually no recreation areas at all, and few resources like swimming pools or tennis courts. We have to do something about zoning to protect our residential areas and still provide for businesses and, possibly, some light industry. And, on top of it all, more and more cars are using Mohawk as a thoroughfare from one place to another in the county, so our roads are being choked up and are becoming a safety hazard. This job is too big for part-time lay volunteers—or underpaid amateurs. We need professional management, and a lot of it!"

Mr. Bruno did not agree. He felt that Mohawk could handle its problems with the same highly democratic machinery that it had always had, but he did feel a great concern about the calibre of people named to elective and appointive office. The town, he felt, was loaded with talented men and women who would be willing to give time and energy if they could be persuaded to do so. The citizens, he was sure, would have the wisdom to elect them if their names appeared on the ballot.

It was because of this interest in the efficient and progressive management of Mohawk that Mr. Bruno was especially worried about the condition of the Republican Town Committee. Since elections were on party lines, the committee played an important—if not a crucial—part in the selection of candidates for elective and appointive office.

Under the bylaws of Mohawk, the voters of each party were required to assemble in a caucus to select their Town Committee. This committee, by the rules laid down by the caucus, was then charged with the responsibility of recommending a candidate from the party for each position on the ballot. Thus, anyone who wanted to become a member of the School Committee, for instance, first found it advisable to apply to the Town Committee for its endorsement, and win his case over any opposition there. Then the Town Committee recommended his name to the party caucus, and the caucus officially made the choice—usually following the committee's lead. In some instances, an individual defeated in the caucus would demand a party primary, or run against the caucus nominee in the final election as an Independent; but in fact this very rarely happened and even less rarely proved to be a successful approach for a candidate.

It was, then, the task of the Town Committees of both parties to choose and, in some instances, to find and attract the best possible candidates for local office. For the Republicans this responsibility was particularly important because of their majority position in Mohawk.

In fact, the power of the Republican Town Committee went beyond the selection of local elected candidates. Because they were the majority party, they made recommendations to the Town Council on all town appointments, and almost always found their suggestions accepted. They named the official candidates for state assemblyman from Mohawk, and selected the Republican delegates from their town to as many as five district, county, and state conventions to choose candidates for other state and county offices. With a Republican President, they even found themselves having to approve or disapprove local Republicans being considered for federal appointments.

Finally, as the main organized political support for members for the Town Council and the School Committee, they found themselves constantly called on for comments on pending Mohawk problems, though these conversations generally were informal and between individuals.

In addition to this governmental responsibility, of course, the Town Committee generally was in charge of campaigns. They raised an average of $40,000 in presidential years, registered voters, ran tours and meetings for candidates, canvassed door-to-door for votes, distributed literature, placed advertisements in the papers, organized mass telephone campaigns, and got out mailings. On election day itself, they set up an elaborate checking system at the polls to make sure that Republican voters actually came out to cast their ballots, telephoned and called for any one who had not yet appeared, offered transportation to the voting places, and provided baby-sitting services for women who wanted to vote. All this activity was carried on by volunteers.

Francis Bruno was impressed by these functions, but even more intrigued by the possible contributions to the general management and organization of the town which he felt the Town Committee could make if it were well organized. He saw, for instance, a great potential in study groups to look at outstanding town issues from a long-range point of view, since the Town Council and School Committee were so occupied with day-to-day details that they had not time or energy for long-range planning.

Furthermore, he was worried that the town of Mohawk might change its charter to a nonpartisan form of government unless the voters felt that they were getting efficient and competent service from their Republican Town Committee in the areas where it had a direct effect on municipal personnel and policies.

Finally, as Mr. Bruno told a case writer from the Harvard Business School, "This thing was in such a mess—and I must admit I am challenged by anything that is really a shambles. It seemed to me that I could contribute some tried-and-true business methods and straighten out the situation to everyone's benefit."

But Bruno was under no illusions about the problems, nor the amount of time and work involved. He had already participated in local politics. Some seven years before, just after he moved to Mohawk, he had become very interested in the Eisenhower-for-President movement. During the spring of 1951, long before there was any organized Citizens for Eisenhower, and even before Ike had expressed his willingness to be a candidate, Bruno had established a group to back his candidacy composed of Democrats, Republicans and Independents.

This activity brought him into a head-on collision with the local Town Committee, the county chairman, and the Republican State Committee, all of whom were rabid Taft supporters. These men and women, with long service in the Republican party, had achieved positions of some prominence and influence—the Town Committee chairman, for instance, later became a top officer of the Electoral College. They bitterly resented the brash newcomer who was elbowing his way into their preserve, and they heartily disagreed with his liberal proclivities.

Nevertheless, Bruno rolled up his sleeves and spent many long hours building support for Eisenhower in town. He rallied around him many fellow newcomers, most of whom had not been active in politics before, and linked them with many of the old-time residents of the town who had resented the domination of the local Republican organization by the more conservative commuters.

The battle was a rough and time-consuming one. The Town Committee spread the story that Bruno was a Communist, or worse; local merchants refused to give him space for a headquarters; he was called an upstart who was politically ambitious and trying to "muscle in" where he didn't belong. The showdown came in the meeting of registered Republicans of Mohawk called to select delegates to the national convention from the area. Though the Town Committee wanted to instruct the delegates to vote for Taft, and so recommended, Bruno and his amateurs defeated their recommendation in an upset decision.

Bruno was then asked to run the Eisenhower-Nixon campaign in Mohawk by the Town Committee, but this more really amounted to an abdication of responsibility by the Town Committee, which apparently decided that if Bruno "was so smart, let *him* run it." At any rate, they refused to participate at all. In the course of the pre-election drive, Bruno had a session with them during which he accused them of sitting out the fight, and pointed out that they had refused to contribute or raise $1 for the effort, thus straining his relations with the committee still more.

In due course, his employers in the city heard about the fracas and, though they made no formal moves, it became obvious that they were not pleased. He was new with the company and, while they were correctly bipartisan officially, the fact was that most of Bruno's associates were pro-Stevenson and some even went so far as to solicit funds for the Democrats in the office. Happily, few people in Mohawk knew Bruno well enough to have found out where he worked, so the company's name was not involved, but this possibility always existed, and Bruno's employers were presumably concerned about it.

When the campaign was over, Bruno was glad to be out of it. While he found participation highly rewarding and interesting—not to say exciting—he had been badly bruised by the attacks; the old guard was still in control of the party machinery, and his company still seemed chilly to his political activities. Furthermore, the expenditure of time and effort had been enormous, and the pressure built up on his youngsters in school and his wife in her social contacts had been a real strain.

They became almost outcasts for a while because of the strong pro-Taft environment—and, later in the campaign, bore the brunt of attacks by the local Democrats. Consequently, he had kept aloof and rejected several overtures that had been made to him to seek office or support candidates.

Looking back on the 18 months he had spent on the Eisenhower campaign, he thought it had all been worth while, however. "Politics is an entirely different world from business," he told the case writer. "In this special world, business approaches can be helpful. But the businessman has to realize that you don't tell people in politics, you listen; and that team play is even more vital than it is in industry; that it isn't just intelligence that counts, but the ability to take punishment and engage in give-and-take; and that many professionals really take this activity seriously and are idealistic about the importance of what they are doing. They believe in what they call 'the practice of government,' and take pride in their political activity whatever their status in life may otherwise be. They are not usually appreciated by the average citizen, but they play an indispensable part in making democracy work. Any businessman who thinks that the politician—or the people, for that matter—are waiting breathlessly for him to deign to participate better take another look. You have to earn your spurs in politics, just as you do in anything else."

As he considered the advisability of geting back into "this special world," he recalled his earlier experiences. It soon became clear that many of them would be repeated; in fact, as soon as the word began to get around that he might be a candidate for Town Committee chairman, the rumors started. He was accused of being anti-Catholic, pro-birth control, opposed to women on the town committee, an opportunist, ruthless, an interloper, and so on. The Town Committee would obviously take an inordinate amount of time and painstaking work to patch up. Its communications were bad, its meetings infrequent and disorganized, the process of nomination of candidates for the senior offices often degenerated into a brawl. (A recent contest, for instance, had ended in a tie between a wealthy, quiet local merchant and an unreliable ex-Socialist lawyer who had always been on the wrong side of every issue.)

The committee had recently started to take "flash votes" without quorums; there were no subcommittees; there was no real machinery set up to make the committee truly representative; many members were apathetic; and it was in bad repute with the townspeople. If he was to be successful in his efforts, he would have to be totally committed to the job, give up virtually all his other outside interests, and cut even deeper into his family life.

Finally, he was not at all sure how his company would look on his active participation. By now he was well identified with his firm in the public mind in Mohawk. and it would be difficult to keep their name out of it. Furthermore, he had assumed very heavy executive responsibilities which demanded a great deal of him, and he would clearly have to make some sacrifices here if he planned to do the job in Mohawk that needed to be done.

As the story about his possible candidacy became widespread in Mohawk's political circles, the committee started to choose up sides. It became obvious very quickly that his friends' estimates of his strength were doubtful, at best, and that he would have to make a real fight for the job if he wanted it. As Bruno sized up the situation, he could count on between ten and fifteen votes, but he needed a majority, not just a plurality of the 36 votes to win. The opposition began to crystallize against him, even though he wasn't a candidate; some of the "antis" called on him to tell him he should make a formal announcement that he was not available "in order to save yourself the embarrassment of being clobbered in public." Lined up against him was one old-time committee member who really wanted the job. As the infighting became fiercer, Bruno found it increasingly difficult to decide what to tell his friends on the committee when they came back for his decision.

The Sinda
Lumber Company[1]

Late in September 1954, Edwin H. Sindall, 3rd, president of
The Sindall Lumber Company, held an interview with Robert L.
Payton, assistant to the vice president for resources. Payton requested that
he be given a six-week leave of absence, with pay, to accept an invitation
to work as a full-time volunteer on the campaign staff of Congressman
Arthur F. Bryson, Republican candidate for the United States Senate in
the forthcoming elections.

The Sindall Lumber Company is a medium-sized firm with headquarters in a state in the Pacific Northwest. Just over fifty years old, it
was founded by the grandfather of its current chief executive and substantially diversified by his father. Originally the company was largely
occupied with the purchase and cutting of timber which it sold to wholesalers. Later it acquired facilities for processing the lumber and, still
later, started to manufacture doors, window frames, and other prefabri-
cated items for the building industry. By 1954, the manufacturing end of
the company had become its major source of revenue, although it continued to purchase timber rights, cut and process lumber, and sell the
finished **boards.**

The firm sells its goods all over the West Coast, and has timber
rights in three states. Employing 1,500 people, it is one of the most important suppliers of doors and window frames in the area. Family owned

[1] This case was made possible by the cooperation of a business firm which remains anonymous. It was prepared by Dan H. Fenn, Jr., under the direction of Professor Paul W. Cherington. Copyright © 1959 by the President and Fellows of Harvard
College.

and controlled, it has been consistently successful at adapting itself to the changing circumstances and needs of the housing industry. Sindall Lumber does a small amount of business with the federal government.

An alumnus of the Harvard Business School in the class of 1947, Payton went to work for Sindall immediately upon his graduation. When a friend asked him what he did for the company, he explained his job in these words:

> I pick up almost anything that comes along. Recently, for example, I devoted all my time to union negotiations, traveling between our cutting operations, this office, and the headquarters of several of our competitors to make sure that our bargaining positions are coordinated. I am not doing the actual negotiating with the union myself, but I am responsible for supplying the background material on which our decisions and arguments will be based.
>
> Once this job wound up, I went back to the facts and figures of our resources program. I survey possible land for exploitation, keep track of our reserves, and make recommendations for the vice president on the timing, location, quantity and quality of our purchases.
>
> I suppose, in short, you could call me a jack of all trades in the resources and industrial relations fields.

Mr. Sindall knew that Payton, a native of the state in which the company headquarters was located, had been extremely active in a number of civic organizations for a long period of time. However, he also was aware of the fact that Payton had never been especially interested in politics, and consequently was somewhat surprised at the request for a leave of absence to work in a campaign.

In the course of the discussion, Sindall discovered that Payton's only direct contact with Congressman Bryson had been at a luncheon meeting earlier in the year when a group of local businessmen had gathered to meet with the prospective candidate and form a paper committee which would provide some publicity and a skeleton organization to be activated if and when it was needed. Several of the more prominent members of the group were friends and associates of Payton's, and they knew of his leadership role in other community projects so they had invited him to join in the effort for Bryson.

Payton went on to explain that there had been little need for his services in the early stages of the campaign. Bryson's immediate objective had been the Republican nomination, determined at a primary early in September when the voters in each party chose their candidates. Since he had no substantial competition, he won the race handily.

However, Payton continued, after the primary several of his friends called on him to ask for his help. They indicated that the organization needed an able, vigorous young man to serve as a full-time advance agent for a whistle-stopping tour of the state. Consequently, Payton told Mr. Sindall, "they asked me if I could possibly arrange a leave from the last week of September to Election Day in November and take on the assignment."

"At first," Payton commented, "I had some real doubts about my ability to do the job. After all, I have no political experience or acquaintances. But my friends convinced me that this would be no handicap; that I would catch on fast enough. Then, they told me that they are having a lot of trouble trying to round up campaign workers who have both the time to do a job for them and enough potential ability to do it well."

The task of recruiting workers for this particular campaign, it appeared, was especially difficult because Congressman Bryson was not given much of a chance to win. His Democratic opponent, Edwin L. Johnson, was a former United States Senator who had retired voluntarily six years before, only to return to active politics when his successor became ill toward the end of his term and announced his intention to withdraw.

Mr. Sindall broke in at this point: "Do *you* think Bryson can win?" he asked Payton.

"Well," Payton replied, "I think he has an uphill fight on his hands, but personally I believe he has a fair chance of making it." He then proceeded to analyze the political situation and the candidates involved.

Senator Johnson, a farmer, was a well-known political figure with a strong and experienced organization. Though his group had deteriorated somewhat during the years he had been out of politics, it was being reassembled quickly and his long-time, statewide political experience was likely to stand him in good stead according to political analysis.

Furthermore, he was backed by labor—though not with great enthusiasm because he tended to be somewhat "unpredictable" in his voting—and by liberal organizations like the Americans for Democratic Action. He was not noted for his intellectual power, had been recorded in several unpopular votes during his Senate service, and was clearly out of favor with the business community of the state which considered him unqualified and too "New Dealish," as some of the state's leading business executives expressed it.

Bryson, too, had been in public service for some years but had never before been a candidate for statewide office. A veteran of the state legislature, he had served seven terms in Congress. He was an early supporter of Eisenhower, former deputy chairman of the Republican National Committee, and a member of both the Eisenhower and Dewey campaign staffs.

A lawyer, he had distinguished himself as an author of legal treatises and as a practicing attorney. He characterized himself as a "moderate Republican, where the human element is involved, but a regular old

Scrooge when it comes to the taxpayer's dollar." A friendly newspaper columnist described Bryson in these words:

> He has a strong dedication to principles, but does not stubbornly and dogmatically sacrifice long-term strategy by refusing to compromise on short-term tactics. His one theme song has been that his vote is not owned by any group or anyone. He is known as a man of real intellect, an enthusiast about promoting and strengthening the free enterprise system.

Congressman Bryson's chances for election were reduced substantially in the eyes of the political experts by the fact that the state was electing a governor at the same time. The Republican nominee was an unknown businessman without political experience who had emerged as a compromise candidate after a particularly stormy primary, while the Democrat was the well-known, highly respected mayor of one of the state's leading cities.

Payton indicated to Mr. Sindall that the prospects did not overly discourage him. Rather, he said: "the more I find out about Congressman Bryson, the more I like him. He is a good family man, active in his church, fair minded, and well liked by all kinds of people."

"Furthermore," he said, "I am really challenged by this assignment and by the chance to learn something about politics. And finally I really think that businessmen have an obligation to participate actively in politics, to support the principles and candidates in which they believe."

In considering Payton's request, Mr. Sindall first thought about it in relation to his company's role in various community activities. The firm had no determined policy, in this area; rather, Mr. Sindall, as president, examined each situation individually as it arose. However, he did have some general guidelines which he followed in ruling on these specific cases.

When his father was president, no executives were allowed time off to work on any community projects, nor were they encouraged to take on nonbusiness, civic responsibilities on their own time. As a result, Mr. Sindall felt that the company's reputation in the cities where it operated had suffered drastically.

Believing in the need for good comumnity relations, the new president urged his managers to join in community endeavors. He suggested that they participate in nonpartisan town politics, serve with the Red Cross and United Fund, become directors of local banks, and so on. Further, he was receptive to requests for a reasonable amount of time off to pursue such activities.

He himself became very active in the affairs of the city where the company headquarters was located. For five or six years he spent 20 per cent of his time on a number of projects which, in his words, "didn't bring in any new orders or increase our bank balance, but did get me on a first-name basis with people in the major companies of this area. I suppose that, somehow, this work may be useful from a business standpoint in the future. But at any rate it did help our reputation in the community."

One of Mr. Sindall's principal interests was public education, and he had served as chairman of a citizen's action group for the public schools. He had been especially alert to projects which were designed to improve the quality of instruction and the facilities, and, at the same time, take advantage of various specialized federal grant programs like the School Lunch Program, vocational education, and Public Law 874 which made money available to cities affected by major government defense installations.

In recent years, he had become increasingly concerned about the amount of his own time which he was spending on community projects and hesitant about releasing any of his four top executives for large-scale endeavors. For example, he had refused to lend any of them to the local United Fund to serve as president, or as chairman of the annual fund drive, although he had encouraged them to serve in every other post in the organization. "A small company like ours," he explained, "just cannot afford to let its key men go because each one of them is so crucial to the efficient and profitable management of the business."

Politically, Mr. Sindall was a strong Republican and was pleased when any of his managers became involved, on a part-time volunteer basis, in Republican party politics. Consequently, when the general superintendent of his main manufacturing plant, who was a Republican county chairman, asked for permission to run for mayor of his town, Mr. Sindall had given his approval with the condition that he must do full justice to his company responsibilities even if he were to be elected.

Because of his firm Republican convictions, Mr. Sindall did not feel that he would look on any similar requests from Democrats with approval. "I think the Republicans are better because the Democrats are more likely to give the country away," he told the case writer from the Harvard Business School. "Consequently, if someone had come to me asking for time off to work for Senator Johnson, or to run for office as a Democrat, I would not grant his request. It seems to me that the only effective way for management to fight unionism in politics is to throw its weight on the Republican side. Giving time off to Republican candidates or workers in preference to Democrats is one way to do it."

"Furthermore," he continued, "as a staunch Republican myself, convinced that my party is right and is better for The Sindall Lumber Company, I would be a hypocrite if I used either my own resources or those of the company to help out the opposition."

While he would not want the company identified in any way with the Democrats, Mr. Sindall felt that a man's politics, like his religion, is still a personal affair. "If someone wants to vote Democratic or work for the Democrats, I might try to influence him by presenting the arguments on the Republican side," he explained, "but I certainly would not hold that against him in terms of promotion or compensation."

Mr. Sindall's interest in politics, as he expressed it, "arises purely because I believe in good government. I have never used political help in securing anything for The Sindall Lumber Company, and never would. I consider it dishonest to ask politicians for assistance, and would shut the doors of this company before I would ask for favors."

At the end of his interview with Payton, Mr. Sindall said he would consider the request and reply before the end of the day. As soon as Payton had left his office, Mr. Sindall called Stuart Broderick, vice president for resources of the company and Payton's immediate superior, to find out whether the leave would present serious manning problems to his department.

Mr. Broderick indicated that Payton's absence would mean some temporary reassignment of duties, and an increased work load for himself and several other people. "However," he concluded, "this is not an insuperable obstacle for us. I guess we could work something out if we had to."

Payton's request, while it met Mr. Sindall's criteria of supporting Republicans, did present him with some unique questions which he had not faced before. In the first place, Payton was asking for a full-time leave of absence with pay for political service. Secondly, it involved federal instead of local or state office; and, thirdly, it was obvious that Payton was becoming more deeply and, perhaps, permanently involved in politics than any of the company's headquarters executives had been before.

General Electri
and Practical Politics

The following material has been reprinted with the permission of the General Electric Company as a contribution to a better understanding of the private enterprise system.

* * *

EMPLOYEE RELATIONS NEWS LETTER
For Circulation Among General Electric Management

May 28, 1956

POLITICAL HELPLESSNESS OF BUSINESS HURTS EVERYBODY

We are always pleased to consider that we Americans are privileged to live under the finest form of government that man has yet devised. We are pleased, too, to consider that our form of government was designed to promote the freedom of people in free markets, the free flow of commerce, and a free business system of incentives and competition for the benefit of all.

But we are disturbed, as we scan the current political picture, to observe some events and trends that seem destined to impair the ability of our economic system to operate in the long-range best interests of everyone. We think, for instance, that much that is happening will restrict, rather than enhance, the ability of businessmen to make possible an ever-rising standard of living for the American people. And curiously, perhaps, we think that businessmen themselves are to blame for much that's going wrong.

What seems to us most fundamentally wrong as we survey the political scene is this: It's good politics to be anti-business. Or, as one observer facetiously put it, "baiting business bags ballots."

This isn't a brand new phenomenon, of course. The Washington bureau chief of one of the nation's great wire services recently pointed out that "in the past two decades, there has been a political trend toward deriding, if not discrediting, business." He goes on to say, however, that businessmen's "troubles with the politicians often are their own fault."

We agree. And even though the problem may not be new, we think it deserves re-examination. So, briefly, we'd like to discuss with you its causes, its implications for the future, and what, if anything, can or must be done about it.

The Voter's View

It might seem logical, perhaps, to expect general agreement among the beneficiaries of the free enterprise system that a business is an estimable institution. Business, after all, is the principal source of the incomparably high standard of living we Americans enjoy. Business is not only the source of those material goods and physical services that can make lives richer and happier, but an instrument also of a rising level of rewarding spiritual living. A housewife freed by a machine from the drudgery of hand-washing of dishes or laundry can reach out for more humanly constructive things to do for others and for greater spiritual satisfactions from her own life.

People know this, of course. They know, too, that it is they—the customers of a business—who determine whether that business shall succeed or fail. They know that if a business provides a product or service they don't want, the business will fail. They know that the better a business can do what they want done at a price they'll pay, the more it prospers and grows. In short, the people know that a business succeeds only as it serves. Yet at the polls, they are thought to vote in droves for the candidates who say the interests of the people are opposed.

These voters, who are *economic* men, must have been led to believe that, as *social* men, they must go to the polls and vote against their own interests. They make it "good politics" to pillory business. Why?

Behind the Voters' View

There is no simple answer, of course. But in history, psychology, and current events, there are some guides.

In the first place, there are and presumably always have been businessmen foolish enough to short-change the public to gratify their personal ambitions. It could hardly be argued that the architects of the trusts a half-century ago were mainly motivated by a desire to serve the people. Nor can it be argued that every businessman today operates in the balanced best interests of all concerned. But there's no evidence that the proportion of crooks among businessmen is any higher than in any other group of people, whether masons or lawyers or public officials or factory workers. In fact, as a businessman's responsibilities mount, those giving him that responsibility tend to put character and social responsibility more and more at the top of the requirements he must meet. But businessmen have let the inevitable exceptions be blown up unchallenged into an appearance of being the rule.

As to big or successful business particularly, there's another explanation for widespread public suspicion. People feel—all other things being equal—that success begets power, and that power is too likely to be used for evil purposes. The more successfully a business manages to serve and please people, the bigger it grows and thus the more the public tends to suspect it.

The little fellow, of course, is the darling. He's the politician's pet, because there are more of him who vote than there are big or successful fellows. Americans' hearts naturally go out to the underdog. But once the little fellow gets big, he's suddenly considered dangerous. And this is true even if his bigness stems from unusual ability and determination to do humbly what people want done in the way they want it done.

Another reason why the businessman is in the doghouse is the quite logical one that a lot of smart and articulate people very profitably devote their lives to putting and keeping him there. These are the people who through ignorance or maliciousness dedicate their lives to convincing people that the welfare of the public and the welfare of business are incompatible. While these anti-business people try to take the credit for the good results flowing from our free enterprise system, they continue to seek to destroy it by creating a welfare state in which everyone would be a little man except for federal functionaries and themselves.

These are the outright opponents of business, call them statists, socialists, collectivists, or at best, people just envious of others' usefulness and success. They're enormously effective in discrediting every success that business achieves through serving the public. They will continue to be so, as long as businessmen continue to sulk silently in their tents and don't give the public the facts not only of the good "economic" merchandise they supply but also of the wonderful "social" merchandise they throw in.

The Politician—Leader or Led?

The result of these natural tendencies and external pressures on people's thinking is that most every politician thinks the voters are convinced that what's good for business is bad for them and vice versa. That's why politicians, who generally seek to mirror the minds of the majority of their constituents, find it so useful to assault business. And it will pay off at the polls as long as the people who know the truth don't bother to explain it to the voters.

So the fact is that the voters' orientation generally controls the votes of politicians, just as our customers' likes and dislikes control the design of our products. This is the essence of economic or political democracy, and this is quite right. Neither our political system nor our business system can tolerate runaway disregard of public sentiment.

Yet there is something quite fundamentally wrong when, as now, the political system turns up sponsoring attacks on the business system. When the institution of American politics promotes defamation of the institution of American business, the long-range welfare of all the people is severely threatened. This is no special interest problem. This is everybody's problem.

Business, of course, deserves a good share of the blame for creating the problem and allowing it to continue unsolved. For while business has made sure its products pleased the public, it has not taken similar pains to deserve and get general understanding, approval and support for the economic system that encourages business to serve the public so well.

What's the Evidence?

Now what's the evidence for all this? Where's the proof that voters average anti-business, that politicians typically tag along, or that business is, in fact, the target of attack?

A Gallup poll last fall gave ample proof of the voters' lack of confidence in businessmen. The pollsters asked people which of three types of men they would most like to see as the next President of the U. S.—a man who usually sides with business, who usually sides with labor, or who usually follows a middle-of-the-road policy? The middle-of-the-roader came out well ahead, but the man who usually sides with labor polled more than three times as many votes as the man who usually sides with business.

Now any politician who studied these statistics might well conclude that his welfare depended (1) on proclaiming he's a "middle-of-the-roader" while (2) favoring the "labor" viewpoint three-to-one over the business view. Thus, if his opponent is not smart enough to do the same thing, he captures the allegiance of the vast majority of the electorate and becomes a shoo-in.

In Washington, the search for issues for the fall vote-harvest is spawning more than 100 Congressional investigations. As you have surely noticed, many are quite openly dedicated to digging up dirt about successful businessmen.

The election year attacks on successful businesses are taking many forms. A graduated tax to punish business success in pleasing people is being urged. Socialized power advocates among the legislators are trying to prove that government support of private power production is designed to benefit "business" and is therefore wicked. Television networks have been under attack. Businessmen in government jobs have been harassed. Aircraft manufacturers have been under fire. And so on. Business should certainly be open to proper public scrutiny at all times. But too often the obvious intent of political investigators is to add to and cash in on anti-business prejudices.

Not a Party Proposition

The Democrats, of course, are in charge of these investigations, because they control both houses of Congress. But they have no copyright on the notion that it's good politics to assault business—or to court the foes of business in hopes of gathering votes.

The Republicans, too, think they see political value in capitalizing on the average voter's responsiveness to attacks on business. If the Republicans controlled Congress this year, they might find it equally advantageous to rake business over the coals. The G.O.P. has sought more money for every major program to regulate business. And Republican representatives are reportedly absenting themselves from hearings when businessmen are testifying. So it's not a party proposition at all—just a matter of taking political advantage of existing public opinion.

This strategy, of course, is by no means confined to Washington. In a recent electrical industry strike, five state governors, representing both political parties, intervened on the side of the union to do seemingly unwarranted damage to the company. One state government astonishingly labeled the strike a "lockout," even though action of this kind could hardly fail to kill off thousands of present jobs there and scare off thousands of other potential jobs in that state for years to come. Yet the actions were obviously judged to be "good politics" for the moment.

So much for the evidence. These items are but shreds. To the average voter, and hence to the average politician, successful businessmen have let themselves be made to seem antisocial badmen. However good and popular their products, however important their contribution to the nation's living standards, it's good politics to harass them. It pays off at the polls.

Is Business in Politics Now?

This might not be important if business and politics were wholly separate. But the businessman who says he's not involved in politics is kidding himself—dangerously. He may not be active in party politics. He may not read what's going on in his State Capitol or in Washington. He may not even vote.

But whether he's politically inert or not, a businessman is in politics up to his ears. In this era in which big government delves deep into the lives of everyone, affecting his welfare from birth to death, no businessman can logically say that what politicians do or fail to do is strictly their affair—not his. A head-in-sand approach to the ill repute of business with both the public and the politicians can only endanger business and all the people business serves.

What Must Be Done

What's to be done? How can the people be shown that the function of a good business is to serve them, not to take advantage of them? How can business get it across that the size of a company is a measure of its competitive success at serving people, not of its ability to oppress them? What can business do, not selfishly but with the public interest in view, to bring about favorable public attitudes toward the wonderfully productive role of business in our society?

Finally, how can the politicians be shown that failing business is bad politics, the route to retirement—not to re-election?

Fortunately for the nation, there is an answer. And the answer is not to try to silence the opposition. In our democracy, the right of anyone to seek his ends through lawful means should be unquestioned. To argue that the opposition to business has no right to fight is to undermine our democratic system.

A Two-Part Program

The answer to businessmen's political problems is to get politically important themselves—to convince the public and its representatives that for the good of everyone, businessmen also must be listened to, encouraged and treated fairly. The road to political effectiveness lies along a two-part program of *first* deserving and getting the respect of a majority of the people, and then, *second,* of making sure that businessmen's ideas of right and wrong are forces to be reckoned with by any politician intent on getting elected or re-elected.

Part 1—Deserve and Get Public Support

Part one of the program is nonpolitical. But it's an essential prerequisite for *political* effectiveness, as for operating effectiveness as well. This means businessmen must behave right, make sure no general complaints about business are justified, and make equally sure any exceptions to this are cleared up promptly and voluntarily. They must turn out good products, and advertise and price them fairly. They must pay their people right, and treat them right. They must do an ever-better job of satisfying people's proper hopes for dignity and extra human satisfactions from their work.

Businessmen must go out with a two-way proposition of doing what they ought to for their communities in return for equal consideration from those communities. Business must be a good local taxpayer, asking no bargains. It must contribute generously to local charities. It must help support other community businesses all it can by making its purchases locally.

Then businessmen must make sure their intentions and their deeds are known and understood. They must explain their business and all business to their employees and neighbors, so they know the problems and needs and challenges of business, and the great rewards for all that successful business can provide. They must help all concerned learn sound economics and acquire needed political sophistication.

They *must train management and other employees to be ready spokesmen* who ably and continuously tell the *positive* story of the economic and social good that business does.

They must thus get the public to withhold judgment and refrain from any precipitate action, while the full facts on controversial issues are being secured and objectively weighed.

This is Phase One: To make sure business first deserves and then gets the respect, understanding and warm approval of the people. Once the voters understand that the success of American business is tied tight to their own needs and hopes for richer, fuller lives, it can no longer be good politics for politicians to be anti-business.

Part II—Influence Votes

Phase Two of making business politically important demands that politicians be convinced that the considered testimony and recommendations of businessmen can and will influence the voting of the politicians' constituents. The big reason now that union officials are thought to be so important politically while businessmen are usually so impotent is that rightly or wrongly the politicians figure union officials can and do influence votes, while businessmen can't and don't. Unlike Phase One, this is a program of direct political action, but centering on issues rather than candidates or political parties. It is a non-partisan program of publicly and effectively supporting what is in the public interest and opposing what is not.

Businessmen and others allied to protect the public interest can be effective in direct political action. There's no excuse for defeatism when the ingredients for political effectiveness are obvious and at hand. It can be made good politics to be on the side of business when an informed public is shown that business is for what the public really wants and needs.

The ingredients number only five.

1. *Good Issues.* Obviously, business must never support any other kind of cause. Management must simply develop the ability to recognize what is in the long-range best interests of everyone and what is not, and then put the issue promptly, squarely and directly before the voters.

2. *Money.* Too many politicians figure unions are now the sole source of enough money to win elections. This is foolish. If businessmen and like-minded people will alert enough people to raise money from individuals on a strictly legal, ethical basis, there'll be no trouble at all getting all that's required. Meanwhile, a lot of people will have become interested, because however small their contribution, they'll get a sense of participation in a good cause.

3. *Mass Communication.* Effective political action, just like any other effective merchandising, requires getting the basic sales story across to the ultimate consumer, this time the voter. The voter can no more be expected to vote for a cause he knows little or nothing about than a customer can be expected to buy an unknown product. Selling businessmen's ideas on public affairs forthrightly through mass communication—and just as courageously rebutting misrepresentation—will also discourage the opposition from making false claims because of the certainty of being exposed.

4. *Leg-Work Organizations.* Just as infantrymen must mop up after an artillery barrage and salesmen wrap up the job begun by advertising, so active *local* leg-work organizations are essential to finishing the work done up to a point by mass communication. As any effective precinct captain knows, political success depends in the last analysis on leg-work by scores of individuals who are alert, articulate, sold on the justice of their cause, and who can do the final persuading *and get out the vote of the right individuals on election day.*

5. *Speaking Up.* As a part of Phase One, businessmen from big names on down must become active, competent, known and accepted in making their views known, whether in print or by word of mouth, before big or small groups, in debates on television or before city governments, or at Congressional or state government hearings. In Phase Two, to personalize the mass communication, to inspire the precinct leg-men, and to turn back instantly any new last-minute misrepresentations, businessmen must *learn how* to draw on the skill and credibility they developed in Phase One (Phase Two is too late) to make compelling and *winning* public appearances on the particular issues—and then *make* them.

These are the things businessmen need to do to get over their helplessness and become important in the political arena. There's nothing revolutionary in any of them. As you can see, they are borrowed direct from successful product marketing. They're just the things the opposition has borrowed from commercial sales training and has been employing so effectively against business all along.

Formula for Failure

This is no challenge to take over government and run it for the special advantage of business. To the extent that businessmen or farmers, labor officials or lawyers or any other group can get the power to run the government in their special interest, democracy has failed. Nor is this a call to action, or reaction, to undo the great social progress that has accompanied the great economic progress of the decades past. It is a call to correct misinformation and keep it corrected.

The path of progress for all Americans lies not in letting any group of citizens gain undue power. Yet this seems the trend today. The foes of business, a special interest group, are gaining steadily in power and prestige. And no American dedicated to preserving both our political and our business systems can ignore this threat to the balanced best interests of all groups and individuals in the whole public.

"The only thing necessary for the triumph of evil," said Edmund Burke, "is for good men to do nothing."

COMMUNITY AND GOVERNMENT RELATIONS BULLETIN
For Circulation Among General Electric Management

September 17, 1964

POLITICS, THE COMPANY, AND YOU

During any period of intense political activity—like this presidential election year of 1964—there will inevitably be questions about the relationship of the Company and its employees to the political process.

- *Does General Electric favor one political party over another . . . one candidate over another?*
- *Are General Electric employees free to go to work for the candidate and party of their choice?*
- *Why does the Company speak out on politically controversial issues? And what about employees doing the same?*

These and numerous other related questions touch on matters of legitimate concern to both employees and the public. It is useful, therefore, to seek to answer them clearly and completely.

What follows is not new. It has been said before in many ways and in many places. It is said again now in the interest of enlarged understanding among any who may have some cause for uncertainty.

The Company Is Non-Partisan

Any discussion of General Electric and the political process must begin with one fundamental fact:

The Company has been, is, and will be strictly non-partisan; it neither supports nor endorses any political party or candidate.

In addition to federal and state statutes which broadly prohibit political contributions or expenditures by corporations, there is a long-standing conviction in the Company, as expressed through its officers and managers, that the Company exists chiefly for economic and social purposes, and that partisan politics is the proper business of individual citizens who singly or bound together for political purposes, should be free to think, speak and act as they choose. Only in this way can the integrity of representative government be preserved.

Still the Company has a relationship to the political process and it proceeds from the concept that a workable democracy requires widespread informed participation.

"Those who won our independence," said Supreme Court Justice Louis Brandeis, "believed . . . that the greatest menace to freedom is an inert people, that public discussion is a political duty, and that this should be a fundamental principle of American Government."

Providing Information on Public Issues

For many years, General Electric has sought to contribute constructively to the discussion of public issues by providing information—and occasionally taking a Company stand—on certain questions that have an impact on the business.

Recently, for example, the Company has joined in the debate over taxes, international trade and tariffs, patent rights and penalty payments for overtime work.

On such matters, General Electric, through its officers, managers and other qualified employees, has a special competence of knowledge and experience to contribute and an obligation to speak out so that decisions are taken in the light of all available facts. To stand mute would impede the workings of a democracy which rests on confidence in the ability of the representatives of an informed electorate to arrive at sound judgments on public questions.

Obviously, many of these business-related issues are fraught with political overtones and controversy. The Company's participation in the discussion of them, however, does not reflect a political partisanship; it simply is an attempt to add facts, correct misinformation, and to supply constructive ideas where there is often a vacuum.

As Thomas Jefferson wrote in 1820:

"I know of no safe depository of the ultimate powers of the society but the people themselves; and if we think them not enlightened enough to exercise control with a wholesome discretion, the remedy is not to take it from them, but to inform their discretion."

Encouraging Employees to Be Politically Active

General Electric's non-partisanship among parties and candidates in no way abridges the right of its employees, as individual citizens, to actively work for the party and candidates of their choice. In fact, the Company has long encouraged this kind of responsible citizenship. Without widespread individual support, political parties and candidates will become dependent on, and ultimately tied to the interests of an ambitious, working minority.

However, freedom of political activity and association, like freedom of religion, must be carefully preserved as a matter of personal, voluntary choice. General Electric does not in any way suggest what party or candidate employees should support.

At the same time, it should be made very clear that employees who do participate in the political process do so as individuals, speaking and acting for themselves and not as representatives of the Company.

Specifically, there are four kinds of voluntary political activity which the Company seeks to encourage.

Being Informed

The only solid foundation for any kind of political activity is to be informed about issues, candidates, and the political process itself—the function of various organizations and how they mesh to perpetuate representative government.

To this end, the Company has conducted seminars in practical politics in which local political leaders of both parties discuss the intricacies of politics and government at all levels.

Plant newspapers and other employee communication media equip employees with facts about elections, biographies of candidates and information on business-related public issues.

Competing candidates for public office frequently tour factory and office areas, meet and talk with employees or hold rallies at the plant gates.

Registering and Voting

In an attempt to motivate more people to exercise their franchise, the Company has provided fact sheets on registration and voting regulations and conducted "Register and Vote" campaigns at many locations.

Further, the Company in most locations, observes a paid holiday on Election Day, thereby making it considerably more convenient for employees and their families to cast their ballots.

Supporting a Political Party or Candidate

Parties and candidates have a continuing—and often urgent—need for volunteers to do work of all sorts, and for individuals to provide the financial backing necessary to conduct an adequate campaign.

This year, in response to President Kennedy's Commission on Campaign Costs, General Electric has launched a Company-wide non-partisan effort to encourage all employees to support—with their dollars—the political party or candidate of their personal choice. This "Dollars for Citizenship" program dramatizes the importance of individual political contributions, and then provides a convenient—and private—opportunity for employees to respond as they choose. The Program has been endorsed by both the Democratic and Republican National Committee chairmen, and by scores of other political leaders around the country.

Also this year, as in the past, employees are being alerted to the many other ways an individual can contribute through volunteering his time and talents to political organizations. Over and above giving and raising money, people are needed to help man the voting places, prepare and mail out campaign literature, poll precincts and do all the other varied and exciting work that is required in a successful campaign.

This kind of voluntary effort is, of course, the great sustaining force of our political parties.

Government Service

Actual participation in the government—filling an elective office or serving in an appointive position—is a highly commendable form of political activity by those employees who are qualified and interested. And the Company generally encourages it, and will, where necessary, attempt to arrange special work scehdules and leaves of absence.

Literally hundreds of General Electric employees—from factories and offices around the country—are currently engaged in government service, ranging widely from local school boards to state legislatures, and discharging important duties in the Peace Corps and the Office of Economic Opportunity (the War on Poverty).

These public-spirited individuals are helping to continue a tradition established by top General Electric officials, who have a long and distinguished record of voluntary public service in appointive positions.

From 1920 to 1940, both Gerard Swope, president, and Owen D. Young, chairman of the Company, held appointive positions in Republican and Democratic Administrations. Mr. Young was frequently mentioned as a possible candidate for President on the Democratic ticket in 1928.

During World War II Charles E. Wilson, then president, and Ralph J. Cordiner, who later became chairman and chief executive officer, served President Roosevelt on the War Production Board, while Philip D. Reed, then chairman, was a leading member of the U. S. Economic Mission in London.

After the War, Mr. Wilson became chairman of President Truman's Committee on Civil Rights, and later was named by the President as the first Director of the Office of Defense Mobilization during the Korean War.

In 1956-57, Mr. Cordiner served the Eisenhower Administration as chairman of the Defense Advisory Committee on Professional and Technical Compensation.

And currently President Johnson has appointed Fred J. Borch, president of the Company, to serve on the National Citizens Committee for Community Relations, carrying forward General Electric's long history of commitment to equal opportunity rights for all citizens. Vice President Virgil B. Day is serving the Department of Labor on the Management Advisory Committee on Wage Stabilization and Labor Disputes. And Dr. Guy Suits, another Company vice president, is serving on the House Research Management Advisory Panel.

GUIDELINES TO POLITICAL ACTIVITY BY EMPLOYEES

There is much that General Electric and its employees can do to contribute to the vitality and strength of our representative government.

Because the Company must necessarily remain strictly non-partisan, its activities are confined to the job of analyzing, informing and encouraging. The vital element of direct involvement in the partisan work of political parties and support of candidates has to be left to individual employee-citizens.

In order to help maintain this clear distinction, there are long-standing guidelines to the participation of employees in political activity. These guidelines, recently restated, and reviewed by the Executive Office, are designed to reaffirm and preserve the Company's non-partisanship while protecting the right and freedom of individual employees to engage in political partisanship.

I. General Statement

Widespread, informed participation in the political process is the key to successful democracy. General Electric employees have the right and are encouraged to support the political party or candidates of their choice. The Company, however, is and must remain non-partisan; it does not and will not support or oppose any party or candidate. Accordingly, as employees exercise their political freedom, it is important that they do so in a manner that makes it clear they are speaking and acting as individuals and in no way as representatives of the Company.

II. Partisan Fund Raising

In the solicitation of contributions to or for a particular candidate, political party or similar organization:

- No employee shall solicit such contributions from any other employee who reports to him or is below his level in the Company organizational structure.
- No Company representative shall designate, appoint or instruct a Company employee to act as a solicitor of other employees for such contributions.
- Employees, who as individuals, undertake to solicit such contributions from other employees shall do so only under conditions which make it clear to the solicited employee that he is under no Company compulsion or pressure to make any contribution.
- Employees who solicit their contributions on their own time even if on Company property must so conduct such activities as not to interfere either with their own work and responsibilities to the Company, or with the work and responsibilities of other employees.

- Employees who solicit such contributions shall not, through the use of General Electric's name or stationery, or otherwise, indicate or imply to any person that the solicitation is approved or supported by the Company.

III. Partisan Use of Company Funds or Facilities Barred

No officer or other employee shall make, authorize or approve the contribution or expenditure of Company funds or use of Company facilities directly or indirectly for the purpose of aiding or supporting a particular party or candidate for political office, in any Federal, State or Local election (including party conventions, primary elections and general elections). This does not necessarily prohibit allowing opposing candidates equal opportunity for plant visits, gate rallies, etc.

IV. Non-Partisan Programs

The Company may conduct from time to time programs designed to encourage all employees to register and vote, be informed on public issues and support the party and candidates of their choice. Such programs—to be implemented only after appropriate managerial and legal review—will be entirely non-partisan, voluntary and conducted in a manner which will permit each employee to choose freely, to participate or not, and will protect the confidentiality of his action.

V. Employees in Public Office

Some employees, of course, may wish to run for public office, or hold appointive public office or work in the political campaigns of others.

Such service as an elected or appointed public official or other personal political activity may require the employee's full time or part of the employee's time during normal working hours.

- Where the employee's full time is required, the Company may grant leaves of absence (without compensation) and with suitable benefit plan arrangements.
- Where part of the employee's normal working hours are required, effort will be made to arrange special work schedules which will permit the employee's absence without interfering with his Company work. Where such special work schedules cannot be arranged without a reduction in total hours worked by an employee, the employee's pay will be reduced proportionately.
- Vacation periods may, of course, be used by employees for partisan political activities.

General Electric employees who become elected or appointed to public office hold this office responsible to their constituents and their consciences, and do not serve as representatives of the Company, and the Company will seek to avoid any conflict of interest.

In those instances when the government requests the loan of an employee to serve without compensation, and this employee has a special competence to work in the public interest, appropriate arrangements can be made to facilitate such service.

VI. Speaking Out on Public Issues

Just as the Company respects the right of employees to participate in the party of their choice, so it respects the right of employees to hold and to publish such opinions on public issues as they may choose. However, on public issues which can significantly affect the business environment generally or the Company in particular, General Electric's officers and managers have both a right and an obligation to develop and publish opinions on behalf of the enterprise as a whole. Obviously, the opinions so expressed, on behalf of the Company, and by other individual employees may not be the same.

When an employee chooses as a private citizen to advocate publicly views on public issues inconsistent with a view espoused by the Company (or on public issues where the Company has espoused no views and where the employee's views could mistakenly be considered the Company's) the employee should make plain that his opinions are his own. This is no infringement on either the Company's or the individual's right to freedom of speech, but it is intended as protection of this right for both.

These considerations as to individual employee's political activity do not, of course, exhaust the questions that may arise in this increasingly important area. In those situations not clearly covered by these guidelines, employees and their managers should seek the guidance of local Company counsel.

PART NINE

SPECIAL SITUATIONS

Communications
Research Laboratories[1]

On Tuesday, October 8, 1963, Mr. Howard Roach appeared at the employment office of CRL's Laboratory in Metro, Pennsachusetts in response to a "Help Wanted" advertisement for an IBM tab operator which he had read in the *Metro Times.*

The receptionist gave Mr. Roach an employment registration card to fill out. Upon completing the card, Mr. Roach was asked to have a seat in the waiting room while waiting for an interviewer to see him.

Shortly thereafter, Mr. C. E. Bronzo called Mr. Roach into his office. After preliminary introductions and chitchat, Mr. Bronzo started to discuss Mr. Roach's training and experience. It soon developed that Mr. Roach was a well qualified candidate for employment. These are the highlights of his background:

In July, 1943, at the age of 18, Mr. Roach enlisted in the U. S. Army. While in the Army, Mr. Roach took advantage of many educational opportunities. His primary effort was devoted to the study of electronic data processing equipment and accounting procedures. As a result of his studies, Mr. Roach rapidly advanced through the enlisted ranks. He retired from the Army in August, 1963, with the permanent rank of Chief Warrant Officer.

Mr. Roach is thoroughly familiar with the various IBM tabulating machines which CRL has in its Metro office. He knows how to operate, wire, and troubleshoot the machines.

Now that Mr. Roach has retired from the Army, he wishes to secure a position with a large "blue chip" company. He is only 38 years old, and

[1] This case was prepared by Mr. C. E. Babcock under the direction of Professor Donald Grunewald.

feels he can be a very useful employee. It is his intention to complete requirements for his BA degree, and to eventually become a systems analyst.

Mr. Roach stated that, "He is aware of the fact that he would have to start in a relatively 'menial' position and work his way up."

At the conclusion of the interview, Mr. Bronzo informed Mr. Roach that he would be informed of CRL's decision by mail within a few days.

Mr. Bronzo dictated a reply to Mr. Roach on Thursday, October 10. In his letter, Mr. Bronzo informed Mr. Roach that he had not been selected for the position. (A copy of the body of the letter to Mr. Roach is attached as Exhibit One.)

On Friday, October 25, a Mr. H. R. Rockwell of the State Commission against Discrimination (commonly known as SCAD) called on Mr. Bronzo. Mr. Rockwell stated that he was "investigating an *age* discrimination complaint lodged against CRL by a Mr. Howard Roach." Mr. Rockwell requested that he be allowed to see all records pertaining to Mr. Roach's application for employment. Mr. Bronzo arranged to have them sent directly to Mr. Rockwell. Mr. Rockwell also requested that Mr. Bronzo execute a sworn statement relating his part in the "Roach Affair," and that it be sent by registered mail to his office within three days. (A copy of this statement is attached as Exhibit Two).

Mr. F. D. Lincoln, personnel director of CRL, was informed by Mr. Bronzo of all aspects of the situation. He approved the action taken by Mr. Bronzo to date. He informed Mr. Bronzo that if formal charges were brought against CRL, he was to be notified immediately.

On Wednesday, November 13, Mr. Bronzo received a notice from SCAD that a representative from CRL was required to appear at a formal hearing to be held at 9:30 a.m. on Monday, December 2. Mr. Bronzo immediately notified Mr. Lincoln of this action.

As personnel director, Mr. Lincoln is responsible for determining what policy CRL is to follow in this case, and to review existing policy to see if such a problem can be avoided in the future.

CRL is a wholly owned subsidiary of a major, privately owned United States communications utility. Its primary responsibility is to provide communication research and development services to its parent company and "corporate sisters."

In addition to the Metro Laboratory, CRL has three more large facilities in a nearby state. It also operates branch laboratories in five other states in the northeastern, southern, and midwestern parts of the country. CRL employs in excess of 14,000 personnel. They are distributed as such:

Metro Laboratory	1,700 plus
Mentor Laboratory	4,500 plus
New City Laboratory	3,000 plus
Elkton Laboratory	3,500 plus
Branch Laboratories	1,100 plus

These 14,000 personnel are distributed within the following occupational classifications:

Technical Staff	3,000 plus
Assistant Technical Staff	4,000 plus
Administrative Staff	1,000 plus
Clerical	2,000 plus
Plant Operations [2]	3,000 plus

As of October 31, 1963, CRL had assets in excess of $100 million. Its operating budget for 1963 is expected to exceed $335 million. Since CRL is a nonprofit organization, all monies expended for assets and operating costs are provided by the parent company.

CRL has a reputation of being a "good" place to work. There has never been a major strike conducted by the unionized plant operations personnel. It is considered to be one of the outstanding industrial research organizations in the world. Because of the many startling discoveries made at CRL and the manner in which they are utilized, its image is constantly in the public eye. Also, because of its affiliation with its parent utility, many local, state, and national political bodies maintain an active interest in CRL's activities.

Mr. Lincoln is not sure what course to pursue. Over the years with CRL, Mr. Lincoln has been a staunch advocate of fair employment practices. In fact, he is CRL's representative reporting "Plan for Progress" facts to the President's Committee on Equal Employment Opportunity. It has also been, since 1941, a firm policy (stated very clearly in the General Executive Instructions) that CRL will not practice employment discrimination because of race, creed, color, religion, or *age*.

On the other hand, Mr. Lincoln has also advocated that an applicant not be hired if he is unqualified for a particular job, or if he is so overqualified for a particular job that a personnel or personal problem is likely to develop. Mr. Lincoln is sure that Mr. Roach was not rejected because of his age. On the other hand, Mr. Lincoln acknowledges the fact that Mr. Roach is a competent tab operator.

What should Mr. Lincoln do?

Exhibit One

Communications Research Laboratories

Dear Mr. Roach:

Since your recent visit to the Laboratories, we have had your candidacy under active consideration.

Many factors influence such consideration, the most important being the mutual suitability of an applicant and a particular position.

---

[2] Represented by the CWA of the AFL-CIO.

After carefully reviewing your previous education and training, in light of the specific requirements of the available position, I regret to inform you that at this time I can not offer you encouragement concerning employment. However, I will retain your application in our reference file in the event I can suggest a suitable opening in the future.

We thank you for your interest in the Laboratories, and wish you good luck in the future.

Very truly yours,

Exhibit Two

Communications Research Laboratories

Statement from Mr. C. C. Bronzo

Mr. Howard Roach was interviewed by me on Tuesday, October 8, 1963. The purpose of this interview was to determine if Mr. Roach was qualified for a position in our Accounting Organization as an IBM Tab Operator.

After thoroughly interviewing Mr. Roach myself, I discussed his qualifications with Mr. V. T. Capunza,[1] who is the Manager of our Tabulating Department. We concluded that Mr. Roach was extremely overqualified for the position, and that it would not be in his or our best interests to offer him the position.

I accordingly notified Mr. Roach by my letter of October 10, 1963 that I could not offer him encouragement concerning placement at this time.

Sworn to: Signed by:

[1] Fictitious name.

Mahrud Foods, Inc.

The new general manager of the central kitchen of Mahrud Foods, Inc. is wondering what action, if any, he should take with respect to the problem of where the firm's large delivery trucks should be parked when not in use. Mahrud Foods owns and operates a chain of 23 low-priced cafeterias and four retail shops that sell prepared foods in a large midwestern city. Much of the food is prepared in a central kitchen and trucked to the cafeterias and retail shops in the firm's own ten large delivery trucks.

The problem first arose two years ago when the city passed an ordinance prohibiting the parking of trucks on the city streets during the hours from 11 p.m. to 5 a.m. in order to facilitate street cleaning. Fines of ten dollars per violation were established by the ordinance.

Mahrud Foods had always parked its trucks overnight on the street in front of the central kitchen before the ordinance was passed. At the time the ordinance became law, management had investigated the costs of buying a nearby lot for parking purposes. This lot, the only one available in the vicinity, had a price of $50,000. This high price for the lot, plus the costs of resurfacing the lot, and the high real estate taxes on the lot (estimated at $1,500 per year) had led management to reject this solution to the problem. Leasing space in an existing parking lot would cost the company about $75.00 per week. Parking the trucks outside the city in a neighboring suburb without an overnight parking ordinance would involve labor costs of over $100.00 per week plus additional fuel costs, as the suburb was a 20-minute drive from the city and the workers would have to be paid for this extra driving time. Another alternative would be to continue to park the trucks on the street and pay for violations whenever the trucks were ticketed by the police.

The police precinct captain is a friend of the assistant manager of Mahrud's central kitchen. The assistant manager solved Mahrud's parking problem by providing the precinct captain with free groceries each week and free coffee to all patrolmen who stopped by the kitchen from time to time. In return for these favors, the police overlooked the daily violation of the city parking ordinance. The groceries and coffee cost Mahrud about $25 per week.

The new general manager of the central kitchen is somewhat disturbed by the present parking arrangements entered into by the assistant manager. He is uncertain, however, of what action, if any, he should take with respect to the parking problem. The empty lot is still available and the other alternatives mentioned above are also available, including a continuation of the present arrangement.

Lynn Cocktail Lounge [1]

William Lynn has investigated the possibilities of opening a cocktail lounge at North Municipal Airport of Centre City in the state of Rocky Mount.

Rocky Mount is a state similar to New Mexico or Arizona. Metropolitan Centre City has a population in excess of 500,000. The tourist trade provides the main source of income in Centre City. During the winter season, its many hotels and motels attract a large clientele from tourists seeking to escape the rigors of winter in their home states. The headquarters of one railroad and the western division office of a second are located in Centre City. Centre City has little other industry. The agricultural processing center for the state of Rocky Mount is located in a city more than 300 miles from Centre City. There is relatively little agricultural activity in the Centre City area.

Lynn had been approached by a friend, who is vice president of Consolidated Airlines, about the possibilities of opening a cocktail lounge in the Consolidated Airlines terminal building at North Municipal Airport. Consolidated is a large national airline which handles about 30 per cent of the airline passenger business into and out of Centre City. A small feeder airline, West Central Airways, also serves Centre City by means of North Municipal Airport. Its terminal building is immediately across the street from the Consolidated Airlines terminal. However, the West Central Airways terminal building is a very small one, with no

[1] This case has been reprinted with permission from *Cases in Business Policy*, edited by Donald Grunewald, which was published by Holt, Rinehart and Winston © 1964.

room for a cocktail lounge. An inspection of the West Central terminal and a talk with West Central Airways officials convinced Lynn that the latter's terminal could not be expanded to provide a competing cocktail lounge. The proposed location of the cocktail lounge in the Consolidated Airlines terminal faces the West Central Airways building. Therefore, Lynn believes the cocktail lounge would attract travelers from both airlines.

Three other airlines serve Centre City by means of South Municipal Airport. They handle about 60 per cent of the airline passenger business into and out of Centre City. Centre City is also served by three railroads and two national bus companies.

Lynn's whole business career has been spent in the food and beverage service industries. He had worked for a nationwide chain in this industry for over 20 years before branching out on his own. He currently owns three profitable drive-in restaurant concessions on a turnpike. Because of Lynn's reputation as a successful businessman, his friend at Consolidated came to him first before talking to one of the national chains. Lynn was intrigued by his friend's proposal. The space in the terminal was formerly rented to a gift shop, which was liquidated after the former owner's death. It could be converted to a lounge seating fifteen people at the bar. Space would also be available for a few tables and a juke box. Lynn estimated that the space could be converted, fixtures acquired, and an adequate inventory purchased for a total investment of about $25,000. Lynn had a capable man in mind who was available to manage the lounge and act as head bartender. Other employees could readily be hired. Consolidated would be paid a fixed monthly rental plus 2 per cent of all sales.

On the basis of his experience in the industry, Lynn believes that the lounge could operate to yield a good profit. He would build the lounge into a smooth-running operation and then sell out to a national food service chain after a year or two, in order to make a capital gain. Similar operations have been sold to national chains at other airports for between $100,000 and $150,000. Lynn knows that the national chains would be eager to buy his lounge if it proved successful.

After some investigation, Lynn applied for a license to operate a cocktail lounge. Alcoholic beverage licenses in Centre City are under the control of the city License Board. Board members are appointed by the mayor, with the consent of the City Council. For many years, Centre City politics has been dominated by A Party. The B Party has not controlled the City Council since 1880 and has not elected a mayor since 1907. The current B organization is practically nonexistent. In effect, the A Party primary serves as the election in Centre City. The dominant A organization, often called a "machine," has been virtually unopposed in the primary for over thirteen years.

The chairman of the city License Board told Lynn that his application for a license would be denied unless he made a campaign contribution of $16,000, to be divided as follows: $6,000 to the mayor and $2,000 to each of the five members of the City Council. Lynn, a registered member of A Party, rebelled at this type of political "contribution."

Lynn believes that a strong two-party system is best for the nation and the A Party. If the A Party faced strong competition, Lynn believes it would nominate its most capable candidates in order to win. Lynn is not impressed with the caliber of the A Party in Centre City.

The state of Rocky Mount is also dominated by the A Party. Lynn decided to appeal to the state chairman of the A Party to see what he could do. However the chairman said he was powerless to intervene in a "local" matter.

Lynn is currently uncertain about what he should do next. He could buy a license from an existing license holder. Such a procedure would be honored by the city License Board. However, the going rate for purchasing licenses is in excess of $25,000. Or, he could decide not to pursue the project further. Finally, he could make the political "contribution" and be awarded a new license. Lynn is aware that political contributions are not tax deductible for federal income tax purposes.

Follansbee Steel
Of
Follansbee, West Virginia

At the end of November, 1954, Republic Steel's management, headed by Charles M. White, president, said it was at a loss to understand why the purchase by it of the machinery and equipment of the Follansbee Steel plant would be an important factor in the failure of Follansbee to continue in business, or why such a purchase could be considered an appropriate subject for investigation by any federal administrative agency or executive branch of the government.

Republic's part in the sale agreement was "in no sense the purchase of a going business" the statement said, for Follansbee's management had already told its stockholders that the firm could not profitably continue in business as a nonintegrated steel company under present market conditions. Morover, said Republic, two of Follansbee's chief customers were at the time installing equipment which would eliminate their reliance on a converter of cold rolled sheet steel.

In regard to fears of unemployment in Follansbee, Republic said, "Predictions have been grossly exaggerated." Arguing that more than a third of the steel plant's employees did not live in the community, and the town itself was in the heart of an important industrial area, Republic said, "At worst the unemployment situation may be only temporary, and nearly all the employees of the Follansbee mill will receive pay which will tide them over for the time being."

[1] Northwestern University cases are reports of concrete events and behavior, prepared for class discussion. They are not intended as examples of "good" or "bad" *administrative or technical* practices. Copyright 1955, Northwestern University. This case reprinted with the permission of Northwestern University.

Republic said that transfer of the mill's equipment to Gadsden, Alabama, "will in all probability give greater stability of employment to more people than will become temporarily unemployed as a result of Follansbee's failure to continue in business at its present location."

In reply, the Citizens' Committee of Follansbee, headed by Mayor Frank Basil, sent an open letter to Mr. White, challenging his contention that Republic's sales agreement "was in no sense the purchase of a going business." The citizens' group pointed to two other offers to take over the company or its assets, both of which had been turned down by Follansbee directors. The two prospective buyers, the latter said, had faced the defect which the mill had as a nonintegrated plant and would remedy it, not by liquidation, but by expansion.

"As we see it," Mayor Basil's letter continued, "the main threat to the continued existence of our mill does not come from its nonintegrated character and alleged obsoleteness. It comes rather from much more powerful companies which are interested in swallowing competitors." The last point was being studied by the Senate Anti-Monopoly Subcommittee. Mr. White said he was at a loss to understand why its purchase should have been the subject of such investigation.

What had alarmed the people of the town of Follansbee (population 4,435) was the announced intention of the Follansbee Steel Corporation to sell the bulk of its assets to Frederick W. Richmond, a New York financier. Mr. Richmond had intended, in turn, to sell most of the production facilities to Republic, and Republic planned to move the equipment to Gadsden, Alabama. The mill had been operating in the town of Follansbee for 142 years. "The plant employs 90 per cent of the town's work force," said Mayor Frank Basil. "This deal will spell disaster for us. There won't be anything left here to keep this town alive."

"It is the 4,500 shareholders," said Mr. Richmond, "who are going to be hurt, and not the employees of Follansbee. The employees can only lose jobs that are already partially lost or in jeopardy.

"If the mill were to continue as it has in the past year for a further period of time, not only would the employees find themselves without jobs, but the stockholders could easily find themselves without working capital and without sufficient funds to operate the mill any longer." He pointed out that two of Follansbee's largest customers, Empire Steel Corporation and Newport Steel, were installing their own cold-rolling equipment, and that early in 1955 Follansbee would lose most of what little business it still had.

"As far as I am concerned," said Mr. Richmond, "whether the deal is eventually consummated or not is a matter of degree. Neither I nor my associates can lose money. We can make some if the deal goes through. The people I feel sorry for are the stockholders of Follansbee, whose assets are being dissipated and whose position is being jeopardized by the unwarranted interference of wholly irresponsible people in the affairs of the corporation."

At stake in the struggle for Follansbee were two cold-reducing mills, one cold-finishing strip mill, two continuous cold sheet mills, tinning pits for long terne sheets and auxiliary equipment, all of which were located in Follansbee. These facilities employed several hundred workers from Follansbee, and the town received about two-thirds of its tax revenue from the plant. The company's operating troubles, which had caused it to lose $106,820 before taxes in the quarter which ended September 30, 1954, were said to stem from the fact that it was a non-integrated steel company. It had to buy semi-finished steel from other firms, and then sell some of its finished products in competition with the same firms.

Frederick W. Richmond, the central figure about whom the controversy revolved, was thirty years old in 1954. By that time he had already made himself a multimillionaire. *Time* magazine dubbed him a "tycoon, junior grade."

Richmond was originally from Boston. At Harvard, while taking the Navy's wartime V-12 officer training program, he ran a one-man tax consultant service. Shipped to the Pacific before finishing Harvard, he came out of the war, as he put it, "a radioman, third class, and a crap-shooter, first class."

After the war ended he finished his schooling at Boston University and later used $1,400 of Navy dice winnings to start an ad sales office. (While at Harvard he had drummed up ads for the Harvard *Lampoon*.) He then switched to export-import trading, in which his first big deal was with an Argentinian who wanted half a million yards of a certain type of cloth. Richmond found the cloth at the War Assets Administration, and bought it with credit from a Boston bank for which his father did legal work. On the resale he cleared $40,000. Then he expanded his line to steel and chemicals.

By 1948, when Richmond was twenty-four, he had a suite of offices on Fifth Avenue in Manhattan, and his business was grossing $11,000,000 a year. Then, after suffering losses in the recession of 1949, he decided to leave the export business to become a financier.

With the help of money from friends he started by buying W. Ralston Company, a small New Jersey paper converter for $550,000. He later sold it at a profit. Then in rapid succession he picked up five more companies, including Brubaker Tool of Millersburg, Pa. (price $600,000); Toledo's Baker Brothers, manufacturers of automatic factory equipment for Ford, General Motors, and others ($1,500,000); Detroit's Gear Grinding Machine Company ($1,600,000).

In 1954, Richmond headed syndicates buying Pennsylvania's Birdsboro Steel Foundry and Machine Company ($4,000,000), Hydraulic Press Manufacturing Company ($4,000,000), and Detroit's Republic Gear Company ($2,700,000). As he put it, "I look for situations where the stock is being traded at a price which is sufficiently low so that my offer to the stockholders, while under the book value, is still more than the price at which the stock is being traded." He had become, as one business associate called him, "a speculator in companies—specifically companies which could be bought for less than their asset value." Richmond was secretive about his associates, who varied from deal to deal. For those who would join him, he had a word of caution: "My enterprises are strictly venture capital. It's not like buying DuPont bonds."

Richmond's first offer on the Follansbee deal, which had been accepted by Follansbee's directors in August, 1954, had been to buy their properties and sell them to an integrated steel company. He said that he had contacted eighteen steel companies in a vain search to find someone who would keep the mill in Follansbee before turning to Republic's offer to buy the plant and move it to Gadsden. The move would eliminate the jobs of 653 workers at Follansbee, but Republic had offered to re-employ 150 of them at Gadsden. Richmond promised to continue to operate Follansbee's sheet metal division at Follansbee, employing 290 persons.

In the Follansbee deal, Richmond had offered the company a gross price of $9,286,260 for the bulk of Follansbee's assets. Included in these assets was $4,030,405 in cash and bills receivable, leaving the out-of-pocket cost to Richmond only $5,255,855. By selling the mill to Republic for $1,500,000, and selling Follansbee's inventories for another $3,090,000, Richmond would have reduced his net outlay to a mere $665,855.

Richmond would also receive a tax refund of $970,000 due to Follansbee for 1952 and 1953 losses, which would have given him a cash profit of $304,145 on the series of transactions. Besides, he would still own the balance of Follansbee's properties, including the Federal Stamping and Enameling Division, which had a book value of $6,574,249.

The directors of Follansbee intended to merge the remaining corporate shell of the Follansbee Corporation, whose only asset then would be about $9,300,000 in cash, with two midwestern concerns, Frontier Chemical Company of Wichita, Kansas, and Consumers Company of Chicago, both of which were controlled by Clint Murchison, a Dallas, Texas, oil and cattle multimillionaire. Murchison was reputed to be one of Texas' richest oilmen. Estimates of his fortune ranged as high as half a billion dollars. He owned barge lines, insurance companies, ranches, bus lines, office buildings, banks, and farms. Frontier Chemical produced chlorine, caustic soda, muriatic acids and other industrial acids which it distributed throughout the West and Midwest. Consumers Company produced sand, gravel, stone, ready-mixed concrete and other building materials which it sold in the Chicago area. The merger was to be by an exchange of stock, and the merger plan called for changing the name of Follansbee Steel Corporation to Union Chemical and Materials Corporation.

Mr. Stephen Rooth, representing the Murchison interests, stated that the reasons that Murchison was interested were: first, to find a marketplace for the equity which he had in the two companies (he would acquire Follansbee's listing on the New York Stock Exchange); second, it would provide capital for the expansion of the chemical business; third, the significance of the loss carry-forward, which would be lodged in the surviving corporation.

In presenting his case before the Federal District Court in the injunction suit which followed, Mr. Abraham Pinsky, attorney for the Citizens' Committee, pointed out that Republic was also getting, in addition to the physical assets set out by the proxy statement, patents, trademarks, and records. Included were the sales records of almost $25,000,000 of Follansbee's business, with the names of customers and specifications of their requirements. Republic also intended to take over the entire Follansbee sales force, its sales offices and office equipment, and the good will attached to these facilities.

On October 26, 1954 Judge Herbert S. Boreman of the Federal District Court of Wheeling, West Virginia issued a restraining order temporarily blocking the sale of the Follansbee assets to Frederick Richmond. The injunction, which was obtained by 47 minority stockholders holding a total of 1,550 shares of Follansbee's total of 464,331 outstanding common shares, prevented the management from voting proxies approving the Richmond offer at the next stockholders' meeting. The plaintiff contended:

1. That proxy statements mailed to stockholders on the sale and merger proposals failed to disclose arrangements by which certain of the Follansbee Steel officials were to remain in the employment of the continuing corporation, namely: Marcus A. Follansbee, president, and John J. Harding, vice president, were to be retained by the new Murchison company as consultants at annual salaries of $15,000 each; and that the law firm of William B. Paul, one of the Follansbee directors, was to be retained as legal counsel.

2. That the proxy solicitations failed to disclose that Mr. Richmond had agreed to indemnify the Follansbee directors and officers against possible liability in a $6,000,000 pending damage suit brought against the company by one Rex Murdock, a major Follansbee stockholder.

3. That the proxy statements failed to bring to the attention of the stockholders two other offers: one, an offer by Cyrus Eaton of Cleveland and Louis Berkman of Steubenville to purchase the stock, and second, an offer by Mrs. Aline Warner of New York to purchase the assets.

4. Both of the undisclosed proposals included stipulations agreeing to continue operations of the Follansbee mill in Follansbee, West Virginia.

Marcus Follansbee denounced the Eaton-Berkman group. He charged them with "trying to capture the entire company at a bargain price" and said that they had initiated "trumped-up court actions" in an effort to kill the pending sale to Richmond. "This eleventh-hour court action," said Mr. Follansbee, "is an unscrupulous attempt to sabotage the proposed sale and merger, ostensibly on behalf of the Follansbee stockholders, but actually on behalf of certain mysterious persons who are trying to scuttle the Richmond deal and expect to pick up the resulting debris at a much lower price."

Spokesmen for the Follansbee Steel management denied that they had received bona fide offers to buy the company, either from Mrs. Aline Warner or from Louis Berkman and Cyrus Eaton. Mrs. Warner said that her offer had been made by telephone and telegram. The Berkman-Eaton offer had been made by mail.

The minutes of the stockholders' meeting of November 1, 1954 showed the following passages:

MR. PINSKY: There have been bona fide offers submitted by Messrs. Eaton and Berkman. What is your ruling on that?
CHAIRMAN FOLLANSBEE: We do not feel that the Eaton-Berkman offers were in such form that the directors could consider them.
MR. PINSKY: Who is "we"?
CHAIRMAN FOLLANSBEE: The directors.
MR. PINSKY: Let's have the minutes of that action.
CHAIRMAN FOLLANSBEE: The minutes are not written up.
MR. PINSKY: Do you have any memorandum of the minutes?
CHAIRMAN FOLLANSBEE: They are not here.
MR. PINSKY: Will you produce them?
CHAIRMAN FOLLANSBEE: I will, some time.
MR. PINSKY: Will you produce them now, at this meeting?
CHAIRMAN FOLLANSBEE: No.

The initial Eaton-Berkman offer, which had been made through their attorney, Joseph A. Patrick of New York, without disclosing the names of the principals, was to purchase 51 per cent of the stock at $21 a share, which would give 51 per cent of the stockholders about $1.00 more for each of their shares than the Richmond offer. The Follansbee directors refused to present this offer to the stockholders, and criticized it for "giving preference to 51 per cent of the stockholders at the expense of the remaining 49 per cent." The subsequent Eaton-Berkman offer was to purchase 51 per cent of the stock now at $21 a share, and the remaining 49 per cent at the same price within a year.

Mr. Cyrus Eaton had substantial and varied business interests. He was chairman and president of the Portsmouth Steel Corporation, chairman and president of West Kentucky Coal Company, and chairman of the Chesapeake and Ohio Railway. He was also a director of Cleveland Cliffs Iron Company and Sherwin Williams Company. He had been, at times, a director of Republic Steel Corporation, Youngstown Sheet and Tube Company and other concerns. Mr. Eaton's office issued the following statement in connection with his Follansbee offer:

> Because of Mr. Eaton's past record in saving several essential industries in Ohio for their home communities, West Virginia governmental and business interests have asked his help in working out an agreement among the parties concerned to keep Follansbee in operation in its home city. On that basis Mr. Eaton has become interested in the matter. In 1946, when Portsmouth, Ohio was threatened with becoming a ghost city by the removal of the local works of the Wheeling Steel Corporation, Mr. Eaton stepped in and formed the Portsmouth Steel Company. The property was enlarged and improved and today is in successful operation with 7,000 employees.
>
> In 1926 Mr. Eaton gave his personal check for $18,000,000 to save the Trumbull Steel Company, Warren, Ohio from liquidation. Later he made Trumbull the cornerstone of the nation's third largest steel producer when he combined it with a number of steel companies to form the Republic Steel Corporation.
>
> Two years ago, in June, 1952, Mr. Eaton advanced a loan of $7,600,000 to 850 employees of the *Cincinnati Enquirer,* which enabled them to buy the paper and preserve their jobs. It had been planned to merge the *Enquirer* with another newspaper.

Mr. Eaton insisted that his interest was purely philanthropic. "My main purpose," he said, "is to act as peacemaker between the Richmond group and the others, to work out some deal that will keep the mill operating where it is." Would the SEC, he asked, kindly order a resolicitation of stockholders so that they might make a democratic choice?

Mr. Louis Berkman was an ex-steel scrap man in his early forties, who had broadened his activities in recent years to steel producing and steel rolling. He was president of Louis Berkman Co., which operated iron and steel plants through ownership of subsidiaries and divisions, including Parkersburg Steel Company, Parkersburg, West Virginia; Blast Furnace Division, Martins Ferry, Ohio; Ohio River Steel Division, Toronto, Ohio; and Superior Sheet Steel Division, Canton, Ohio. The Ohio River Steel Division had been the Toronto Works of the Follansbee Steel Corporation until 1950, when Follansbee had sold it to Berkman. Among the people of the Follansbee community Berkman had a reputation for being a manipulator of steel companies, a sharp trader, and a hard driver of his labor force.

Mrs. Aline Warner was the wife of a New York broker who had substantial means of her own. Speaking on her behalf, Mr. Miles Rubin, her attorney, said that her original interest in the Follansbee mill had been a financial motivation; she felt that the mill could be made to earn a profit, and that she could make some money on the deal. Later, said

Mr. Rubin, when she visited the town, the townspeople won her sympathy, and when she saw what intrigue was going on, she determined to defeat it. In evidence of the good faith of Mrs. Warner, and substantiating her ability to perform, Mr. Rubin exhibited the following confirmation of a telegram:

1954 OCT 28 AM 8 24

MARC FOLLANSBEE
FOLLANSBEE BLDG PGH
IF RICHMOND DEAL WITH YOU IS NOT CONCLUDED OR EXTENDED I WOULD OFFER NINE MILLION FOUR HUNDRED THOUSAND DOLLARS FOR IT WITH IMMEDIATE DEPOSIT IN ANY BANK DESIGNATED BY YOU OF FIVE HUNDRED THOUSAND DOLLARS STOP MY ATTORNEY MILES RUBIN AT 115 BROADWAY NEW YORK PREPARED TO MEET WITH YOU ON MOMENT'S NOTICE
ALINE WARNER   DUBLIN ROAD   GREENWICH CONN

At the stockholders' meeting of November 1, 1954, at which the stockholders voted on acceptance of the proposed Richmond deal, Marcus Follansbee refused to entertain any offer but the Richmond one. The minutes of that meeting showed the following exchanges:

MR. PINSKY: On October 2, 1954 in Brooke County Court you stated that you would submit offers to the stockholders and be glad to submit them.
CHAIRMAN FOLLANSBEE: Substantial offers.
MR. PINSKY: You did not say substantial offers. You are breast beating.
CHAIRMAN FOLLANSBEE: I said I would accept bona fide offers from substantial people and we do not have bona fide offers.
MR. MILES RUBIN: Have you informed the directors and stockholders of the receipt of a telegram to you by Mrs. Aline Warner offering to purchase the assets for nine million four hundred thousand dollars?
CHAIRMAN FOLLANSBEE: I have informed the directors and the press has informed the stockholders.
MR. RUBIN: Have you informed the directors and stockholders that five hundred thousand dollars has been deposited in the Guarantee Trust Company of the City of New York to stand as a deposit on her offer?
CHAIRMAN FOLLANSBEE: I have informed the directors and the press has notified the public.
MR. RUBIN: Do you consider Mrs. Warner's offer to be higher than Mr. Richmond's?
CHAIRMAN FOLLANSBEE: Not substantially so, no.
MR. RUBIN: Do you consider 25 cents a share to be a substantial increase?
CHAIRMAN FOLLANSBEE: No, I do not.
MR. RUBIN: Did you state under oath in the action brought by the minority stockholders that if a higher offer were made you would submit it to the stockholders?
CHAIRMAN FOLLANSBEE: I did, if a bona fide offer, and I do not consider your telegram a bona fide offer. We have everything spelled out in the Richmond purchase agreement.

MR. RUBIN: Did you notify the directors that Mrs. Warner's offer specified that she would contract on the same terms as included in the Richmond contract, including time limitations in such contract?

CHAIRMAN FOLLANSBEE: I did.

MR. McCAMIC (minority attorney): How did the directors vote?

CHAIRMAN FOLLANSBEE: The directors voted.

MR. McCAMIC: How did the directors vote?

CHAIRMAN FOLLANSBEE: The majority of the directors voted.

MR. McCAMIC: What was that majority?

CHAIRMAN FOLLANSBEE: I do not think it is important what the majority voted.

MR. McCAMIC: Are you refusing to answer?

CHAIRMAN FOLLANSBEE: Yes.

Mr. Pinsky later argued before the Federal Court that this stockholders' meeting had been an arbitrary and violent suppression of corporate democracy or suffrage. "It seems to be the universally accepted notion," he said, "that at a meeting of the equitable owners of a business any proposition touching their interests may be raised. One cannot read the record of this stockholders' meeting without being impressed by the fact that each attempt to present the two other offers in this case was promply ruled out of order."

Challenged to show what inquiry had been made into Richmond's ability to perform, the Follansbee management asserted that they had made careful investigation. The data in the dossier they exhibited consisted of eight items, mostly newspaper clippings. Except for three *New York Times* articles and one *Fortune* story which were dated prior to their contact with Richmond, the articles had datings after contractual relations with Richmond had been established. In the Dun and Bradstreet report contained in the file, the data on some of his earlier adventures in business had been withheld.

In his argument before the Federal Court, Mr. Pinsky dwelt upon the inability of Richmond to perform. "The comparison of Richmond with the other offerors," he said, "puts the odium of nonsincerity on Follansbee. Aline Warner put up $500,000 and her ability to cover the balance is undisputed. Eaton-Berkman deposited $1,000,000. On the other hand, Richmond agreed to put up $500,000, then refused to do so, and finally Follansbee settled for $300,000." Mr. Pinsky exhibited evidence to support his claim that Richmond would not have been able to conclude the deal without the aid of Republic Steel. "Richmond," he said, "was a weak reed to lean upon. Without the Republic deal he could not go forward and complete his contract. It is clear now that he was never able to operate the mill. His promises in that respect were the purest moonshine. The record affirmatively shows that Follansbee knew of his instability."

As evidence of the agreement to continue the employment of certain officials, Mr. Pinsky exhibited the following letter:

February   , 1954

Mr. M. A. Follansbee, President
Follansbee Steel Corporation
Gateway Center
Pittsburgh 22, Pennsylvania

Dear Mr. Follansbee:

I transmit herewith an offer addressed to Follansbee Steel Corporation to acquire certain assets of the Corporation. Manifestly it is of the first importance to me that if the sale is consummated, the purchasing company shall have the benefit of the services of the present management. In order to assure this, I propose that if the transaction is consummated:

1. the new company shall enter into five year management contracts, on suitable terms, with such of the present top officers of the corporation as you will indicate to me are essential to the continued successful operation of the enterprise;
2. the new company shall retain the present attorneys and independent auditors of the Corporation.

Very truly yours,

FREDERICK W. RICHMOND

Questioned about this offer by the SEC, Mr. Moses, a partner in the law firm of Paul, Rock and Moses, the Follansbee attorneys, said that there had been such an offer, but it had never been accepted. Asked whether the offer was still outstanding, he said this involved the legal question of how long an offer is outstanding, but he admitted that it had never been rejected. The amount of compensation being considered for the attorneys was $1,000 a month. While this was the same as the amount of their retainer while with Follansbee, it was pointed out that their total compensation from the company had been close to $50,000 a year.

Mr. Richmond had claimed that the services of the management of Follansbee and its attorneys were essential to him because of their knowledge of the business. In his argument before the court, Mr. Pinsky pointed out that upon merger all of the business and assets of Follansbee would be gone. Consumers and Frontier would also cease to have any legal existence. Union Chemical would be the surviving corporation, not in the steel business in which these men were experienced, but in the chemical and building supply business.

The union president of the Follansbee local of the CIO was of the opinion that the employees would not stand for a cut in wages under any circumstances. If cutting wages to make the mill a profitable operation was an alternative to going out of business, he believed that his men would rather lose their jobs altogether than take a cut. He based his opinion on what had happened at Louis Berkman's Toronto Steel

Works, two miles up the river from Follansbee. Berkman had smelted scrap iron into billets there, and during the war it had been a profitable operation. After Korea, when war work ceased and it became a losing operation, Berkman proposed to scale down rates. The employees refused to take any cut, the mill closed, and had remained closed ever since.

A Follansbee merchant who had raised $6,000 to finance the Citizens' Committee proxy fight said that there were other reasons for the uncompromising attitude of the mill employees. Many of them, he said, had bought homes, cars, television sets and household appliances on time payment accounts. They had obligated themselves to the full extent of their paychecks, and they felt that they could not afford to take any cut.

A Follansbee clergyman who had been a leader in the citizens' campaign was convinced that the threat of widespread unemployment was very real. The crux of the problem, he pointed out, was that the average Follansbee employee was 55 years of age, and that many employees had thirty or forty years of service. Their lives were so deeply rooted in the community, he said, that they could not be persuaded to consider moving to another part of the country to find jobs. It was these employees who were in danger of becoming permanently unemployed.

Mrs. Celia Humes, president of the Bank of Follansbee and herself a longtime resident of Follansbee, agreed. There were many families in town, she said, whose incomes had been from the mill as long as the mill had been in existence. Mrs. Humes thought that the provincialism of the natives of a West Virginia mill town was difficult for an outsider to appreciate. Many of these people, she said, had never in their lives been further than five miles from Follansbee.

The manager of a steel mill in Steubenville, just across the river from Follansbee, thought that most of the Follansbee people might find employment over the next several years, but some of the older men would find it difficult ever to find a job again. Each mill, he said, was required by its union contract to re-employ first those of its former employees who had been laid off. For the past several years every local mill had such a waiting list, and would therefore be unable to accommodate any Follansbee people.

Mayor Frank Basil asserted that losing the mill would have a very direct effect on the municipal government. The mill supplied about two-thirds of the income of the city through real estate and gross sales taxes. Also, those expenditures which required the approval of voters, he said, would fail to receive their approval if there was general unemployment. Without the mill income, the police force would have to be cut to two men, street lighting would have to be curtailed, and other city services would have to be cut, regardless of whether these services were needed or not.

Some of the members of the Citizens' Committee were dismayed at the apathy displayed by the employees themselves in the face of the impending crisis. Perhaps, said one committeeman, the employees did not realize how critical their situation was. Few of them took any active part in the campaign. It was only a small group of businessmen and civic leaders who took an earnest inerest in the fight.

Marcus Follansbee was generally unpopular among the towns-people, who resented his absentee management and felt that he gave their problems little consideration. The Follansbee family was now in its third generation. John Follansbee, the founder, had had three sons, who failed to get along in harmony, and therefore he split his estate and willed each of them a steel plant. None of them cared to live in small towns where their mills were located. When Marcus came into his inheritance, he moved the Follansbee headquarters to Pittsburgh. Thereafter he seldom came to Follansbee. There were times when he visited the mill only once in a two-year period. Nevertheless, detailed operations were controlled from Pittsburgh. Tales were told of how every truck shipment from the mill had to be dispatched from Pittsburgh. Operating the headquarters office in Pittsburgh had cost $546,000 in 1954.

*   *   *

On October 25, Democratic Representative Wayne L. Hays of Ohio called for a Justice Department investigation of the proposed sale of Follansbee to Richmond to determine whether antitrust laws would be violated. The Congressman asserted that the entrance of Republic Steel in the sale arrangements "appeared to be a violation of the Clayton Anti-Trust Act." He said that the competition of Follansbee in a large steel-producing area would be eliminated if the sale were to take place. Rep. Hays' district bordered on the West Virginia state line, and a number of his constituents were employed by Follansbee.

On November 17th a Senate Anti-Monopoly Subcommittee composed of Senator Langer (Rep., N.D.), Senator Kilgore (Dem., W.Va.), and Senator Kefauver (Dem., Tenn.) met in Washington with Governor William C. Marland and Attorney General John Fox of West Virginia. The committee said, in a statement, that "there is reason to suspect that acquisition of Follansbee may well violate antitrust laws."

J. Sinclair Armstrong, Securities Exchange Commissioner, announced that the SEC might step into the proposed sale to Richmond. "We've been investigating this case," he said, "to determine whether SEC proxy rules were violated. The fact that the integrity of our proxy rules is challenged is very serious. The staff of my commission has spent more time on this case than on any other during 1954."

On December 1, Frederick Richmond asserted that he was still willing to place $3,850,000 in escrow toward his planned $9,286,620 purchase of Follansbee assets. In an effort to save his deal, he offered to keep part of the plant operating, and Republic offered to continue some of the other departments to see whether they could be profitably operated in Follansbee. As a last resort, Richmond made this offer to the town: he would pay a full year's salary to an executive secretary if the townspeople would form a promotional organization to lure new industry into Follansbee.

In Cleveland, Mr. Eaton reiterated his offer to buy Follansbee. He promised not to dismantle any of the company's equipment at Follansbee, and repeated his intention to keep it operating at its present location.

Mrs. Aline Warner announced that she would press her fight to have her offer of $9,400,000 considered. Mrs. Warner said that she would operate the plant, or have it operated for her, in Follansbee. She said that her plan would be not to move anything, or to close up anything. She questioned whether Mr. Eaton's promise to keep the plant in Follansbee was "only a guarantee through the newspapers, or whether it was stipulated in the contract."

The Port of New York Authority[1]

A new jetport for the New York-New Jersey metropolitan area

On December 14, 1959, the Port of New York Authority made public a preliminary report concluding that the Great Swamp area of Morris County in New Jersey offered the only practical site on which to build a much-needed new jetport for the northern New Jersey-New York metropolitan area. According to the Port Authority, studies on which the report was based had been under way since early in 1957. These studies confirmed that the capacity of existing airports would be reached by 1965, at which time an additional major airport would be needed. It was indicated that the Port Authority's recommendations as to possible locations for the proposed jetport were guided by several basic considerations, including proximity to the traffic generating area, airspace, and the primary requirement of protection of airport neighbors from excessive noise.

The Port Authority's preliminary estimate of costs indicated that the proposed new jetport could be constructed for a total cost of about $220,000,000. Basic to the mandate of the two states for the accomplishment of the planning and development of the Port of New York by the Port Authority is the principle that facilities be provided on a self-supporting basis. The Port Authority which was set up by a compact between New York and New Jersey and approved by the U.S. Congress has no power to levy taxes or assessment.

The compact provides that the Port Authority shall not pledge the credit of either state. However, on the basis of experience with existing airports, the Port Authority felt such a project could meet the self-

[1] This case was prepared by Mr. Robert D. Kirkup under the direction of Professor Donald Grunewald.

supporting requirement. The port compact directs the Port Authority to "make recommendations to the legislatures of the two states or to the Congress of the United States . . . for the better conduct of the commerce passing in and through the Port of New York, the increase and improvement of transportation and terminal facilities therein, and the more economical and expeditious handling of such commerce."

In the preliminary report, the Port Authority stated that it was prepared to carry its preliminary studies forward to the point of definitive recommendations with respect to the financing, development, and operation of a great new major airport in northern New Jersey. They would be made with the cooperation of the many other governmental agencies, civic groups, airlines, etc., and final recommendations would then be submitted to the governors and the legislatures of New Jersey and New York for their consideration.

During May, 1961 the Port of New York Authority submitted to Governor Robert B. Meyner and the Legislature of the State of New Jersey, and Governor Nelson A. Rockefeller and the Legislature of New York, "A Report on Airport Requirements and Sites in the Metropolitan New Jersey–New York Region." In addition, a copy of each of the following consultant's reports were sent to the governors' offices, to the Secretary of the Senate and the Clerk of the Assembly of the State of New Jersey, and to the Secretary of the Senate and the Clerk of the Assembly of the State of New York: C-E-I-R, Inc., *The Economic Relationship of Air Transportation to the Economy of the New Jersey–New York Metropolitan Area;* Hammer and Company Associates, *Economic Effect of a New Major Airport, New Jersey–New York Metropolitan Area;* H. O. Walther, *A Study of the Impact of Airports on the Market Value of Real Estate in the Adjacent Areas;* R. Dixon Speas Associates, *Transport Aircraft Development Trends and Passenger Schedule Patterns;* Stanley H. Brewer, *A Projection of Air Cargo Growth for the Port of New York Authority Airports 1960–1980;* Booz, Allen & Hamilton, General Aviation Forecast; Airborne Instruments Laboratory, *A New Major Airport New York–New Jersey, Volume I—Airspace, Volume II—Airport Capacity;* Landrum and Brown, *Study of the Effect of Airport Accessibility on Realization of Air Passenger Potential, New Jersey–New York Metropolitan Area;* National Weather Forecasting Corporation, *A General Climatographical Survey of the Land Area Within An Eighty Mile Radius of the New Jersey–New York Metropolitan Area.*

In the letter accompanying the Port Authority's report, it was restated that the Port Authority has no power whatever, and therefore can have no plans whatsoever, to construct another airport. No recommendations or statutory proposals would thus be included, but the report would set forth the technical and engineering facts and conclusions bearing on the need for and the practical locations of any new airport.

The Preliminary Report tentatively evaluated fifteen sites. This number was increased to seventeen in the final report to include McGuire Air Force Base and Lebanon Forest in southern New Jersey. All sites were found to be feasible from an engineering standpoint except Site 5, Caldwell, where flood-control consideration would preclude the development of a major airport, and Site 6, Jersey Meadows, where adjacent obstructions would prevent the development of adequate runway configurations. Construction costs, although varied, would not render unfeasible any of the seventeen sites. The controlling criteria, therefore, became airspace and accessibility.

In Airborne Instruments Laboratory's report on airspace was included the following:

"In a highly developed terminal complex determining the location for a new airport is a task that can be accomplished only after extensive analysis and even then only with some compromise of the ideal. Aircraft operating under instrument flight rules (IFR) consume enormous segments of the airspace, and airports must be located so that traffic of one in no way interferes with or impedes traffic of another. Consequently, for optimum use, airports must be many miles apart."

It was found that even the best locations studied would require careful re-arrangement of traffic patterns. The relative merit of each location was therefore based on:

1. How minor the restrictions would be that would have to be imposed.

2. The over-all effect of such restrictions on the movement of air traffic in and out of the area.

3. The over-all effective increase in air traffic capacity that would result.

Airport accessibility in terms of time, distance and fares from traffic-generating centers is a vital consideration in airport site selection. Favorable accessibility is essential to realization of the region's air commerce potential and to the development of sufficient traffic to make any airport economically feasible.

In the preliminary report, the Port Authority stated: "The proposed site in Morris County meets all of the requirements for a new major airport to serve the New Jersey–New York area, and it is the only potential site in the areas which does so."

This conclusion was further substantiated on the basis of the second report. It was declared that the site is practical because it is west of the heaviest concentrations of air traffic. Traffic to and from the southwest and west could thus be routed with minimum conflict with traffic to other airports; access to and from the south and northeast would be available with very little circuitous routing, and airspace could be cleared for holding areas in the vicinity.

The site was found to be a good location with respect to the region's traffic-generating areas and would not result in any significant reduction of use by potential air passengers. With existing and proposed highways, travel time by automobile would be approximately 25 minutes to downtown Newark and 44 minutes to the Lincoln or Holland Tunnel. Running time for airport buses would be 47 minutes to the West Side Airlines Terminal in Manhattan, at a fare of about $1.45 and for non-stop rail service to Pennsylvania Station, New York, about 50 minutes, at a fare of about $1.65. Nonstop monorail service between the airport and Manhattan would take about 32 minutes and would require a fare of $7.

Several other reasons can be given for choosing the Morris County site. There is enough land in the Great Swamp area to permit a 10,000-acre airport, which would be large enough to provide sufficient areas for the protection of local residents and businessmen from excessive aircraft noise. The center of the new airport would fall outside of the required 32-by-80-mile buffer zone around Newark Airport and far away from the corresponding buffer zone around any other existing airport in the vicinity. The desirability of the site from the standpoint of airspace has been confirmed by the Federal Aviation Agency. There are no major urbanized areas or highways running through the site, nor are there any any public buildings or industrial developments of any description.

Despite the residential structures in some of the westerly areas of the site, the fact remains that there are fewer structures and a smaller population than would be found in a potential airport area of this size anywhere else in the metropolitan region. All efforts would, of course, be made in the design of the airport to assure that a minimum number of these residences would be affected; and the whole purpose of including extensive areas within the airport boundaries is to overcome and avoid the noise problem in the neighborhoods around the airport site.

The basic design requirements for the proposed jetport were developed by the Aviation Planning Division of the Port Authority based on the information developed by its own staff and outside consultants.

The plans called for four runways laid out in a dual parallel configuration, each 12,000 feet long with sufficient land area allowed for possible future extension up to 14,000 feet. Also included were a 1,400,000-square-foot passenger terminal, a 14,000-car-capacity parking lot, aircraft maintenance facilities, tank storage for 24 million gallons of fuel, control tower facilities, an operations building, post office, commissaries for the preparation of flight meals, and a hotel. There would be 72 loading positions for passenger aircraft and twenty for cargo planes.

For the purpose of analysis, the development of the new jetport could be broken down into three stages. First, the primary construction stage could conceivably take place from 1965 to 1970. During this period at least $35 million would be spent for labor and another $70 million for materials and equipment, much of this being absorbed by the local economy. The jetport opening and early operational stages would make up the second stage, which would be from 1970 to 1980. The third stage, after 1980, would be the level of optimum operations.

The reactions of state and local officials, business groups, and the community as a whole to such a proposal as the building of a jetport in the immediate area is indeed interesting to observe.

A short while after the preliminary report was released by the Port Authority, this headline appeared on the front page of the *New York Times*: "Jet Age Threatens Rural Way of Life." This was accompanied by three pictures of a town and rolling country estate which supposedly would be wiped out if the jetport were allowed to be built in the Great Swamp. The article described the area as a region of homes with rail fences, some of which antedated the Revolution, of estates with winding drives, and as a region where under a light snowfall the terrain of hills and dells takes on the enchantment of a Christmas card.

The opposition to the proposed jetport by local residents was immediate and vigorous. At a meeting in Far Hills, New Jersey, a Port Authority spokesman received an antagonistic reception when he came to outline the agency's plan. The 200 persons in attendance had to be called to order several times, as every one wanted to make his objection heard. A woman warned that the Port Authority should be prepared for many lawsuits if plans materialized based on a New York Supreme Court ruling permitting residents to sue the Thruway Authority for damages to property values because of loss of peace and quiet.

The Morris County Planning Board went on record as opposing the jetport, stating that the many disadvantages outweighed the advantages. The board felt that outside interests rather than Morris County residents would be the only receivers of possible benefits. Other disadvantages mentioned included the substantial change that would occur in the character of the community, the prospect of increased taxes without return on ratables, putting an end to a County Park Commission plan to make a wildlife preserve out of part of the area, and the serious effect on flood control and water supply which the building of the jetport might produce.

The results of a poll conducted in Morristown by Fairleigh Dickinson University students is of some interest. Although 55 per cent of the residents surveyed were opposed to the jetport, while 45 per cent indicated they were in favor or neutral, the majority felt that their town would not be hurt. Four out of ten expressed fear of noise nuisance, but two-thirds felt that the value of their property would not be affected.

The main opposition to the plan came from the Jersey Jetport Association. The association, made up of homeowners and other opponents, projected a $176,335 campaign to fight the building of a jetport in the Great Swamp. The chairman of the group, Republican U.S. Representative Peter Frelinghuysen, Jr., declared that the Port Authority had completely ignored the feeling of the people and also criticized Governor Meyner for not joining the fight against the Morris County location.

The one group that did approve of locating a jetport in Morris County was the Netcong Business Leaders. This organization, with 55 members, stressed the economic impact that the jetport would have in the community and saw the project as a buffer against future economic depression.

The possibility of establishing a jetport in the Great Swamp of Morris County was doomed from the very beginning by the attitudes taken by New Jersey's political leaders. Both houses of the legislature overwhelmingly went on record as being opposed to the proposal, as did gubernatorial candidates James P. Mitchell and Richard J. Hughes. Perhaps if this issue had not arisen in an election year, the legislature and the candidates would not have been so overwhelmingly opposed to the Morris County site. It appears that the politicians were afraid of losing the votes of those persons from North Jersey opposed to the jetport and also of those persons from South Jersey who felt that a new jetport located in the pine barrens would be a valuable economic asset to the development of the southern half of the state.

Another interesting development concerning the controversy over the proposed jetport was the public hearing on Senate Bill No. 218, which was held before Governor Meyner in the Assembly Chamber of the State House during July, 1961. Senate Bill No. 218 reads as follows:

> 'Be it enacted by the Senate and General Assembly of the State of New Jersey:
> 1. No airport for usage by air carriers engaged in interstate air transportation, overseas air transportation, or foreign air transportation, shall be constructed in the counties of Morris, Hunterdon, Somerset, Union, Essex, Warren, and Passaic; provided, however, that this act shall not apply to any existing airport or future extension thereof which is presently served by air carriers certified by the Civil Aeronautics Board or airports operated and maintained by the United States Government as military installations.
> This act shall take effect immediately.'

Governor Meyner, in examining Bill No. 218, felt that a question of constitutionality was involved in choosing seven counties and excluding all others, and also that some federal questions might possibly be raised. He felt that of more importance, however, was the question of whether it should be decided at that time if there should be no new airports in those seven counties.

During the long and noisy hearing it appeared that no one was able to offer any sensible solution to the problem. As Governor Meyner said, "simply signing the bill will not eliminate the problem of the uncertainty . . . an issue of this sort is likely to last for quite a while."

Since Morris County is outside of the Port Authority District boundaries, the bistate agency would need to have the approval of both the New York and New Jersey legislatures before it could begin to carry out any of its plans. With the passage of Bill No. 218 into law and the attitude of the New Jersey Legislature, it appeared practically impossible that the Port Authority would ever be able to establish a jetport in the Great Swamp of Morris County.

In December, 1961, spokesmen for the Jersey Jetport Site Association in Morris County issued a joint statement announcing victory "for the foreseeable future" in their battle to block the Port Authority's plan. The two-year campaign against the proposal had cost $224,000, of which $155,000 was raised by public subscription. The remaining $69,000 consisted of county and municipal funds spent for technical studies.

George K. Bott, chairman of the Jetport Association's advisory council, said that the bulk of the money had been spent for technical studies, public relations, and legal fees, with the remainder having gone for such things as rent, heat, and light.

Thus, the problem of providing adequate airport facilities for the future remains unsolved. The Port of New York Authority, despite some of the justifiable criticisms leveled against the agency, has performed its duty and can do no more. The question now becomes one of who will help assume the responsibility for seeing that the aviation industry maintains its role in helping to keep the New Jersey and New York metropolitan area the greatest center of trade and transportation in the world.

Port Authority officials have consistently stated that:

> "The Port Authority has no power whatsoever, and therefore can have no plans whatsoever, to construct another major airport. . . . Our duties in this field under the Port Compact are simply to study and to report. . . . The only authority in the world that can authorize the construction of a new terminal airport anywhere in this metropolitan area is the authority of the people through their elected representatives in Trenton and Albany."

The only other location that would appear suitable for building a jetport is in the pine barrens of Burlington County in South Jersey. Unfortunately, the problems of airspace and accessibility have yet to be overcome. Site 13, the Mount Holly–Burlington A site, and the better of the two Burlington County sites evaluated by the Port Authority, lies mainly within Chesterfield and North Hanover Township, about sixty miles from New York City. It has the great disadvantage of requiring crossing of the busy airways to the west, and it would also require the abandonment of McGuire Air Force Base and the associated military climb corridor before it could ever be fully developed. It has been suggested that a spur from the New Jersey Turnpike at Bordentown might be constructed which would shorten ground travel time to New York City somewhat, but it is still estimated that to reach midtown Manhattan would take about ninety minutes by bus or rail, with fares of about $2.90 and $3.90 respectively. Nonstop monorail or helicopter service is presently considered unfeasible, largely because of the excessive fares which would have to be charged.

The main point in favor of the Burlington County site is that Governor Hughes, the Burlington and nearby Ocean County Planning Boards, the Boards of Freeholders, and a majority of the State Legislature are convinced that the new jetport should be built there. They point out that there are over 25,000 acres of land available at the site of which 16,000 acres are already owned by the state. (Twenty-five thousand acres constitute about 40 square miles, which is almost as large as the entire land area of Hudson County.) There is probably no place in New Jersey where one could get the necessary amount of land cheaper. With such a large expanse of land, noise problems could be minimized and safety control would be better. The area is also known to have an unusual degree of freedom from fog. A new jetport would be a definite economic boost to the development of South Jersey and would result in a further buildup of the New York–Philadelphia industrial corridor across northeast and central New Jersey.

The main obstacle in the way of proceeding with the plans to have the jetport in Burlington County has been the Federal Aviation Agency. The FAA had, from the beginning, recognized the need for a new jetport, but had firmly rejected the Burlington County site on the basis of airspace requirements. However, the FAA finally agreed to turn its computers to the problem, and in early 1963 a study was completed at a cost of approximately $1 million.

The results of the FAA study were not encouraging. Although it did not rule out the possibility that some day a jetport could be built in Burlington County, it did state that it could not approve the site because of the impossibility of coming up with a solution to change satisfactorily the air corridors and airspace requirements for the existing major private and military airports.

A less serious obstacle in the way of the jetport is the question of what agency would raise the necessary funds to complete the project and undertake the responsibility for its operation. It is extremely unlikely that the Port of New York Authority would be willing to finance the project, based on its opposition to having the jetport such a great distance from New York. New Jersey and Pennsylvania could cooperate in creation of a bistate authority to do the job, but one of the objections to the Burlington site is that nearby Philadelphia already has International Airport which is "hungry for business and cool toward competition." It is doubtful whether an authority representing only a few counties in South Jersey would be able to raise the sizable amount of capital required.

APPENDIX A

Burlington Jetport Issue at End, Hughes Concedes[1]

Gov. Hughes conceded yesterday he has come to the end of the line in his advocacy of Burlington County as a jet airport site.

"I don't see anything else I can do for it," he told the *Star-Ledger.* "I don't know any group or agency or person to whom I can appeal."

Because he has reached this decision, Hughes indicated, he asked the Port of New York Authority last week to study two new airport locations, both in North Jersey. One is near Bearfort in northwestern Passaic County at the Sussex County line. The other is at Bowling Green, west of Picatinny Arsenal near the Morris-Sussex County border.

The Governor believes that he completely fulfilled his 1961 campaign pledge to try to locate a fourth great metropolitan area airport in the Burlington-Ocean pinelands.

"I stood on my head," Hughes said. "I went to the White House. I went to the Federal Aviation Agency. And when the FAA agreed to make a simulation study for the Burlington site, I raised a fuss until they included environmental factors, too.

"At first, they had planned to study only air traffic factors. But I convinced them to include a study of the weather and topography."

The simulation study found the weather and topography fine for an airport. But last June 15 FAA slammed the door on Burlington because, it ruled, the study showed it could not fit into the heavily traveled air traffic pattern.

The FAA rejection also included the Pine Island site in Orange County, New York.

Despite the rejections, Hughes noted, he and Gov. Rockefeller of New York joined in asking the Port Authority to re-evaluate the FAA's study, both for Burlington and Pine Island.

PA Reaffirms Veto

Hughes said he felt so strongly about Burlington County that he insisted the authority, in restudying the site, should use a consultant who had never entered the authority's airport picture before.

Nevertheless, last week, the Port Authority reaffirmed FAA's rejection of both Burlington and Pine Island.

But while Hughes then asked the authority to study the Bowling Green and Bearfort sites in North Jersey, Rockefeller stood pat on Pine Island. Rockefeller, Hughes noted, said he still hopes for a jetport there "if no better site comes up."

"But that's what I'm banking on," Hughes said, "that we've got a better site. I flew up to inspect all those sites two weeks ago. Pine Island is no good. There are two mountains, 900 feet and 1,100 feet high, called Mt. Adam and Mt. Eve, which come at you just before you'd land."

Hughes said the Port Authority would take about a year to run its studies of Bowling Green and Bearfort, which were not included in PA's list

[1] Reprinted from Volume 50, No. 321 of the *Newark Star-Ledger* with the permission of the *Newark Star-Ledger.*

of possibilities in 1960 when it urged an airport in the Great Swamp of Morris County.

Overlooked

Why did the Port Authority overlook Bowling Green and Bearfort when it ran its original studies?

"I don't know why the Port Authority never found these," Hughes said. They were advanced by his own Department of Conservation and Economic Development.

During the 1961 gubernatorial campaign, retiring Gov. Meyner announced for the Great Swamp site, which enraged Morris County interests. Hughes, it is said, had hoped to keep the issue quiet. But he found himself in a box. To soothe Morris voters, he announced against the authority's proposal.

In view of the final rejection of Burlington County, does Hughes now regret having placed himself so flatly on record against the Great Swamp?

"No," he said. "No regrets. The Great Swamp is not a good site, anyhow. I've been told by many pilots that it's in a bowl and would be dangerous to land. It would cost $50 million just to drain.

"Moreover, it is just outside the perimeter of the air pattern. It's just about on the line. It would also be a great annoyance and nuisance to thousands of residents."

Await Blitz

Many observers feel that the Port Authority is simply awaiting an opportune moment to launch another blitz in behalf of the Great Swamp. Hughes doesn't believe this.

"They've given up," he said. "I don't think the Port Authority has any hope for the Great Swamp."

The reporter observed there is some feeling that the Port Authority was pretty arbitrary about rejecting certain sites. Since it's the creation of New York and New Jersey, couldn't the two states get together and compel it to build on a specified site? In short, why let the Port Authority call the shots?

"That's a very mistaken viewpoint," Hughes answered vigorously. "I'm directing the Port Authority unilaterally to make this study of Bearfort and Bowling Green and they're going ahead because I asked them.

"To picture the Port Authority as a tyrant is popular politics. It's our Port Authority. We asked them for the truth on Burlington and they told us the truth."

Could the state or some other agency build a new airport, leaving the Port Authority out of the picture?

Hughes said he knew no other agency which could finance it, particularly in its early money-losing years.

Has Hughes considered McGuire Air Force Base, which Senator Case now espouses?

"Yes," answered Hughes, "I went to the Pentagon about the time I was elected. I could get no hope. Besides, it is subject to many of the same objections as Burlington."

Finally, Hughes was asked if the metropolitan area actually needed a fourth airport.

Again a vigorous "yes". Within three or four years, the three present airports will be overcrowded, Hughes said.

APPENDIX B

THE PORT OF NEW YORK AUTHORITY
111 Eighth Avenue—at 15th Street, New York, N.Y. 10011

Lee K. Jaffee   FOR RELEASE: Upon Receipt
Director of Public Relations   January 16, 1964
Telephone—620-7541

New York, Jan. 16—A study of possible sites for a major airport to serve the New Jersey–New York Metropolitan Area was authorized today by the Commissioners of The Port of New York Authority as requested on December 30 by Governor Richard J. Hughes of New Jersey and Governor Nelson A. Rockefeller of New York. Announcement of the Commissioners' action was made by Chairman S. Sloan Colt following the monthly Board meeting at 111 Eighth Avenue.

The Governors' request for the study was made following the Port Authority's report to them that the development of a major airport at Burlington, New Jersey, or Pine Island, New York, was not feasible. The Burlington–Pine Island re-evaluation also was made at the request of the two governors.

The new study will cover the Bearfort area of West Milford Township, Passaic County, and the Bowling Green area of Jefferson and Sparta Townships on the Morris-Sussex County border in New Jersey, and any other sites which may be considered practicable. The study will be completed in about a year.

Consulting services will include aerial photography, topographical and boring surveys, meteorological studies, hydrographical surveys and other professional services. It is estimated that these consulting services will cost about $380,000. This estimate may be somewhat reduced if the Port Authority finds it feasible to use meteorological data available through the Federal Aviation Agency, the United States Army and the Weather Bureau.

In a statement following receipt of the re-evaluation report, Governor Rockefeller noted that consideration of Pine Island could not be completely foreclosed until a more satisfactory site was found. He said: "Obviously, it is imperative to meet anticipated traffic needs that a new jetport be available by 1970. I am, therefore, asking the Port Authority to study other available locations in the region and earnestly hope that the Port Authority will come up with a recommendation that can lead to action and a solution of the prob- at the earliest possible time."

At the same time, Governor Hughes expressed his disappointment at the report of the re-evaluation with respect to the Burlington site. He stated: "The judgment, at all stages, has been uniform: the pinelands site is incompatible with some of the most heavily traveled air corridors in the world and the air safety problems involved appear to be insuperable; added to the ground distance from the population centers it would be designed to serve, this factor of air safety would rule out any hope of a Burlington jetport."

The Governor emphasized his continued opposition to "the establishment of a jet airport in the Great Swamp area of Morris County, Hunterdon County or any other settled residential area where the community would be disrupted by such a development."

Governor Hughes noted that he previously had directed Commissioner Robert A. Roe of the New Jersey Department of Conservation and Economic Development to look into the possibility of alternate sites in the event that the Burlington area might be found unfeasible. He stated that as a result, Commissioner Roe suggested two alternate locations in Northern New Jersey as "promising sites" for a new major airport. One of these sites is near Bearfort in northwest Paassaic County at the Sussex County line, and the other near Bowling Green, west of Picatinny Arsenal near the Morris–Sussex County border. Consequently, he requested that the Port Authority also undertake studies of the feasibility of a new major airport at these locations.

APPENDIX C

THE PORT OF NEW YORK AUTHORITY
111 Eighth Avenue—at 15th Street, New York, N.Y. 10011
Tel: 620-7271
EXECUTIVE OFFICES
Austin J. Tobin
Executive Director

October 27, 1964

Hon. Richard J. Hughes
State House
Trenton, New Jersey

My Dear Governor:

When the Port Authority's re-evaluation of the Burlington (New Jersey) and Pine Island (New York) sites, made at the request of your Excellency and Governor Rockefeller, was formally transmitted on December 30, 1963, you issued a statement expressing disappointment at the re-evaluation as it applied to the Burlington site, but recognizing that the air traffic problems involved, to say nothing of the basic problem of accessibility, would rule out any hope of a Burlington jet airport. You advised us, however, that Commissioner Roe and his staff, with your permission, had made a check of possible alternate sites. These general surveys led to the suggestion of two possible locations in northern New Jersey. These proposed sites were Bearfoot and Bowling Green. You requested, therefore, that the Port Authority undertake further studies of the practicability of the construction of the necessary new airport at either of these locations, and advised us that you had discussed this request with Governor Rockefeller. These studies were to determine and analyze the climatological, hydrological, site preparation and construction factors with respect to both sites. You will recall that in your letters and instructions to us you anticipated problems in these areas because of the completely unknown engineering and technical factors involved, and you specifically requested us to probe them in depth.

Accordingly, the Commissioners of the Port Authority, at their meeting on January 16, 1964, authorized studies of the practicability of a major terminal airport in the Bearfort area and the Bowling Green area.

In accordance with your request that the Governors' offices be kept advised from time to time as to the progress of these studies, I wrote to you on February 24, 1964, outlining the organization of the study of the two sites. Early in August 1964, I sent a further progress report to Commissioner Roe and to Dr. William Ronan, Secretary to Governor Rockefeller.

Since that time, the work and reports of two of the consultants have been completed.

One of these reports is from our consultant, the Walsh Construction Company, on preparation of possible sites for a major airport in the Bearfort–Bowling Green area of northern New Jersey.

We also have received a report on factors applying to water supply at both sites, prepared by Hazen and Sawyer, Engineers.

Our final and complete report on these two sites will be ready for transmittal to you and to Governor Rockefeller by the end of the year, as scheduled when our study was authorized on January 16. In the meantime, these two consultants' reports on basic factors of our study have provided us with information of such critical importance that, in keeping with your directive, I am transmitting these two consultants' reports to Governor Rockefeller and to you in advance of a final report.

I should note that in addition to these two consultants we retained the Aero Service Corporation of Philadelphia to develop five foot contour topographic maps of both sites from aerial photographs; Alpine Geophysical Associates, Inc., of Norwood, New Jersey, to make a geophysical study to determine the ratio of soil quantity to rock, the thickness of the soil and the character of the rock at both sites; the National Weather Forecasting Corporation, which is collaborating with Professors Havens and Shulman of Rutgers University to establish weather patterns in the area of the proposed sites, making hourly observations around the clock for about one year of weather in those areas, including visibility, ceiling, surface winds, temperature and humidity.

As you will note from the attached copy of the Walsh report on the preparation of possible sites at Bearfort and Bowling Green, the terrain at both of these sites would require major and costly excavation and related operations.

At Bearfort Mountain, the "total predicted bid" at 1964 prices is $213,855,000. At the Bowling Green site a bid of $167,471,732 would have to be anticipated. The consultant tabulated these bids as follows:

Bearfort Mountain Site

Tabulation of Predicted Bid Prices

		Quantity	Unit	Unit Price	Total
1.	Constructing Interior Access & Quarry Roads	—	—	$ —	$ 3,788,462
2.	Clearing & Burning	3,309	Ac.	$ 720.000	$ 2,382,480
3.	Stripping for Fills	1,714	Ac.	$1,388.000	$ 2,379,032
4.	Rock Excavation	91,784,000	C.Y.	$ 1.576	$144,651,584
5.	Fill in Place	116,200,000	C.Y.	$ 0.226	$ 26,261,200
6.	Final Dressing	—	—	—	$ 1,112,302
7.	Mobilization *	—	—	—	$ 33,279,940
			Total Predicted Bid		$213,855,000

Bowling Green Site

Tabulation of Predicted Bid Prices

		Quantity	Unit	Unit Price	Total
1.	Constructing Interior Access & Quarry Roads	—	—	$ —	$ 3,743,777
2.	Clearing & Burning	2,964	Ac.	$1,099.000	$ 3,257,436
3.	Stripping & Grubbing	2,964	Ac.	$2,120.000	$ 6,283,680
4.	A. Rock Excavation	67,696,000	C.Y.	$ 1.394	$ 94,368,224
	B. Earth Excavation	3,777,000	C.Y.	$ 0.516	$ 1,948,932
	C. Rock Borrow	2,028,000	C.Y.	$ 1.223	$ 2,480,244
5.	Fill in Place	92,647,000	C.Y.	$ 0.228	$ 21,123,516
6.	Final Dressing	—	—	—	$ 1,302,646
7.	Mobilization *	—	—	—	$ 32,963,277
			Total Predicted Bid		$167,471,732

* Heavy construction equipment (purchase price less salvage value).

The completion of a major airport at Bowling Green or Bearfort, both of which involve long term site preparation problems, would extend into the 1970's. Site preparation alone would take six or more years and the construction of runways an additional length of time. For the purpose of this study, therefore, 1964 costs have been escalated by item and in detail over the construction period at the rate of 3-1/8 per cent per year. In other words, escalation has been limited to the actual period of construction for each major item (e.g. the actual period of site preparation, the actual period of runway construction, terminal construction and the like).

Thus the following tabulation represents our estimates of the total cost (including the cost of engineering, administration and interest during construction) of a completed major airport at the Bearfort and Bowling Green sites:

	Bearfort	Bowling Green
Land Acquisition	$ 12,000,000	$ 28,000,000
Site Preparation	385,000,000	302,000,000
Airport Construction and Water Supply	423,000,000	434,000,000
	$820,000,000	$764,000,000

At our present interest rate, the minimum annual debt service requirement to carry obligations of this magnitude would vary from $55.7 million at Bowling Green to $59.8 million at Bearfort. This would mean that sums nearly equal to our *gross* revenues from all Port Authority airports in the year 1963 would have to be available *after* the payment of all operating expenses for the Port Authority to meet its minimum legal requirements for the purpose of issuing bonds for the financing of either project.

By way of comparison about $420 million has been spent to build and develop Kennedy International Airport. A very large element in the substantial added cost of developing an airport like Kennedy at the Bearfort and Bowling Green sites is attributable to the necessity of excavating many million cubic yards of hard, granite gneissic rock, devoid of seams or significant weathering. The only feasible method would require the drilling and blasting, and the filling in of valleys and of low areas with many million cubic yards of the excavated rock. Although the general geological character of these sites was previously known, the detailed boring samples and seismographic studies by our consultant first disclosed the fact that practically 100 per cent of the necessary excavation at the Bearfort site consisted of granite and gneissic rock and that about 94 per cent at the Bowling Green site consisted of similar hard granite. Similarly, only after our consultants developed a detailed contour map of both sites and determined the geophysical characteristics of the site areas, was it possible for our engineers and consultants to calculate and balance out volumes of excavation and fill which revealed the tremendous quantities of rock that needed to be excavated by drilling and blasting and which would then require classification and transportation for use as fill.

Our estimates indicate that an airport at either site operating at its full capacity of 350,000 aircraft movements annually from the day the airport opened could not possibly provide funds to meet the foregoing minimum debt services requirements. Therefore, if an airport at either site were to be constructed and operated by the Port of New York Authority, a lump sum capital subsidy of $300 to $400 millions, or annual operating subsidy of comparable proportions would be indispensable.

I know that you and other New Jersey officials have been particularly concerned with the factors applying to water supply at both sites. For your full information, I am attaching the report received from Hazen and Sawyer. This consultant's conclusions are as follows:

1. An adequate water supply could be obtained for an airport at either of the sites under consideration. The most favorable project at Bearfort would cost $875,000 to build and $137,000 per annum for fixed charges and operations. At Bowling Green, the initial cost would be $1,520,000 and annual expense $402,000. None of the figures include the cost of water storage or distribution at the airport. The Bearfort costs include the purchase of raw water from the State of New Jersey at an estimated price of $30 mg; the Bowling Green costs include the purchase of raw water from Jersey City at $200 per mg and the cost of water to compensate Newton for watershed area lost to the airport. The estimates are necessarily tentative, pending negotiations with the proper officials when the airport project reached a more definite stage.

(Note: These costs are within reasonable limits for a major commercial airport and would not constitute a major cost factor.)

2. An airport at Bearfort would reduce the yield of Newark's Pequannock River system by approximately 310,000 gpd, and an airport at Bowling Green would reduce the Jersey City supply by 550,000 gpd. The 310,000 gpd at Bearfort represents only .3 of 1% of Newark's present total supply while the 550,000 gpd at Bowling Green represents slightly more than .7 of 1% of the Jersey City water supply. The annual compensation to be paid for these losses (at $200 per mg) would be $22,600 to Newark or $40,000 to Jersey City, depending upon the site selected.

3. Construction and grading of the airport must be arranged to minimize erosion and large storm water holding basins must be provided at the head of all streams to prevent excessive deposits of silt and sand in the streams and lakes below during construction. These basins would not intercept fine particles of clay and silt, and turbid or muddy water must be expected for some distance downstream at times of heavy runoff during the period of construction. The turbidity would be noticeable while construction was in progress and might interfere with recreation in the smaller ponds near the airport. Some turbidity would reach the inlets of the larger lakes and reservoirs on occasion, but this would settle out and not affect the quality of water drawn from the lower end of reservoirs. Erosion would cease upon completion of the airport, but the storm water holding basins should be maintained permanently for treatment of surface flows from the pavements.

4. Waste treatment and disposal facilities for sanitary sewage and hangar waste at the Bearfort site would cost $600,000 to construct, with an annual expense of $50,000 for fixed charges and operations. Similar facilities at Bowling Green would cost $1,145,000 to construct, with a annual cost of $108,000 or $124,000, depending upon whether or not Federal Aid was available. These facilities would be designed and built to divert the treated effluent from the watersheds of Newark and Jersey City to the Walkill River below water supply intakes.

5. Removal from the site or pretreatment of hangar and wash rock wastes would be necessary before these wastes were discharged to the airport sewerage system. The extent of such pretreatment would depend upon the

tenant airlines' operations at the airport and the cost is not included in our estimates.

6. With the precautions recommended, surface runoff from the airport runways, taxiways, and aprons would have negligible effect on downstream water supplies or recreational use of lakes.

7. Ground water supplies, public or private, located in the valleys below either site would not be affected by an airport.

8. From the standpoint of water supply and waste disposal the Bearfort site could be served at less cost than Bowling Green. From the standpoint of protecting state water resources, however, development of the Bowling Green site would have less overall effect because the drainage area below is already subject to housing, recreation, and other commercial developments.

Our preliminary estimates as set forth in this letter will be amplified in our complete report which will be ready for transmittal to you and to Governor Rockefeller by the end of the year.

Sincerely,

Austin J. Tobin
Executive Director

REA Express

William F. Harnden is credited with being the "First Expressman," inaugurating service between Boston and New York in 1839. Within the next twenty years, many competing express companies were formed, including, among others, Adams Express (1840), American Express (1850), Wells Fargo & Co. (1852), and the Pony Express (1860). By 1917, intense competition had reduced the number of express companies to seven major organizations. Because of World War I transportation problems, the federal government ordered them unified as the American Railway Express Company in 1918. This company was purchased by a group of American railroads in 1929 and was renamed Railway Express Agency. In 1960, the organization was renamed REA Express to reflect its all-modal capacity.

REA Express is essentially a small-shipments business, providing service by air, rail, highway, and water to more than 20,000 communities in all fifty states, plus part of Canada. Its operations include Air Express service with 37 airlines, international service to and from 87 foreign countries, and carload service for strawberries and other perishable from the West Coast, the southwest and the state of Louisiana. REA Express maintains 8,100 offices and terminals and coordinates all modes of transport to link shippers and consignees with pickup and delivery at all principal points in the United States and internationally throughout the free world.

REA had over 30,000 employees in 1963. Its payroll approximates $180 million a year, or about half a million dollars a day. The company also has more than 7,000 commission agents who represent REA in smaller communities.

In 1963, REA handled over 67 million shipments of all types, representing a total of more than 105 million shipment pieces. REA uses some 13,500 pickup and delivery trucks, tractor trailers, and other types of automotive equipment. In geographic coverage, REA is the largest common carrier in private transportation. In 1961, REA formed REA Leasing Corporation, which leases containers and trailers to 61 railroads for use in piggyback operations.

REA is now the only express company existing and regulated under Part I of the Commerce Act and the only company offering air express service. REA first came under federal regulation in 1906. In addition to federal regulation by the ICC, CAB, Federal Maritime Commission, and the FCC, REA is regulated by fifty state regulatory agencies.

REA has many private competitors, notably United Parcel Service and the bus express package service operated by Greyhound. In addition, there are about 18,000 private-enterprise regulated companies, partially or wholly in the small shipments field, as well as unregulated competitors.

However, REA's main competitive worries do not come from its business competitors. REA Express and its predecessor companies have been faced with competition from the United States Post Office for many years. In the nineteenth century, the express companies competed with the Post Office in carrying the mails until Congress made this business a postal monopoly.

Modern competition between the Post Office and the express companies began on January 1, 1913 with the inauguration of parcel post. At that time, there were few good roads, and transportation between rural areas and the major cities was a grave problem. Congress recognized the needs of the rural resident who did not have private transportation facilities conveniently available. Accordingly, bills to establish a small parcel service—beyond the few pounds then mailable—were introduced in Congress in 1912.

The Postmaster General gave his views relative to the purposes and provisions of the Senate's bill (which would permit Post Office carriage of parcels not exceeding eleven pounds or 72 inches in length and girth combined) as follows:

> The delivery of parcels to the limit of 11 pounds on all rural routes and within the delivery limits of free carrier offices will effect both an economy and a public convenience, as it will enable the inhabitants of the rural sections to use the mail for the transportation of the various small products of the farm, garden, and orchard, and at the same time to have delivered to them any of the smaller articles of necessity purchased in the towns without the time and expense incident to a trip of several miles for a trifling purchase.
>
> In my judgment the proposed measure will benefit all classes of the people except those carriers now engaged in the business of transporting small wares. While the patronage of these will be lessened, it will have

the effect to limit their business to the more weighty freight, which is distinctly the business of such carriers.

Shortly thereafter, Congress passed the proposed bill authorizing the eleven pounds, 72 inch parcel post service, effective January 1, 1913. In order to prevent this new postal service from becoming a permanent charge upon the general taxpayers, for the benefit of those who were most likely to use it extensively, or the mail order houses, provision was made for the revision of the schedules and rates whenever "the experience of the Postmaster General" indicated that they were such as "permanently" to render the cost of the parcel post service greater than the revenue therefrom. Thus, Congress manifested an intent to make an important distinction between fourth class (parcel post) and other classes of mail, its purpose being to make the parcel post self supporting. To insure against the Post Office's setting rates that would yield a profit and to insure that parcel post would not be extended beyond the point necessary to furnish transportation facilities which the express companies could not furnish, the Act of 1912 provided that changes in rates were to be subject to the consent of the Interstate Commerce Commission after investigation.

Despite the probable intent of Congress to confine the parcel post system to the transportation of small packages and to refrain from unnecessary competition with other carriers, this policy was soon departed from by administrative action. On August 15, 1913, the Postmaster General raised the weight limit in Zones 1 and 2 to twenty pounds, and on January 1, 1914, it was raised to fifty pounds in Zones 1 and 2 and to twenty pounds in Zones 3 through 8.

Although a Congressional Committee investigated these revisions in 1914 and found that the changes had been "issued without sufficient consideration for the needs of the service and of the facilities available," additional changes that increased size and weight were brought about in subsequent years through administrative action. In addition, the Postmaster General reduced the rates initially established by Congress, despite the fact that the Post Office had no cost accounting system and no means of assessing the adequacy of revenues on any class of mail. These increases in weight and size limits and rate reductions were made without public announcement of what had been proposed, and interested parties were given no opportunity to be heard. Consent of the ICC was secured by a single exchange of letters.

The effect of parcel post on private enterprise express companies was not long in coming. The United States Express Company, one of the principal express carriers of the pre–World War I era went out of business on June 30, 1914, a year and a half after the parcel post system was established. President Roberts of U.S. Express stated:

> We cannot stand it (parcel post competition) as at present constituted when it is carrying parcels of almost unlimited weight. We would have

continued, however, if the members of the parcel post had not threatened to extend it to consume the express business, increasing the weight of parcels carried and reducing the rates.

From 1918 until 1931, the weight limits were set at seventy pounds in Zones 1, 2 and 3 and fifty pounds in Zones 4 to 8, and the dimension limit at 84 inches. In 1931, the weight limit was set at seventy pounds for all zones and the dimension limit was increased to 100 inches. This was the first time that the ICC held public hearings on the question of size and weight limits. The increased size and weight limits now permitted the handling of many articles of merchandise, including small furniture items such as end tables, cabinets, benches and telephone sets, mirrors; also ironing boards, incubators, breeders, wash tubs, dry goods, hardware, and other articles previously packed in two or more packages. While the mail order houses were the chief proponents of these increased size and weight limits, they opposed rate increases proposed for Zones 1 through 3 and were successful in delaying them, despite a 25.9-million-dollar deficit on parcels handled in these zones in fiscal 1930.

When the seventy pounds and 100 inches limits were established in all zones, no provision was made to restrict these limits to traffic moving to and from the farms and small communities. As a result, parcel post became increasingly competitive with REA and other private carriers.

During the period of rising costs after World War II, all private carriers had to increase their rates. While the Post Office also had rising costs, action to increase parcel post rates was long delayed, and the rate increases that were eventually made failed to reflect the full impact of these increased costs. In the period from 1946 through 1959, REA had aggregate general rate increases of 260 per cent; in the same period the Post Office aggregate rate increases were only 163 per cent.

Thus, with this increasing disparity in rates, more and more of the heavier commercial shipments formerly handled by REA and other private carriers were diverted to parcel post. The following figures demonstrate what happened:

Year ending June 30	Number of LCL Express Shipments	Number of Parcel Post Pieces at Zone Rates
1946	220,463,444	821,226,867
1947	214,737,874	936,418,134
1948	167,289,420	992,517,251
1949	120,382,497	1,048,920,633
1950	97,240,405	1,008,631,565
1951	82,194,291	1,046,944,222

Since express shipments average just a little less than two pieces each, the loss of express volume is roughly comparable with the gain in parcel post. The kind of packages that were diverted is disclosed by an examination of the changes in parcel-post volume in the various weight brackets comparing the fiscal years 1947 and 1951:

Weights	Parcels Handled		Increase	
	1947	1951	Number	Per cent
1-20 lbs.	880,510,660	955,397,706	74,887,046	8.50
21-40 lbs.	45,412,123	74,440,373	29,028,250	63.92
41-70 lbs.	10,102,900	17,106,143	7,003,243	69.32

The deficit on fourth-class mail increased from $56,083,873 in 1947 to $131,140,928 in 1951—an increase of 133.83 per cent. Parcels weighing more than twenty pounds represented only a small fraction of the total number handled—but the larger packages demanded a disproportionate share of space in post offices, vehicles, and railroad cars. Handling the increasing volume of the larger packages undoubtedly added to operating costs of the Post Office Department.

This shift from REA and other private carriers to parcel post had multiple effects. It clearly benefited the mail order firms and other large commercial users of parcel post and express facilities, who paid lower rates to parcel post. The shift crippled REA and forced the layoff of approximately 40,000 express employees. Taxpayers were also affected as reported deficits on fourth-class mail during 1946–1951 amounted to $560 million, a greater deficit than in the period 1926–1945.

Beginning in 1949, Congressional committees began to study the problems of parcel post rates and competition with private transportation companies. Senate Report No. 1039, 82nd Congress which was submitted to Congress on October 19, 1951 stated:

> The benefits of low-cost service are illusory if part of the total cost of transportation is borne by the general taxpayers. If shippers do not pay the full cost of the transportation service they use, traffic generally is diverted from transportation media inherently better able to serve them. A lavish subsidy system distorts user preference to such an extent that it soon becomes impossible to evaluate the inherent advantage of any form of transportation.

In report No. 1006 (dated September 24, 1951) the House Committee on Post Office and Civil Service recommended that a bill be passed to correct inequities between parcel post and the private carriers:

> It is apparent that the problem of the Government agency competing with private business to the point that that private business, the Railway Express Agency, is being irreparably damaged, cannot be met by rate increases alone. In the opinion of the committee, however, it can be met by a restatement of congressional policy with regard to parcel post service and a return in part to the size and weight limits originally approved by Congress when parcel post was established to provide a small delivery service to areas which are not serviced by other transportation facilities.

In the judgment of the committee this legislation evidences the policy of the Government that it refrain from competition with legitimate private business. However, it does retain the principle upon which parcel post was established that all elements of our economy and all of our people shall have transportation facilities whereby they can obtain necessary goods and ship the products of the farm.

The legislation will be advantageous to the Post Office Department and will represent a savings by eliminating the handling of heavy and bulky parcels. The large packages which must be handled outside of mail sacks occupy a large amount of space in post offices needed to process first-class mail. They also require special handling since they are not adaptable to the parcel post slides and other mechanical equipment installed in the post offices. In addition, these large heavy parcels crush smaller parcels passing through the mail, causing an excessive cost in rewrapping and damage.

Shortly thereafter, following a unanimous recommendation by both House and Senate Committees, the 82nd Congress by voice vote enacted Public Law 199, which became effective on January 1, 1952.

Public Law 199 affected only parcels moving from one first-class post office to another. In such cases, dimension limits are fixed at 72 inches. The weight limit is forty pounds to Zones 1 and 2 (up to 150 miles), and twenty pounds to Zones 3 to 8 (beyond 150 miles). Public Law 199 does not alter previous regulations affecting parcels sent to or from second-, third-, or fourth-class post offices, or addresses on rural or star routes. It does not change regulations on parcels containing baby fowl, live plants, trees, shrubs, and agricultural commodities (not including manufactured products thereof) moving between post offices of any class.

The new law had an almost immediate affect on REA. The number of less-than-carload shipments handled by REA in 1952 was more than 14,300,000 above those handled in 1951. Motor carriers, L.C.L. freight, freight forwarders and airlines also received some diverted traffic. It is impossible to state precisely how much traffic was diverted from parcel post to REA and other private carriers, since undoubtedly some parcels were repackaged in smaller units still acceptable to parcel post.

Proponents of an expanded parcel post began to attack P.L. 199 shortly after its passage. They introduced H.R. 73 in the 84th Congress to repeal P.L. 199 and to permit larger weight and size limits. Similar bills were introduced in the 85th Congress. Those in favor of repealing P.L. 199 claimed that if shippers again were permitted to send freight via parcel post between larger cities and towns, the postal deficit would be lowered. They claimed that the Post Office Department has lost millions of dollars in potential revenue due to the abandonment of this service.

REA and others in favor of retaining P.L. 199 claimed that the government would have to spend millions of dollars for new and expanded facilities and would have to meet other increased operating costs including transportation costs involving greater bulk for the heavier freight-type packages if such service was restored. In a rate increase case in 1953, the ICC stated:

> We are unable to agree with the protestants that an increase in traffic, especially such as might result from restoration of the former size and weight limits, would insure against recurring deficits. In the fiscal year 1951 the number of parcels carried was 27% greater than it was in the fiscal year 1946, but in the same period the deficit estimated for fourth-class mail rose from $42,415,355 to $131,140,928.

Opponents of P.L. 199 also claimed that parcel post made a profit of $122,000,000 in 1952. The basis of this claim is the argument that first-class mail is the principal line of the postal establishment and that all other classes of mail and service are mere byproducts. Accordingly, incremental cost accounting should be applied. Under such an accounting system, first-class mail, it is argued, should bear the fixed expenses of the postal establishment, and the other classes should pay only the added costs that they create.

REA spokesmen claimed that the adoption of this type of accounting could result only in greatly increasing the postage rate on first-class mail for the purpose of benefiting those who would use the other classes of mail. The Post Office Department itself rejected the incremental cost theory in a report entitled "Financial Policy for the Post Office Department," March 31, 1954, as follows:

> . . . the Post Office was neither established nor is now operated primarily to carry first-class mail. Furthermore, it is the considered judgment of top accounting authorities and economists that incremental costing methods are invalid as a basic costing approach for the postal establishment today.
>
> Such a line of reasoning collapses entirely before the fact that first-class mail—the principal line—accounts for only 7% of the total weight and bulk of the mail handled by the Post Office; second-class mail is responsible for 22%; third-class for 6%; and fourth-class for 59%.

One of the leaders in the campaign to repeal P.L. 199 was the National Retail Dry Goods Association. This organization conducted a vigorous campaign to organize opposition to P.L. 199, on the grounds that P.L. 199 unfairly increased the selling, packing, and transportation expenses of commercial shippers. The staff manager of the Traffic Group of the National Retail Dry Goods Assoication stated in 1953 "NRDGA spearheaded a move which culminated in the formation of the National Committee on Parcel Post Size and Weight Limitations." Other groups active in pushing for repeal of P.L. 199 included The National Council on Business Mail, Inc. and the Parcel Post Association. These groups basically represented mail order houses and certain other commercial users of parcel post. Other groups backing repeal of P.L. 199 included the postal workers unions and from time to time officials of the Post Office Department. Congressman Broyhill (R., Va.) was one of the chief proponents of repealing P.L. 199. Congressman Broyhill, however, had little seniority on the House Post Office and Civil Service Committee.

Hearings were held in January, 1954, by a Subcommittee of the House Committee on the Post Office and Civil Service, under the chairmanship of Mrs. St. George (R., N.Y.) to obtain the views of interested parties on size and weight limitations of parcel post. The testimony of witnesses representing large users of parcel post in almost all instances amounted to a request for the repeal of the law and the restoration of the size and weight limits which existed prior to January 1, 1952. Testimony in support of retention of P.L. 199 was given by several REA officials, by the president of the Association of American Railroads, by the secretary-treasurer of the American Short Line Railroad Association, by the president of the National Association of Railroad and Utilities Commissioners, and by a member of the Georgia Public Service Commission. Congressman Murray (D., Tenn.), ranking minority member of the House Committee on Post Office and Civil Service in the 84th Congress, and chairman of the Committee in the 85th and succeeding Congresses, opposed repeal of P.L. 199.

REA and the railroads were not the only opponents of repealing P.L. 199. The directors of the Chamber of Commerce of the United States in March 1955 voted to take a position for retention of the present parcel post size and weight limits (e.g., retention of P.L. 199) as being consistent with the Chamber's existing policy declarations covering its stand against unfair government competition with private enterprise. The local Cartage National Conference, representing motor truck freight carriers, not only voted to oppose repeal of P.L. 199 but also advocated further weight and size restrictions on parcel post service. The Teamsters Union, which had organized United Parcel Service, editorialized in their magazine, *The International Teamster*, against changes in size and weight limits. Other support for retention of P.L. 199 came from (among others) the California Trucking Association, Inc.; the Transportation Association of America; The Brotherhood of Railway and Steamship Clubs, Freight Handlers, Express and Station Employees; the Special Committee on Cooperation with the I.C.C. in the Study of the Railroad Passenger Deficit Problem; and the National Association of Motor Bus Operators.

In addition to the usual legislative work by its own and allied representatives in Washington, the REA undertook an extensive public relations program which included sample editorials for newspaper editorial reference or direct use, articles in the REA *Employee Bulletin,* network radio and newspaper press releases, advertisements in major national magazines, and several special pamphlets—"A Case for Private Enterprise (Public Law 199–82nd Congress)" and "The Truth about Parcel Post."

The 2nd edition of "The Truth about Parcel Post" states the position of REA Express with respect to size and weight limits:

A parcel post service conforming to the original concept, that is, one handling small packages and extending into the area not adequately served by private carriers, is a great convenience to the rural users and should be continued. But it (parcel post) should not be permitted to engage in unnecessary and unfair competition with private enterprise. If government competition is permitted in the field of transportation, which business field is next? And where would it stop?

Unfair government competition with private enterprise can never be justified—let alone on the basis of damaging results to the taxpayer, to a substantial private enterprise industry and to the principles of private enterprise so that a relatively few business units may enjoy low operating costs.

Private carriers . . . offer an abundant variety of transportation facilities, competently operated in fair competition with each other. No single carrier (or type of carrier) is in a position to monopolize all the traffic. Where these services are available, there is no justification for the Post Office Department to engage in the tranportation of large, heavy parcels. It is strangely contradictory that the very commercial interests who urge the repeal of Public Law 199 would be the first to defend their rights vigorously if the Government of the United States sought to establish mail order or retail businesses to compete with them—at below-cost prices underwritten by the United States Treasury.

For example, the American Retail Federation has alleged that the Government competes unfairly and unnecessarily with its members. Its representatives protested competition from service post exchanges and commissaries. . . .

Clearly these groups are either for or against government competition depending on their own convenience.

Contrary to American principles of fair play, many of the commercial shippers seeking repeal of Public Law 199 practice a double standard.

The public relations campaign, coupled with legislative efforts and support from the executive branch of the government (particularly during the Eisenhower administration) together with continued postal deficits on fourth-class mail, led to the defeat of all attempts to repeal P.L. 199 and alter size and weight limits.

REA Express has other competitive problems with the Post Office besides size and weight limits. As of 1963, the average weight per piece of surface express shipped on REA was about thirty pounds and of air express, about 25 pounds. President William B. Johnson of REA Express testified in 1963 before a Congressional hearing that a recent nationwide field study shows that 29.5 per cent of REA's total business is now mailable, despite size and weight limits. Mr. Johnson stated:

. . . under present rules and regulations the Post Office stands ready to capture, right now, almost one-third of our present business. Can there be any doubt that we compete? Can there be doubt that as the parcel post subsidy increases, the diversion of our business into Government service will likewise increase? Can there be doubt that unlimited subsidy for parcel post means ultimate destruction for a carrier which must cover its costs to survive and which can lose 30% of its business to the Federal Government? . . .

Thus, the question of parcel post rates is of vital importance to REA Express.

Despite the success in reducing size and weight limits with P.L. 199, Railway Express had a difficult financial period in the 1950's. REA was threatened by liquidation or nationalization in late 1958 and early 1959 when the New York Central considered pulling out of REA because the agency was losing over $35 million a year. On July 7, 1959, hearings were actually held on Senate Resolution 8, which provided for federal acquisition and operation of the company as part of the Post Office Department.

REA's owners, 67 of the country's largest railroads, installed a new management for REA in 1959, headed by William B. Johnson. The new management averted both liquidation and nationalization as a result of a drastic revision of all of REA's basic transportation agreements and by reorganization of every phase of the business. Prior to 1959, REA functioned as a nonprofit cooperative or agent of the railroads. Since the reorganization, the agency has been required to pay its way or die. REA has responded well to the profit and loss system to date. The new management succeeded in ending the deficits by 1962. In the fiscal year July 1, 1962–June 30, 1963, REA had a consolidated gross income of $394.1 million and a consolidated net profit after taxes of $3.4 million.

In the three years since 1960, REA has instituted three rate increases which together average about 40 cents a shipment or 25 cents a piece of business, largely to cover a profit squeeze owing to repeated wage increases. During the same three years, parcel post has also had wage increases, and its deficits have grown, but there has been no rate increase. Thus, the disparity in rates between REA and other private carriers and parcel post has been increasing. In the period 1946–1959, REA general rate increases aggregated 260 per cent; parcel post rate increases for the same period aggregated only 163 per cent.

REA and other private carriers have attempted to bring public attention to their rate problems vis-a-vis parcel post in recent years. REA has utilized news releases, items for editorial reference, articles in its *Employee Bulletin,* excerpts from the Second Hoover Commission Report, and a series of advertisements in major magazines to make its position known to the public and to Congress. Examples of some of these are shown in Exhibits 1 through 12.

The Chamber of Commerce and other groups supported these efforts to require parcel post to operate on a break-even basis. In 1955, the chamber stated:

Charges for parcel post service should be sufficient to cover all costs incurred by the government in the performance of this service. Such costs should be determined under sound commercial accounting practice. . . .

The chamber backed its statement up with an article in its *Washington Report,* which called for the inclusion of indirect costs such as retirement pay for parcel post workers, the reasonable value of space provided in government buildings and use of other properties and facilities, including depreciation and maintenance expenses in computing the costs of parcel post. All of these indirect expenses, amounting to approximately $50 million a year, are currently excluded as costs for rate-making purposes. Other groups such as the National Associated Businessmen, Inc., the Citizens Committee for the Hoover Report, and the many groups that backed the fight to save P.L. 199 also support REA in its attempt to prevent below-cost competition from parcel post. The same groups, led by the commercial mail order firms, that oppose the present size and weight limits also have opposed attempts to raise parcel post rates to cover all their costs. On the recommendation of Postmaster General Day, Congressman Murray (D., Tenn.), chairman of the House Committee on Post Office and Civil Service, introduced H.R. 5795 in Congress in 1963. Present law requires a reasonable balance between parcel post revenues and direct costs. A deficit not exceeding 4 per cent of cost is allowed by law because it is recognized that it is impossible for parcel post to break even exactly in any one year. As originally introduced, H.R. 5795 would remove the requirement that the parcel post deficit not exceed 4 per cent (or about $33 million at current levels of operation). No new limit on the deficit would be substituted and the Postmaster General would no longer have to certify that the limit has not been exceeded. H.R. 5795 would do nothing about raising parcel post rates or reducing deficits. It would legalize all present and future parcel post losses, with no known limits and cancel out the present responsibility of the Postmaster General and the ICC for adjusting rates to reduce losses. The Postmaster General needed some Congressional action, if he wished to avoid a large rate increase. The efforts of the Postmaster General were supported by the large mail order firms.

Mr. William B. Johnson, president of REA Express, testified against the passage of H.R. 5795 before the House Committee on Post Office and Civil Service. He first reviewed the history of REA and its competitive problems with the parcel post service. He then pointed out the objections to H.R. 5795 and the possible consequences to REA of its passage. Mr. Johnson stated that below-cost parcel post rates could take as much as 30 per cent of REA's present business, costing REA up to $63 million of annual revenue. This would probably lead to the failure of REA. Mr. Johnson stated:

> If REA, a nationwide common carrier dependent on small shipments, becomes unable to continue in private enterprise, will Congress vote to nationalize or subsidize it so that its *other services* can be continued for the public? . . . about 7 million pieces of our traffic are commodities not acceptable by parcel post. These include so-called "wet freight" requiring icing, such as fresh vegetables, fish, lobsters, etc. Also included

are explosives, corpses, live animals of all kinds, jewelry, coin, valuable minerals, acids, radio-isotopes, liquor, etc. Who would handle this business, which is marginal and costly?

About 45 million pieces of our business is not acceptable now by parcel post because of size limitations, and about 16 million because of weight limits. If below-cost price competition by parcel post makes us financially unable to handle these 61 million pieces, and we are not nationalized or subsidized, will the parcel post size and weight limits be expanded, as sought by some for the past 12 years? Is H.R. 5795 just an oblique approach to the old size and weight question?

Mr. Johnson included with his testimony several charts and exhibits. Case Exhibit 13, "Some Advantages of Parcel Post over Private Enterprise Transportation," Exhibit 14, "REA Express Business Vulnerable to Unlimited Parcel Post Subsidy" and Exhibit 15, "Zone Rate Parcel Statistics," are reproduced from his testimony.

Management of REA decided to oppose H.R. 5795 as originally written but believed it was necessary to suggest some other immediate solution to the present parcel post deficit. With a 4 per cent tolerance, as under present law, or about $33 million, there is a remaining deficit (in 1963) of $113 million. One way to meet this deficit would be to increase rates. REA proposed three possible solutions, all involving rate increases. A rate increase of 19 per cent or thirteen cents per piece of total zone-rate fourth-class mail would cover this additional $113 million deficit. Perhaps the rate would have to be raised two cents more to take care of any diversion of business from parcel post owing to higher rates.

Another solution would be for Congress to raise the permissible deficit from 4 per cent to 6 per cent ($33 million to $50 million). This would necessitate a rate increase of only 16 per cent or eleven cents per piece to cover the remaining deficit plus another one cent to take care of any diversion of business.

A third solution would be to double the present permissible deficit or subsidy to 8 per cent ($33 million to about $67 million). This would necessitate a rate increase of thirteen cents or ten cents per piece to cover the remaining deficit.

As a result of the testimony by REA officials and other opponents of H.R. 5795, as originally drafted, the House Committee on Post Office and Civil Service drafted a compromise, whereby the 4 per cent maximum on the permissible deficit would be suspended for three years in exchange for a Post Office promise to make a rate increase on parcel post after the suspension took place. The Report, No. 387 of the House Committee, is reproduced as Exhibit 16 of this case. The Senate Committee on Post Office and Civil Service, under the chairmanship of Senator Olen D. Johnston (D., S.C.), also reported out the compromise bill.

Management of REA must decide what further action, if any, it should take with regard to the revised H.R. 5795. Should it oppose the revised bill? If REA makes this decision, can it stop passage of the bill at this late stage? How? Will other groups, normally allied with REA, go along with a decision to oppose the revised H.R. 5795? These groups include the trucking industry, freight forwarders, the railroad industry, including the short-line railroads, the bus industry, all of railway labor, the transportation regulatory commissioners of various states, the Transportation Association of America, the National Businessmen's Association, the U.S. Chamber of Commerce, and other carriers in the small shipments field, as well as various customers such as the Florida citrus industry, the seafood industry, the nursery industry, the electronic industry, the publishing industry, and other manufacturers.

On the other hand, if REA decides not to oppose the three-year suspension, should it take any action at this time toward a long-range solution of some kind of the rate problem? Management must also consider the long-run future of such other problems as size and weight limits, the inclusion of indirect costs in the parcel post rate base, etc. Ultimately, management must answer the question: Can a private enterprise firm successfully compete with a government agency over the long run, or should it get out of such business, and, if so, how?

EXHIBIT ONE

**A Report to the Congress
by the
Commission on Organization of the
Executive Branch of the Government**

PARCEL POST

The parcel post system has had a long and tangled legislative history since it was established in 1912. Congress always has been concerned with the possibility that it might compete with private enterprise; and in reporting the original bill the Senate Committee on Post Office and Post Roads said:

> Neither has the public had in mind Government ownership of express companies nor the absorption of the heavy transportation business handled by express companies at the present time. We have endeavoured to provide the service for which there has been a general demand.[1]

Congress in at least two ways sought to minimize the potentiality of detrimental competition resulting from the service, first, by limiting the size and weight of packages, and second, by providing that the charges for service should be sufficient to cover costs.

The original law restricted the service to packages of not more than 11

SOURCE: Excerpt from May 16, 1955 Hoover Commission Report: BUSINESS ENTERPRISES.

[1] 62nd Cong., S. Rept. 955, p. 16.

pounds in weight, and a combined length and girth of no more than 72 inches. On a number of occasions the Postmaster General, with the approval of the Interstate Commerce Commission, increased the size of acceptable packages. By 1931 the weight of packages had been increased to 70 pounds in all zones and the combined length and girth was increased to 100 inches. These size and weight limitations continued in force until January 1, 1952,[2] when Congress, by law passed in 1951, reduced the maximum weight to 40 pounds in the first two zones and 20 pounds in the other zones, and reduced the size of packages to 72 inches, girth and length combined, with certain exceptions as to these weights and sizes.

The original law provided a rate schedule and authorized the Postmaster General to revise the rates with the permission of the Interstate Commerce Commission. The rates fixed by Congress in 1912 were not increased significantly until 1925, and the service in the late 1920's was practically paying its own way. However, despite great increases in costs, rates remained relatively unchanged until January 1, 1949, when a new scale imposed by Congress became effective. Under this new schedule the charge for the first pound was approximately twice what it had been in 1913.

The cost of the parcel post service exceeded revenues by an ever-increasing percentage, rising from about 9 per cent in 1930 to 16 per cent in 1946. Despite rapidly rising costs after 1946, the Postmaster General was unwilling to ask the Interstate Commerce Commission to approve of rate increases sufficient to avoid a deficit. As a consequence, Congress, by the act of September 27, 1950,[3] provided that before the Postmaster General could expend any money appropriated by Congress for the Post Office, he must certify that he has submitted to the Interstate Commerce Commission proposals for such increased rates as will be sufficient to pay the cost of fourth-class mail service. As a result of this law, rate increases became effective in 1951 and 1953.

Although Congress required the Postmaster General to submit rates that would cover the total cost of the service, deficits have still continued. The deficit increased from $99,011,000 in 1949 to $131,141,000 in 1951 and to $151,497,000 in 1953. This represented about 24 per cent of the cost of the service. The deficit for 1954 is estimated to be about $29,218,000.

In addition to the direct costs chargeable to the service, sizeable indirect costs are not considered in determining the losses resulting from handling parcel post. These include contributions to the Government retirement fund, and to employees' compensation, custodial costs and depreciation. These total about $151,000,000 according to the Post Office Department.[4] No official estimate has been made of what portion of these indirect costs should be allocated to parcel post.

This failure of parcel post rates to cover the full cost of service constitutes a subsidy to the users of parcel post. Thus the Subcommittee of the Senate Committee on Interstate and Foreign Commerce reported in 1951:

[2] Act of October 10, 1951, Public Law 199, 65 Stat. 610.
[3] Public Law 643, 64 Stat. 1050.
[4] U.S. Post Office Department, Financial Policy for the Post Office Department (1954), pp. 162-163.

In the opinion of the subcommittee there is no justification for the action of the Government in subsidizing its own parcel post service in competition with private railway express service. A subsidized Government transportation service in competition with a nonsubsidized private service cannot be squared with the declared national transportation policy. In addition, the deficit which stems from railway express service has the same harmful effect on the national defense as other types of passenger-train service deficits.[5]

RECOMMENDATION NO. 11

That the Postmaster General shall, if the current rates do not cover all costs of the parcel post services (including indirect costs), seek a further increase of rates.

PUBLISHED AS A MATTER OF PUBLIC INTEREST
BY RAILWAY EXPRESS AGENCY, INC.

EXHIBIT TWO

Natural Progress?

In following the work of the Hoover Commission, we are reminded of a remark attributed to Thomas Jefferson—"The natural progress of things is for liberty to yield and government to gain ground."

The latest report on government competition with private business should be required reading for anyone concerned with free enterprise and the dangers of "creeping socialism." It is significant that the proportion of public to private wealth has doubled in the last twenty-five years. While our economy is expanding at a healthy pace, government has been growing twice as fast. The commercial enterprises of the Defense Department alone are valued at over $15 billion, and the total business and industrial enterprises of the government are estimated to be worth between—believe it, or not—$25 and $50 billion. Between 2,000 to 3,000 government functions are competing with private business.

Not only do these commercial activities of the government compete unfairly with private business, but they pay no taxes and little or no interest on the capital, seldom charge depreciation and, among other things, deprive federal, state and local governments of taxes which private enterprises would pay. The Commission says that many of these activities can be turned over to private business at a great saving, and warns that socialism isn't creeping any longer—it is running full blast. The government is operating paint factories, laundries, retail stores, mines, railroads, and thousands of similar commercial enterprises—all competing with private business with the taxpayers picking up the tab. Even the parcel post system, by operating at below-cost rates, has taken business away from private carriers which must operate at a profit. A strange situation indeed when we consider our high standard of living and our industrial strength are based upon free enterprise and open and fair competition.

[5] 82nd Cong., 1st sess., S. Rept. 1039, p. 54.

Recommendations have been made by the Commission which, if passed by Congress, will do much to balance the budget, save the taxpayers billions of dollars, and reverse the trend toward socialism. Mr. Hoover calls for the pressure of American common sense to secure action on these proposals by Congress. But you and I must let our elected representatives know we want them to act. All the good intentions in the world are useless unless something is done. Now it is up to us . . . and Congress.

EXHIBIT THREE

INFORMATION
COPY

From
News Bureau
Railway Express Agency
219 East 42nd Street
New York 17, N.Y.

Murray Hill   6-7900

FOR RELEASE IN PUBLICATIONS DATED
WEDNESDAY, NOVEMBER 5, 1958, OR LATER

PARCEL POST RATES PROPOSED BY POST OFFICE
NOT SUFFICIENT, SHOULD BE RAISED TO COVER FULL
COSTS, EXPRESS HEAD SAYS

Agency President Says Failure to Include at Least $78 Million of Costs
of Other Government Agencies in Rate Proposals to ICC Imposes Unfair Burden on Taxpayers, Constitutes Discrimination Favoring Mail
Order and Other Commercial Parcel Post Shippers

NEW YORK—Recently proposed increases in parcel post rates fall far short of meeting the requirement of the Federal law and should be properly increased before submission to the Interstate Commerce Commission, Alfred L. Hammel, President of Railway Express Agency, said in a statement filed yesterday (Nov. 4) at Washington with the Post Office Department and released here for publication today.

Failure to establish rates that will produce revenue adequate to cover the full cost of handling fourth-class mail, he asserted, imposes an unfair burden on the taxpayer and constitutes unjust discrimination in favor of the mail order concerns and other commercial users of the parcel post. The formal statement was filed in accordance with a Post Office provision for the filing of the views of interested parties prior to the Department's submission of proposed rates to the ICC.

Certain substantial annual costs amounting to at least $78.2 million for zone rate parcels and catalogs, in particular, Mr. Hammell noted, have not been included in the Post Office Department's computations on which the proposed increased rates are based. They were published in the Federal Register on October 4.

"I refer specifically," he said, "to those costs paid or assumed by other Government Agencies for services, facilities and other benefits provided for fourth-class mail in the operation of the Post Office Department." "The mere fact that these costs are paid by other Government Agencies," Mr. Hammell said, "does not excuse the Post Office Department's failure to include them in its rate-basing studies. These expenditures are just as much a part of the cost of handling fourth-class mail as are those paid from the Post Office Appropriation."

Mr. Hammell's statement noted that revenues from present rates on zone parcels and catalogs, as estimated by the Post Office, amounted to $518 million. On the other hand, he observed, present Post Office budgetary expenditures plus the other conservatively estimated costs of government, exceed those revenues by more than $166 million.

Quoted by Mr. Hammell in support of his position was a portion of a March 25, 1957, letter of Assistant Postmaster General Hyde Gillette to the Postmaster General in which "factors properly applicable in postal rate making" included "costs of postal services paid by other government agencies, such as retirement contributions, workmen's compensation, unemployment insurance and custodial and other costs for public buildings."

Another quote referred to by the express company president was that of Former Deputy Postmaster General Maurice H. Stans to a Senate Subcommittee on August 16, 1957, in which he said, "The original legislation creating a parcel-post service specified, among other things, that revenues should be adequate to pay the full costs."

The ICC has the authority to either approve or disapprove the specific fourth-class rate proposals as filed by the Postmaster General.

* * *   1104058

EXHIBIT FOUR

Government is no place for...

"LEMONADE ECONOMICS"

LEMONADE 2¢

PARCEL POST

Most children make money on lemonade stands—"profits" are high and prices are low. That's because lemons, water, sugar, ice, and utensils come from mother's kitchen and are not included in the cost.

But that's hardly the way to operate our Government's parcel post system which, by law, is supposed to pay its own way. It not only competes unnecessarily and unfairly with private carriers but requires taxpayers to make up the difference between low rates and higher costs.

Post office reports do not include annual costs in excess of $43 million attributable to 4th class mail which are paid by other Government departments, nor do they include annual interest charges on the accumulated deficit of $1.2 billion from parcel post operations.

Commercial customers of this "lemonade stand" operation naturally find Government's services "cheaper." That's why they seek to perpetuate and even extend their special advantage at everyone else's expense.

There *is* something that can be done about it.

The Hoover Commission, along with many others, has recommended legislation to the present Congress which would require parcel post shippers to pay *all* the costs.

**For a free copy of an informative booklet,
"The Truth about Parcel Post," address
The Public Relations Division**

RAILWAY EXPRESS AGENCY, INC.

219 East 42nd Street, New York 17, N. Y.

A PRIVATE ENTERPRISE IN THE PUBLIC SERVICE

EXHIBIT FIVE

EXHIBIT SIX

WHAT'S WRONG WITH THIS PICTURE?

Far-fetched, you say? Why should the government be in the automobile business? It shouldn't . . . but . . .

Why should the government be in the *shipping* business? It *is* . . . through the handling of commercial traffic in the U. S. Government Parcel Post system.

Unfair competition? Yes. Private firms fully capable of handling commercial traffic are forced to compete with the government in this field. Established primarily to supply transportation facilities in rural areas, parcel post now transports a great volume of commercial traffic between cities and towns where pri-

vately operated transportation facilities are more than adequate.

In the spirit of fair play and of America's free enterprise system, we should not permit the government to be pressured into expanding its commercial shipping business where private enterprise firms are equipped to perform the service. As the Hoover Commission reports say, "The private enterprise system is the basis of the military strength of this Nation and of its unparalleled standard of living."

For a free copy of an informative booklet, "The Truth About Parcel Post," write to:

The Public Relations Division of

RAILWAY EXPRESS AGENCY, INC.

219 East 42nd Street, New York 17, N. Y.

A PRIVATE ENTERPRISE IN THE PUBLIC SERVICE

EXHIBIT SEVEN

EXHIBIT EIGHT

WHAT'S WRONG WITH THIS PICTURE?

The Hoover Commission along with others has recommended legislation to Congress which would require parcel post shippers to pay rates that would cover all costs, including *indirect* expenses in maintaining this service.

Yet many months after the submission of this report, parcel post is operating in direct and unfair competition with the private shipping industry —and it still loses money.

No business can hope to compete successfully with the government—nor should it have to on such a basis! Under the system of free enterprise, private industry has made America the most powerful nation in the world. Let's keep it that way!

Send today for your free copy of the information booklet, "The Truth About Parcel Post." Write to:

The Public Relations Division of

RAILWAY EXPRESS AGENCY, INC.

219 East 42nd Street, New York 17, N. Y.

A PRIVATE ENTERPRISE IN THE PUBLIC SERVICE

EXHIBIT NINE

On thousands of streets and at railroad stations and express terminals all over the country, scenes like this are repeated many times a day.

The efficient operations of the Railway Expressmen . . . on train and truck, railroad or terminal platform and at the local airport . . . have long been part of the American scene.

Since its beginning in 1839 . . . advancing with the early railroads, the overland stage, and the Pony Express, and keeping pace with today's streamlined trains and aircraft . . . express service has played an important and continuing part in the progress of our nation.

In normal times, the Agency carries anything and touches the lives of everyone. In times of crisis, the complete and dependable service of Railway Express has transported blood for the Red Cross, serum to combat epidemics, key materials for national defense.

Year after year, as the world's most extensive private enterprise transportation system, a great tradition of service to the public is carried on . . . the American way.

For a free copy of an informative booklet, "The Truth About Parcel Post," address The Public Relations Division

RAILWAY EXPRESS AGENCY, INC.

219 East 42nd Street, New York 17, N. Y.

A PRIVATE ENTERPRISE IN THE PUBLIC SERVICE

EXHIBIT TEN

EXHIBIT ELEVEN

EXHIBIT TWELVE

THE TAXPAYER WOULD **SHUDDER**

The average taxpayer would be likely to shudder if he fully realized how the Federal Government spends some of his money.

A case in point: *Reported 4th class mail (parcel post) losses 1926-1954 total more than 1.2 billion dollars.* But that is not the complete picture.

The Post Office Department admits its reports do not include all the expenses paid by the Government for 4th class mail operations. The unreported expenses have been estimated at more than $43 million annually. No private business can compete with government—let alone at below-cost, taxpayer-subsidized rates.

The Hoover Commission, after thorough studies, made note of the serious issue of government competition and past Congressional efforts to reduce it. It has recommended to the present Congress a further step—that continuing taxpayer subsidies to parcel post shippers be wiped out through rate increases adequate to cover all costs.

One year's debt interest paid by taxpayers, on reported past deficits alone, amounts to more than $33 million.

There is no more reason to subsidize someone else's shipping costs than to help pay his rent, electric or other business expenses.

**For a free copy of an informative booklet,
"The Truth About Parcel Post," address
The Public Relations Division**

RAILWAY EXPRESS AGENCY, INC.

219 East 42nd Street, New York 17, N.Y.

A PRIVATE ENTERPRISE IN THE PUBLIC SERVICE

EXHIBIT THIRTEEN

SOME ADVANTAGES OF PARCEL POST OVER PRIVATE ENTERPRISE TRANSPORTATION

THE POST OFFICE DEPARTMENT ...

... pays no taxes of any kind.

... pays no fees for licenses or permits.

... is in the federal government retirement plan, rather than the more costly Social Security or Railroad Retirement.

... pays no interest on debt.

... does not need to obtain truck rights.

... is not regulated by the 50 states.

... is not subject to strikes or work stoppages interrupting the service.

... has space priority and can control rail service.

... makes no payment for loss and damage except on insured parcels, for which an extra charge is made.

... does not handle certain costly commodities.

... has no worries about credit in the financial community.

EXHIBIT FOURTEEN

REA EXPRESS BUSINESS VULNERABLE TO UNLIMITED PARCAL POST SUBSIDY

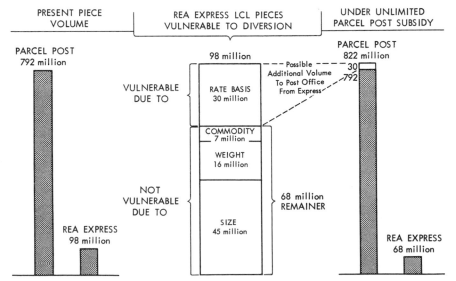

EXHIBIT FIFTEEN

ZONE RATE PARCEL STATISTICS - FROM POST OFFICE DEPARTMENT COST ASCERTAINMENT REPORTS

For the Fiscal Years Ended June 30 - - 1947 Through 1962

Year	One-Pound Pieces*	2- to 70-lb. Pieces	Total Pieces*	Total Weight in Pounds	Revenue	Cost	Deficiency-D or Surplus-S
1947	168,743,057	767,282,626	936,025,683	5,103,876,462	$223,256,088	$264,064,331	$ 40,808,243-D
1948	178,928,669	813,588,582	992,517,251	6,241,893,456	257,427,242	321,391,872	63,964,630-D
1949	172,921,291	875,999,342	1,048,920,633	7,300,454,387	337,664,503	427,709,397	90,044,894-D
1950	158,641,699	849,998,866	1,008,631,565	7,187,990,533	380,820,198	445,022,716	64,202,518-D
1951	159,816,768	886,127,454	1,046,944,222	7,484,512,409	401,756,222	524,441,780	122,685,558-D
1952	167,368,852	879,206,751	1,046,575,603	6,564,687,596	446,927,336	586,375,980	139,448,644-D
1953	159,189,927	883,742,239	1,042,932,166	6,069,572,014	451,429,819	590,772,571	139,342,752-D
1954	154,658,778	840,091,739	994,750,517	5,754,073,868	543,414,822	553,783,687	10,368,865-D
1955	149,210,398	799,009,766	948,220,164	5,421,815,065	550,707,179	537,115,898	13,591,281-S
1956	155,237,385	817,570,940	972,808,325	5,257,533,723	552,201,156	580,566,746	28,365,590-D
1957	163,228,216	812,391,649	975,619,865	5,237,992,821	543,236,772	582,050,703	38,813,931-D
1958	154,038,179	796,894,361	950,932,540	5,151,904,064	539,349,270	630,819,297	91,470,027-D
1959	7,940,514*	849,180,644	857,121,158*	5,200,374,923	531,365,761	638,539,976	107,174,215-D
1960	--	839,891,207	839,891,207	5,161,570,637	561,135,414	661,202,478	100,067,064-D
1961	--	800,366,207	800,366,207	4,724,760,389	578,656,114	690,339,162	111,683,048-D
1962	--	792,305,672	792,305,672	4,705,484,928	575,753,366	681,723,443	105,970,077-D

* Zone Rate Parcels weighing between 8 oz. and 1 pound were reclassified as Third Class Mail matter effective August 1, 1958 (PL 85-426)

EXHIBIT SIXTEEN

88th Congress 1st Session	HOUSE OF REPRESENTATIVES	Report No. 387

THREE-YEAR SUSPENSION OF RESTRICTIONS ON WITHDRAWAL FROM TREASURY OF POSTAL APPROPRIATIONS

June 13, 1963.—Committed to the Committee of the Whole House on the State of the Union and ordered to be printed

Mr. Murray, from the Committee on Post Office and Civil Service, submitted the following

REPORT

(To accompany H.R. 5795)

The Committee on Post Office and Civil Service, to whom was referred the bill (H.R. 5795) to repeal the provisions of law relating to the fixing by the Postmaster General, with the consent of the Interstate Commerce Commission, of rates of postage on fourth-class mail, and for other purposes, having considered the same, report favorably thereon with amendments and recommend that the bill as amended do pass.

AMENDMENTS

The committee proposes two amendments to the bill—an amendment to the text and an amendment to the title.

AMENDMENT TO THE TEXT

The amendment proposed to the text of the bill strikes out all after the enacting clause and inserts in lieu thereof a substitute text.

This substitute text, which consists of one section, provides for the suspension for a period of 3 years—from July 1, 1963 to June 30, 1966— of a provision in Chapter IV of the Supplemental Appropriation Act, 1951 (31 U.S.C. 695).

This provision is to the effect that, on and after September 27, 1950, none of the funds appropriated to the Post Office Department from the general fund of the Treasury shall be withdrawn from the Treasury until the Postmaster General has certified in writing that he has requested the consent of the Interstate Commerce Commission ot the establishment of such rate increases or other reformations as may be necessary to accomplish the following purposes:

First, to insure that the revenues from fourth-class mail service will not exceed by more than 4 per cent the costs of such service.

Second, to insure that the costs of such service will not exceed by more than 4 per cent the revenues from such service.

This provision of the Supplemental Appropriation Act, 1951, is set forth in that part of this report under the heading "Matter for the Information of the Members of the House of Representatives".

This provision of the Suppplemental Appropriation Act, 1951, is predicated upon the existing fourth-class mail rate reformation authority which was originally set forth in section 6 of the act of July 28, 1916 (39 Stat. 431) and which is now contained in the last paragraph of section 207(b) of the act of February 28, 1925 (43 Stat. 1067), as amended by section 7 of the act of May 29, 1928 (45 Stat. 942; 39 U.S.C., 1958 ed., sec. 247). Although such section 207(b) directs the Postmaster General to seek reformation in certain instances, this directive was not in fact carried out until the enactment of the Supplemental Appropriation Act, 1951, which enforced compliance with the provisions of the last paragraph of section 207(b) of the act of February 28, 1925, as amended.

The committee emphasizes that the mandate for the Postmaster General to seek fourth-class mail reformations under section 207(b) of the act of February 28, 1925, will continue in full force and effect. Such section will continue to constitute a directive to the Postmaster General to seek reformations, with the consent of the Interstate Commerce Commission, which will insure that the revenues from fourth-class mail are sufficient to cover the costs thereof. In this connection, it should be observed that the Postmaster General has stated his intention to submit a petition to the Interstate Commerce Commission in the near future in order to obtain the consent of the Commission to "a reasonable increase in the present zone rates applicable to parcel post and catalogs."

AMENDMENT TO THE TITLE

The Amendment proposed to the title of the bill is as follows: Amend the title so as to read:

> A bill to provide a three-year suspension of certain restrictions in the Supplemental Appropriation Act, 1951, on the withdrawal from the Treasury of postal appropriations.

The purpose of this amendment to the title of the bill is to provide a title which will reflect the provisions of the text of the bill, as proposed to be amended by the committee.

PURPOSE

The purpose of this legislation is to provide for the continuance of essential postal services by granting the Postmaster General temporary relief from an existing statutory requirement which can operate to prevent the withdrawal from the Treasury of funds for any postal operation unless such relief is granted. This existing statutory requirement is the paragraph contained in Chapter IV of the Supplemental Appropriation Act, 1951, referred to above.

STATEMENT

Enactment of this legislation is necessary to assure that all postal services now available to the American public will be provided without interruption due to lack of necessary funds or other causes. The postal establishment faces a critical situation in this respect. The Postmaster General has officially reported, in effect, that the existing law requires him to perform an impossibility and that under the appropriation limitation cited above, he will be unable to withdraw any funds from the Treasury to operate the postal establishment after June 30, 1963, unless granted relief from the limitation.

In summary, a combination of several different statutes lays down a mandate that expenses on fourth-class mail may not exceed revenues by more than 4 per cent, but at the same time bars the postal establishment from profitable traffic in large packages between first-class post offices which otherwise would tend to make up for losses incurred in handling small packages originating at or destined to other classes of post offices. This leaves the Postmaster General but one possible means, under his parcel post reformation authority (39 U.S.C., 1958 ed., sec. 247), to gain needed additional revenues, and that is to increase parcel post rates with the consent of the Interstate Commerce Commission.

Although by law expenses may not exceed revenues by over 4 per cent, the extraordinary changes that have taken place in the national economy and the national transportation complex have brought the parcel post operation to a point where in the fiscal year 1962 parcel post expenses exceed revenues therefrom by 24.6 per cent. Thus, it is evident that a rate increase—the only avenue open to the Postmaster General—averaging at least 20.6 per cent would be necessary to comply with the 4 per cent limitation, even if it could be assumed (and it cannot) that an increase of such magnitude would not price the parcel post service out of a substantial part of its traffic and cause an even greater deficit.

Parcel post volume has decreased to a marked extent in each recent year under the present parcel post rate structure, and it is evident from experience following earlier rate increases that the rate of progression of decrease in volume will be sharply accelerated with any new parcel post rate increase. The Postmaster General and other postal authorities testified that the point of diminishing returns for any new rate increase— beyond which resultant losses from diversion of traffic would outweigh any possible new revenues—is in the close neighborhood of a 13 per cent average increase. That is to say, any parcel post rate increase averaging more than 13 per cent at this time would be self-defeating since the resultant traffic loss would increase the deficit rather than reduce it.

The committee is in unanimous agreement that it is imperative to grant the relief provided by the committee amendments to meet the immediate emergency and permit withdrawal of funds from the Treasury to continue all postal services now available to the public. This relief through temporary suspension of the statutory limitation on withdrawal of funds from the Treasury, will have the great value of substantially maintaining the status quo in parcel post operations until the Congress can complete a thorough study of the entire parcel post operation and arrive at an appropriate decision with respect to parcel post cost-revenue relationships, methods of adjusting parcel post rates, and other pertinent related matters.

Approval of the committee amendments, therefore, are definitely in the public interest. Prompt action is essential to assure uninterrupted and efficient postal service, and the enactment of this legislation will injure no one. Suitable parcel post rate adjustments still will be permitted, without the intervention of an arbitrary rate-fixing requirement (such as now exists) that is wholly inconsistent with long-recognized and proved standards for the regulation of rates. Private enterprise carriers of package traffic will be afforded equal protection since they, too, will continue in the status quo in relation to parcel post service. It is noteworthy, in this connection, that representatives of many such carriers testified before the committee as to their very profitable and expanding business operations, and one of the large private enterprise carriers, REA Express, disclosed that within the last 2 years it has improved its position from a serious loss operation to one promising reasonable return on investment.

SIZE AND WEIGHT LIMITATIONS

It is to be emphasized that enactment of this legislation will have no effect whatever on the maximum size and weight limits prescribed by the Congress in Public Law 199, 82nd Congress (39 U.S.C. 4552). Such section 4552 preempts the field so far as concerns the authority of any department or agency (or official thereof) to increase maximum size and weight limits on parcel post beyond those specified by the Congress therein. Interstate Commerce Commission so ruled in denying a Postmaster General's petition for rate adjustments and increased size and weight limits (Docket No. 33750) in a final decision of March 7, 1963. This decision is supported by the opinion of Judge Leonard P. Walsh, U.S. District Court for the District of Columbia, in *Railway Express Agency, Inc.* v. *Day,* C.A.No. 1202-62, filed October 26, 1962.

FINAL POLICY DECISION BY THE CONGRESS

In reporting this legislation, the committee recognizes its obligation to conduct a thorough and painstaking review of the entire parcel post operation, with special attention to cost-revenue relationships, proper rate levels, prevention of unjust Government competition with private enterprise, the public convenience and necessity, and other related matters—exclusive, however, of size and weight limitations which already have been settled by the Congress. Such review will be directed to arriving at a final decision, in due time but within the 3-year suspension period, as to the considerations subject to review. It is the committee's expectation that it will be enabled, during this period, to develop and present for the approval of the Congress, a sound and permanent policy for the entire parcel post operation which will be consistent with the interests of the public, private transportation enterprise, and the postal service.

ADMINISTRATIVE REPORTS

The official recommendation of the Postmaster General, embodied in H.R. 5795 as introduced, a supplemental letter from the Postmaster General, and the official report of the Interstate Commerce Commission on H.R. 5795 follow.

* * *

OFFICE OF THE POSTMASTER GENERAL

Washington, D.C., April 4, 1963

Hon. John W. McCormack
Speaker of the House of Representatives
Washington, D.C.

Dear Mr. Speaker:

There is forwarded herewith a draft of legislation to repeal the provisions of law relating to the fixing by the Postmaster General, with the consent of the Interstate Commerce Commission of rates of postage on fourth-class mail.

This proposal is a part of the Post Office Department's legislative program for the 88th Congress and the Bureau of the Budget has advised that, from the standpoint of the administration's program, there is no objection to the submission of this proposal for the consideration of the Congress. It is recommended that this proposal be enacted by the Congress.

Sincerely yours,

J. Edward Day
Postmaster General

Enclosures:
Draft of legislation.
Statement of purposes and need.

* * *

A BILL To repeal the provisions of law relating to the fixing by the Postmaster General, with the consent of the Interstate Commerce Commission, of rates of postage on fourth-class mail

Be it enacted by the Senate and House of Representatives of the United States of America in Congress assembled, That (a) section 6 of the Act of

July 28, 1916, 39 Stat. 431; and the last paragraph of section 207 (b) of the Act of February 28, 1925, 43 Stat. 1067, as amended by section 7 of the Act of May 29, 1928, 45 Stat. 942 (39 U.S.C., 1958 ed. 247), are repealed.

(b) The paragraph under the heading "General Provisions" under the appropriations for the Post Office Department contained in Chapter IV of the Supplemental Appropriations Act, 1951, 64 Stat. 1050, as amended by section 213 of the Postal Rate Increase Act, 1958, 72 Stat. 143 (31 U.S.C. 695), is repealed.

Sec. 2. Administrative actions taken in accordance with the provisions of law repealed by this Act shall remain in full force and effect, notwithstanding such repeal.

Sec. 3. Section 2303(b) of title 39, United States Code, is hereby amended by deleting that part of the last sentence which reads: ", including any adjustment pursuant to the provisions of section 207(b) of the Act of February 28, 1925, relating to reformation of classification (39 U.S.C., 1958 ed. 247)."

Sec. 4. (a) Section 2305 of title 39, United States Code, is hereby repealed.

(b) The Table of Contents of Chapter 27 of title 39, United States Code, is amended by deleting "2305. Effect on fourth-class mail rates."

* * *

OFFICE OF THE POSTMASTER GENERAL
Washington, D.C., April 23, 1963

Hon. Tom Murray
House of Representatives, Washington, D.C.

Dear Congressman: In response to your inquiry of today, I am glad to furnish the additional information you requested.

On April 4, 1963, I submitted to the Speaker of the House of Representatives the draft of proposed legislation to repeal the provisions of law relating to the fixing by the Postmaster General with the consent of the Interstate Commerce Commission, of rates of postage on fourth-class mail.

The enactment of this proposed legislation will have no effect whatever on Public Law 199, 82nd Congress (now contained in sec. 4552 of title 39, United States Code) nor on the parcel post size and weight limits prescribed therein. I do not plan to propose any change in that law nor in the size and weight limits.

If the Congress enacts the legislative proposal submitted with my letter of April 4, 1963, I do plan then to submit an additional legislative proposal to provide for a reasonable increase in the present zone rates applicable to parcel post and catalogs.

Sincerely yours,

J. Edward Day,
Postmaster General.

* * *

INTERSTATE COMMERCE COMMISSION
Washington, D.C., May 24, 1963

Hon. Tom Murray
Chairman, Committee on Post Office and Civil Service
House of Representatives, Washington, D. C.

Dear Chairman Murray: Your requests for comments on a bill, H.R. 5795, introduced by you, to repeal the provisions of law relating to the fixing by the Postmaster General, with the consent of the Interstate Commerce Commission, of rates of postage on fourth-class mail, and for other purposes, and on a somewhat similar bill, H.R. 2525, introduced by Congressman Morrison to vest in Congress the exclusive authority to set rates of postage for fourth-class mail have been referred to our Committee on Legislation. After consideration by that Committee, I am authorized to submit the following comments in its behalf:

Both bills would repeal the administrative authority contained in 31 U.S.C. 695 and 39 U.S.C. 247, which, in effect, requires the Postmaster General to maintain, subject to the consent of the Interstate Commerce Commission, a parcel post rate structure that will return the cost of the service within 4 percent; and, in effect, would vest in the Congress exclusive authority over rates of postage for fourth-class mail.

From your personal experience as a participant in a proceeding before the Commission last year in Docket No. 33750, "Reformation of Rates and Other Conditions of Mailability of Fourth-Class Mail," and in dealing with the general subject over the past decade or more, we know you will appreciate the position the Commission has been placed in since passage of the original act in 1912.

In the first place, we believe that the existing division of authority over the mail rate structure, i.e., Congress prescribes rate on the first three classes and the Postmaster General, with the Commission's consent, prescribes the rates and other conditions of mailability on the fourth class, tends toward piecemeal and unbalanced consideration of subjects which are interrelated. Thus, as you are aware, the expenses of the Post Office Department on all classes of mail and service are largely joint, with the allocation of revenues and expenses being made among the several classes by tests or samplings. It would appear, therefore, that consideration of the whole matter by one body would be preferable from a public point of view.

Secondly, and of more direct interest to the Commission, is the fact that our function in these matters has been misunderstood by some, as evidenced in the above-cited proceeding, which is an indication that the statutes are not as clear as they might be. Indeed, after 1 year of experience under the original statute, the Commission in its 1913 Annual Report to the Congress, at pages 79-80, closed its discussion of the new parcel post law with a recommendation that "be relieved of all duties in connection with the parcel post. If that is not done, the duties to be performed by the Commission, as well as the standards to be applied to it, should be more clearly stated."

In spite of the lack of clarity, upon presentation of the various proposals through the years by the Postmaster General for our consideration, we have endeavored to perform our duties under the existing statutes with the utmost dispatch.

In view of the foregoing, we believe that the involved bills present a broad policy question which is appropriately reserved for congressional determination. Accordingly, we take no position on the merits of these bills. We urge, however, that careful consideration be given to possible adverse competitive impact upon existing nongovernmental transportation facilities for parcel delivery that could result from the contemplated legislation. This could be assured by a declaration of congressional intent that parcel post service should continue to supplement rather than compete with nongovernmental operations in the parcel post field.

However, should either bill receive favorable consideration we suggest that by amendment or through clarification in the committee's report, the intent of the Congress to deal with the entire fourth-class mail structure, including matters relating to weights and sizes of fourth-class mail, should be affirmatively indicated.

Respectfully submitted.

Abe McGregor Goff,
Acting Chairman, Committee on Legislation
Rupert L. Murphy.

* * *

MATTER FOR THE INFORMATION OF THE MEMBERS OF THE HOUSE OF REPRESENTATIVES

The provision of the Supplemental Appropriation Act, 1951, which is suspended by the bill from July 1, 1963 to June 30, 1966, inclusive, is set forth below.

The paragraph under the heading "General Provisions" under the appropriations for the Post Office Department contained in Chapter IV of the Supplemental Appropriation Act, 1951 (64 Stat. 1050), as amended:

> Hereafter, none of the funds appropriated to the Post Office Department from the general fund of the Treasury shall be withdrawn from the Treasury until the Postmaster General shall certify in writing that he has requested the consent of the Interstate Commerce Commission to the establishment of such rate increases or other reformations (in addition to any specific increases or other reformations heretofore or hereafter authorized or prescribed by law), pursuant to the provisions of section 207 of the Act of February 28, 1925, as amended (39 U.S.C. 247), as may be necessary to insure (1) that the revenues from fourth-class mail service will not exceed by more than 4 per centum the costs thereof and (2) that the costs of such fourth-class mail service will not exceed by more than 4 per centum the revenues therefrom: Provided, That the foregoing shall not be construed to require any increase in the postage rate, established by the Act of April 15, 1937 (39 U.S.C. 293c), for publications or records furnished to a blind person.